# British Culture and the First World War

# British Culture and the First World War

Experience, Representation and Memory

**TOBY THACKER**

Bloomsbury Academic
An imprint of Bloomsbury Publishing Plc

B L O O M S B U R Y
LONDON • NEW DELHI • NEW YORK • SYDNEY

**Bloomsbury Academic**
An imprint of Bloomsbury Publishing Plc

50 Bedford Square  
London  
WC1B 3DP  
UK

1385 Broadway  
New York  
NY 10018  
USA

www.bloomsbury.com

**BLOOMSBURY and the Diana logo are trademarks of Bloomsbury Publishing Plc**

First published 2014

© Toby Thacker, 2014

Toby Thacker has asserted his right under the Copyright, Designs and Patents Act, 1988, to be identified as Author of this work.

All rights reserved. No part of this publication may be reproduced or transmitted in any form or by any means, electronic or mechanical, including photocopying, recording, or any information storage or retrieval system, without prior permission in writing from the publishers.

No responsibility for loss caused to any individual or organization acting on or refraining from action as a result of the material in this publication can be accepted by Bloomsbury or the author.

**British Library Cataloguing-in-Publication Data**
A catalogue record for this book is available from the British Library.

ISBN: HB: 978-1-4411-2163-9  
PB: 978-1-4411-8074-2  
ePDF: 978-1-4411-3058-7  
ePub: 978-1-4411-3437-0

**Library of Congress Cataloging-in-Publication Data**
Thacker, Toby, 1957–
British culture and the First World War: experience, representation and memory/Toby Thacker.
pages cm
Includes bibliographical references and index.
ISBN 978-1-4411-2163-9 (hardback) – ISBN 978-1-4411-8074-2 (pbk.) –
ISBN 978-1-4411-3058-7 (epdf) – ISBN 978-1-4411-3437-0 (epub)
1. World War, 1914–1918–Influence–Great Britain. 2. World War, 1914–1918–
Great Britain–Literature and the war. 3. World War, 1914–1918–Great Britain–
Music and the war. 4. Great Britain–Social life and customs–20th century.
5. Popular music–Great Britain–1910–1921–History and criticism. I. Title.
DA577.T43 2014
940.3'1–dc23
2014004135

Typeset by Deanta Global Publishing Services, Chennai, India

# CONTENTS

*Acknowledgements* vi
*List of illustrations* viii
*List of maps* xi

Introduction 1
1 'The blessings of peace' 11
2 August 1914 33
3 The call to arms 53
4 January–June 1915 79
5 July–December 1915 101
6 January–September 1916 123
7 September 1916–July 1917 147
8 August–December 1917 171
9 January–July 1918 193
10 August–November 1918 213
11 1919–23 231
12 'We will remember them' 249
Conclusion 273

*Notes* 285
*Archival sources, newspapers, journals and magazines* 323
*Further reading* 326
*Index* 350

# ACKNOWLEDGEMENTS

A number of people and institutions have helped in the writing of this book, which has been a long time in the making. Many of the ideas developed here have sprung from an undergraduate course on 'Britain and the First World War', which I taught first at Swansea University, and which has evolved further at Cardiff University. I must record my thanks to Noel Thompson, my then head of department at Swansea, who encouraged me to develop the idea of a course examining both the military history of the war and also its artistic representation, and to successive generations of students at both universities who have sharpened my understanding and spurred me to explore new aspects of the British experience of the war.

I am indebted to the staffs of all the libraries and archives in which I have worked for their great help in identifying and finding relevant source materials. Many have been generous with their time in discussing individual sources and in trying to locate the rights holders for particular papers. I wish to thank particularly Peter Keelan and Alison Harvey who have been so helpful in opening up the varied resources of the Special Collection at Cardiff University Library to me.

I am also grateful to the trustees of a number of literary estates who have generously allowed me to quote from previously unpublished private papers, and to libraries and museums which have allowed me to reproduce pictures. I wish to thank Professor Jon Stallworthy, trustee of the Rupert Brooke Estate, for permission to quote from the papers of Rupert Brooke at the Archive Centre, Kings College, Cambridge; the trustees of the Seven Pillars of Wisdom Trust for permission to quote from the papers of T. E. Lawrence in the Bodleian Library, Oxford; the Estate of Michael Ayrton for permission to quote from the journals of Henry Nevinson in the Bodleian Library, Oxford; the authorities of Somerville College, University of Oxford, for permission to quote a poem from the Margaret Kennedy Collection and to reproduce a photograph of students and dons at the college in 1914; the executor of the Edward Thomas Estate for permission to quote from papers in the Edward Thomas Archive at Cardiff University; the Elgar Birthplace Museum for permission to quote from the papers of Edward and Alice Elgar held there; the trustees of the David Jones Estate for permission to quote from the papers of David Jones at the National Library of Wales, Aberystwyth, and to reproduce a drawing now held at the Museum of the Royal Welch Fusiliers; Laura Ponsonby for permission to quote from the papers of

# ACKNOWLEDGEMENTS

Hubert Parry and to reproduce photographs held at Schulbrede Priory; the Wellcome Library, London, for permission to reproduce photographs; and the Glenside Hospital Museum, Bristol, for permission to reproduce photographs. Quotations from Vera Brittain's 'Great War Diary', from her correspondence, and from her poems are included by permission of Mark Bostridge and Timothy Brittain-Catlin, literary executors for the Estate of Vera Brittain, 1970. Extracts from the unpublished letters of Paul Nash in the Tate Gallery Archive are © Tate Trustees, and are reproduced here by permission of Tate Trustees. I am grateful to the trustees of the Spencer Estate for permission to reproduce previously unpublished quotations from the letters of Stanley Spencer at the Tate Gallery Archive, and to Faber & Faber for permission to reproduce quotations from Geoffrey Keynes (ed.), *The Letters of Rupert Brooke* (London: Faber & Faber, 1968). Every effort has been made to trace copyright holders and to obtain their permission for the use of copyright material. The publisher apologizes for any errors or omissions there may be in the above list and would be grateful if notified of any corrections that should be incorporated in future editions of this book.

Many scholars and friends have helped to develop my ideas and understanding in conversation, by suggesting lines of enquiry, and by supplying me with books and articles. In no particular order, I would like particularly to thank Kevin Passmore, Tracey Loughran, Chris Williams, Karen Arrandale, Helen Ashton and Christopher Mitchell. I am grateful to Ian Dennis and Kirsty Harding for drawing the maps.

It would have been impossible for me to have explored in any depth the Welsh experience of the First World War without the active help of a number of Welsh-speaking colleagues and students. I wish to record my thanks to Eluned Lewis, Sioned Treharne and Siobhan McGurk, who helped with the difficult task of translating Welsh-language poems, and also to Martin Wright, Bill Jones and Gethin Matthews. Colin Hughes very kindly shared with me his unique knowledge of the Battle of Mametz Wood. Others have helped similarly with particular areas: Dr Claire Wilkinson of the Cheltenham Ladies College helped me with a number of Greek and Latin allusions, and I wish to acknowledge my larger debt to two great interpreters of Elgar, Stephen Jackson and Tim Morris, who have both helped me enormously in understanding him as a man and a composer. Laura Ponsonby and Kate Russell were generous not only in throwing open the private papers of Hubert Parry and his relatives to me at Schulbrede Priory, but also in providing hospitality there. Special thanks go to Susan who has put up with me through the whole period I have worked on this book, and accompanied me on many excursions to sites associated with it.

I am grateful finally to all at Bloomsbury who have helped in the preparation of this book, especially to the anonymous readers who made such positive and helpful suggestions for improvement to it. Any errors remaining are my own.

Toby Thacker, Gloucester, 2014

# LIST OF ILLUSTRATIONS

Figure 1  Leading figures of the English Musical Renaissance 13
Papers of Hubert Parry, Schulbrede Priory.

Figure 2  Suffragettes parade in Littlehampton in 1913, led by Lady Maude Parry 15
Papers of Hubert Parry, Schulbrede Priory.

Figure 3  Red Cross nurses leaving for the front, August 1914 39
Hammerton, J. A. (ed.), *The War Illustrated Album de Luxe: The Story of the Great European War told by Camera, Pen and Pencil* (London: Amalgamated Press, 1915–17).

Figure 4  Refugees on the quayside at Ostend 40
*The Times History of the War* (London: Printing House Square, 1915–20).

Figure 5  Highnam Court 44
Papers of Hubert Parry, Schulbrede Priory.

Figure 6  *In the Dread Talons*; the German capture of Antwerp, October 1914 49
*Western Mail*.

Figure 7  The call to arms 54
George Elam newspaper cuttings collection, Cardiff University Library.

Figure 8  Marines of the Royal Naval Division in Antwerp, October 1914 58
Hammerton, J. A. (ed.), *'I Was There!' The Human Story of the Great War of 1914–1918* (London: Waverley Book Company, 1938).

Figure 9  A British Expeditionary Force operating theatre near Boulogne 64
Wellcome Library, London.

LIST OF ILLUSTRATIONS ix

Figure 10  *The Two Roads*; Lloyd George's view of the war, December 1914  69
*Western Mail.*

Figure 11  Students and dons at Somerville College, Oxford, October 1914  73
Somerville College, University of Oxford.

Figure 12  Beaufort War Hospital, 1915  92
Glenside Hospital Museum, www.glensidemuseum.org.uk.

Figure 13  Zeppelin damage in London  98
Hammerton, J. A. (ed.), *'I Was There!' The Human Story of the Great War of 1914–18* (London: Waverley Book Company, 1938).

Figure 14  A German shop attacked by crowds in London  107
*The Times History of the War* (London: Printing House Square, 1915–20).

Figure 15  Wounded soldiers arriving at the Beaufort War Hospital  110
Glenside Hospital Museum, www.glensidemuseum.org.uk.

Figure 16  Convalescent soldiers and staff at Beaufort War Hospital  112
Glenside Hospital Museum, www.glensidemuseum.org.uk.

Figure 17  The 'convalescent depot' at Boulogne  114
Wellcome Library, London.

Figure 18  Richard Nevinson, *In the Observation Ward*, 1916  115
*Modern War Paintings by C. R. W. Nevinson*, with an essay by P. G. Konody (London: Grant Richards, 1917).

Figure 19  Faisal with officers  132
*The Times History of the War* (London: Printing House Square, 1915–20).

Figure 20  The Royal Welch Fusiliers resting before the attack on Mametz Wood  139
Hammerton, J. A. (ed.), *The War Illustrated Album de Luxe: The Story of the Great European War told by Camera, Pen and Pencil* (London: Amalgamated Press, 1915–17).

LIST OF ILLUSTRATIONS

Figure 21   The manuscript of 'Jerusalem'   142
Papers of Hubert Parry, Schulbrede Priory.

Figure 22   A dressing station in Macedonia   156
Hammerton, J. A. (ed.), *The War Illustrated Album de Luxe: The Story of the Great European War told by Camera, Pen and Pencil* (London: Amalgamated Press, 1915–17).

Figure 23   David Jones, *A Boche Machine Gun*, September 1917   176
Reproduced with permission of the David Jones Estate.

Figure 24   Scene from the Ypres Salient   180
Hammerton, J. A. (ed.), *The War Illustrated Album de Luxe: The Story of the Great European War told by Camera, Pen and Pencil* (London: Amalgamated Press, 1915–17).

Figure 25   Allenby enters Jerusalem   185
Hammerton, J. A. (ed.), *The War Illustrated Album de Luxe: The Story of the Great European War told by Camera, Pen and Pencil* (London: Amalgamated Press, 1915–17).

Figure 26   A Rolls Royce in the desert   198
Hammerton, J. A. (ed.), *'I Was There!' The Human Story of the Great War of 1914–1918* (London: Waverley Book Company, 1938).

Figure 27   A mine exploding on the Hejaz railway near Deraa in 1918   218
Hammerton, J. A. (ed.), *'I Was There!' The Human Story of the Great War of 1914–1918* (London: Waverley Book Company, 1938).

Figure 28   The memorial to Hedd Wyn in Trawsfynydd   252
Author's private collection.

Figure 29   Mametz Wood and the memorial to the 38th (Welsh) Division   265
Author's private collection.

Figure 30   The Hedd Wyn memorial, Hagebos   270
Author's private collection.

# LIST OF MAPS

Map 1   The German invasion of Belgium and France  45
Map 2   The Retreat from Mons  46
Map 3   Antwerp and First Ypres  49
Map 4   The Ottoman Empire in 1914  76
Map 5   The Dardanelles and Gallipoli  81
Map 6   Neuve Chappelle and Aubers Ridge  82
Map 7   The Battle of Loos  103
Map 8   The Battle of the Somme  126
Map 9   The Arab Revolt  131
Map 10  The Battle of Arras and the Nivelle offensive  151
Map 11  Salonica  157
Map 12  Passchendaele  172
Map 13  The German offensives of 1918  195
Map 14  The Allied offensives of 1918  215

# Introduction

This book is about the British experience of the First World War, the way that experience was represented, in different media, and how those representations fed into the broader construction of memory of the war. There is now a long and distinguished tradition of writing in the English language about how the war was imagined, a tradition focused initially on the poetry and literature which emerged from the war, and which has then fed into a broader cultural history which accepts that the behaviour of both individuals and modern states are, in the words of Priya Satia, 'shaped by the cultural imagination'.[1] From its beginnings, this is a body of scholarship which has given undue prominence to the group of writers whose poems and memoirs were produced largely in the 15-year period between 1920 and 1935, the 'literature of disillusion'. The focus on writers who represented the conflict as horrible, futile and destructive chimed with a larger societal revulsion against war and militarism, and with the iconoclastic and anti-miltaristic mood of the 1960s and 1970s. The memoirs of Edmund Blunden, Robert Graves, Siegfried Sassoon and Vera Brittain, which spoke of separation and loss, of pointless suffering, and the destruction of an old order, came to be seen as the authentic representations of the conflict, and their voices became the representatives for the 'doomed youth', the 'lost generation' which had fought and died in the trenches.[2] The First World War came to be seen as an epochal event in British history, a watershed separating an earlier age of self-confidence and optimism from one of insecurity and cynicism.

Since the 1990s, there have been significant developments, as from different directions, historians of different types have revisited this terrain, and sought to challenge these deeply entrenched paradigms. Military historians have challenged the idea that the British Army in the First World War was led by unimaginative generals, and have tried instead to celebrate the 'forgotten victory' of 1918, when the German Army was forced from its long-held positions on the Western Front, and compelled to surrender.[3] Those looking at international relations have argued that far from being accidental or pointless, the British involvement in the war was the result of a careful calculation based on a traditional understanding of British interests, and that it prevented the German domination of the continent of

Europe, a domination which, while not genocidal, would have prefigured in many ways the Nazi occupation of the 1940s.[4] Historians of women, and of gender, have challenged the long-accepted idea that women were emancipated as a result of the war, and have argued that the changes in women's lives during the war resulted rather in a renegotiation of citizenship, which while registering significant advances, did not alter the fundamental balance of power relations in a deeply gendered society.[5] Cultural historians have pointed to the striking differences between the post-war 'literature of disillusion', and the way the war was actually represented while it was happening, typically as a heroic conflict between good and evil, a struggle for civilization itself.[6] This has been reflected in a reappraisal of that much misused term, 'propaganda', and increasingly historians are discarding the idea of a top-down (and sinister) process of manipulation in favour of a horizontal model, in which support for the war effort was produced and articulated by individuals and institutions outside the government.[7] In a welcome development, historians have begun to look beyond London and England, and to explore regional variations in the experience of war in Britain.[8] As we approach the 100th anniversary of the First World War, the paradigmatic understandings which have dominated our understanding of the conflict have been dethroned, and there is an exciting reappraisal of the British experience of the war.

This book takes a twin-track approach, seeking to provide a broad reconstruction of the British war effort and to chart within this the experiences of a group of selected writers, painters and musicians. Although it may seem unnecessary to those with a detailed grasp of the military history of the war to recount major campaigns and battles, I believe that this is vital to any cultural history. Far too many cultural histories of the First World War provide either inadequate or inaccurate context, using quotations from letters, diaries and works of art without any clear sense of relationship to what was happening at the point when these were produced. I also follow a rigidly chronological approach. Although historians have the benefit of hindsight, those living during the war did not. Until the early days of August 1914, it was not clear to even the most informed contemporaries, let alone to more ordinary members of the British public, whether they would be drawn into the developing European crisis. Once war was declared on 4 August, few had any idea how the conflict might develop; virtually none imagined the stalemate in the trenches which was to become the central experience of conflict for most British soldiers. As we shall see, during 1915 and 1916 there were widely held expectations, which today appear entirely misplaced, that successful offensives might bring a rapid end to the war. By 1918 these had largely been replaced by a dull expectation that the war would extend at least into 1919 and possibly well beyond that. Although for the most part the war was fought away from Britain, the public mood at home was sensitive to developments in different theatres and changed from week to week. There were distinct points of crisis, one as early as the last week of August, and the beginning of September 1914, when news began to emerge of the retreat from Mons, and of German atrocities in Belgium, and this provoked an immediate surge in voluntary recruitment. By 1915 there was a recognition that the war – already being called 'the Great War' – would be protracted and bloody, and there was a deeper moment of national crisis in April and May, provoked by the failed attacks in Flanders and the Dardanelles, the first Zeppelin raids on Britain, and the sinking of the passenger liner *Lusitania*. There was a different and separate sense of reappraisal in November 1915 as it became clear that the offensive at Loos had been unsuccessful. We may detect a grim hardening of mood through the latter part of 1916 and into 1917 as the war ground on, seemingly without end, and a bleak despair which came to a head in the spring of 1918, when successful German offensives on the Western Front coincided with the 'Maurice Debate' in parliament, and the moral hysteria around the 'Billing Case'. For many individuals, the most significant points in the war did not coincide with these broader developments, but might be related to a particular event outside them.

So that we may more accurately contextualize individual experience, I have tried also to provide some sense of how the British public was informed about major developments in the war, a topic which would merit a larger study in its own right. News about the war reached the public in many different ways, and it is unwise to generalize about this. Newspapers were the primary source of information, and although for much of the war their reporting was one-sided and ludicrously optimistic, historians who have looked in detail at individual publications have recognized that they also published a great deal of accurate information. Although for most of the war the predominant tone in British newspapers was nationalistic and heroic, often using the 'high diction' which cultural historians of the 1970s and 1980s saw as a deliberate obfuscation,[9] from the start of the conflict newspapers also published reports and letters which depicted gruesome details of the horrors of trench warfare, and of the privations suffered by soldiers and civilians alike in different theatres. Similarly, although letters from serving soldiers and sailors were supposed to go through a process of censorship, there were many gaps in this. Officers' letters were not so strictly censored, and as we shall see, in many cases combatants were able to communicate remarkably freely with relatives and friends at home. As Michael Roper has noted, there was an outpouring of letter writing during the war as individuals were separated geographically and emotionally from their normal circumstances, leaving not only a rich resource for historians, but providing many at home with a counterpoint to the official representation of the war in the newspapers.[10]

Why focus on the fortunes of a group of creative individuals? These were people for whom the whole issue of representation was of central importance. Whether they were writers of poetry or prose, illustrators or painters, or composers of music, the individuals at the heart of this study thought constantly about how to transmute their life experience into different forms of art. For the most part they wanted to write, or paint, or make music not only as a means of personal expression, but to communicate with others, and to influence them. They were therefore concerned not only with different subjects, but with forms, idioms and styles. The years before 1914 had witnessed an extraordinary ferment of ideas in all the arts, and this had affected almost all of the individuals selected here, compelling them to think and to rethink how best to express themselves. The outbreak of war brought further artistic challenges, in addition to those which artists faced in common with other adult members of society. Was the war a suitable subject for artistic representation? If it was, did it call for new forms of representation? Was there a special obligation for artists to become involved, and to experience war at its sharpest? Was there a patriotic duty to support the war effort? Or indeed to challenge, and even oppose it? As the war developed, and it became ever more apparent that the conflict was on an unprecedented scale, and was exposing people to experiences of an altogether new order, these artistic questions became more challenging.

Although all my subjects faced fundamentally similar questions of representation, in other ways their experience was widely different, and is used here to illuminate many of the broader aspects of war for the British people. Only three of the group, Rupert Brooke, Paul Nash and T. E. Lawrence, could be identified as young junior officers from the social elite whose representations have come to dominate British memory of the war, and of those three, Lawrence served far from the Western Front. Three others, the Welsh-language poet Ellis Evans, the painter Stanley Spencer and the illustrator and the writer David Jones, served as private soldiers in the infantry. Two, Vera Brittain and Kate Finzi, served in the role in which females could most closely parallel young soldiers, as volunteer nurses in military hospitals. For two of the group, Richard Nevinson and Stanley Spencer, a dominant experience of the war was as medical orderlies in military hospitals. A great deal has been written about female nurses in the war, but male nurses have been overlooked. The two composers in the group, Edward Elgar and Hubert Parry, provide several different perspectives on the war. Both were too old to do military service and, therefore, could not participate directly in the war. Elgar, who had thought deeply about the role of the composer in society – and indeed been deeply saddened by the rather gloomy conclusions he drew about the role of the composer in *British* society – oscillated between introspection and a desire to act as a national voice, and felt after August 1914 a huge obligation to compose music which would support the war effort. Intriguingly, his most important composition of the war years, and his most personal contribution, would be a work, not of patriotic celebration, but one of mourning. Parry did not feel such a strong obligation to compose to support the war effort, but in his role as Director of the Royal College of Music he felt a duty to speak publicly to his students about how they should react to the war.

Socially and geographically, the eleven artists selected came from very different parts of Britain. One, Hubert Parry, was effectively a member of the aristocracy, although Rupert Brooke, through his circles of friendship, similarly mixed with aristocrats and with members of the governing class. Several, including Paul Nash, Richard Nevinson, Vera Brittain, Kate Finzi and T. E. Lawrence, were from solidly bourgeois backgrounds, although even here we should note important variations. Vera Brittain's conventional upbringing in provincial Buxton was a world apart from that of members of her class brought up in London; T. E. Lawrence was at a deep level *déclassé*, and several experts on him have pointed to the tensions he felt because of his illegitimate birth, and the sense of his father's lost aristocratic status. David Jones, Stanley Spencer and Edward Elgar were from lower-middle-class families. Although Elgar had by 1914 moved upwards socially both through marriage and through public recognition, he never overcame a sense of social inferiority which derived from his humble origins as the son of a piano-tuner from Worcestershire. Ellis Evans was from a farming family in the mountains of North Wales, had left school at the age of 14 and was firmly rooted in one of the cultural and linguistic communities most remote from mainstream British society in 1914. We should bear in mind also how almost all individuals experienced the First World War largely through their contact with significant others, with lovers, close relatives and friends. These close relationships could take an individual into social worlds which they themselves had not previously known, and frequently had a profound effect on how they experienced the war. Intriguingly, several of this group of artists, including Parry, Nash and Nevinson, had close contacts through their wives and mothers with the suffragist movement. Parry, through his daughter and her husband, was brought into close contact after 1914 with the anti-war movement. Richard Nevinson was able to join the pacifist Friends Ambulance Unit in Flanders early in the war because of his father's connections. Conversely, Edward Elgar was throughout the war affected by his wife's straightforward and strongly voiced patriotic convictions.

I have deliberately included creative individuals working in different art forms to challenge existing accounts which tend to treat these art forms separately. Different academic disciplines, and sub-branches within these disciplines, have evolved their own criteria for analysis, typically acting in isolation from one another. To this day, the overwhelming emphasis in cultural histories of Britain and the First World War is on the written word, and it is only recently that we have seen the long-standing preoccupation with those who were critical of the war challenged, and more attention paid to those who supported it.[11] There is now a flourishing branch of art history which examines the representation and memorialization of the war by painters, but this has been led by those interested in the avant-garde, and frequently tends to judge artists by aesthetic criteria. In this view, artists using modernist idioms to represent the war have been singled out for attention, and the use of more traditional idioms has been seen as regressive and unworthy.[12]

Music has suffered from the long-standing perception of it as an abstract art form, one inexplicable without an adequate technical knowledge and vocabulary, and it has been left to a few courageous musicologists working more recently to try to redress this by placing works composed between 1914 and 1918 in social and political context.[13] I hope in this study to consider words, visual images and music in the same way, as representations in the broadest sense, and to overcome the artificial barriers between them which have been thrown up by specialist disciplines.

It is important to stress that I do not imagine this group of artists to be in any sense completely representative of British society in 1914. One would need a much larger group of people to put forward even the most flimsy claim to presenting some kind of cross section of such a diverse and multifaceted population. Nor are the individuals in the group presented as necessarily the 'greatest' or most important practitioners of their art. Several – and I think here of Elgar, Jones, Evans and Spencer – would be considered by specialists as leading exponents in their artistic field, but others, like Finzi, have been neglected by posterity. Several, including Nevinson, Nash and Brittain, owe their fame very largely to their representations of the First World War. Nor can such a small group have had direct experience of all the theatres in which the First World War was played out. Several served as front-line soldiers in the quintessential locus of the war for the British, on the Western Front, in Flanders and on the Somme. Lawrence's war was of course in the very different setting of Arabia, in the Hejaz and the Levant. Spencer served for 2 years in Macedonia, and Vera Brittain spent time nursing in Malta, before taking up the same role in Etaples during the Passchendaele offensive. Rupert Brooke died on his way to action in Gallipoli. Kate Finzi spent 18 months working as a nurse in Boulogne, part of the vast army of men and women which supported the fighting soldiers on the nearby front line. Elgar and Parry spent the war years in Britain, where like so many of the civilian population, they anxiously followed the war news and devoured letters and reports from the fighting fronts. None of the group were aviators, and none served at sea. There will therefore be little about these aspects of the war in this book. Perhaps more surprisingly, given the radical inclinations of several in the group, and the deep sense of association with the Celtic world felt by Ellis Evans, David Jones and T. E. Lawrence, none appear to have taken a close interest in Irish affairs. There will be little mention here of Ireland or Scotland, although I hope that the emphasis on Wales and on Welsh culture will serve to challenge any sense of 'British' experience as something confined to England and the English.

A final reason for focusing on creative artists is a prosaic one, the simple wealth of evidence they leave behind them. In addition to their poems, drawings, paintings and musical compositions, most of the individuals selected here have left copious records of their war experience in letters and journals of various kinds. Theirs was an extraordinarily literary society, where many men and women kept diaries, and wrote letters almost every day. In this group, Vera Brittain, Kate Finzi and Hubert Parry have left substantial diaries; Lawrence, Elgar and Brooke more fragmentary ones. Lawrence wrote lengthy reports on his activities as a liaison officer during the Arab Revolt. Rupert Brooke and Edward Elgar wrote many letters, often of an intimate and revealing nature. Stanley Spencer is the only one of the group who produced virtually no artistic work during the war, but he was a prolific and idiosyncratic letter writer, and has a left a detailed contemporary record of his experience. Richard Nevinson left virtually no letters or journals, but his father was a conscientious diarist, and faithfully recorded many details about his son's life during the war. Similarly, Elgar's wife Alice kept a daily diary in which she commented frequently on her husband's activities, his health and his changing moods. The evidential trail is weak is only one case, that of Ellis Evans, and it is correspondingly more difficult to reconstruct his personal trajectory through the war years.

Throughout, I have privileged the use of contemporary sources in reconstructing both the events of the war and the experiences of my subjects. Far too many historians and biographers indiscriminately mix primary and secondary source material in constructing their own narratives, and to support their arguments, and I have sought wherever possible to avoid this. It is now well established that in the British case, testimony about the First World War produced after 1918 frequently differed radically from that produced during the war, and it is all the more necessary to distinguish sharply between these. Secondary sources, produced by biographers and historians, must be treated with even greater suspicion. Unfortunately, biographies of artists are often hagiographic in tendency, and whole traditions of biography have grown up around some of the better known subjects of this study which have emphasized certain aspects of an individual's life or character, while obscuring others which might cast that individual in a less flattering light. Published editions of correspondence, and of diaries, have often been edited, often with similar intent. Inaccuracies which appear in one secondary account are frequently then replicated in subsequent ones. T. E. Lawrence expressed this problem with characteristic vigour in a letter to Robert Graves, written in 1927, referring to the second-hand interpretations of his own wartime career being put about by the American Lowell Thomas: 'Butter of the Lowell Thomas sort does not keep very well. And its quotation at tenth hand is painfully rancid'.[14] I hope that the reader here will find here fresh material to challenge the rancid mythology of the First World War. Of course, any diary, letter or artistic representation is not an unmediated reflection of experience. Even if produced only hours after an event, there is a distance and, therefore, necessarily a reconstruction of that experience, one which is normally fashioned in anticipation of a particular audience. But this testimony is far more direct, and typically much less self-conscious, than something produced months, years or even decades later. Wherever possible, I have used unpublished primary sources or have used these to cross-reference published primary sources. Where these documents have not been dated by their author, but the date is clear from the content, I have indicated this in parenthesis in my notes. Where I have, in the absence of contemporaneous material, had recourse to later testimony, to a post-war memoir, or a secondary source, in reconstructing a particular event or development, this is indicated.

I hope that this book will help to collapse or at the least to challenge some distinctions which have become reified in much existing literature on the First World War. One is that between soldiers and civilians, a distinction observed by many participants in the war. Rupert Brooke observed soon after joining the Royal Naval Division in 1914 that he felt himself to be under a 'special seclusion and reserve', separate from civilians;[15] Kate Finzi, who as a young female volunteer managed to get to what she called the 'war zone' in Belgium very early in the war, was similarly preoccupied with a sense of the distinction between the men and women serving there, and the population at home in 'Blighty'. Both, we should note, were enthusiastic volunteers who were bitterly critical of those unwilling to follow their example. By the middle of the war this distinction between soldiers and civilians was felt so sharply that many from the 'war zone', when back on leave in Britain, found themselves completely unable to communicate with people there and longed to be back with others who shared their experience. This distinction has particularly preoccupied those looking at the history of women, as it tends to separate the male combatants in the war from all others who lived through it. Much ink has been expended in trying to argue that, for example, the experience of female nurses in military hospitals was similar to that of men in the line, and that the trauma they suffered should be considered in the same way. In this study I do not intend to create a hierarchy of victimhood by drawing borders between the experience of those who fought in the front line, or who experienced the consequences of violence as nurses, or who had to live with it in their imagination.

Another social distinction observed by Kate Finzi during the war, and one which was given a different emphasis after 1918 by writers like Vera Brittain, was that between young and old. Finzi noted with sympathy the frustration of older people in Britain who wanted to contribute more to the war effort, but were prevented by their age; in a shift which parallels many others after 1918, Brittain in her post-war memoir imagined the war was a cynical trick played upon the young by the old. Historians have for decades now been preoccupied with class, race and gender as 'categories of analysis', and these have served to structure many valuable works. They have in the process typically overlooked age. The overwhelming emphasis of historical research on the First World War has been on young people, largely men, reaching adulthood in 1914. They have even been labelled the 'generation of 1914', as if people of other ages had no reaction to the war, or none of equal significance. The study of individuals of very different ages, as undertaken here, will hopefully highlight what an important factor this was in the way that people experienced and responded to the war. Younger adults – like

Finzi *and* Brittain in 1914 – were far more likely to see the war as an opportunity for excitement and adventure, and it is perhaps no coincidence that the youngest member of the group selected here, David Jones, who was 18 when the war broke out, was one of the most enthusiastic to join up. There is a significant difference in the reaction of someone like Rupert Brooke, nearly 10 years older, on the surface more settled and established, but who saw the whole idea of enlistment and participation in a much more complex light. People of a different generation altogether, like Elgar and Parry, had an entirely different perspective. Put very crudely, young adults tended, not unnaturally to be most concerned for their own fate, while older people tended to take a wider view, thinking more of others and of society as a whole.

Similarly, I hope that by paying particular attention to Wales as well as to England, this book will challenge easy assumptions about regional and national differences. The briefest consideration of the fate of Ellis Evans, from a Welsh-speaking rural community in the mountains of North Wales, will highlight the problems of any totalizing narrative of 'Britain' in the war, but we need equally to guard against a reactive tendency to imagine that everything in Wales was different. Adrian Gregory has recently presented evidence to argue that there was considerable opposition in Wales to the war in August 1914, but it is relatively easy to find an equal body of contemporary evidence, particularly from urban South Wales, to suggest that there was widespread support for the war there.[16] If we consider the case of a young recruit to the Royal Welch Fusiliers like David Jones, the picture becomes more complicated. There is still debate among scholars as to whether, or how far, Jones was 'Welsh' or 'English'. He served alongside 'Taffies' from North Wales, and Cockneys from London, both types of soldier immortalized in his later memoir *In Parenthesis*, and he was surely only one of millions of people in Britain in 1914 whose ancestors came from very different parts of England, Scotland, Wales and Ireland, to say nothing of other countries.

If one of the purposes of prosopography is, by studying a small group of similar people, to advance generalizations which might be applicable to much larger groups, this book, by looking at a very disparate group, might suggest the dangers of generalization. There will be one unifying theme: the emergence of disillusion. From the work of scholars like Janet Watson we know that the British were fighting very different wars before and after 1918. This study will confirm the argument that there was broad support for what was perceived as a just war across British society between 1914 and 1918, and that in the decade after 1918, this view of the war changed dramatically, as earlier belief in the righteousness of the British cause was challenged by scepticism about pre-war 'secret diplomacy', about the veracity of claims of German 'barbarity', and by cynicism about the patriotic rhetoric which dominated public discourse during the war.[17] By looking at individuals, this study will suggest that disillusion came to them at different points in time, and that the first manifestations of a broader public consensus after 1918 were apparent in individual representations produced earlier in the war.

On the day before the British declaration of war against Germany on 4 August 1914, *The Times* spoke of Britain being drawn 'into the vortex of European militarism'.[18] Over the next 4 years more and more individuals used this same metaphor to describe the war, and indeed to suggest that those who emerged from the vortex would not emerge unchanged. In the decades since, it has become a commonplace to imagine 1914 as a watershed in British history, the dividing line between a prosperous, calm and self-confident society, and one characterized by decline, insecurity and a loss of innocence. This book will neither confirm these over-complacent assumptions, nor suggest new meta-narratives to replace them. It will argue that we need to revisit the contemporary testimony of those who experienced the war, to recover the dominant tropes they used, and not merely to dismiss these as naïve and misguided. In the process we may come to a better understanding of why so many British people were willing to go, most of them voluntarily, into the vortex, and of what happened to them there.

# CHAPTER ONE

# 'The blessings of peace'

On 30 April 1914, a new anthem by Britain's foremost composer, Sir Edward Elgar, was given its first performance at St Paul's Cathedral in London. *Give unto the Lord* was a setting of Psalm 23, the product of a composer at the height of his powers, who had taken the musical language of late-Romanticism to its expressive limits. Originally intended for a large choir and a full orchestra, the anthem displayed Elgar's extraordinary ability to set words to music, and in so doing to heighten their sense and impact. Following the words of the psalm, the anthem changes in mood from one moment to the next: declaring that 'the voice of the Lord is full of majesty', Elgar creates a solemn mood of imperial pomp; portraying the Lord 'who strippeth the cedars bare', he generates a turbulent and stormy atmosphere. After moving through a gamut of emotions, the piece arrives at a stunningly tranquil conclusion, as the choir repeats the last line of the psalm, 'The Lord shall bring his people the blessings of peace.' George Martin, the director of the choir at St Paul's to whom the work was dedicated, wrote to Elgar to thank him: 'every note of it', he wrote, 'so dignified and so sincere'.[1]

Elgar was not alone in 1914 in looking for peace. Britain was a great trading nation, at the height of imperial and maritime supremacy. Apart from the difficult but relatively confined conflict with Boer settlers in South Africa between 1899 and 1902, the country had not fought in a major war since the 1850s. Its small professional army had fought numerous colonial wars, but the population at home had been insulated from these, confident in the power of the Royal Navy to shield it from any enemies. The international situation in Europe indeed seemed relatively peaceful, after the Balkan Wars in 1912 and 1913, and the mounting tensions of the naval race with Germany between 1906 and 1912. Most people who took an interest in public affairs were preoccupied with problems at home, notably the ongoing campaign of suffragists for women to be granted the vote, and by the threat of conflict in Ireland between Republicans seeking Home Rule in the South and Loyalists wishing to remain united with Britain in the North.

## The artists

Edward Elgar is one of the most misunderstood of major composers. To the lay public in Britain he is known as a caricature, composer of 'Land of Hope and Glory' and other pieces typically used to dignify great patriotic occasions, such as the opening of the Olympic Games in London in 2012, or the funeral of Margaret Thatcher in April 2013. This vision is complemented by the visual image still familiar from the years when his moustachioed figure, in front of Worcester Cathedral, ornamented the Bank of England's £20 note. Elgar's association with the First World War is less known, although visitors to the biggest British military memorial outside the country, at Thiepval on the Somme, will hear his famous 'Nimrod' theme from the *Enigma Variations* of 1899 played at the interpretative centre there. Elgar had been born into a lower-middle-class family at Broadheath, near Worcester, in 1857 and was 57 years old in 1914. By that time he had travelled far from his humble origins, having been knighted in 1904 and given membership of the Order of Merit in 1911. In 1889 Elgar had married Alice Roberts, the daughter of a general, and in 1912 they had moved into a mansion in Hampstead, where Alice sought to maintain a lifestyle commensurate with Elgar's unofficial status as the nation's composer laureate.

Behind the façade Edward Elgar was a man of contradictions. He never overcame a sense of social inferiority derived from his humble background and the sense of being an outsider to British society that came with being a Roman Catholic. It had taken him the best part of 20 years to establish himself as a professional composer, having started as a humble violin teacher and conductor of the orchestra of Worcester's lunatic asylum. He was a profoundly nervous man, prone to hypochondria, and – for all the outward trappings of success – he felt misunderstood as a composer. He was intensely conscious that, of the arts, music had the lowest profile in Britain, and he was fully aware that the British public responded most enthusiastically to his more accessible works, such as the *Pomp and Circumstance Marches* written in 1901. In contrast he felt that the public did not understand his more serious works, those written as he characteristically put it, from 'his insidest inside'. The incomprehension which in 1900 had greeted the work now universally regarded as his great religious masterpiece, his oratorio setting the words of Cardinal Newman's poem, *The Dream of Gerontius*, had cut him to the quick and had made him terribly reluctant ever again to expose his deepest feelings to the public. Conversely, the way in which Arthur Benson's patriotic words for 'Land of Hope and Glory', grafted onto his *Pomp and Circumstance March No. 1*, had been adopted as an unofficial national

FIGURE 1 *By 1914 the 'English Musical Renaissance' was well under way. From left to right: Edward Elgar, Edward German (standing), Dan Godfrey, Alexander Mackenzie, Hubert Parry (standing) and Charles Stanford.*

anthem had rekindled in him a desire to act, as he wrote in 1904, 'as the old troubadours or bards did. In those days it was no disgrace for a man to be turned on to step in front of an army and inspire them with a song.'[2]

Anyone working with the huge surviving correspondence to and from Elgar cannot fail to be struck by how many letters he received from well-wishers, friends and from unknown members of the public, thanking him for his music.[3] It seems that no amount of encouragement could overcome Elgar's inner doubts, and his conviction that God was against great art. It was a conviction strengthened in 1912 when Elgar's choral setting of O'Shaughnessy's poem of the same name, *The Music Makers*, effectively a personal statement of his position as a composer, was received with a distinct lack of critical warmth. In the next two years, Elgar, now well into middle age, was frequently depressed and unwell. He was torn between intense longing for privacy and the desire for public recognition; between his love of the countryside and his wife Alice's aspirations for him to cut a figure in London society; and between deep religious feeling and a sense that God was indifferent to the fate of men. He was indeed fortunate to be supported unreservedly by Alice, who constantly championed his music, and who tolerated his intense emotional reliance on the friendship of younger women, notably that of Alice Stuart-Wortley, the 'Windflower' to whom Elgar confided his innermost thoughts.

George Martin's gracious tribute to the anthem *Give unto the Lord* had brought little consolation to Elgar in 1914, who had hoped that the anthem would also be performed at the Worcester Festival that year. When it was not, he wrote to the Festival's director, in typically self-lacerating vein: 'I have been wondering if I am really wanted at all.'[4] Alice Elgar, ever solicitous, planned a holiday to Scotland with her husband and their daughter Carice, hoping that a bracing climate and country pursuits would help to restore Elgar's spirits. On 19 July they left London by train. Elgar was not easily satisfied by the different places they visited in Scotland; Alice's diary records how they travelled to the islands of Mull, Iona and Staffa, moving on to Inverness, back to Lairg, then to Dingwall, before finally finding suitable accommodation at Achnasheen in Ross.[5] It was in this remote highland setting that they first heard the rumours of a European war. Elgar was horrified, writing to Alice Stuart-Wortley on 2 August: 'How truly awful all the news is – I cannot think of anything else – we get very little news & I have been wiring to London as trains are hours late – posts very vague and newspapers scarce & old: thanks for those you sent – we shall remain here until the 9th & longer if we can so please write as often as you can & tell me news, not only of the war, for which I hunger.'[6]

Charles Hubert Hastings Parry was older than Elgar, born in 1848, and is, similarly, often misunderstood. If Elgar felt himself to be outside the British establishment, Parry most definitely did not. He had inherited a substantial country house with an estate at Highnam Court near Gloucester and married Maude Herbert, the sister of the Earl of Pembroke. As an adult, Parry claimed the rare distinction of being on terms of friendship with four different prime ministers. Parry made his way professionally first as a historian of music, and only later as a successful composer. He became a leading light of the Three Choirs Festival, where so many important works of the new school of English composers were promoted, including in 1889 Parry's eight-part choral setting of Milton's 'At a Solemn Musick', a celebration of the union of words and music known to generations of choral singers in Britain as *Blest Pair of Sirens*. Parry was also influential as a teacher, and in 1895 was appointed Director of the newly formed Royal College of Music. He was knighted in 1898.

He stood therefore at the heart of the 'English Musical Renaissance' of the late nineteenth century; he played a significant part in raising the profile of music in British cultural life, and in helping a generation of younger composers, including Vaughan-Williams, Howells, Finzi and Ivor Gurney. Parry was greatly influenced by German music and philosophy, notably through his teacher Edward Dannreuther, and personally welcomed Wagner to London when he visited in 1877. Parry's own music was stylistically indebted to late-Romanticism, but was always gentle and lyrical, never overbearing. He displayed a particular gift for writing extended melodies, several of which have gained enduring popularity with the British public. An example is 'Long Since in Egypt's Plenteous Land', written for the oratorio *Judith* in 1902, but much better known as the hymn setting 'Dear Lord and Father of Mankind'.

The success of Parry's ceremonial works, such as the anthem *I Was Glad*, first performed at the coronation of Edward VII in 1902, have contributed to a misleading image of him as a royalist, even an imperialist. This has been strengthened recently by the performance of several pieces of his music at the wedding of Prince William to Kate Middleton in 2012. We can gain a different insight into his character and history from a postcard sent by George Bernard Shaw to Elgar in 1920, after Parry's death. 'P.', he wrote, 'was a damned nice chap, and if he had been a little less nice, he would also have been a little less damned'.[7] Parry, with all the advantages conferred on him by birth, and by education at Eton and Oxford, was actually a free-thinking radical, who from an early age identified himself with the progressive wing of English politics. His wife Maude was a fervent suffragist, and through her Parry was closely involved with the most controversial social and political movement of the era. His eldest daughter Dorothea married Arthur Ponsonby, a Liberal MP who chaired the party's Foreign Affairs Group, and Parry's friendship with Ponsonby was to bring him into close association with further strands of dissent in 1914.

Parry's personal life was not as successful as his professional career. His wife Maude was eccentric and capricious, frequently ill, and, unlike

FIGURE 2 *Britain was a society in flux before August 1914. Here, women demonstrate in Littlehampton to be allowed to vote, led by Lady Maude Parry, wife of the composer.*

Alice Elgar, she had frankly little interest in music. Although Parry was remarkably indulgent towards her, his marriage was not altogether happy. His own health was not good, and he was prone to depression. As he grew older he took refuge not only in music, and in work with his students at the Royal College, but also in philosophy. He developed an ambitious scheme to write a study of philosophy which would put forward a theory of progress wedding aesthetic, political and social ideas, and increasingly this project provided a refuge from the taxing realities of his personal life. Parry was also a sailor. He bought a 21-ton yawl in 1896, which was rebuilt and named the *Wanderer* in 1903, and he enjoyed the opportunities this provided for exploring the coastline and its wildlife. In July 1914 he was preparing the *Wanderer*, which was berthed at Littlehampton, for his annual journey to the west coast of Ireland. On 18 July he took the *Wanderer* for a day's sailing in the Solent, where the British Navy was gathered. He wrote in his diary: 'Had a good sight of the huge fleet assembled for review and of the aeroplanes circling above it.'[8]

After this, Parry, who was nothing if not busy, had to return briefly to Highnam to attend to his estate. He found that the army wanted to use three of his fields for manoeuvres, and, closer to his heart, that a number of trees had been damaged in a recent storm. He then returned to Littlehampton to prepare the *Wanderer* for its forthcoming expedition. Other matters were though intruding on his attention. On 31 July he wrote that he had heard from Arthur Ponsonby about 'war fever & universal war preparation. He very busy as Chairman of a section of the Liberal Party opposing our being drawn in. He spoke with the warmest admiration of Edward Grey, of his coolness & patience, & clear headedness. But many people seem to have gone crazy.'[9] Parry continued with his plans, but found the *Wanderer*'s skipper worried that they would not be allowed to leave harbour because of the rumours of war. On 3 August they set sail, but, as Parry wrote: 'We were stopped by a Navy steam launch who told us to alter our course as we were going over dangerous ground & would have a shot fired at us, if we went any further.'[10]

If Elgar and Parry were representatives of a generation which had come to maturity in the late Victorian era, Rupert Brooke had been clearly identified as one of the rising stars of an entirely new cohort. There is such a mythology around him, even now, that it is difficult to get beyond the legend of the golden-haired Apollo, the beautiful young poet who charmed and beguiled men and women alike. As a starting point we should draw on the comment made in 1964 by James Strachey, who knew Brooke intimately at Rugby School and then at King's College Cambridge, before the two broke apart in 1912: 'Rupert wasn't nearly so nice as people now imagine; but he was a great deal cleverer.'[11] After a brilliant career at Rugby and Cambridge, Brooke had by 1914 become established as a poet and a scholar of considerable promise. A volume of his poems had been published in 1911, and he was one of 17 writers featured in the first of a new series of anthologies, *Georgian Poetry*, published in 1912. He was awarded a Fellowship at King's College in March 1913.[12] While an undergraduate at Cambridge he had been admitted to the select company of the 'Apostles', and he had since then been a prominent member of the social and literary circles known as the Bloomsbury Group, and the neopagans. He flirted with involvement in the Fabian Society. One of Brooke's many admirers was Eddie Marsh, the editor of *Georgian Poetry* and secretary to Winston Churchill, then First Lord of the Admiralty. Marsh was an influential patron of the arts, who cultivated the friendship of young writers and painters, providing them with encouragement, food, drink and hospitality at his rooms in Raymond Buildings in London. Through Marsh, Rupert Brooke was introduced to aristocratic and political circles. He became a good friend of Violet Asquith, the daughter of the Prime Minister. Gifted with charisma, good looks and intellect, Brooke appeared to enjoy all the advantages life could offer to an Englishman of the Edwardian middle classes.

He had also, through the Cambridge Apostles and his intimacy with members of linked social circles, been one of those privileged to escape from the confines of Victorian sexual conformity. Many of his friends were homosexual or, as he probably was, bisexual, and several enjoyed a degree of sexual freedom which was denied to most young people in Britain until the 1960s and after. But Rupert Brooke's attractiveness and charm had brought him problems, and by 1914 his personal life had become desperately confused. After experimenting with homosexual relationships, Brooke had fallen in love with several young women, notably Noel Olivier and Katharine Cox, but in both cases, approaching intimacy and commitment, the relationships had fallen apart. Brooke experienced a breakdown in 1912 after difficulties in his relationship with Ka Cox, and following this his tendencies towards self-loathing, misogyny and anti-Semitism became increasingly marked. He became stridently anti-feminist; and his writings from 1912 onwards display a fascination with death and confusion about his future. In 1913 Brooke embarked on a long visit to America, and then to Hawaii and Tahiti, partly in an effort to cast out his inner demons. During the visit he had further relationships with women, and he appears to have experienced a degree of fulfilment in a sexual relationship with a Tahitian woman, Taatamata.

Brooke returned to England in June 1914, yearning to re-enter the social and artistic maelstrom he had left 12 months previously, to renew some of his old friendships and to make new ones. Taking up his fellowship in Cambridge appears to have been the last thing on his mind. He spent much of June and July 1914 living at Eddie Marsh's in London, going, as so many did that summer, to the Russian ballet and meeting with other artists. Marsh delighted in bringing together creative spirits from hitherto separate spheres, and Brooke met an incredibly diverse and rich series of people in these weeks. They included writers such as D. H. Lawrence and Siegfried Sassoon and painters such as Paul Nash, Stanley Spencer and Henri Gaudier-Breszka. Briefly, Brooke stayed in Gloucestershire with the 'Dymock Poets', Wilfred Gibson, Lascelles Abercrombie, Edward Thomas and Robert Frost. Marsh introduced him to Winston Churchill and to the Prime Minister, Henry Asquith. Together they attended a private performance by the pianist Denis Browne at 10 Downing Street.[13] Brooke also met again with old flames like Katharine Cox, and the actress Cathleen Nesbitt, and he started a love affair with Lady Eileen Wellesley. During June and July he was writing intimate letters to all three women.

On the surface Brooke appears to have been one of a glittering elite, enjoying the last golden summer before Europe was plunged into war. But behind the dinners and shows, the discussions of poetry and aesthetics, the flirting and pouting, he was deeply unfulfilled. His many letters from this period reveal him as sexually frustrated, bitter about his past, uncertain about his future, and conscious that his youth was slipping away. He planned to visit his mother in Rugby on his 27th birthday on 3 August, and after this, to stay with friends in Norfolk, then perhaps to go on a brief sailing or walking holiday with his friend Jacques Raverat; beyond that his life had no apparent direction. Raverat was the unfortunate recipient of some of Brooke's most unpleasant letters from this period, including one where he wrote: 'I have no respect for young women. I have as little as a sick man has for that gruel which he has to take to keep him alive. I know all about them. And I hate them.' He added: 'You'll be relieved to know that I pray continually. Twelve hours a day, that I may, sometime, fall in love with somebody. Twelve hours a day that I may *never* fall in love with anybody. Either alternative seems too hellish to bear.'[14] In another letter to Raverat in July 1914 Brooke vented his loathing for Jews, his contempt for London society and his ill-feeling towards an earlier passion, Noel Olivier, writing: 'It's so *BLOODY* being celibate.'[15] He was angry with Cathleen Nesbitt because she could hardly fit him into her crowded acting schedule, and despite having showered her with protestations of love and adoration, wrote from his mother's house in Rugby: 'But you talk bloody rot about us not getting to know each other better. What in hell do you mean?'[16]

Clearly, Brooke was a very troubled young man, frustrated above all by his failure to build successful relationships with those closest to him. He knew that his extraordinary magnetism attracted men and women to him, and he was aware that he exploited this, sometimes quite shamefully. He knew also that he was a talented poet, but in common with others, he faced the challenge of escaping from the dead hand of Victorian romanticism and finding a distinctive idiom which might reflect a rapidly changing world. By the end of July 1914 he appears to have been living almost from day to day, flitting from one person to another and from one idea to another. The rumours of a European war, and of the possibility of Britain being dragged into it, which he heard from Eddie Marsh before he left London for Rugby, added a new element to his mental turmoil.

In contrast to these established figures, 21-year-old Vera Brittain in 1914 could only dream of being a creative artist. Born in 1893 in Newcastle-under-Lyme, Brittain's father was the director of a business producing high-quality paper.[17] The Brittains moved with Vera and her younger brother Edward to Buxton in Derbyshire in 1905, and there they lived a life of conventional provincial respectability, models of bourgeois propriety. Vera had, though, from an early age dreamt of becoming a writer, and as she matured she adopted ideas of female autonomy which were completely at variance with her parent's expectations of a conventional marriage. She was intelligent, earnest and thoroughly imbued with Victorian ideals of self-improvement. According to her later recollection, in 1911, while still at St Monica's boarding school for girls in Surrey, she read Olive Schreiner's *Woman and Labour* which awoke in her the ideal that women might become 'the equal and respected companions of men'.[18] Back with her parents in Buxton after leaving St Monica's, Brittain became increasingly discontented with the prospect of marriage, and with the round of dances, tea parties and games of tennis where she was expected to meet a suitable partner. Her discontent with this lifestyle was focused not on concerns about economic justice, or about poverty, but solely on the intellectual and creative limitations it imposed on women of her class. She was totally inexperienced sexually.

We can gain some sense of how far removed Brittain was from the currents of metropolitan life out in the Peak District from the fact that, for all her desires for female autonomy, she had no contact whatsoever with the campaign for women's suffrage. For all her developing discontent with established gender roles, she quite enjoyed aspects of her privileged lifestyle; she loved fine clothes and enjoyed amateur dramatics, dancing and tennis. She still attended church with her parents and, despite her growing doubts about orthodox Anglicanism, developed something of a crush on a young curate. Brittain had begun to think seriously about going to university, and after attending a summer school at Somerville College, Oxford, in August 1913, she resolved to try to get a scholarship there in 1914. Showing characteristic determination and discipline, she studied intensively, trying to bring her Latin, Mathematics and English up to the standard required, and in March 1914 she was awarded an Exhibition of £20 a year for 3 years to study English at Somerville. She still had to pass the Senior Entrance Exam in July, but she secured her parents' reluctant and somewhat baffled acceptance to her plans to study. The first colleges for women at Oxford, including Somerville, had been established in the 1870s, but women students there, although allowed to take undergraduate examinations, were still not allowed to gain a degree from the university.

Vera Brittain was close to her brother Edward, 2 years younger than herself, who had been sent to public school at Uppingham. Edward was a sensitive boy, a violinist who harboured ambitions to compose music, and it was through him that Vera met Roland Leighton in April 1914. Leighton was the captain of his house, an outstanding scholar and Colour-Sergeant of the Officer Training Corps. Like Edward he was also an aesthete, interested in literature and poetry, and Vera was immediately attracted to this self-confident, even arrogant, young man. They shared a passion for Olive Schreiner's books, and an earnest relationship between them, tinged with suppressed sexual feeling, developed around conversations and letters about literature and religion. The two met again at the Uppingham School Speech Day on 11 July 1914, and Brittain revelled in the atmosphere and ceremonial there. She saw in the public school emphasis on developing 'character' a reflection of her own intense desire for self-fulfilment. In her diary she wrote: 'For girls – as yet – there is nothing equivalent to a public school for boys – these fine traditions & unwritten laws that turn out so many splendid characters have been withheld from them – to their detriment.'[19] Leighton made a clean sweep of the school prizes, and as he and Edward were both due to go to Oxford in October, it was with renewed enthusiasm that Vera took the Senior Examination on 20 July. Fondly she imagined going to the university to study alongside them. Five days later, while she waited to hear the results, she noted in her diary how conversation with friends after tennis had turned to other matters, 'chiefly the European crisis, which has suddenly come nearer owing to Austria issuing what is practically an ultimatum to Servia'.[20]

Dreaming of escape from provincial conformity, Vera Brittain had no experience of the extraordinary artistic ferment in London of the years before 1914. In no field was this excitement more apparent than in painting, where the impact of modernism coincided with the emergence of an exceptionally talented group of young British painters, most of whom studied at the Slade School of Drawing, Painting, and of Sculpture. Here they were exposed not only to an austere diet of traditional life drawing and sharp criticism from the professor of drawing, Henry Tonks, but to the most radical ideas about art coming from continental Europe. Three of these young painters are selected here for analysis – Richard Nevinson, Paul Nash and Stanley Spencer.

Richard Nevinson was born in 1889 and grew up in a remarkable intellectual environment. His father Henry was a notable Liberal journalist and war correspondent; his mother Margaret was a prominent campaigner for women's suffrage and Poor Law reform. Their house in Hampstead was a centre for agitated political debate, and young Richard Nevinson was exposed to a range of cosmopolitan influences as he matured.[21] Coincidentally he was sent to school at Uppingham, which Vera Brittain's brother Edward later attended. Although she was swept off her feet in the summer of 1914 by her experience of Uppingham's Speech Day, Richard Nevinson as a young boarder experienced another reality. He loathed the conformity, bullying, sexual abuse, corporal punishment and militarism at the school, and it confirmed him as a rebel against the establishment. He took refuge in painting and drawing, and extended holidays in Europe gave him the opportunity to see modernist paintings there. Between 1909 and 1912 Nevinson studied at the Slade alongside contemporaries such as Stanley Spencer, Mark Gertler, Paul Nash and Ben Nicholson. He also met young women like Dora Carrington, Barbara Hiles and Dorothy Brett. These three generated scandal by cutting their hair short in 1911 in a deliberate gesture of defeminization.

In his later autobiography Nevinson portrayed student life at the Slade, a mixture of earnest aestheticism, wild partying, promiscuity and social rebellion, marked for him by an intense but unhappy relationship with Dora Carrington. After leaving the Slade, Nevinson spent time in France, meeting some of the leading lights of the European avant-garde, such as Severini and Modigliani, and becoming familiar with the work of others like Kandinsky. He claimed to have met Lenin in Paris, knowing him to be 'a revolutionary of some sort'.[22] From an early age Nevinson had been prone to various illnesses, notably rheumatism, and he developed a brittle temperament, alternatively extroverted and flamboyant, then withdrawn and even paranoid. During a health cure in – of all places – Buxton, Nevinson met Kathleen Knowlman, later to become his wife. By 1913 he was gaining a reputation as one of the modernist painters associated with Percy Wyndham Lewis and the Rebel Arts Centre in London, but it was his involvement with the Italian poet Marinetti which brought him to wider public attention.

Filippo Marinetti was the self-styled leader of the 'Futurists', a group proclaiming a belief in a future to be dominated by movement, energy, dynamism and machines, and contempt for the past, or 'passé-ism'. Together with other Italian artists Marinetti had published a 'Futurist Manifesto' in Italy in 1909, and in 1910 and 1912 he visited London to propagate his ideas there. Marinetti's group also espoused the idea of war as 'the only hygiene in the world', seeing it as an elemental opportunity for regeneration.[23] In April 1914, Richard Nevinson and Wyndham Lewis jointly invited Marinetti to London for a series of events which attracted huge publicity. Famously, at the Dore Galleries, Marinetti presented a show of his poetry during which Nevinson banged a big drum from behind the stage. Nevinson then joined with Marinetti to issue a 'Futurist Manifesto' which was published in *The Times*, *The Observer* and the *Daily Mail* early in June. Nevinson claimed that he used to visit theatres and shower copies of the manifesto onto audiences from the galleries. The text repeated many ideas from Marinetti's original, introducing a deliberately offensive critique of the British establishment with a lyrical call to 'English artists', to 'strengthen their Art by a recuperative optimism, a fearless desire of adventure, a heroic instinct of discovery, a worship of strength and a physical and moral courage'. It spoke of 'a violent incentive for creative genius', but notably did not repeat Marinetti's original description of war as an aesthetic and purifying force. Nevinson foolishly claimed in the 'Manifesto' the endorsement of several other young artists,[24] and this led to confrontation at a dinner a few days later, where a speech by Nevinson was heckled, and which degenerated into a brawl. Nevinson then attended a 'Grand Futurist Concert of Noises' at the Coliseum in London, where Marinetti sought to translate his ideas into sound, using 10 special 'noise tuners'. Ironically, at a later performance, Marinetti added a recording of Elgar's music 'to bring a little melody into the act', a move which was received 'in stony silence'.[25] All of this sound and fury was accompanied by pictorial art. Nevinson exhibited several of his works with London Group in mid-June, attracting more publicity and some scathing criticism.

One of these paintings, entitled *Arrival*, displays the pictorial language which Nevinson had been developing, inspired by Marinetti, Severini and other Futurists. In it Nevinson represented an ocean liner reaching port, but, in Cubist fashion he broke up the planes of the liner, the dockside and the sea, fragmenting the picture, allowing him to contrast the movement of a huge modern ship with the stasis of the dockyard, and to suggest the dynamism of modern life. Tiny human figures appear in the painting, but are overwhelmed by the enormous ship, and the movement around them. Nonetheless, the painting is far from totally abstract. *The Times*' review was typically sceptical: 'Mr. Nevinson', it stated, 'used to be a painter with a modest talent, but now he is like a singer with a small voice who has taken to shouting'.[26] Nevinson had also alienated himself from the other avant-garde artists whom he had offended by attaching their names to his 'Futurist Manifesto', and who now went on to proclaim themselves a separate group called 'Vorticists'. Nonetheless, his 'shouting' had brought him great publicity. He was recognized as 'the eminent English Futurist' and had made himself something of a celebrity.[27] The idea of 'Futurism' became widely known, if associated in many minds with nothing more than gaudy colours and unusual geometric shapes. In the popular press it was used to generate humour, but already its influence was penetrating into design, being used for curtains, furnishings and clothing. It would not be long before camouflage artists working for the military were applying Futurist techniques to break up the outlines of ships and aircraft.

A characteristic pattern had been established, in which Nevinson sought publicity in provocative ways, often consciously giving offence to others, while at the same time feeling that he was misunderstood and misrepresented, both by conservatives and radicals. Describing himself in his later autobiography as 'high-spirited and bursting with energy', Nevinson nonetheless claimed also that he was 'a serious, and even a grim, hard worker'.[28] By the end of June 1914, Marinetti had returned to Italy, and Nevinson left London with his mother to visit the south of France. Their efforts at relaxation were frustrated by an increasingly anxious mood there and, in July, by talk of war with Germany. They reached Paris after 'a terrible journey across France in the burning heat with neither food nor drink, jammed in like cattle with the soldiers', to discover that the government had ordered mobilization and that it was almost impossible to change their money into French francs. It was with some relief that they boarded an express at the Gare du Nord, and then a cross-Channel ferry crowded with Americans, to get back to England.[29]

The art of Nevinson's contemporary, Paul Nash, was entirely different. Where Nevinson was interested in machines, movement, force and sought to engage a wide audience, Nash was an inward-looking, spiritual young man, interested above all in landscape, trees and with what he perceived as the special feeling of certain places. He was also from a middle-class background, and, like Nevinson, he had taken up drawing at school, where he had suffered from bullying. Growing up in London, it was in the open spaces of Kensington Gardens that Nash claimed 'I came upon my first authentic *place*.'[30] Although Nash's parents intended him to pursue a career in the navy, he was obviously unsuited to this, and they allowed him to follow his art instead. He studied at the Slade in 1910 and 1911, but did not find the atmosphere there congenial. Intriguingly he described Nevinson as the 'school bully, in a playful sort of way, on a mental, rather than a physical, plane'.[31] After leaving the Slade Nash was lucky to be encouraged by several older men, who gave him advice, and bought his works. One of these was Gordon Bottomley, one of Marsh's 'Georgian' poets, who was to remain a lifelong supporter.[32] Through William Richmond Nash showed some of his drawings at the Carfax Gallery in London in November 1912, which brought him a much-needed £30, and the envy of some other aspiring artists.[33]

In 1913 Nash was introduced to Margaret Odeh, the daughter of a clergyman, and very soon the two became engaged. Margaret had studied at Cheltenham Ladies' College and then at St Hilda's College, Oxford. She had joined the suffragettes and worked for the Tax Resistance League, which supported women who refused to pay their taxes because they were not eligible to vote. Through Margaret, Paul Nash was introduced to a world of activism which was entirely new to him, but he remained an observer rather than a participant in politics. He was close to his younger brother Jack, also an aspiring artist, and they had a joint show of their works in London in November 1913. Both were invited to join Roger Fry's Omega Workshops, which were established to bring modernist artistic ideas into design and furnishings. At this stage, Paul Nash's drawings were almost exclusively of trees and of landscapes, but he was gaining a modest reputation.[34] His models were Rossetti and Blake.

In March 1914 Nash met Eddie Marsh, who with characteristic generosity invited him to stay, and introduced him to other artists and writers. On 9 July Nash breakfasted in Raymond Buildings with Marsh, Rupert Brooke, W. H. Davies and another young poet, Siegfried Sassoon. Nash was planning a holiday together with his brother Jack and with Margaret Odeh, intending to stay for some of the time with Gordon Bottomley and his wife in the Lake District. On 16 July they left London, spending the next fortnight travelling from the Bottomley's cottage at Carforth to Grasmere, Thirlemere, Keswick, Penrith, and through the Kirkstone Pass to Pooley Bridge. Nash was exhilarated by the grandeur of the mountains, the gills and torrents, and the picturesque buildings, 'All hanging on the edge of precipitous places, all grey and ruinous'. The party then visited the art collectors Michael Sadler and John Rutherston, and marvelled at the works they had assembled. Paul Nash was excited to see one of his drawings hung in the company of drawings by Rossetti, Whistler, Bone and Hokusai. He might have sold another drawing to Rutherston, he wrote, 'if War had not just broken out & caused everyone to think twice about buying a thing'.[35]

By common consent, the most gifted of this generation of young artists at the Slade was the unworldly figure of Stanley Spencer, forever associated with the village of Cookham in Berkshire. Spencer was born there in 1891, the eighth of nine children who survived; his father was the village organist and a music teacher. The family lived in a semi-detached house, Fernlea, in an atmosphere of religious piety, love of nature and reverence for the arts, above all music and literature. Cookham lies on the River Thames to the west of London, but in the late Victorian period was still remarkably isolated. When the river rose, the village was turned into an island, surrounded by flooded meadows, heightening this sense of detachment. Stanley was brought up with his younger brother Gilbert in an incredibly sheltered way, educated at home, and rarely travelling outside the village. From an early age he developed an intense spirituality; he and Gilbert associated familiar scenes and people from Cookham with the Bible stories they were steeped in. Both loved drawing, and as they grew older, the family gradually accepted that they would try to become artists. If the world that Stanley Spencer grew up in was confined physically, culturally it was not. His oldest brother Will was a brilliant pianist, and there was always music in the house, typically Bach, Handel, Beethoven and Schubert, as well as literature. Spencer's imagination was formed by 'Everyman classics' as well as by his father's Bible readings. At the age of 16 he was allowed to study at the nearby Technical Institute in Maidenhead, and in 1908, he was admitted to the Slade. His parents came to an arrangement whereby Stanley could travel in to the school every day on the train, and return home in the evening. At the Slade, Spencer was known, inevitably, as 'Cookham'.[36]

At the end of his first year, Spencer was awarded a scholarship for another 2 years at the Slade. During this period he developed and brought together the themes which would dominate his life and his art, his intense spirituality, his love of nature, of Cookham, and an as yet unrequited sexual longing. He started to produce drawings and then paintings of scenes and people from Cookham which not only alluded to the Bible, but represented episodes from it, as if the life of Christ had been played out in rural Berkshire. Spencer always painted from his own direct experience, and his work combined a childlike intensity with a unique spiritual radiance. Although as a student Spencer had met other artists, and his reputation had spread, he still loved Cookham, and when he finished at the Slade, he simply continued painting in the family dining room at Fernlea. Between 1912 and 1914 he produced several paintings which brought him attention. Typically, he was spotted by Eddie Marsh, who met him in November 1913. Marsh wrote to Rupert

Brooke that he and 'Cookham' had 'got on like a house on fire', adding that 'he writes delicious letters'.[37] Spencer was indeed a prolific and idiosyncratic writer. He cared little for spelling and punctuation, but corresponded, often at great length, with his brothers and sisters, and with an increasing range of artistic friends. He wrote frequently to fellow Slade students Jacques and Gwen Raverat, and also to Henry Lamb, an older artist. Marsh travelled to Cookham, where he bought Spencer's painting *The Apple Gatherers* for £55. In April 1914 Spencer spent a weekend with Marsh in London, who was now considering publishing a volume of *Georgian Painters* as a companion to *Georgian Poetry*. This led on 10 July to a meeting at Raymond Buildings with Rupert Brooke. Spencer wrote: 'He is a good man, & I think he must be an English man, must be.'[38] Spencer was clearly a little overawed, but need not have been. Brooke was the first to confess that he knew little about painting. The two got on well, and they agreed to meet again. Spencer was working on a self-portrait in Marsh's bathroom, and undoubtedly enjoyed the Bohemian atmosphere surrounding his new patron.[39] Typically, he missed his engagement with Brooke at Marble Arch. Spencer returned to Cookham, where he continued working on his self-portrait.

If Nevinson, Nash and Spencer were beginning to establish themselves as professional artists, a younger man in London from a less prestigious educational background could as yet only dream of this. David Jones had left the Camberwell School of Arts and Crafts in the summer of 1914 at the age of 18, but he had already resolved to dedicate himself to fine art. Born in 1895 to a Welsh father from Anglesey and an English mother from London, Jones had studied under the direction of A. S. Hartrick since 1910, combining a focus on drawing from observation with courses on English literature. He grew up in a late-Victorian atmosphere where, as Paul Fussell has written, 'aestheticism and religion met for mutual enrichment'.[40] In certain ways, one is reminded of Spencer's background, with its combination of earnest piety and respect for high culture. The Jones family was frugal but not poor. David Jones' father James was a printer working for the *Christian Herald*, and both parents were committed to aspirational respectability. As an adolescent David Jones read widely, drinking in not only Shakespeare, Milton and the Bible, but heady draughts of Victorian medievalism. At Camberwell he read the English Romantic poets and Bede and Gildas, as well as *The Anglo-Saxon Chronicle* and the *Song of Roland*. As a result, many of his drawings used medieval imagery and symbolism, even when presenting contemporary scenes.

Although Jones left after his death a vast collection of letters, very few survive from before 1919, and we thus know little about his inner state in the years before the war.[41] We know that he was high-spirited and enjoyed taking part in tableaux recreating medieval scenes; he was, in Thomas Dilworth's words, 'evidently a bit of a dandy'.[42] There has been much debate about whether, or how far, David Jones was 'Welsh', and unsurprisingly there are different views about this. Through his father, Jones was introduced to

Welsh mythology and history, and he proudly thought of himself as being Welsh in spirit. He read a translation of the mythological Celtic tales called the *Mabinogion* and numerous histories of Wales in English. Although his father was a Welsh speaker, David Jones was not. His later friend René Hague was unequivocal: 'It was a great sorrow to David that he was cut off . . . from a Wales for which he had no more than a sentimental love. . . . Of modern Wales he had little or no knowledge. . . . Worst of all, in spite of years of application he could never learn the language.'[43] Jones himself confessed as much, when in his later memoir, *In Parenthesis*, he differentiated between his fellow soldiers in the London Welsh, referring to some as 'the genuine Taffies'.[44] Towards the end of his life, Jones spoke of his situation just before the war, which, he said, came as 'a simplification'.[45] He was a young man with a profoundly romantic and historical imagination, and with vague ideas about becoming an artist. In his own later words, he was 'an innocent uninformed boy'.[46]

We know even less about Ellis Evans, who certainly was a 'genuine Taffy'. Evans was born in 1887 to a Welsh-speaking family in the village of Trawsfynydd in North Wales, the oldest of 11 children. Shortly after his birth the family moved to a farmhouse outside the village, Yr Ysgwrn. Ellis left school at 14 and stayed with family, working on the farm, looking after the sheep. This is an area which is still largely Welsh-speaking, and which although only 100 miles as the crow flies from Cardiff or Birmingham, is extraordinarily remote, cut off from the rest of the world by mountains and the sea. Ellis Evans was by all accounts a dreamer, and according to accounts written after his death, started writing poetry at the age of 11. In the Welsh tradition, poetry is not something associated with a bourgeois elite, but is a possession of the ordinary people. It is an important element of the *eisteddfod*, a cultural festival where entries in different art forms are presented and judged. Welsh strict-metre poetry is a form where the music of the words, the rhythm, alliteration and balance are as important as the meaning. The most highly esteemed poems combine a high level of technical accomplishment with feeling and inspiration, achieving a degree of linguistic complexity which is difficult for even well-educated Welsh speakers today to appreciate fully. Welsh poets were traditionally given a bardic name when they had achieved a certain standing, and it is a testimony to Ellis Evans' success that in 1910, having won a chair at the Bala Eisteddfod in 1907, he was given the bardic name of Hedd Wyn, which is usually translated as 'Blessed Spirit'. After this he won prizes at a succession of local *eisteddfodau*. Clearly he worked extremely hard on his poetry, inspired by the wild and dramatic scenery around him, and he soon gained a remarkable mastery of the elements of strict-metre verse.

Ellis Evans did not keep a diary, and only a handful of fairly prosaic letters to and from him have survived. Much of what we know about him derives from later reminiscences and should be treated with caution.[47] He was much influenced by Shelley and the English romantic poets. His poetry was pastoral and lyrical, untouched by the currents of modernism. Although he attended the Welsh Independent Chapel in Trawsfynydd, there is conflicting evidence about how far, as a young adult, he was still an orthodox believer.[48] He was in a relationship with Lizzie Roberts, a local teacher, but with no income of his own, he could not think of marriage. He was encouraged in his poetry by J. Dyfnallt Owen, a minister who later became a pioneer of Welsh nationalism, and one of the stories about Ellis Evans which laid the groundwork for a later mythology derives from him. It suggests that Evans was steeped in the Welsh nonconformist tradition which held soldiering and militarism to be sinful. Apparently in the summer of 1914, before the war, the army was carrying out practice artillery firing in the mountains near Trawsfynydd, and the concussion from this broke some of the windows in the village chapel. In a recollection first published in March 1918, Dyfnallt recalled how, 'when I recounted the whole affair of the senseless firing, there was a wild light in Hedd Wyn's eyes; and there was no-one as eloquent in his opposition towards the defiled abomination that prostituted the vale as he'.[49]

We similarly know little about Kate Finzi, who apart from her 'War Diary', published in 1916, has left few written traces. She was born in 1890, the eldest daughter of a wealthy mercantile family of Sephardic Jewish origin, now naturalized, and living in North London. Kate's mother was a cultured woman from a German family, who played the piano well and wrote music herself. The Finzi family was one which valued creativity and the arts, and Kate's youngest brother Gerald, who was born in 1901, went on to become one of the most respected English composers of the twentieth century. Kate was brought up in a cosmopolitan environment and was taken by her mother on frequent European holidays, where she was able to improve the French and German she had learnt at home and at school. Like Vera Brittain, Kate was sent to a boarding school for girls. For all the Finzi family's material advantages, they were not strangers to ill fortune. Kate's father died from cancer in 1909, and one of her younger brothers, Douglas, died from pneumonia in 1912. Another brother, Felix, committed suicide in 1913. In the summer of 1914, Kate's mother was on holiday in Switzerland with her two surviving sons. Kate, aged 24, was old enough to stay alone in London.[50]

If we know little about Ellis Evans and Kate Finzi, we find ourselves with T. E. Lawrence in the position of Lytton Strachey, who, looking at the Victorians, cried: 'We shall never understand them! We know too much!' Every significant detail of Lawrence's life has been told and retold, by himself, by friends, relatives, admirers, detractors, historians and by psychoanalysts. Lawrence liked to create mystery around himself, to exaggerate, to invent and to obscure. The legend of 'Lawrence of Arabia' which has flourished ever since the final days of the First World War has complicated the picture further. The literary industry based on Lawrence is now complemented by websites dedicated to constructing and deconstructing the mythology around him. Lawrence liked, during the 1920s, to compare himself to a crab, using a protective outer covering to conceal the inner person.[51] Even his family name, he maintained, was merely 'an assumption', and so he cast it aside and took another.[52] It is genuinely difficult now to know whether some of the most significant events in the formation of the legend of 'Lawrence of Arabia' ever happened at all, or to what extent they are mixtures of truth and fiction. In darker moments, Lawrence was ready to confess that he had irremediably muddled the historical record of his own life. He wrote in 1934: 'There is no truth in me; so there can be little truth in my books as in those written about me.'[53]

Lawrence was, fortunately for the historian, a great writer and has left a significant body of letters and contemporaneous notes in addition to his later published work, and it is from these that we must try to construct, as far as possible, an accurate record of his experience of the First World War. We know that he was born in 1888 and that he was the illegitimate son of Thomas Chapman, an Anglo-Irish gentleman, and his former maid, Sarah Junner. Seeking anonymity in a society which had little tolerance for such a union, the family, taking the name Lawrence, moved several times before settling in Oxford. There 'Ned', the second of six sons, went to the City of Oxford High School and then to Jesus College, Oxford, to study history. Even the tales of his schooldays are littered with disputed accounts of various episodes, but it is clear that Lawrence grew up as an extraordinarily focused, ascetic and driven young man, with a passionate interest in medieval history and a deeply rooted desire to achieve some great purpose. Like so many 'great Victorians', Lawrence was influenced by his mother's ambitions and desire to control her sons. One result of this was his lifelong antipathy to women or, more precisely, to the idea of any sexual contact with women. Lawrence learnt some of the pleasures and pains of self-denial as a small child, and even as an adolescent, and then a student, he schooled himself to go for long periods without food and sleep, and to balance these deprivations with extended periods of study or physical exertion. The Harvard psychoanalyst John Mack has argued convincingly that Lawrence was 'inuring himself for some great task ahead', and that his student days in Oxford 'may also be looked upon as a period of intellectual, physical, and emotional preparation'.[54]

Unlike all the other artists in this study, whose ambitions were focused on creativity, and who had no desire to change the world through politics, Lawrence developed a passionate early interest in warfare, and in international affairs, encouraged by a Fellow at Magdalen College, David Hogarth, who was also Keeper of the Ashmolean Museum in Oxford. Hogarth encouraged Lawrence to travel and to think of the future of the British Empire. In 1909 and 1910 Lawrence went for the first time, ostensibly to prepare a dissertation on medieval castles, to the Middle East. Travelling widely in what is today Syria and Lebanon, and was then still part of the far flung Ottoman Empire, Lawrence developed an interest in archaeology which led to his subsequent engagement with a British Museum expedition to the ruins of the Hittite city of Carcemish on the Euphrates. Lawrence developed a fascination with the Arabs and their culture, and a close personal relationship with one young Arab man, Salim Ahmed, known also as Dahoum. He learnt to speak Arabic and applied himself with his usual extraordinary concentration to learning about the different tribes he came into contact with.

Virtually all of the Middle East in the early twentieth century was still nominally under Ottoman rule, but other states had ambitions for the region and sought to shape events there. The British controlled Egypt and the vital strategic link of the Suez Canal between the Red Sea and the Mediterranean. The French had deep-rooted aspirations to control Lebanon and Syria; the Russians hoped to expand south from the Caucasus and to gain access to the Mediterranean from the Black Sea; and Germany sought to gain economic influence in the region by developing the Berlin–Baghdad railway. The oil wells of Mesopotamia, in what is now northern Iraq, were taking on a new strategic importance which few people yet appreciated, as ships turned from coal to oil propulsion. The decision taken in 1911 to adopt oil as the principal fuel for all future ships of the Royal Navy gave the British a greatly heightened interest in maintaining access to these wells, now being exploited by the Anglo-Persian Oil Company.

As a young man learning about the region, armed with a deep sense of history, Lawrence appreciated the strategic importance of the Middle East. In common with most contemporary British observers, he viewed the Ottoman Empire as corrupt, despotic and ripe for dissolution. He was strongly francophobe and cherished an idea that the Arabs, under British tutelage, might soon throw off the shackles of Turkish rule. Following his mentor David Hogarth, he took it for granted that his archaeological work should be combined with service to British imperial interests, and even as a young man Lawrence developed a heady sense of how he might contribute to high-level discussions of strategy and politics. Priya Satia sees him as one of a socially connected group who saw in the open spaces of the desert opportunities for British imperial expansion which also chimed with their aesthetic, historical and philosophical imagination. In Lawrence's case, it also provided scope and focus for his literary ambitions.[55] More practically, as an archaeologist Lawrence learnt to manage large groups of Arab workers, mediating among them and imposing authority upon them, with force if necessary.

In January 1914 Lawrence went from Carcemish to spend 6 weeks with a Palestine Exploration Fund team which was surveying the Sinai desert on the instructions of Lord Kitchener, the British Agent and Consul-General in Egypt. The Sinai desert, then without roads or railways, lay between Palestine and the Suez Canal, and had come under British control in 1906. Lawrence and his colleague Leonard Woolley were asked to produce their survey, with maps, under the title *The Wilderness of Zin*, partly to disguise its production for military purposes. In June 1914 Lawrence returned to Oxford do background research on previous travellers to the Sinai before the publication of the survey. With a characteristic sense of biblical precedent, Lawrence wrote that he and Woolley had 'explored the desert of the exodus, looking for the footprints of the children of Israel'.[56]

There has been endless debate about whether Lawrence was working for British Intelligence before the First World War, but much of it is misplaced. Most academics, archaeologists and engineers working in the Middle East at this time saw it as part of their patriotic duty to report on developments they witnessed which might affect the strategic situation. What distinguished Lawrence was the seriousness with which he devoted himself to study of the region, its history, its culture and its contemporary mores. He was already planning a book about seven great cities of the Middle East which would weave together these themes, intending to call it *Seven Pillars of Wisdom*. He also had dreams of starting a printing press dedicated to the production of fine editions, which would seek to revive ancient traditions of craftsmanship in printing and bookbinding.

This group of writers, painters and composers was obviously not representative of British society in the summer of 1914. Rather, they point to its diversity, in gender, class, age, region and even in language. What is striking is how unprepared they were for the outbreak of war and for the challenges this might bring. None of them, with the exception of Lawrence, who had had some dealings with German archaeologists and engineers in the Middle East, was hostile to Germany. On the contrary, several, including Elgar, Parry, Finzi and Brooke, had travelled in Germany and had learnt to love aspects of its culture. Elgar's music had indeed been sometimes better received in Germany than in Britain, and it had been championed in Britain by German musicians and art lovers, above all the conductor Hans Richter. Parry was deeply imbued with German philosophy and music. Brooke had stayed in Germany for some time in 1912 and liked to deploy German words and phrases in his letters. Nevinson, Spencer and Finzi were from families with close ties to Germany.

Of the group, only Lawrence was interested in war and in military matters. From his historical reading, he accepted that war was one of the ways in which nations and groups of people interacted, and as a believer in the civilizing virtues of British imperialism he wanted to see the extension of British interests in the area he was fascinated by, the Middle East. The young David Jones was steeped in late Victorian medievalism, with its tales of chivalric and knightly conflict, but this was a world away from the calculations of generals and admirals in the early twentieth century. Elgar, although a British patriot to the core of his being, was not a man of violence. Nevinson, for all his noisy public enthusiasm for speed, movement and energy, had not embraced the Futurist idea of war as a necessary hygiene, and neither he nor any other in the group had seen war as offering a way towards new kinds of artistic representation. Several of the group, including Spencer, Nash, Parry, Brittain and Ellis Evans, were distinctly averse to violence and were by nature gentle and spiritual.

All these individuals, young and old, male and female, had grown up in an age with a belief in ideals of progress. Some, and here Elgar, Lawrence and Brooke stand out, were troubled by their perceptions of the changes around them. Stanley Spencer and Ellis Evans appear to have been extraordinarily insulated from contemporary currents in social life and in the arts, but the others, conversely, were embracing change. Vera Brittain and Kate Finzi were both taking advantage of the new educational opportunities becoming available to young women of the middle classes. Nash, Nevinson and Parry were closely involved with and sympathetic to the suffragettes though women who were close to them. Parry was committed to a philosophical ideal of human betterment; more prosaically, Elgar, Lawrence and Nevinson were, in different ways, fascinated by new technological developments. Curiously, although several of the group were churchgoers and had been brought up in conventionally Anglican families (with the exception of Elgar, who was a Roman Catholic, and Evans, who was a nonconformist), all were by 1914 either agnostics or committed to broader, more unorthodox ideas of spirituality. All were sensitive to aesthetics, to beauty and to refinement. All had enjoyed the blessings of peace, but this was about to end.

# CHAPTER TWO

# August 1914

When news reached Britain at the end of June 1914 that the heir to the Austrian throne, Archduke Franz Ferdinand, and his wife had been assassinated in Sarajevo, there was widespread horror at what was perceived as a terrorist outrage. The Prime Minister, Henry Asquith, the Foreign Secretary, Edward Grey, and the King, George V, conveyed their sympathy to the Austrians. There was no clear sense, as *The Times*' correspondent reported from Berlin, of how foreign relations might be affected by the killing. Things changed a month later, as Asquith wrote to his young confidante, Venetia Stanley: 'Austria has sent a bullying and humiliating Ultimatum to Servia, who cannot possibly comply with it, and demanded an answer within 48 hours – failing which she will march.' He was still hopeful that Britain need not be involved though, adding 'Happily there seems to be no reason why we should be anything more than spectators.'[1] Across Europe, there was agreement with Asquith's assessment that the Austrian ultimatum was intended to provoke war with Serbia. We know now that the Austrians had secured from Germany a declaration of support if they went to war against Serbia (the infamous 'blank cheque'), and reckoned on a successful punitive war which would strengthen their position in the Balkans, but this was not yet obvious to the public in Britain.[2] With Asquith's consent, Edward Grey suggested a Great Power conference to resolve the dispute between Austria and Serbia, but the Germans rejected this immediately.

Britain's position in the system of European alliances in 1914 was extraordinarily complex. After a long period of 'splendid isolation' in the nineteenth century, Britain had concluded an 'Entente Cordiale' with France in 1904. Subsequently, joint plans had been developed to respond to a possible German attack on France. These plans, further developed after the Agadir crisis in 1911, envisaged that a British force might be sent to northern France to fight on the left wing of French forces covering the borders with Germany and Belgium. More significantly, in 1912, Edward Grey had overseen joint naval talks which shared responsibilities between the British and French fleets. The British were to concentrate in the North Sea, and the French in the Mediterranean. This allowed the British to keep a clear superiority in numbers of capital ships over the newly developed German fleet in the North Sea, and the French to concentrate their own strength against Austria and Italy, but it also left the British with some sense of obligation to defend the north French coast. Grey and Asquith were fully aware, as the crisis developed in the final week of July 1914, of the implications of these military contingencies, and both were clear in their minds that if Germany attacked France, Britain would not be able to stand aside.

On 30 July the Russians started the cumbersome mobilization of their forces after Austria declared war on Serbia the previous day. Russian assurances to Germany that their mobilization was directed only against Austria were not accepted, and initial complacency about an Austrian war on Serbia started to turn to panic there. German war plans demanded an immediate response to Russian mobilization, envisaging that France could be defeated by a powerful attack through Belgium before the Russians could sufficiently concentrate their own forces to attack Germany. All sides sought assurances from Britain about how it might react to a larger European conflict. The Germans hoped that the British would stand aside (as they had done in 1870 during the Franco-Prussian war); the Russians, and particularly the French, sought assurances from Britain that it would not.

There was strikingly little appetite for war in Britain at this stage. The dispute between Austria and Serbia did not engage British sympathies on one side or another. Senior politicians in the Cabinet, including the Chancellor, Lloyd George, were opposed to intervention; the City of London feared the disruption of trade; academics, intellectuals and artists had no desire to be seen as allies of Tsarist despotism in Russia; in parts of Britain with a strong socialist tradition there was admiration for German trade unionism. The whole situation was changed by the German invasion of Belgium, which directly threatened British interests. A long-standing principle of British foreign policy was that no one Power should dominate the north European coast, and the prospect of the German fleet operating from Antwerp, Ostend, Zeebrugge, and even Dunkirk and Calais, was not one which any British government in 1914 could have contemplated with equanimity. It had long been known that a German attack on France might be partly directed through Belgium, and in August 1914 this materialized. On 29 July, the Germans had asked Britain for an assurance that it would stand aside if Belgian neutrality was infringed, but Edward Grey had refused, countering instead with a request to both France and Germany to respect Belgian neutrality. On 3 August the Germans declared war against France, and entered Belgium, claiming that they had to forestall a similar French move. Asquith's relief was palpable. He wrote to Venetia Stanley: 'The Germans, with almost Austrian crassness, have delivered an ultimatum to Belgium and forced themselves onto their territory.'[3]

At 2.00 p.m. that day, Edward Grey spoke to a packed House of Commons and outlined the British position. He explained that Britain had no obligation to help France, but that 'because of the feeling of confidence and friendship' between the two countries, the northern and western coasts of France were 'absolutely undefended'. He declared plainly his own feeling that if a foreign fleet were to attack these undefended coasts, 'we could not stand aside'. He then spoke of 'the more serious consideration – becoming more serious every hour . . . the question of the neutrality of Belgium'. Grey explained how his requests to the French and Germans that they should respect Belgian neutrality had been accepted by the French, but rejected by the Germans; and he told the House how it appeared that an ultimatum had already been presented by the Germans to the Belgians, demanding the free passage of German troops through Belgium. He concluded that if Britain refused to intervene to help either Belgium or France, 'we should, I believe, sacrifice our respect and good name and reputation before the world, and should not escape the most serious and grave economic consequences'. After finishing, in a dramatic moment, Grey was passed a message from the Belgian Legation in London, and he read it to the House. It confirmed his earlier understanding that a German ultimatum had been given to the Belgians and that the Belgians were 'resolved to repel aggression by any means'.[4]

Grey's speech, which effectively presented the case for British intervention, was very well received across the political spectrum. He was followed by John Redmond, the Irish Nationalist leader, who declared that in the event of war, both Irish Nationalists in the South and Unionists in the North of the island would rally behind the government.[5] *The Times* welcomed the decision of the Commonwealth Dominions to stand by Britain, even at the cost of being drawn into 'the vortex of European militarism'.[6] It was now widely accepted that it was only a matter of time before Britain would be at war. Opinion in Asquith's Cabinet had been transformed by the German treatment of Belgium, and only two Ministers, John Morley and John Burns, resigned their posts. On 4 August the British government issued an ultimatum to Germany, stating that unless immediate assurances were given to respect the neutrality of Belgium, Britain would 'feel bound to take all steps in their power to uphold the neutrality of Belgium and the observance of a Treaty to which Germany is as much a party as ourselves'.[7] No one in London appears to have thought that the Germans would back down, and at 11.00 p.m. the chiming of Big Ben marked the expiry of the ultimatum. The German Chancellor, Theobald von Bethmann-Hollweg, had indeed been perplexed by the British attitude, memorably describing the Treaty referred to in the ultimatum in his final conversation with the British ambassador in Berlin as a 'scrap of paper'.[8]

Insofar as we can reconstruct the views of the writers, painters and musicians who are the focus of this study, their attitudes to the developing crisis – ranging from indifference and incomprehension through to enthusiasm for war – tell us much about broader British opinions. For most of July 1914 they, like the rest of the country, had little sense of the gravity of the Sarajevo assassinations and shared the general sense of calm in international and even domestic affairs. Rupert Brooke, arriving back in Britain from his long travels in June 1914, was struck by this, writing to an American friend that, with the exception of Ireland: 'Everything else is rather stationary. No strikes, no wars, no nothing.'[9] Undoubtedly the mood in Britain changed dramatically in the last days of July 1914, and hardened after the German invasion of Belgium. This was an age in which people got their news almost exclusively from newspapers, and their presentation of the developing crisis was hugely influential. There is now a deeply rooted popular assumption in Britain that the outbreak of war was greeted with enthusiasm, with cheering and even with euphoria, but this is difficult to sustain in any kind of detailed analysis.

There was a wide range of reactions in Britain to the declaration of war with Germany, from apathy and indifference through to excitement and exultation. Grey's gloomy observation as he looked out from the Foreign Office that 'the lamps are going out all over Europe; we shall not see them lit again in our lifetime' is frequently quoted.[10] Less well known is Asquith's blunt statement to Venetia Stanley that 'The whole thing fills me with sadness . . . we are on the eve of horrible things.'[11] There was a broad consensus on the righteousness of Britain's cause. This was clearly expressed by the *The Times* on 5 August: 'We are going into the war that is forced upon us as the defenders of the weak and the champions of the liberty of Europe.' This was not only 'the cause of right and honour', but 'also the cause of our own vital and immediate interests'.[12] The *New Statesman*, which had urged caution as late as 1 August, stating that we might face 'a catastrophe', declared on 8 August that Britain had 'never gone to war with cleaner hands'.[13] There was widespread apprehension and even horror at the prospect of war. The newly established literary journal *Welsh Outlook* spoke for more than just Wales when it declared that 'the tragedy is too stupendous. . . . And yet it is necessary'.[14]

## Engagement or inertia: the challenge for individuals

Of the artists selected for this study, Rupert Brooke was the first to realize that the prospect of war would change his life, one way or another. Before leaving London at the end of July 1914, he was taken on 30 July by Eddie Marsh to dine at 10 Downing Street, and here he met Winston Churchill for the first time.[15] Presumably, the prospect of war with Germany was a topic of conversation, and it appears that Brooke was thinking hard about it. With characteristic insight he saw that, however he reacted, it would not be possible to remain unaffected. The next day he wrote from Rugby to

Stanley Spencer: 'But this damned war business. . . . If fighting starts, I shall have to enlist, or go as a correspondent. I don't know. It will be Hell to be in it; and Hell to be out of it. At present I'm so depressed about the war, that I can't talk, think or write coherently.'[16] He then explored the same idea in a letter to Eileen Wellesley, asking 'If war comes, should one enlist? Or turn war correspondent?'[17] Brooke clearly shared the discomfort of many intellectuals at the prospect of fighting on the Russian side, as he wrote to Jacques Raverat: 'Everything's just the wrong way round. *I* want Germany to smash Russia to fragments, and then France to break Germany. Instead of which I'm afraid Germany will badly smash France, and then be wiped out by Russia. France and Britain are the only countries that ought to have any power. Prussia is a devil. And Russia means the end of Europe and any decency.'[18] On 4 August, still unsure whether his further holiday plans would materialize, Brooke went to stay with Francis and Frances Cornford on the Norfolk coast at Cley.

Here, Brooke heard on 5 August that Britain had declared war on Germany. He wrote to Cathleen Nesbitt: 'I'd slept badly – and when I did sleep, dreamed horribly – all night; because I felt badly about the war.'[19] He spent the next couple of days on the beach, thinking about what he should do. He claimed on 6 August that he had tried, but failed, to get a post somewhere as a war correspondent,[20] and he expressed his uncertainty to his friend Dudley Ward, who had managed to return to England with his wife from Germany: 'What are you going to do? I want something to do.'[21] Brooke now abandoned his holiday plans and returned to London to stay with Marsh and to try to 'go off with the Army or Navy, in some capacity.'[22] There he found, as many other young men were doing, that it was not easy for one with no particular qualifications to get an exciting or interesting post in the military. He spent the next few days going from one office to another, putting his name on waiting lists. Brooke also wrote a revealing essay which was published in the *New Statesman*, pretending to describe the reactions of 'a friend' on hearing the news of the war. Although he showed an awareness of the potential shallowness and vulgarity of a patriotic response to the war, Brooke, surely speaking of himself, described his friend sitting on a beach, reflecting on what he should do, and realizing that 'as he thought "England and Germany," the word "England" seemed to flash like a line of foam'. The idea of 'enemies and warfare' on English soil 'sickened him'. Notably, Brooke described this sense of patriotic resolve as akin to 'holiness' and concluded: 'To his great disgust, the most commonplace sentiments found utterance in him. At the same time he was extraordinarily happy.'[23]

He was unwilling to join the Territorials, where he feared being posted on garrison duty somewhere in Britain, and he quickly abandoned the idea of being a war correspondent. He wrote to Eileen Wellesley, who appears to have advised him against this, that it was 'a rotten trade' at a time when people were 'offering their lives for their country, not for their curiosity'.

Describing his reluctance to become 'a part of a mere machine', he continued: 'I wanted to use my intelligence. I can't help feeling I've got a brain. I thought there must be some organizing work that demanded intelligence. But, on investigation, there isn't. At least, not for ages. I feel so damnably incapable. I can't fly or drive a car or ride a horse sufficiently well . . .'[24] A week later he was still 'chasing elusive employment'. He told Cathleen Nesbitt 'I really think I shall get a commission (Territorial probably) through Cambridge,' and that in the meantime he had been drilling 'on the chance of getting into a London corps as a private'. The whole 'insupportable stress' had left him feeling like 'a useless rag'.[25]

Stanley Spencer's reaction to the outbreak of war was even more torturous. Living in a small village, and with a parochial outlook on the world, he did not spend much time analysing the causes of the war, or Britain's strategic position. Although he was as unmilitary a character as can be imagined, Spencer knew that he was physically fit and eligible for service. Even before 4 August, Rupert Brooke's letter declaring his intention to get involved had thrown Spencer into turmoil. Once war was declared, he found it difficult to concentrate on his painting and expressed his confusion to several people. On 11 August he wrote to Ottoline Morrell, ironically soon to be at the centre of a pacifist circle, that he and his brother Gilbert were 'very bothered about this war: we certainly ought to help but. . . . It is not the fact that we might have an unpleasant time; it is that it means a complete disorganization of our work & perhaps ruination to it'.[26] The next day he wrote in similar vein to Henry Lamb, echoing Rupert Brooke: 'It is intolerable to be out of it: I can not think. If you know of anything either Gil or I could do, let us know. . . . When I feel the horror of the war most is when I go to bed.' Ruminating further, Spencer added: 'What ghastly things those Liege [sic] forts are: there seems to be no sport in war now.' His sentence was interrupted by a small sketch of the steel cupola of a fort, with guns projecting from it.[27]

Ironically, given the desire of men like Brooke to see action, it was a young woman in this group of artists who was first to get to the war zone. The Executive Committee of the British Red Cross Society met on the first day of war but decided at this stage that no 'Surgeons, Nurses, or Orderlies' should be called up 'for service abroad' and that no applications 'under these heads' should be considered.[28] This decision was quickly reversed, because on 7 August Kate Finzi was enrolled by the Red Cross as a 'dresser' in the 56th London (Marylebone) Division of the Voluntary Aid Detachment, or VAD.[29] The VAD was established in 1909 as a 'supplement to the Military Medical Organization of the Territorial Force on home service',[30] when it was imagined that the women in it would help to provide food, drink, shelter and comfort for soldiers, perhaps with some first aid if necessary. Finzi's very early enlistment in August 1914 can be explained not by solely her enthusiasm, which was shared by many other young women, but by her background. 'Dressers' were usually third- or fourth-year medical students, and she was also probably chosen because of her ability to speak some French and German.

As the German Army invaded Belgium, pushing before it a wave of civilian refugees, the Red Cross in Britain was presented with a humanitarian crisis. In the first three weeks of the war, it despatched seven medical teams – largely composed of women, and including about 100 dressers – to Belgium to offer help to these refugees and to wounded soldiers.[31] We know that Kate Finzi was in one of these parties, but from her published diary, we learn only that her 'once flourishing Red Cross detachment' left behind its 'energies and equipment alike' at the 'enforced evacuation of Ostend'.[32] From other surviving Red Cross documents, it appears that Finzi was in one of the groups which left Britain on either 15 August or 19 August, and which was evacuated from Ostend 2 months later, shortly after the fall of Antwerp. This begs the question of why Finzi did not write any more about this episode in her published diary. It may well have been because these first Red Cross units sent to Belgium were in fact able to achieve very little, arriving in a country which they hardly knew, and which was being enveloped in chaos as the Germans advanced. We know that the first group, sent out on 12 August, reached Brussels and promptly fell into the hands of the German occupiers.

FIGURE 3 *Red Cross nurses leaving for the front, August 1914. Ironically, female volunteer nurses, including Kate Finzi, were able to leave for the 'war zone' in August 1914 before men who volunteered for the armed forces.*

Most of this group were repatriated to Britain through Scandinavia later in the year.³³ One party was sent to Antwerp, and it managed to get back to Britain after that city fell. Finzi's group probably achieved little before it was forced back on to one of the last ships leaving Ostend for England on 17 October. We do know that Finzi's ardour was undiminished. Only days after her return to England, she and another Red Cross colleague left London, 'to the accompaniment of a cheery chorus of rag-times' from 'recruits in a neighbouring carriage'. From Southampton, they took a ship carrying the Irish Regiment to Le Havre. The sight of these 'fine strapping fellows going out to meet their fate' provoked Finzi to wonder whether the war was 'a great game' or 'a great slaughter'.³⁴ She would soon find out.

Vera Brittain, following events hour by hour from rumours, and from the newspapers she could get hold of in Buxton, was similarly unable to restrain her youthful excitement. Her diary during these days frequently replicated the tone and the language of *The Times*. On 4 August she wrote: 'Late as it is & almost too excited to write as I am, I must make some effort to chronicle the stupendous events of this remarkable day. The situation is absolutely unparalleled in the history of the world. Never before has the strength of each individual nation been of such great extent, even though all the nations of Europe, the dominant continent, have been armed before. It is estimated that when the war begins *14 millions* of men will be engaged in conflict. Attack is possible by earth, water & air, & the destruction attainable by the modern war machines used by the armies is unthinkable & past imagination.'

FIGURE 4 *Refugees on the quayside at Ostend. Thousands of Belgian refugees, as well as Red Cross volunteers like Kate Finzi, were evacuated from Ostend in the chaotic days after the fall of Antwerp.*

Brittain also realized that war would have an immediate impact on her and on others around her. She wondered whether her plans to go to Oxford would be affected; and in considering this adopted a stance which she only gradually realized would become dominant in her experience of the war, writing: 'There is nothing to do now but wait.'[35] By 6 August, after showing her brother Edward and his friend Maurice appeals in the newspapers for young men to enlist, she turned to a more active stance: 'Today I started the only work it seems possible as yet for women to do – the making of garments for the soldiers. I started knitting sleeping helmets, and as I have forgotten how to knit, & was never very brilliant when I knew, I seemed to be an object of some amusement.'[36] Two days later Brittain heard that Roland Leighton was applying for a commission in the Norfolk Regiment.[37]

Edward Elgar had been at Achnasheen in Scotland since 20 July with his wife and daughter. Here they were cut off from the news, and it was only on 1 August that they realized the gravity of the international situation. Elgar and his wife Alice were both patriotic, and Alice immediately took up the fiercely pro-Allied stance which she maintained for the next four years. On 5 August she wrote in her diary: 'Frightfully anxious for news. Had a telegram saying Germany declared war against us. The Govt. proclamation dates war from 11 P.M. on Augt. 4. May God preserve us. Our conscience is clear that we tried all means for peace & waited at our own disadvantage in patience and forbearance. So we can go on with a brave heart.'[38] Elgar decided immediately to return to London, but found that every available vehicle had been requisitioned for the movement of soldiers. His frustration was heightened by seeing contingents of troops moving south. He wrote to the Stuart-Wortleys: 'we were nearly mad to get any news & our friends seemed to fail us thinking, no doubt, that we had moved on. We had intended to do so but we are thirty miles from a station; ... It has been a weird and affecting time: seeing these dear people bidding goodbye but the spirit of the men is splendid – the Seaforths went first – later in the week the mounted Lovat's Scouts rode through. ... I purposely refrained from any rush or excitement but I am returning to London as soon as possible to offer myself for any service that may be possible – I *wish* I could go to the front but they may find some menial occupation for a worthless person.'[39]

Not until 10 August were the Elgars finally able to begin their own journey south on a 'charabanc'; Alice and Carice got back to London late on 13 August; Elgar himself returned only on 14 August, after attempting to see a friend in Leeds. He was immediately plunged into the new context for his music: its relationship to the British war effort. The first events in this increasingly complex and difficult relationship revealed some of the tensions that were to haunt Elgar for the next four years. He quickly became aware how his earlier music might seem out of place. His new orchestral work *Sospiri* was given its premiere at the opening night of the Promenade Concerts in London, and although the conductor

Sir Henry Wood appreciated the work's 'beautiful feeling',[40] others did not feel it was appropriate for the changed times. The critic for *The Times* came up with this strangely curt dismissal of what is now widely considered a masterpiece: 'Elgar's new "Sospiri," an adagio for strings, harp (Mr Kastner), and organ (Mr Kiddle) was played. There is little to be said about this short piece beyond praising its level expression and terseness of expression'.[41] Elgar was hugely sensitive to audience and critical reaction to his works, and cannot have been cheered by this. Nonetheless, 2 days later, he enrolled as a Special Constable at Hampstead Police Station, and was proud to be serving in this way.[42]

If *Sospiri* failed to excite the Proms audience in August 1914, another of Elgar's works had not. His *Pomp and Circumstance March No. 1*, with the words which had been added to it by Arthur Benson, had before 1914 become established as a second national anthem. Whenever a patriotic British crowd gathered, it was likely to break into a rendition of 'Land of Hope and Glory'. The song was naturally performed at the Promenade Concert on 15 August 1914, and Alice Elgar noted: 'Wonderful effect of Land of Hope and Glory. Enormous audience rose. Shouts'.[43] Elgar was, whatever he thought of this, seen as the English composer who spoke for the nation, and he felt duty-bound to react to this public expectation. Only days after the outbreak of war, Elgar was writing to Arthur Benson about a different text for 'Land of Hope and Glory', which would relate more closely to the changed circumstances. Elgar suggested some verses which had been written by an army officer and which spoke of vengeance against Germany. Benson wrote back critically: 'but I'm still not strong on the *vengeance* line, & indeed I don't see what there is to revenge as yet – we have hemmed in Germany tight all round for years, in the goodnatured unsympathetic way in which we Anglo-Saxons *do* treat the world, & the cork has flown out! ... While I do feel *with* all my heart that *bullying* must be stopped – but bullying mustn't be met by bullying – and if we end in being more militaristic than Germany, je *m'y perds*'.[44] Elgar replied that he was quite happy to withdraw the word 'vengeance', but with a clear sense of irritation. He did not fall out with Benson over this, and they quickly agreed on a new text. This described the Germans as 'the braggart sons of scorn' and 'tyrants of mankind'; it urged the British to 'Stand for faith and honour' and to 'smite for truth and peace', clearly reflecting Elgar's view of the conflict. 'Land of Hope and Glory' maintained its enormous popularity right through the war. Nonetheless a pattern was already emerging, in which Elgar was to find it enormously difficult to tailor his music to the demands of wartime, and to the views of others.

He had other things on his mind. On the same day that Benson wrote to rebuke him over his use of the word 'vengeance', Elgar wrote to two of his closest friends about his concern, not for humans, but for animals. Anticipating by nearly a century the now current interest in the fate of horses in the war, Elgar wrote to Frances Colvin: 'How awful it all is – I cannot write of it – oh my horses, my horses – that is what I moan to myself. To others I try to be cheerful & keep our hearts up.'[45] He also wrote what has become a famous letter to his publisher Frank Schuster, telling him that he and Alice were facing 'financial ruin'. He added: 'Concerning the war I say nothing – the only thing that wrings my heart and soul is the thought of the horses – oh! My beloved animals – the men – and women can go to hell – but my horses; I walk round & round this room cursing God for allowing dumb beasts to be tortured – let Him kill his human beings but – how CAN HE? Oh, my horses.'[46]

Hubert Parry was similarly trying to enjoy a holiday when war was declared. His attempts to sail along the south coast of England were frustrated by restrictions imposed by the navy, although the *Wanderer* was eventually allowed to travel as far down the coast as Torquay and Paignton, before Parry gave up and returned to Littlehampton. He too was plunged immediately into a set of personal difficulties which were to become more painful as the war developed. Almost immediately he discovered that his trusted German servant George Schlichtmeyer was not allowed to step off the boat back onto British soil without being interned as an enemy alien, and Parry had to negotiate with Customs officials, who finally allowed Schlichtmeyer to land at Folkestone. Here they saw 'Vast crowds of refugees from Belgium by the Ostend boat'.[47] No sooner had Parry got back to Littlehampton than he was drawn into agitated discussions with relatives and friends. He noted in his diary that a German lady, visiting his wife for tea, 'regaled us with her views of the virtues of the Kaiser & the abominable bias of English newspapers'. It was, he noted with characteristic forbearance, 'Rather a trying business'.[48] Nor was this a merely private affair. Parry, as Director of the Royal College of Music, had to prepare his regular address to the student body there at the beginning of the new term. He quickly decided that he would have to speak about the causes and purpose of the war, and about the position of his students, most of whom were obviously fit for military service. For a man committed to ideals of peaceful progress, and who felt himself deeply indebted to German culture, this was no easy task. It was in a troubled state of mind that Parry returned to Highnam on 12 September and settled down to compose his address.

Parry's response to the outbreak of war was necessarily an abstract and intellectual one. We have seen how young women like Vera Brittain and Kate Finzi turned immediately to the idea of voluntary nursing as an area where they might be directly involved, and how several of the men in this study thought of becoming about war correspondents, special constables or bizarrely, of helping with the harvest, as a way of contributing. One alone, T. E. Lawrence, had a practical sense of what might be to come, and a clearer view of how he intended to be involved. Lewis Namier, later a distinguished historian, was in 1914 a student in Oxford, and he recalls how shortly after the declaration of war he and Lawrence went to practise rifle shooting at an old clay pit in Oxford.[49] We know that Lawrence had experience of using

FIGURE 5 *Highnam Court, near Gloucester, the home of Hubert Parry.*

firearms from his earlier work in the Middle East, where it was common for British travellers and specialists to carry revolvers and to use them to get their way.

Lawrence also apparently wrote to an American contact, Mrs Rieder, a former teacher at the American missionary school in Jebail, to ask if she could buy a Colt .45 revolver and send it to him in England. He was delighted, when on 18 September, he received in the post not one, but two Colt revolvers. In his letter thanking her, Lawrence made it clear that he was effectively waiting for something to happen in the Middle East before committing himself to a clear course of action. He wrote: 'I have a horrible fear that the Turks do not intend to go to war, for it would be an improvement to have them reduced to Asia Minor.' In the meantime, he spoke of 'the horrible boredom of having nothing to do'.[50]

## The BEF in France and Belgium

The British government had declared war on Germany with a plan to help defend France, but little more. It had no clear idea of how it might defeat Germany. Asquith called a 'Council of War', composed of senior Cabinet politicians and representatives from the armed forces, to meet at 10 Downing Street on 5 August; this body quickly agreed to implement the pre-war plans to send a British Expeditionary Force (BEF) to France, and to impose a blockade upon Germany. On 6 August, Asquith's Cabinet was joined by General Kitchener as newly appointed Secretary for War, and he endorsed the view already presented by General Douglas Haig to the War Council that Britain was potentially facing a long war.[51] Kitchener's view was that it might last 3 years or more, and that Britain should set about raising a huge volunteer army to fight on the Continent. This was accepted by the

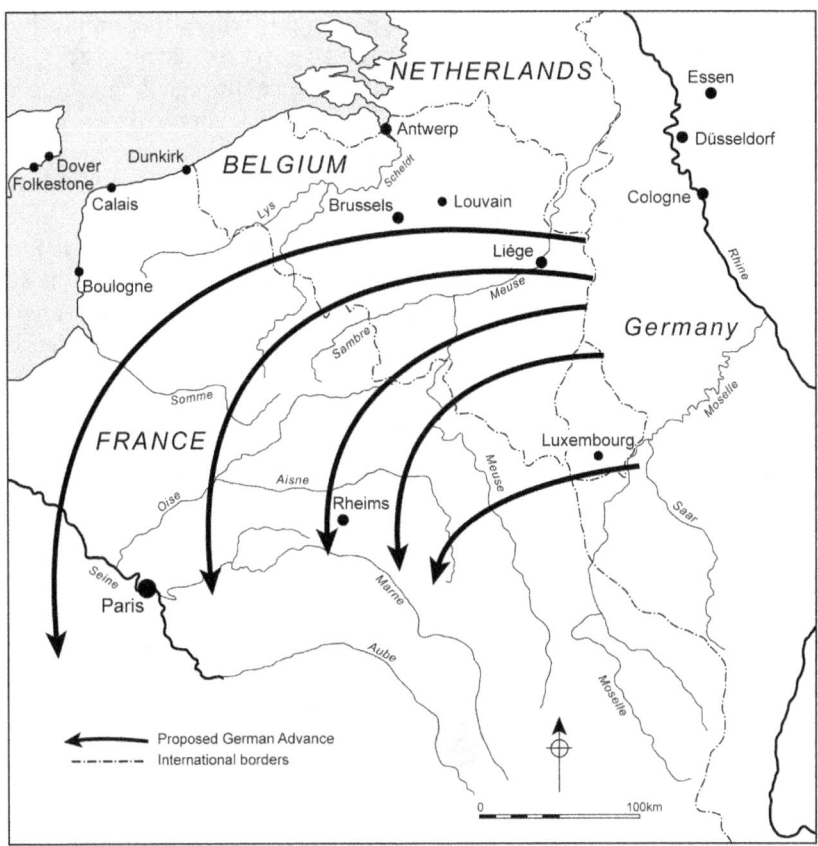

MAP 1 *The German invasion of Belgium and France.*

politicians, and a recruiting programme was immediately started. In fact the first calls for volunteers had already been made.

Britain now had a long-term strategy, underpinned by economic strength: Germany would be weakened by a distant blockade; her merchant shipping would be seized wherever possible on the world's oceans, and if her navy ventured into the North Sea, it would be met by the British Grand Fleet. 'Kitchener's Army' would be recruited, trained and equipped, and would be ready for deployment when the other Powers were exhausted, allowing Britain to dominate peace talks. In the medium term, troops from the colonies and from the Dominions, which had rallied to Britain's side, would be concentrated in Britain and used to strengthen the Expeditionary Force in France.

There was less clarity about the immediate role of the BEF. Although it was transported to France with impressive speed in August 1914, under the protection of the Royal Navy, there was some uncertainty about where precisely it should be deployed. The War Council had sensibly rejected the possibility of deploying the BEF in Belgium, where the supply lines to it from Britain would be more exposed to German naval attacks, but underestimated the rapidity of the German advance through Belgium. Using huge guns, the Germans quickly overwhelmed the Belgian fortresses of Liége and Namur, pushing the Belgian Army and government back into the port of Antwerp, and advancing towards northern France. The BEF was deployed near Maubeuge, and its leading elements met the German Army at Mons, just inside the Belgian frontier, on 23 August. Both sides were surprised, the Germans by the effectiveness of British rifle fire and the British by the size of the forces they discovered bearing down upon them. The BEF, threatened with complete destruction, began a hasty retreat south, fighting defensive actions as it went.

For the next three weeks, the British retreated, in some disorganization. The BEF's commander, General John French, was understandably nervous and thought at one point of retreating south of Paris to escape the oncoming

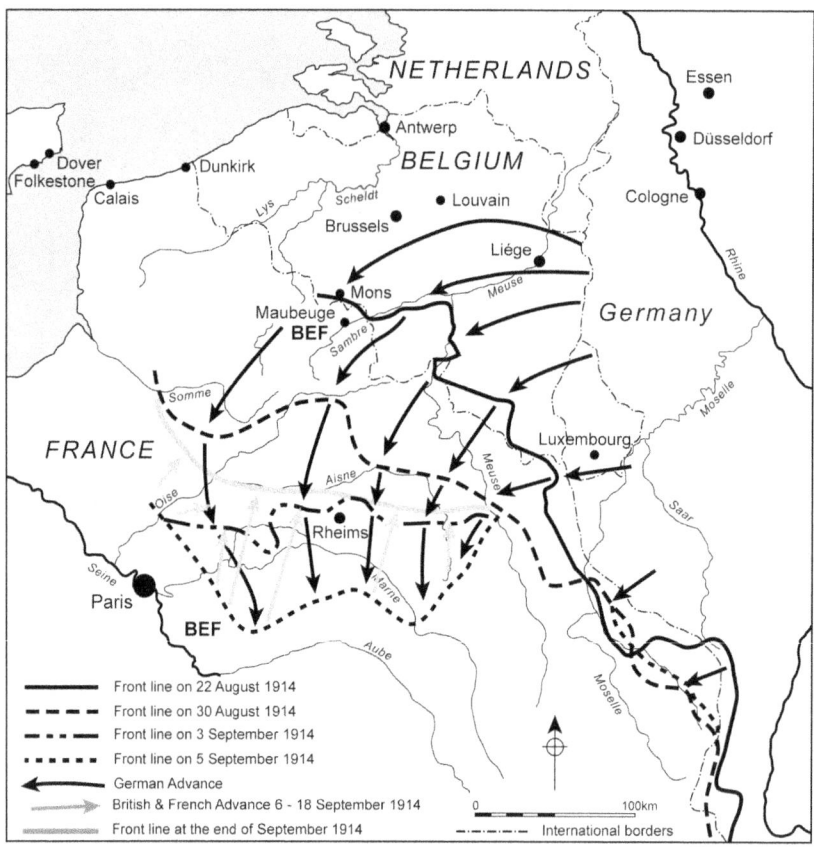

MAP 2 *The retreat from Mons.*

German advance. Fortunately for the British, the German soldiers were equally exhausted by their long marches and were unable to exploit their advantage. In early September the British came to a halt on the River Marne, to the east of Paris, where they joined with retreating French forces on their right and with a newly formed French army on their left. The French counter-attacked on 6 September, and after only days of rest, the British joined them. This – the Battle of the Marne – was a decisive moment in the war. The German attempt to capture Paris, and with it to knock the French out of the war, had failed. Their huge armies, despite their successes in Belgium, and elsewhere along the French frontiers, were exhausted by weeks of marching in hot and dry weather, and they now retreated, looking for suitable defensive positions. They found these in the hills running alongside the River Aisne, and here they dug in. Pursuing British and French troops were able to cross the river, but found that they could not advance against the German positions.

Here, after weeks of fluidity and movement, the characteristic features of warfare on what became known to the British as the 'Western Front' quickly took shape. Both sides discovered that trenches offered the best protection against artillery, which dominated the battlefield. Carefully sited machine guns and entanglements of barbed wire in front of these gave the soldiers in trenches a huge advantage over their attackers. As a dry summer gave way to autumn, heavy rain fell, and mud became the constant companion of the infantry soldier. And the casualties mounted. The first casualty reports from the BEF late in August had listed hundreds of men killed and injured, then thousands. By early October, the British had suffered 'not less than 33,000' casualties.[52]

While the British public anxiously followed the initially fragmentary reports of the 'retreat from Mons', the fighting on the Marne and the stalemate on the Aisne, there had been a significant development in the reporting of the war. On 18 August *The Times* reported that the Germans had burned the town of Burzweiler in Alsace-Lorraine and blown up its factories in retaliation for alleged *franc-tireur* activity. It also reported that the Belgian village of Visé had been burned, reporting: 'The inhabitants have been driven forth, the men being made prisoners and the women and children rendered homeless.'[53] The satirical magazine *Punch* featured on 26 August Bernard Partridge's full-page illustration of a German soldier standing with pistol drawn over the bodies of a woman and a child, in the burning ruins of a Belgian village, with the caption 'The Triumph of "Culture"'.[54] On 3 September *The Times* carried an article on 'The Crime of Louvain', reporting the deliberate sack of the Belgian city and the burning of its university library, on the destruction of villages and on the killing of many civilians. After this, stories of further similar crimes, and other 'outrages' such as rape, the use of women and children as human shields, the shooting of wounded prisoners of war and the destruction of cultural monuments appeared daily in the British press. Successive reports prepared by a Belgian Commission of Enquiry were published in translation in *The Times*. The gendered language of moral outrage used to depict these 'Belgian atrocities' was quickly established in public discourse. The Germans were 'insolent conquerors', 'barbarians', often drunken, or 'Huns'; 'little Belgium' itself was being 'raped'. German protestations of innocence, or that they were acting in self-defence, were dismissed as lies, and their behaviour was caustically summed up as an expression of 'Kultur'. Further substance was added to the newspaper reporting by the arrival of some 200,000 refugees from Belgium before the end of 1914.

Given the subsequent confusion about the 'Belgian atrocities', we need to be very clear about the timing and the accuracy of reports about them. In fact, contrary to the assertion made by Horne and Kramer that atrocity reporting was 'ignored until the third week of the war' in Britain,[55] provincial newspapers had carried accounts of German 'barbarity' in the very first days of the war, adding to the moral outrage felt about the violent invasion of that country. The *South Wales Daily News* reported on 6 August: 'The anger of the population is waxing tremendous owing to the barbarities of the Germans, who not only shot the women and children of Visé, but burned down the town as well.'[56] Vera Brittain reported reading a similar story on 6 August, presumably in another provincial newspaper.[57] Atrocity reporting became much more widespread in late August and September, and truthful accounts rapidly became exaggerated and embellished, not least by wounded soldiers, as we shall see when we turn to individual experience. There can be no doubt that the widespread credence given to reporting of German atrocities in Belgium and France fortified existing feeling in Britain that the war was being fought in a just and righteous cause, just as there can be no doubt that, despite lurid exaggerations, many of these atrocities actually happened.

As the stalemate developed on the Aisne, both sides turned their attention to the north, where in Flanders there were still large areas of open territory. In the final days of September, the Germans renewed their assault on Antwerp, using heavy siege guns, and prompting a desperate appeal for help from the Belgian government for help. Winston Churchill, who had stationed a small group of Royal Marines at Dunkirk in the first weeks of war, decided to send the newly formed Royal Naval Division to Antwerp in a desperate effort to stiffen Belgian resistance, but this initiative was a failure. Almost immediately after the Naval Division arrived in Antwerp it had to be withdrawn, and many of its men were captured. The city was surrendered to the Germans on 9 October, and in the next few days Zeebrugge and Ostend also fell.

The fall of Antwerp was widely seen as a catastrophe in Britain. The German advance along the Channel coast was precisely what Britain had gone to war to prevent. With French agreement, the BEF was withdrawn from the front along the Aisne and rushed by train to Flanders, where it was deployed around the town of Ypres in the only part of Belgium not

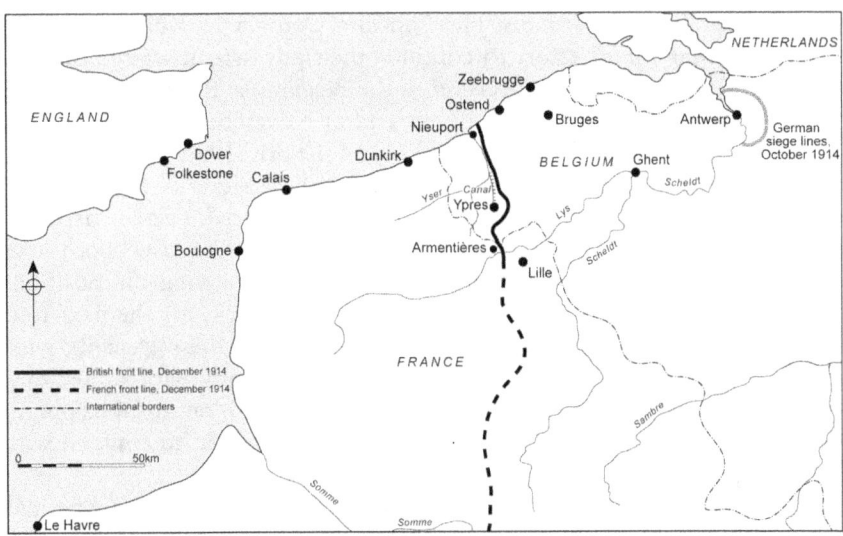

MAP 3 *Antwerp and First Ypres.*

In the Dread Talons.

The German forces take Antwerp—the last stronghold of the Belgians.

*Monday, October 12th, 1914.*

FIGURE 6 *J. M. Staniforth drew cartoons for the Welsh* Western Mail, *and for national newspapers right through the First World War. The deep dismay felt in Britain after the fall of Antwerp is reflected in this cartoon, published on 12 October 1914.*

yet occupied by the Germans. Here, in late October and November, the Germans made a huge effort to continue their advance, thwarted only by desperate resistance and the decision of the Belgians to flood large areas of land between Ypres and the sea. By the end of November, the Belgians had retired to safety behind these inundations, and the British were left occupying a small salient around Ypres, surrounded on three sides by the Germans occupying slightly higher ground. All sides had suffered, British casualties around Ypres coming to some 58,000 men. Here, as on the Aisne, both sides dug trenches, and by December 1914 they were occupying the positions which they would hold, with little significant alteration, for the next four years. In the flat, waterlogged landscape of Flanders, these trenches were in reality little more than ditches which filled constantly with water; they were, as *The Times* reported, 'wretched beyond description; from having to sit or stand in a mixture of liquid mud, the men now had to contend with half-frozen slush'.[58]

It was in these conditions that the strange interlude of the Christmas truce occurred. At many points along the British line on Christmas Eve, German soldiers put small trees out on the parapets of their trenches and sang carols. On Christmas Day, individuals and then groups came out of their trenches, and in places temporary truces were arranged. Drinks, cigarettes and photographs were exchanged and dead bodies were buried. Legend has it that games of football were played between the opposing troops: according to *The Times*, at one point 'a British regiment had a match with the Saxons opposite them, and were beaten, three to two!'[59] On Boxing Day, rain started again after a brief dry spell, and in many places, sporadic firing started again. Higher commanders on both sides were anxious to prevent further fraternization, and made sure, by moving troops around, and by shelling different parts of the line, that the Christmas truce was soon no more than a memory.

The British government did not want war in 1914, and it was with deep reluctance that it entered a European conflict. The Prime Minister and Foreign Secretary had from the end of July realized that if France were attacked it would be difficult for Britain to stand aside, and from that point on Asquith's primary concern had been to maintain the unity of the Cabinet in dealing with the crisis. The German invasion of Belgium not only provided moral grounds for British intervention, but it was also a clear threat to British interests, which dictated that the coast of northern Europe should not be dominated by one foreign country. It was this combination which allowed Asquith to lead his Cabinet, parliament and the British public largely united into a war with Germany. Too many historians and commentators have presented a dichotomy between British strategic calculations and moral feeling, without seeing that these were not exclusive, but could consolidate and fortify one another. To refer to the German invasion of Belgium as providing 'a moral pretext' for British intervention, and to describe the government's reaction to the invasion as 'humbug' are therefore mistaken.[60] No British government in 1914 could have allowed the Germans to take the Channel ports from Antwerp through to Le Havre and establish these as bases for its navy. Asquith, Grey and others also felt a genuine sense of obligation to France and could not have reconciled the admittedly informal commitments they had made with the spectacle of the German Navy operating unhindered in the English Channel. The German invasion of Belgium was seen as a brutal violation of international law. The news of German atrocities in France and Belgium which arrived after the declaration of war strengthened the moral consensus in Britain which saw the war as just and righteous, and helped to elevate it to the status of a crusade.

There were fatal weaknesses in the British position which would cause terrible problems in the future. One was that the obligations to France and Belgium had not been clearly or publicly understood before August 1914, which allowed critics of the decision to go to war to argue that it was the result of 'secret diplomacy'. This was the position taken up by the 'Union of Democratic Control', an organization with which, as we shall see, Hubert Parry was to have a close association. It also permitted both contemporary critics and later historians to argue that the moral outrage expressed over Belgium was insincere, and a cloak for some other motivation. The combination of moral outrage and defence of British self-interest has become increasingly difficult for non-specialists to understand and to sympathize with.

Another problem was that, apart from getting the Germans out of Belgium and France, Britain had no clear war aims in August 1914. As long as the public sense of crusade was maintained, this mattered little, but as the cost of driving the Germans out of Belgium and France grew, the question would arise as to whether that cost was justified, and pressure would grow to find other, perhaps larger war aims. It also, once Germany had occupied most of Belgium and large areas of France, limited the scope for compromise. Britain was committed to what was clearly, by Christmas 1914, an extraordinarily tough military proposition. To conclude terms of peace which left Germany in possession of its gains would be seen as failure.

It is worth noting that none of the individual artists focused on here were hostile to Germany before the 'July crisis'. None wanted war, and some, like Spencer and Brittain, resented its intrusion into their personal lives and the threat it posed to their aspirations. Several of them, notably the composers Elgar and Parry, were great admirers of Germany and its culture. Lawrence viewed German imperial pretensions as potentially in conflict with those of Britain, but he was much more concerned personally with what he perceived as Turkish misrule in the Middle East. He clearly relished the opportunity an international crisis might provide further to undermine the Ottoman Empire. All recognized, with greater or lesser clarity, that the war would change their lives, and although some, like Rupert Brooke and Kate Finzi, would embrace that change, others, like Vera Brittain and Ellis Evans, would do their best to stave it off for as long as possible.

What is most striking now is the enormous confidence with which the government and the British people confronted Germany, armed with no more than a plan for their small army to help defend France, and for the navy to impose a blockade which might take years to impact seriously upon Germany. This confidence was based not on a clear grasp of what a land war with Germany might entail, but on a historical sense of British maritime and imperial supremacy, on the imagined strengths of a peculiarly British character and on a widely shared belief in the righteousness of the British cause. It was a confidence which would be sorely tested in the years to come.

# CHAPTER THREE

# The call to arms

One of the most enduring myths about the First World War in Britain is that when it started, people thought the war would be over by Christmas. There may have been individuals who imagined this, but there is plenty of evidence to suggest that most intelligent people thought otherwise. General Haig told the War Council on 5 August: 'we must organize our resources for a war of several years'.[1] Kitchener, as we know, echoed this on 6 August. That most influential organ, *The Times*, declared: 'From three weeks to three years have been suggested as the probable duration of the contest, and it is evident that few people have given the matter much serious thought.'[2] Above all, the government's immediate decision to raise a large volunteer army signalled its intent to prepare for a long conflict. It was apparent to anyone who considered the different problems involved that it would take at the very least six months, more likely a year or more, to recruit, equip, train and deploy an army of volunteers, and longer still to defeat the huge German Army.

The principle of voluntary recruitment endorsed by the British government had immediate consequences. Initial appeals for volunteers which appeared in the newspapers on 5 August 1914 were soon followed by calls for many more.[3] Across the country public meetings were held where army officers, politicians and priests urged young men to step forward and enlist. Asquith personally led the campaign, speaking in London, Edinburgh, Dublin and Cardiff. Reginald Leete's famous poster of Kitchener, with bristling moustache and pointing finger, appeared in September 1914 and was accompanied by many others. Few historians have considered the less attractive side of the recruitment campaign, how it forced all men of military age (that is to say between 19 and 30 years old) to examine their own consciences, and to justify themselves to all around them. For the 113,000 who joined up in the first three weeks of war, this was a relatively straightforward process.[4] For others, such as Rupert Brooke, David Jones or Vera Brittain's friend

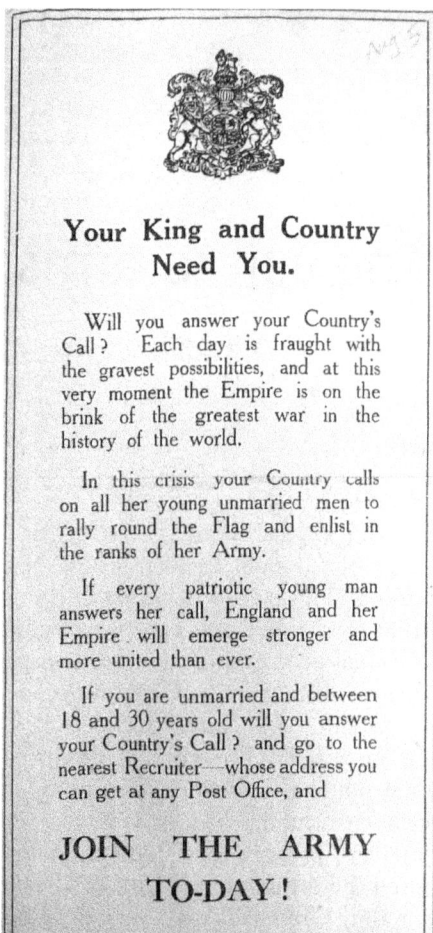

FIGURE 7 *The call to arms. The first call for volunteers in* The Times *of 5 August 1914 was soon followed by more. Similar notices were placed in other national and regional newspapers.*

Roland Leighton, who wanted to enlist, but could not find acceptance in a unit of their choice, the process was dragged out rather longer. For some, like Stanley Spencer or Ellis Evans, the call to arms initiated a prolonged agony of indecision and soul-searching, a conflict that was largely played out internally, but which frequently spilled into family life and into public situations.

The pressure on young men was immense and took many different forms. The newspapers, as well as publishing government notices urging enlistment, printed letters from members of the public denouncing 'shirkers' and 'slackers' who did not enlist, and criticizing friends and relatives who tried to prevent them from doing their 'duty'. This was a strongly gendered campaign, in which 'manliness' was associated with readiness to fight. Posters like 'Women of Britain say Go!' showed women fearfully but proudly watching their menfolk march off to war, and reluctant volunteers were publicly mocked. *The Times* carried a notice in its 'Personal' column on 27 August 1914: 'Wanted, PETTICOATS for all ABLE-BODIED YOUTHS in this country who have not yet joined the Navy or Army'.[5] The *Daily Mail* went further, printing on 11 September a large photograph of young men watching a cricket match, asking why these 'shirkers' were not volunteering. The photograph was sufficiently clear to allow people who knew men in it to identify them precisely.[6] The *Sheffield Daily Telegraph* published a letter, representative of many, from 'A Tommy's Smiling Wife', which stated: 'Now lads, buckle to. If you won't come without being fetched, let's hope it will come to conscription.'[7] Many young women in particular took it upon themselves to harass men in public, presenting them with white feathers, in a gesture which frequently caused lasting humiliation and resentment.

The voluntary approach to enlistment also meant that the 'spirit of August 1914' which historians have explored was very different in Britain from other European countries. This idea is typically understood as a euphoric sense of national community, of shared commitment transcending social divisions, which was seen as replacing a perceived era of decline and moral decay, and there is plenty of evidence to suggest that this was strongly felt in some of the countries going to war in August 1914, notably Germany, Austria and France. In Britain, for many of the population the question of direct participation in the war was horribly fraught.

Hubert Parry was too old for military service, but his students were not, and he had immediately to confront the issue of how to advise them in his college address. After much consideration, Parry had accepted that the British declaration of war was justified by the German invasion of Belgium, but he refused to join in the developing anti-German hysteria. In his address, delivered to the assembled students of the Royal College of Music on 24 September, he outlined his own sorrowful interpretation of recent events. Parry blamed the Prussian Junkers, who were in his view wedded to militarism and the maintenance of class privilege, and had imposed their own narrow creed of force upon the rest of the German population. He spoke of witnessing 'the downfall of a great nation from honour and noble estate', adding that 'it falls painfully to our lot to see them commit the most gigantic crime that has ever been perpetrated by a nation in history – the wilfully sudden declaration of war against France'. This had been followed by 'a crime as base and hideous: the invasion of peaceful, industrious little Belgium, because they thought it was insignificant and incapable of resisting them'. Britain was left with no choice. Reluctantly, Parry concluded: 'If we cannot scotch the war-fiend the world will not be worth living in.'

Parry also developed an idea which was to gain more force later in the twentieth century, and which clearly derived from his conversations with his son-in-law Arthur Ponsonby, who had already, with a few other dissenting Liberals, established the Union of Democratic Control, to campaign for an end to 'secret diplomacy' and for a fair negotiated settlement to the war. Parry argued that 'a truly independent democratic spirit' would never submit to 'such a monstrous system' as prevailed in Germany, and which allowed ordinary people there 'to be driven for the vulgar ambition of Prussia like sheep to the shambles'. Parry tackled head on the question of whether his students should enlist. He said of those who did: 'We feel a thrill of regard for them... moved by fine and honourable motives to face the awful conditions of modern warfare,' but he revealed his own disquiet when he added: 'The world cannot afford to throw away such lives as if they were of no more account than lives which gave no special promise of a rare kind.'[8]

Parry, who already sat on many committees, felt constrained to serve on a newly formed 'Music in Wartime' committee, which, among other things, provided bands to play at recruiting meetings. His carefully prepared position was not easily maintained. From one side he was pushed to support the war effort more wholeheartedly, for example by his irascible colleague and fellow composer Charles Stanford, who, he wrote, was 'full of gruesome stories of German savagery'.[9] From the other, his daughter and his son-in-law urged him to join the Union of Democratic Control and to oppose the war effort. His wife did not help with her changeable moods, one moment spreading what he called 'wild rumours' about German submarines,[10] and the next toying with the idea of going out to Calais and 'and if possible to the "front"!!' The two exclamation marks Parry added to this note in his diary suggest how foolhardy he thought this was.[11]

## Purpose and exhilaration

Rupert Brooke has frequently been used to invoke the 'spirit of August 1914' in Britain, typically through quotations from his war sonnets – even though these did not become known in Britain until March 1915. As soon as war was declared, Brooke returned to London and sought to enlist, but was initially frustrated. But getting a good commission had as much to do with connections as with qualifications, and Brooke was able to call on friends in high places. On 1 September, Eddie Marsh told Brooke that Winston Churchill was forming a Naval Division, and offered to help Brooke and his friend Denis Browne to get commissions in it. Within a few days, after filling out application forms, both men were accepted, and Brooke was thrilled. He revelled in the thought that he was a member, not of the army, but of Britain's 'senior service', and he delighted in the use of nautical terms which prevailed in Churchill's unit.[12]

Behind this façade of patriotic resolve there were more complex feelings. Joining up and losing himself in a great cause appealed enormously to a young man whose personal and sexual life had brought more frustration and disappointment than fulfilment, and to whom the prospect of a don's life in Cambridge was distinctly sedate. He wrote to Ka Cox on 3 September that 'I don't seem to myself to do very much with my existence. And I don't know of anything I want very much to do with it.'[13] The prospect of heroic action with the Royal Naval Division offered a resolution to this crisis. Brooke also faced criticism from former friends and associates who were pacifists, notably several of the Cambridge intellectuals he had earlier consorted with. Several of these, like Lytton Strachey, were now members of the literary group in Bloomsbury; others such as Edward Dent, Maynard Keynes and Gerald Shove were still at Cambridge. For Brooke these circles were linked by the figure of James Strachey, a contemporary with whom he had had a long and intimate relationship, beginning at school in Rugby, continuing in Cambridge, and disintegrating in 1912 when Brooke had broken with several former friends. We know that in August and September 1914 Brooke argued furiously with several of these people about joining up. Once he had found a niche in the Naval Division, Brooke's pro-war stance took on an aggressive tone in which he hit out at former friends. He told Cathleen Nesbitt, again on 3 September, that 'One of the less creditable periods of my life enmeshed me with the intellectuals. I hover on their fringes yet; dehumanized, disgusting people. They are mostly pacifists and pro-Germans. I quarrel with them twice a day.'[14] Shortly after this Brooke wrote to Jacques Raverat about their shared circle of acquaintances, saying that 'the only pacifists & anti-enlisters & pro-Germans' were James Strachey, Gerald Shove, Bertrand Russell and Lady Ottoline Morrell. He recounted an argument in a restaurant between himself and Dudley Ward on one side, and James Strachey and Gerald Shove on the other, calling this 'a lovely scene'.[15]

Brooke was also contemplating death in action, and this brought forth a complex mix of idealism, reflection and self-loathing. In his letters he adopted a flippant tone, appearing to welcome death and criticizing others who feared it; at other points he showed an awareness of how badly he treated friends and lovers. On 20 September he tried to express his contradictory feelings to Eileen Wellesley (who later claimed that she and Brooke were having 'a serious love affair' at this time), writing: 'And another thing (this sounds like a catalogue of German atrocities) I'm really a wolf and a tiger and a goat. I am – how shall I put it – carried along on the tides of my body, rather helplessly.'[16]

A huge attraction for Brooke in joining the Naval Division was the prospect of imminent action. He wrote to Cathleen Nesbitt with breathless excitement after dining again with Churchill at the Admiralty on 23 September: 'Winston was very cheerful at lunch, and said one thing which is exciting, but a *dead* secret. You mustn't *breathe* it. That is, that it's his game to hold the Northern ports – Dunkirk to Havre – at all costs. So if there's a raid on any of them, at *any* moment, we shall be flung across to help the French reservists. So we may go to Camp on Saturday, and be under fire in France on Monday!' He concluded: 'Dear love, I feel so happy in this new safety and brightness'.[17] Four days later, Brooke, together with Denis Browne, joined the Anson Battalion of the 2nd Royal Naval Brigade, with a temporary commission as Sub-Lieutenant of the 15th Platoon, D Company, at Betteshanger Park in Kent. Marsh wrote in his notebook: 'Saw Rupert and Denis off from Charing Cross, in their new uniforms'.[18]

On 4 October, before undertaking more than the most rudimentary training, Brooke and his fellows in the Naval Division – mainly stokers and ordinary seamen, but including other poets, scholars, musicians and the Prime Minister's son Arthur among his fellow officers – were shipped across the channel to Dunkirk, from where they went by train to Antwerp. After only a few hours in trenches, the Anson Battalion had to retreat among tens of thousands of refugees and was lucky to get back to England largely unscathed. The experience had a huge effect on the young poet. For weeks afterwards he wrote about his experiences in Antwerp to friends, and he was also inspired to write five sonnets which subsequently became some of the best known and most influential of all poems produced in

FIGURE 8 *Marines of the Royal Naval Division briefly occupied the trenches outside Antwerp in October 1914; Rupert Brooke was one of the untrained men rushed to the defence of the Belgian city.*

English during the war. Brooke was elevated by the closeness of danger and by the potential imminence of death. He was deeply moved by the suffering of the Belgians, and these dominant strands of his experience in Antwerp were fused in an exhilarating sense of moral purpose. In a letter to Cathleen Nesbitt shortly after his return to London he described what had happened when the Naval Division was disembarked at Dunkirk: 'After dark the senior officers rushed around and informed us that we were going to Antwerp, that our train was sure to be attacked, and that if we got through we'd have to sit in trenches till we were wiped out. So we all sat under lights writing last letters: a very tragic and amusing affair. My dear, it *did* bring home to me how very futile and unfinished life was. I felt so angry.' Confessing that they had not been 'attacked seriously' in the trenches outside Antwerp, Brooke described the retreat: 'But the march through those deserted suburbs, mile on mile, with never a living being, except our rather ferocious looking sailors, stealing sulkily along. The sky was lit by burning villages & houses; & after a bit we got to the land by the river, where the Belgians had let all the petrol out of the tanks & fired it. Rivers & seas of flame, leaping up hundreds of feet, crowned by black smoke that covered the entire heavens. It lit up houses wrecked by shells, dead horses, demolished railway stations, engines that had been taken up with their lines & signals, & all twisted round & pulled out, as a bad child spoils a toy. And there we joined the refugees, with all their goods on barrows & carts in a double line, moving forward about 100 yds an hour, white & drawn & beyond emotion. The glare was like hell. We passed on, out of that, across a pontoon bridge, built on boats. Two German spies tried to blow it up while we were on it. They were caught & shot.'[19]

Some weeks later the same images were still playing in his mind, as he wrote to Leonard Bacon: 'It hurts me, this war. Because I was fond of Germany. There are such good things in her, and I'd always hoped she'd get away from Prussia and the oligarchy in time. If it had been a mere war between us and them I'd have hated fighting. But I'm glad to be doing it for Belgium.' The German invasion of Belgium, Brooke wrote, was 'one of the greatest crimes of history'.[20] But it was clear that he had been uplifted by his experience. He wrote in December 1914: 'And – apart from the tragedy – I've never felt happier or better in my life than in those days in Belgium.'[21]

After years of emotional turmoil, of indecision and unconsummated love, Brooke had found a moral purpose and the chance of redemption. In his letters from this period he used the key terms which then appeared in his five sonnets, speaking of 'safety', of 'beauty' and of 'holiness'. He also developed a keen sense which was to be shared – in different ways – by millions who did military service in the war, of the separation between civilians and combatants. He described this, again using religious language, to Cathleen Nesbitt: 'It's the withdrawal of combatants into a special seclusion and reserve. We're under a curse or a blessing or a vow, to be different. The currents of our life are interrupted.'[22] Brooke's exalted sense of purpose contrasted with his growing contempt for pacifists, and those he felt were not taking the war sufficiently seriously. He felt a strange dislocation between the fighting in Flanders, and Britain, where life appeared to proceed largely undisturbed. He expressed this characteristically in December: 'I'm largely dissatisfied with the English just now. The good ones are all right, and it's curiously far away from us: (if we haven't the Belgians in memory, as I have). But there's a ghastly sort of apathy over half the country. And I really think that thousands of male people don't want to die; which is odd.'[23]

In the sonnets written between mid-October and late December 1914, Brooke chose not to portray in any naturalistic sense his experience of war. He did not write about the sound of the shells, of explosions or of flames; nor did he depict the sufferings of the Belgians which he had witnessed. Instead he used the sonnets to portray an idealized, abstract vision of soldiering, and a meditation on death, which he presented as a release from earthly pains. The sense of catharsis and of a resolution of earlier problems was palpable in the celebrated line 'Now God be thanked Who has matched us with His hour.' In several of the poems Brooke idealized the life the volunteers were forsaking:

> The winds, and morning, tears of men and mirth
> The deep night, and birds singing, and clouds flying
> And sleep, and freedom, and the autumnal earth

In 'The Dead' he wrote:

> Dawn was theirs
> And sunset, and the colours of the earth.
> These had seen movement, and heard music; known
> Slumber and waking; loved; gone proudly friended;
> Felt the quick stir of wonder; sat alone;
> Touched flowers and furs and cheeks. All this is ended.

Brooke linked these images with an imagined England, voicing a deeply felt patriotism:

> If I should die, think only this of me:
> That there's some corner of a foreign field
> That is forever England. There shall be
> In that rich earth a richer dust concealed;
> A dust whom England bore, shaped, made aware,
> Gave, once more, her flowers to love, her ways to roam,
> A body of England's, breathing English air,
> Washed by rivers, blest by suns of home.

In lines which articulated his sense of being part of a proud tradition, Brooke suggested that the country was returning, after unspecified wrong turnings, to its essential role among the nations:

> Blow, bugles, blow! They brought us, for our dearth,
> Holiness, lacked so long, and Love, and Pain.
> Honour has come back, as a king, to earth,
> And paid his subjects with a royal wage;
> And Nobleness walks in our ways again;
> And we have come into our heritage.

In a moment of personal bitterness, Brooke hit out at his former friends and Cambridge associates, describing those who would not enlist as 'sick hearts which honour could not move'. He found poignant images to idealize those who had already 'poured out the red/Sweet wine of youth'. He may indeed have been thinking of someone he knew when he introduced an anonymous figure into the concluding lines of 'The Dead':

> He leaves a white
> Unbroken glory, a gathered radiance,
> A width, a shining peace, under the night.

Brooke's sonnets were first published in the journal *New Numbers* early in 1915.[24] It was not until March and April 1915 that they became widely known, at a moment close to crisis in the national mood, but they have frequently been used to illustrate, and to parody, the mood of Britain at the very outset of the war. To a more cynical age, particularly since the 1960s, they have often appeared ludicrously romantic, and they have been easy targets for satire. Brooke's image of the volunteers as 'swimmers into cleanness leaping' appears particularly misplaced to generations which associate the First World War with mud and blood. Many of Brooke's critics have not been aware that he had actually seen some of the horror of war. Ironically, it was exactly while Brooke was creating this highly abstracted view of warfare that the BEF was sucked into the geographical area which would become the focal point of the First World War for the British Army, and its defining experience of conflict, in Flanders.

Rupert Brooke created an image of war which was notable for an absence of violence: with the exception of the lines 'naught broken save this body/nothing lost but breath' he made no reference to the violence which lay at the heart of every confrontation between the armed forces of the opposed nations. He wrote late in 1914 when the fighting on an increasingly static front line was being conducted with violence unprecedented in history, when, as two French historians have recently observed, shrapnel from heavy shells could cut a man literally in half.[25] The thousands who were injured – if they were fortunate enough to be recovered from the battlefield – presented enormous and sometimes new challenges to the overburdened medical services behind the lines. Bullets and fragments of shells which entered the human body carried with them dirt from the battlefield, in addition to pieces of clothing and even body parts from fellow soldiers. The resulting wounds were terribly prone to infection, especially to tetanus and what was called 'gas gangrene'. This was infection caused by anaerobic bacteria which could quickly spread and destroy large areas of tissue. 'Gas gangrene' gave off a distinctive smell, and the gas produced by the infection gave a crackling sound when pressed. Mortality rates among the wounded in the first months of the war were very high as a result of these infections and because of the entirely inadequate provision of medical facilities. Two artists who, like Brooke, went out to Flanders early in the war have recorded this phenomenon.

On 21 October, as the BEF faced the first heavy assaults outside Ypres, Kate Finzi left London for the second time to serve as a 'dresser' in France. Within a week she arrived in Boulogne, where she found what the normally stolid *Times History of the War* described as a 'crisis'.[26] Thousands of wounded soldiers, British, French, Belgian and German, were being brought into Boulogne by train and by motor ambulance from the nearby fighting around Ypres. The British had at the start of the war designated Boulogne as a base hospital for the BEF but after the retreat from Mons had evacuated all the medical personnel and supplies landed there. When the focus of the fighting switched to Flanders and the Channel coast in October 1914 Boulogne again became the centre for British medical services, but the Royal Army Medical Corps (RAMC), Red Cross and volunteer staff there were swamped by a tide of human suffering. The Red Cross reported that wounded men 'were pouring in at the rate of 2,000 a day'.[27] Hotels and the Casino were quickly turned into hospitals, but even the most basic equipment and supplies were lacking. Wounded men on stretchers, unloaded from trains at the Gare Maritime, were left on the quayside in the rain.

A disused sugar shed next to the station was hastily turned into an improvised casualty clearing station and designated as No. 13 Stationary Hospital. It was here that Finzi was employed; together with six trained nurses, a handful of RAMC doctors and orderlies, and two or three Red Cross surgeons and women doctors, she helped to treat up to one thousand wounded soldiers a day. To start with they had 10 beds and some sacks of straw. Patients were treated on a table made of wooden planks on packing cases.[28] Unlike many other women, who volunteered later, when medical services were far better organized, Finzi saw the most horrible consequences of war in the most chaotic situation imaginable. Her 'War Diary', which documented the development of hospital services in Boulogne, has received comparatively little attention, perhaps because it says little about the emancipation of women, a topic which preoccupies most historians of nursing in the First World War. Finzi unashamedly celebrated the stoicism and diligence of her fellow nurses, who had to work long hours in the most trying circumstances. Hers was also a straightforwardly patriotic account: she never doubted the righteousness of the British cause, and unlike so many who were directly exposed to the horrors of the war, her experience only sharpened her patriotism. Finzi had undoubtedly read about German atrocities before leaving Britain, but now she heard tales of brutality directly from front-line soldiers. She was told about a Belgian girl whose breasts were cut off by German soldiers when she resisted their advances, and heard accounts of Red Cross nurses mutilated. These lurid stories, she wrote, 'alas! seem authentic enough'.[29] Finzi mused about how a country which had produced such great artists and thinkers had now fallen so low, and, like Parry and many others, she blamed 'Prussian militarism'. She contrasted 'Teutonic boorishness' with the kindness of the British, highlighting how she and others tried to care equally for the German wounded who came through the clearing station. Finzi, who could speak some German and was used as an interpreter, related how the wounded German soldiers expected to be shot. One asked her when this would happen. She explained 'whilst dressing his wounds that Britain is a civilized country, and, in contrast to the Huns, does not hit a man when he is down'.[30]

Although on the surface there was a school-girlish cheerfulness and excitement in Finzi's narrative, she also presented an uncompromising view of the violence which had been visited upon the wounded, and of the desperately primitive conditions in which they were initially treated. On 30 October 1914, she wrote: 'Fingerless hands, lungs pierced, arms and legs pretty well gangrenous, others already threatening tetanus (against which they are now beginning to inoculate patients), mouths swollen beyond all recognition with bullet shots, fractured femurs, shattered jaws, sightless eyes, ugly scalp wounds; yet never a murmur, never a groan except in sleep.'[31] Even at this early stage of the war, Finzi recognized that many of the men were suffering from what would now be called mental trauma, but which came to be known in Britain in 1915 as 'shell shock': 'A large percentage of them stammer or have developed a nervous impediment in their speech, owing no doubt to the strain of the past months.'[32] Finzi did not gloss over the appalling conditions in which she had initially to work. She noted that there could be 'no attempt at asepsis in a place so ill ventilated, or, rather, not ventilated at all'. She singled out 'the vermin, against which there is no coping, that in ordinary times one never saw. The men are alive with them, so are we, a fact which necessitates a tremendous "search" at every available opportunity. Even amputated limbs are found to be crawling.'[33] In addition to the gas gangrene and tetanus which posed the greatest dangers to the wounded, Finzi described another medical problem which became more apparent with the onset of winter weather, 'trench feet'.[34] Apparently some doctors at first thought that this was actually frostbite or even an excuse for 'swinging the lead'.[35]

Finzi's narrative was one of triumph over the odds, and she contrasted her new found sense of achievement with what Rupert Brooke might

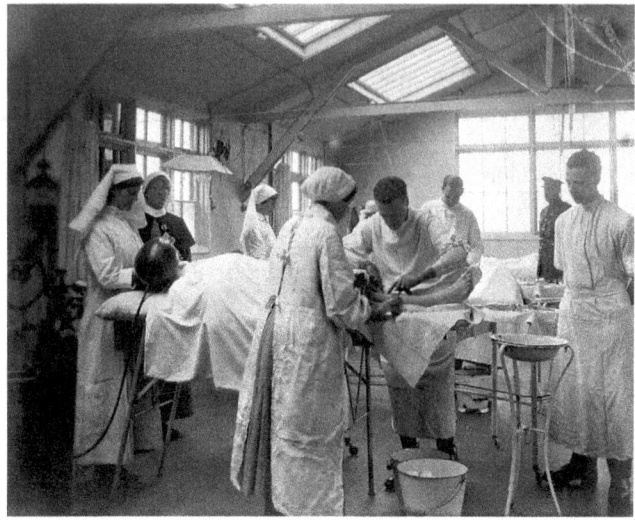

FIGURE 9 *The organized and clean appearance of this operating theatre in Boulogne suggests that the picture was taken after October 1914. Kate Finzi wrote of one such theatre: 'What tales those whitewashed walls could tell!'* (Finzi, Eighteen Months, 1 November 1914, p. 41).

have called the 'little emptiness' of her pre-war life. On 1 November, at a point when despair would have been understandable, she wrote: 'not for a moment do our spirits flag; on the contrary, the worse things grow the more cheerful do we become, the more determined to make the best of things. It is strange that all the years we worked hard to amuse ourselves at home not one brought an eighth of the satisfaction of *this*'.[36]

Through November and December, as the wounded poured into Boulogne in ever greater numbers, the improvised clearing stations and hospitals were gradually improved. Systems of triage were developed, and more orderly arrangements to transfer the seriously wounded back to Britain, and others to convalescent hospitals in France were made. Operating theatres, 'X-ray rooms' and laboratories for the study of infection were set up, and new hospitals were opened, spreading from Boulogne itself to nearby towns such as Wimereux, Etaples, Le Touquet and Abbeville. Boulogne itself became a 'hospital city'. A hospital for Indian soldiers was established in a monastery above the town.[37] A constant flow of casualties was processed; many died and were buried there.

## Nevinson witnesses 'the Shambles'

The early weeks of the war were uncomfortable for Richard Nevinson. As far as can be judged now, he had no desire to join up and fight; his discomfort was increased by awareness of how his Italian Futurist colleagues were agitating for their country to get involved and not to miss the opportunity war offered for a realization of their doctrines. In his later autobiography Nevinson glossed over this difficult period, claiming that he was unmoved by vulgar jingoism, but nonetheless conscious of the 'long-expected outrage on the Belgians'. He stated that 'My own doctor said the Army was out of the question for me,' adding that 'I was pursued by the urge to do something, to be "in" the War; and although I succeeded in the end and was "in" it, I was never "of" it.'[38] From more reliable records, it appears that for the first few weeks of the war Nevinson still tried to concern himself with artistic affairs, but found this difficult. In October his father, who had already been out to the fighting as a war correspondent, recorded in his diary: 'Rich much disturbed about war & the Futurist support of its horror. Declares he will abandon Futurism & call his new movement Mintalitist.'[39]

Richard Nevinson was right to be disturbed. The stupidity of Futurism's doctrine of war as a form of hygiene was being exposed, and his own passionate advocacy of other aspects of the creed – movement, energy, dynamism, machines – appeared insincere if he stayed away from the war. A compromise was provided by his father, who arranged for him to join the newly formed Friends Ambulance Unit, and literally accompanied him to Flanders. This unit had been formed by Quakers in the first days of the war, and over the next few weeks, it gathered trained medical staff, auxiliaries, equipment and vehicles. It left for Dunkirk, accompanied by Henry Nevinson, on 30 October, with no clear idea of exactly what to do upon arrival. The Friends found in Dunkirk a situation very similar to that which Kate Finzi had stumbled into at Boulogne. Three thousand wounded French soldiers had been recovered from the front, only miles away, and left in a disused goods shed at the railway station, a place which soon became known as 'the Shambles'. The unit's official history described the situation:

> They had been there, many of them, for three full days and nights, practically untended, mostly even unfed, the living, the dying, and the dead side by side, long rows of figures in every attitude of slow suffering or acute pain, of utter fatigue or dulled apathy, of appeal or despair.[40]

The French authorities were happy for this group from England to take responsibility for these men. The Friends also established a field hospital in a former convent at Woesten, close to Ypres, and later set up another near Dunkirk at Malo-les-Bains.

Henry Nevinson returned quickly to London and persuaded his son to join the Friends Ambulance Unit. On 10 November he recorded in his diary that he had been 'Early to Red Cross with Rich for his papers';[41] and on 12 November, he wrote that his son was in the uniform of a private in the

RAMC.[42] The next day father and son crossed the Channel to Dunkirk, arriving 'in drenching rain'. They proceeded by motor ambulance to Woesten, where the horizon was 'flickering and winking with shells not far off'.[43] For the next nine weeks, Richard Nevinson worked in Flanders, an experience which left an indelible mark on him and shaped his whole view of the war. As he later mythologized this experience, both in paintings and in prose, it is worth examining what actually happened. Nevinson later emphasized his role as an ambulance driver in Dunkirk, one which clearly suited the Futurist love of machines and movement, and he proudly sent a photograph of himself with his vehicle out to Marinetti in Italy.[44] Images of Nevinson in uniform with the goggles and scarf of a driver have since been endlessly reproduced and featured prominently in his later exhibitions and publications.

In fact, from contemporary sources, it is evident that Nevinson was not a good driver, and although his medal card at the National Archive describes him as a 'Chauffeur',[45] it appears that he spent most of his time in Flanders in the more prosaic role of a medical orderly. An account of the Friends Ambulance Unit in a Canadian medical journal in early 1915 cheerfully said 'what an excellent dishwasher our Futurist painter makes!'[46] It would though be mistaken to see Nevinson as a *poseur* or to play down the gruelling experiences he was exposed to. It is abundantly clear that Richard Nevinson was fearful and nervous, and was faced with horror, danger and hard physical work. On 14 November Nevinson *père* wrote: 'Found Rich had been dressing wounded in the sheds with some success. But his driving of the motor ambulance very poor.'[47] The next day he 'Left Rich fairly happy though very apprehensive about going to the front'.[48] A week later he received a letter from his son about a drive to Boulogne, and a night at Woesten 'When a shell smashed his ambulance'.[49] In mid-December, 'Rich wrote about accident with his motor, knocking over a man in the dark.'[50] Henry Nevinson went back to Dunkirk after this, and found Richard working in 'the Shambles' in a ward of '10 or 12 wounded, some very terrible'.[51] On 22 December he recorded that 'the Shambles' was 'still a miserable sight'.[52] The workers and the wounded there were also exposed to aerial bombardment, which caused Henry Nevinson 'much anxiety'.[53]

It appears that Richard Nevinson was popular among the wounded; his ability to speak French and some German was a help, and he was able to relate to the soldiers. Henry Nevinson records them as saying 'Il ne se moque pas de nous'.[54] But although the young painter may have temporarily mastered his fears, the whole experience was horribly taxing for him, and the wretched winter weather on the Channel coast exacerbated his rheumatism. By the end of January 1915 he had been excused from further service, despite the 'tearful grief of the blessés when Rich came away'. His father wrote on 30 January: 'found Rich just arriving fr. Dunkirk. He and Miss Knowlman at dinner'.[55]

## Conscience, duty and patriotism

Paul Nash, a gentle and spiritual young man, resolved the problem of enlistment in a different way. He was on holiday when the war broke out, and his initial reaction was one of horror. He described to his artistic mentors Gordon and Emily Bottomley how he and his brother Jack had helped farmers who were short of labour, continuing: 'I am not keen to rush off and be a soldier. The whole damnable war is too horrible of course and I am against killing anybody, speaking off hand, but beside all that I believe both Jack & I might be more useful as ambulance & red cross men and to that end we are training. There may be emergencies later & I mean to get some drilling locally & learn to fire a gun but I don't see the necessity for a gentleminded creature like myself to be rushed into some stuffy brutal barracks to spend the next few months practically doing nothing but swagger about di[s]guised as a soldier *in case* the Germans poor misguided fellows – should land.'[56] Nash wrote in similar vein to Eddie Marsh, but, perhaps aware of his close involvement with the war effort through Churchill, was rather more definite, writing about 'ambulance classes and very likely special constable work'.[57] It appears that Nash quickly abandoned these notions, and by the time he next wrote to Marsh, it was to ask if he could stay with him in London, as 'I have just spent a week trying to enlist, and come up then for another try.'[58] Nash's search ended when he was accepted on 10 September 1914 as a private in the Artists' Rifles, a Territorial unit which had been formed originally in the 1860s, and which was accepting men from the professions and the universities, as well as actual artists. Nash wrote proudly to Gordon Bottomley: 'I am now an Artist in a wider sense! having joined the "Artists" London Regiment of Territorials the old Corps which started with Rossetti [,] Leighton & Millais as members in 1860.'[59]

Nash had found a relatively congenial solution, in that this committed him – for the time being – only to home service. The Artists' Rifles were based in London, and he was able to live at home, and go in to drill. He apparently enjoyed the exercise and the open air activity. A fellow recruit who met Nash shortly after enlisting recalled how the men were expected to provide their own uniforms, and initially drilled in their own clothes. Nash was apparently 'dexterous in all his movements, managing his rifle and all the drill with a smart accuracy that won the approval of Captain "Tommy" and the sergeants'.[60] His friend and, later, biographer Anthony Bertram wrote that he doubted whether Nash 'was quite easy in his mind' about enlisting only for home service, and quotes from a letter Nash wrote in October 1914: 'I met Rupert Brook[e] tother day fresh home from Antwerp trenches he said it was marvellous. I expect I should hate the slaughter – I know I should but I'd like to be among it all.'[61]

David Jones, still only 18 years old in August 1914, had less luck enlisting with the Artists' Rifles, but his fate was bound up with the recruiting campaign directed specifically at Welsh men. Fired by patriotism, and supported by his father, Jones tried to enlist in 'a unit called "The Welsh Horse"', but because he knew nothing about horses, he was turned away.[62] On 16 September 1914, as the fighting intensified in France, a group of prominent Welshmen met and proposed to form a London Welsh Battalion,[63] and it appears that Jones heard about this. He must have been one of the first applicants to the London Welsh, as he received a letter dated 17 September from the Battalion's 'Recruiting Office' telling him they were still waiting for permission from Kitchener to form the unit. In the meantime, Jones was invited to a meeting on 'Wales and the War' at the Queen's Hall in London to be addressed by the Chancellor, Lloyd George.[64] This took place on 19 September, when, according to *The Times*, Lloyd George gave 'the greatest speech of his public career', addressing 'an audience composed chiefly of his Welsh fellow-countrymen'. He presented here the themes which would dominate the recruiting campaign aimed at the Welsh: the need to come to the aid of threatened small nations, Belgium, and Russia's 'little brother' Serbia. Lloyd George ended with florid religious imagery, arguing that the war would also lead to moral renewal. It had, he declared, 'reminded us of the great peaks of honour: Duty, Patriotism, and the pinnacle of Sacrifice pointing like a rugged finger to Heaven'.[65] The London Welsh Choir was present to lead the singing of 'national airs' of France, Russia, Belgium and Japan, as well as 'Rule Britannia' and 'Land of Hope and Glory'.[66] Lloyd George met with other Welshmen in Downing Street 2 days later, and it was agreed that he should go to Wales, to call for the recruitment of a 'Welsh Army Corps'.[67]

The campaign was launched by Lloyd George at the Park Hall in Cardiff on 28 September, when he spoke to a large and enthusiastic audience, flanked on the platform by leaders of Welsh local government and by Anglican and Roman Catholic bishops. Nonconformist and trades union leaders were also present. Calling this 'an hour of immeasurable destiny', Lloyd George appealed specifically to Welsh patriotic sentiment: 'A nation whose spirit is roused by the call to its magnanimity and manly qualities, will go into action with all the greater heart, because for centuries its soul has been cleansed from the mere lust for killing.' Calling for another 40,000–50,000 recruits, Lloyd George reassured his listeners that the men would be trained for 5 or 6 months before being deployed.[68] His speech was followed by patriotic leading articles in the Welsh press and by a meeting in Cardiff addressed by the Prime Minister. Here an audience of 8,000 heard Asquith denounce 'hordes who leave behind them at every stage of their progress a dismal trail of savagery, of devastation, of desecration worthy of the blackest annals in the history of barbarism'.[69]

Evidently though, Lloyd George's campaign for a 'democratic army to wage a Holy War' did not run smoothly. Some 50,000 men had already

FIGURE 10 *Staniforth's representation of Lloyd George's view of the war in the* Western Mail *on 3 December 1914 may appear crude today, but his was a view widely shared in Britain through the war.*

volunteered to join the existing Welsh Regular and Territorial Army formations, and these units wanted more men.[70] On 5 October the *South Wales Daily News* reported that there had been only 500 volunteers for the planned London Welsh Battalion, and that the unit could not be attested until there were at least 1,000.[71] This is probably why David Jones, still waiting to hear the outcome of his own application, also tried to join the Artists' Rifles in London. In Wales, there was difficulty getting the wholehearted support of the nonconformist churches; the Welsh National Union of Evangelical Churches, denying that their attitude was unpatriotic, complained that its representatives had been 'cold-shouldered' at the meetings addressed by Lloyd George and Asquith.[72] On 14 October the height requirement for volunteers to the Welsh Army Corps was lowered to 5 feet 3 inches,[73] and although various 'Pals' battalions were formed, by November the *South Wales Daily News* felt compelled to argue that conscription might be necessary if more recruits did not come forward.[74]

Further efforts were made to tailor recruiting to specifically Welsh needs. In December it was announced that there would be a 'Temperance Company' in the 3rd Battalion of the Welsh Regiment and a 'Bantam Battalion' for men between 5 feet and 5 feet 3 inches in height.[75] David

Jones, still trying to find a unit which would accept him, may have benefited from these perceived difficulties. On 12 December he was informed by the Artists' Rifles that he had been found 'physically unfit for military service on account of deficient chest measurement';[76] but the day before this his father heard that application to join the London Welsh was finally approved.[77] Jones was allowed to enjoy his Christmas holiday before formally enlisting on 2 January 1915 as Private Jones, No. 22579 in the 15th (London Welsh) Battalion of the Royal Welch Fusiliers.

The difficulties of recruiting in Wales, especially in rural Wales, are highlighted by the response of Ellis Evans in Trawsfynnydd. As a young man aged 27, he was clearly eligible for military service, but he did not join up. We do not know in any detail how he felt about the war, whether he felt it was not Britain's – or Wales' – business to become involved in a European war, or whether, as has been suggested, he was anti-militaristic. The most direct testimony we have is from a poem he wrote, apparently during the first weeks of the war, called 'Gwladgarwch' or, in English, 'Patriotism'. The poem, which runs to 20 stanzas, replicates many of the most conventional views in Britain after the declaration of war and confirms that, even in the mountains of Merionedd, Evans heard the appeal to Welshmen to support a just war in support of a nation 'under the oppression of foreigners'. It also suggests strongly that he had direct experience of recruitment meetings where local worthies urged men like him to join up.

> 'Our Country and Our Nation' in a tapestry of silver
> Appear on your banners;
> And the national passion in the sound of your marching song
> Awakes leaving its woe and its lamenting
> For freedom and brighter esteem.
>
> You speak clearly from parliament and stage,
> Our need a fire on your lips;
> Are you not our silver tongue
> And are you not the one who will be a shield
> For the privileges of your country and its children?

Another stanza anticipates the sentiments expressed by Rupert Brooke, with religious imagery, and an appeal to an imagined history of chivalrous conduct:

> Again comes the call of patriotism to battle
> As in the days gone by;
> A call on behalf of Britain and her forces,
> A call on behalf of the Lord of Hosts,
> From His shining highness above.

Alan Llywd, an expert on Welsh poetry and on Ellis Evans, writes that he has scoured this poem for traces of irony, but has found none.[78] In an English-language commentary, he calls the poem 'jingoistic', saying that it, and other similar poems, 'meant nothing'.[79] Various reasons have been advanced to explain why Evans would write something like this. He may have felt a duty, as a spokesman for the community, to voice commonly felt views; he may have been hoping to make money or to enhance his reputation. If he sincerely felt these patriotic sentiments, he did not act upon them, although we can safely presume that he was put under pressure to do so. All we know is that he did not enlist.

## Reactions to atrocity

Elgar, as we have seen, was deeply frustrated that his age barred him from military service. In the early months of the war, he reacted by trying to write music that would support the war effort, although no one felt more keenly than he did what a poor substitute this was. He tried writing songs about soldiering in late 1914, but he felt unhappy with this idiom. It is clear from Alice Elgar's diary that she and her husband both followed the war news anxiously, were horrified by the atrocities in Belgium and depressed by the initial successes of the German Army. On 28 August she wrote: 'Heard of destruction of Louvain – utter barbarians. Heard of losses to our beloved army Anxious to do something for Belgian refugees.'[80] A month later, Elgar cut short a visit to his sister. He was apparently 'too opprest [sic.] with the war to stay away'.[81] It was the plight of Belgium which moved Elgar to write his first notable piece of war music, an orchestral backdrop to the recitation of a poem by the Belgian refugee Emile Cammaerts. The poem was called 'Carillon', recalling the musical chimes of Belgian churches destroyed by the Germans, and the work was premiered in the Queen's Hall in London on 7 December. Alice Elgar wrote that it was a 'gorgeous performance' producing 'wonderful enthusiasm',[82] but *The Times* was less fulsome: 'Most of the music', its critic wrote, 'is in the "Pomp and Circumstance" style, and the composer only seems just to touch upon the fringe of the deeper feelings which the poem is intended to arouse. . . . if this is all that the tragedy of Belgium can bring from a musician it seems a small tribute.'[83]

*Carillon* was frequently performed during the war, and a recording Elgar made early in 1915 sold very well. But Elgar did not need *The Times* to point out what he knew only too well himself. Shortly before Christmas he received a letter from a French friend now serving with a regiment of Cuirassiers. He told Elgar how he was working with Canadian horses which had recently arrived for the unit, but we can only wonder now what distress this line might have caused Elgar: 'for the moment I am at the veterinary infirmary – many wounded horses come from the war'.[84]

Vera Brittain, as a woman, was not eligible to join the armed forces; nor was she qualified to join one of the volunteer medical groups going out to the fighting fronts. Her response to the recruitment campaign was played out primarily through her relationships with three men: her younger brother Edward, his former school friend Roland Leighton, and Bertram Spafford, a local man who had earlier proposed to Brittain, but been rejected. Vera encouraged Edward to join up. On the first day of the war she wrote: 'I showed Edward an appeal in *The Times* & the *Chronicle* for young unmarried men between the ages of 18 and 30 to join the army. He suddenly got very keen & after dinner he and Maurice wandered all around Buxton trying to find out what to do in order to volunteer for home service.'[85] But Vera's father was totally opposed to this idea: 'Daddy worked himself into a thorough temper, raved away at us & said he would never allow Edward to go abroad whatever happened.'[86] The next day she went to her first 'St. John's bandaging class'.[87]

Strangely, Vera Brittain felt differently about Roland Leighton. Hearing that he was trying to get a commission in the Norfolk Regiment, she wrote: 'I cannot but think it a terrible waste of good material that such an intellect as that should put itself in readily in danger.'[88] She was still desperately hoping that she would get into Oxford, and that she might study there alongside Leighton. On 21 August she heard that Leighton's application for a commission had been turned down, and wrote back that she was pleased he was 'not going into the Army'.[89] A few days later she heard to her delight that she had passed the Oxford entrance exam. Although her father, who was clearly very agitated, railed about the difficulties this would cause now there was a war on, he eventually consented to her going up. Breathlessly she wrote to Leighton, 'You *will* go won't you?'[90] But he was still set on joining up, and on 29 September, he delivered the first of what was to become a series of hammer blows, saying that he could no longer 'endure a secluded life of scholastic vegetation'.[91] On 7 October he wrote to tell her that he had been accepted for a commission in the Norfolk Regiment.[92]

Vera Brittain's resentment at Leighton's decision not to study may have been partly responsible for her behaviour towards Bertram Spafford, who was still living in Buxton. After attending church on Sunday, 6 September, where she heard a 'fine' sermon on the theme of 'fortitude', Brittain was talking in the Pavilion Gardens with her father and one of his friends, both of them troubled by the news that a British cruiser, HMS *Pathfinder*, had been sunk by a U-boat with heavy loss of life. In her diary she wrote: 'As we sat talking Bertram Spafford came stalking past pushing his mother's bath chair. We all looked at him, contemplating his obvious strength, & suitability for military work, & Mr. Ellis remarked rather contemptuously that he was waiting for a corps of gentlemen. I replied that I had pointed out to him on Saturday that there was now such a corps to be found, but that he had told me he could not leave his "business"!'[93] One wonders how much of this conversation was audible to Spafford and to his mother. Even after leaving home and going to Oxford, Brittain kept an eye on Spafford. On 27 December she wrote about him again in her diary: 'every man of standing has gone from here except Bertram Spafford, who has received various anonymous letters & white feathers which seem to have no effect'.[94] Although there is no suggestion here that Brittain had herself sent white feathers or anonymous letters to this young man, one wonders how she knew that this had happened.[95]

If for Brooke, Finzi and Nevinson the opening months of the war brought excitement and a sense of purpose as well as exposure to horrors, they were for Vera Brittain a terrible anticlimax. She arrived at Somerville College, Oxford, on 9 October 1914, at a strange point in the University's history. Women students were at last allowed to study there – provided they adhered to a strict code of conduct – but they were not yet allowed to take degrees. In her first term, Brittain tried hard to immerse herself in college life, and to a considerable extent, she tried to ignore what was going on in the war. She worked hard to bring her Latin and Greek up to the standard demanded, and she threw herself into other activities, such as singing with the Oxford Bach Choir, which was directed by Parry's colleague Hugh Allen. She joined the Oxford Women's Suffrage Society, and attended lectures given by academics and writers. She soon acquired a reputation at Somerville for being, in her

FIGURE 11 *Students and dons at Somerville College, Oxford, October 1914. Vera Brittain (fifth from left in the first row standing) is smiling bravely in this photograph, but in reality she was deeply disappointed that her brother Edward and his friend Roland Leighton had opted to enlist rather than to take up their own places at the university.*

own words, 'insufferably conceited'.⁹⁶ An older student, Margaret Kennedy, wrote a short poem describing her:

> With neck out thrust, head on one side
> Mouth open, aspect bold
> All freckle-nosed and gimlet eyed
> Oppressive to behold
> 'That bore!'
> (So tight were Vera's lips compressed
> She scarcely ate at all.
> You looked twice 'ere you ever guessed
> They sometimes twitched withal)⁹⁷

It did not help when, at the end of her first term, Roland Leighton wrote, telling her that he doubted now that he would go to Oxford when the war was over, as it would 'seem such a waste of time'.⁹⁸

Stanley Spencer's conscience had been pricked by Rupert Brooke even before the declaration of war. Three weeks on he was still agonizing about joining up and turned to his mentors, Jacques and Gwen Raverat. His letter began bluntly: 'What ought Gilbert and I to do in this war. My conscience is giving me no peace.' As usual in his letters to the Raverats, Spencer talked about his painting, or rather his efforts at painting, as he was clearly unable to concentrate. He then turned back to the theme of enlistment, flagging up a potential resolution to the problem. Spencer wrote that he had heard of a group being drilled by a Sergeant in Maidenhead, 'without belonging to the army'. Adding to this letter before it was finally posted, Spencer admitted that he and Gil had joined this group, but was typically candid. Although it was 'horribly monotonous', they were going to continue, and 'since it looks respectable and eases my conscience considerably I will join this and not the Territorials'. This was clearly not the end of the matter. He continued: 'Advice from you would relieve me greatly, even if you said I ought to go to the front.'⁹⁹

Spencer's dilemma was complicated by his family situation. His brothers Percy and Sydney were keen to join up. His oldest brother Will had a German wife, but was coincidentally back in England for a visit, and was now separated from her. Spencer's mother was resolutely opposed to any of her sons joining up, and in another letter, Stanley described her attitude: 'It is impossible to get her to understand the necessity of men joining. "My dear it's brutality. I hope none of *my* sons will ever kill a man . . .".'¹⁰⁰ We know that recruitment increased substantially in September and October 1914, largely in response to the military situation in France, and in particular, the German capture of Antwerp.¹⁰¹ Certainly the pressure on Spencer did not ease off in Cookham. He wrote again to Henry Lamb in November, hoping that he might help get him and Gil into 'any decent regiment'. He continued: 'There are such a terrible lot of slackers about that I think it is necessary after leaving home and going to Oxford, Brittain kept an eye on Spafford. On 27 December she wrote about him again in her diary: 'every man of standing has gone from here except Bertram Spafford, who has received various anonymous letters & white feathers which seem to have no effect'.[94] Although there is no suggestion here that Brittain had herself sent white feathers or anonymous letters to this young man, one wonders how she knew that this had happened.[95]

If for Brooke, Finzi and Nevinson the opening months of the war brought excitement and a sense of purpose as well as exposure to horrors, they were for Vera Brittain a terrible anticlimax. She arrived at Somerville College, Oxford, on 9 October 1914, at a strange point in the University's history. Women students were at last allowed to study there – provided they adhered to a strict code of conduct – but they were not yet allowed to take degrees. In her first term, Brittain tried hard to immerse herself in college life, and to a considerable extent, she tried to ignore what was going on in the war. She worked hard to bring her Latin and Greek up to the standard demanded, and she threw herself into other activities, such as singing with the Oxford Bach Choir, which was directed by Parry's colleague Hugh Allen. She joined the Oxford Women's Suffrage Society, and attended lectures given by academics and writers. She soon acquired a reputation at Somerville for being, in her

FIGURE 11 *Students and dons at Somerville College, Oxford, October 1914. Vera Brittain (fifth from left in the first row standing) is smiling bravely in this photograph, but in reality she was deeply disappointed that her brother Edward and his friend Roland Leighton had opted to enlist rather than to take up their own places at the university.*

own words, 'insufferably conceited'.[96] An older student, Margaret Kennedy, wrote a short poem describing her:

> With neck out thrust, head on one side
> Mouth open, aspect bold
> All freckle-nosed and gimlet eyed
> Oppressive to behold
> 'That bore!'
> (So tight were Vera's lips compressed
> She scarcely ate at all.
> You looked twice 'ere you ever guessed
> They sometimes twitched withal)[97]

It did not help when, at the end of her first term, Roland Leighton wrote, telling her that he doubted now that he would go to Oxford when the war was over, as it would 'seem such a waste of time'.[98]

Stanley Spencer's conscience had been pricked by Rupert Brooke even before the declaration of war. Three weeks on he was still agonizing about joining up and turned to his mentors, Jacques and Gwen Raverat. His letter began bluntly: 'What ought Gilbert and I to do in this war. My conscience is giving me no peace.' As usual in his letters to the Raverats, Spencer talked about his painting, or rather his efforts at painting, as he was clearly unable to concentrate. He then turned back to the theme of enlistment, flagging up a potential resolution to the problem. Spencer wrote that he had heard of a group being drilled by a Sergeant in Maidenhead, 'without belonging to the army'. Adding to this letter before it was finally posted, Spencer admitted that he and Gil had joined this group, but was typically candid. Although it was 'horribly monotonous', they were going to continue, and 'since it looks respectable and eases my conscience considerably I will join this and not the Territorials'. This was clearly not the end of the matter. He continued: 'Advice from you would relieve me greatly, even if you said I ought to go to the front.'[99]

Spencer's dilemma was complicated by his family situation. His brothers Percy and Sydney were keen to join up. His oldest brother Will had a German wife, but was coincidentally back in England for a visit, and was now separated from her. Spencer's mother was resolutely opposed to any of her sons joining up, and in another letter, Stanley described her attitude: 'It is impossible to get her to understand the necessity of men joining. "My dear it's brutality. I hope none of *my* sons will ever kill a man . . .".'[100] We know that recruitment increased substantially in September and October 1914, largely in response to the military situation in France, and in particular, the German capture of Antwerp.[101] Certainly the pressure on Spencer did not ease off in Cookham. He wrote again to Henry Lamb in November, hoping that he might help get him and Gil into 'any decent regiment'. He continued: 'There are such a terrible lot of slackers about that I think it is necessary for people like me to join; it is sickly in Cookham. I am quite sure I am as strong as thousands who are fighting & the more beastly the stories become the more I feel I ought to go or do something. Gil walks about like a lump of lead.'[102]

Spencer soon noticed 'the difference between the wounded soldiers & the ones not yet gone to the front'. In December 1914, by which time his brother Percy had enlisted, Spencer described a visit of 'men from the Durhams' to Cookham, where it appears they set up a recruiting station in the bicycle shop. He reported how they harassed local men, in North Country accents which sounded outlandish to Spencer: '"I'll even ask thee again wilt th'a be a man & join Kitchener's army? . . . We are British, British!"' Apparently the Durhams had been particularly insistent with a local boy who had already been injured, and 'attacked him with gusto'. In contrast, Spencer wrote, 'The wounded are always quiet & never say a word about our not joining.' Gil was apparently very upset about contemporaries from Cookham who had already been killed and 'goes about like one possessed'. Spencer concluded, specifically addressing the question of whether certain people, such as artists, ought to feel exempt from the general call to arms: 'I do not think that to keep out of the thing because you are valuable in other ways is possible.'[103]

## War in the Middle East

On 3 November, the Ottoman Empire declared war on Britain, France and Russia. Turkish feeling had been outraged by the seizure of two battleships being built for them in Britain, and conversely encouraged by the German step of handing to the Turkish Navy two modern German warships, the *Goeben* and the *Breslau*, which had been in the Mediterranean in August and which had escaped from British warships to Constantinople. The Turkish declaration, which was followed by the proclamation of a *jihad* or holy war against Britain, France and Russia, hugely enlarged the scope of the war for Great Britain, bringing with it new problems and potential gains. The Ottoman Empire still covered much of the Middle East, including the Arabian peninsula, Mesopotamia – today Iraq – the Sinai peninsula, Palestine, Lebanon and Syria. The single line, narrow-gauge Hejaz railway, recently completed with German help and with money raised by subscription from all over the Muslim world, linked Damascus and the heartland of Anatolian Turkey with the distant Holy City of Medina and with Mecca. From Palestine, the Turks could potentially threaten the Suez Canal, the vital artery linking British possessions in the Mediterranean with the Indian subcontinent. Equally, Turkish rule over millions of Arabs had been despotic and corrupt, and both the British and French governments now saw the opportunity to take over parts of the Ottoman Empire. The French wanted particularly to gain territory in Syria and Lebanon, long exposed to French missionary activity, and still linked in the French imagination with a heroic

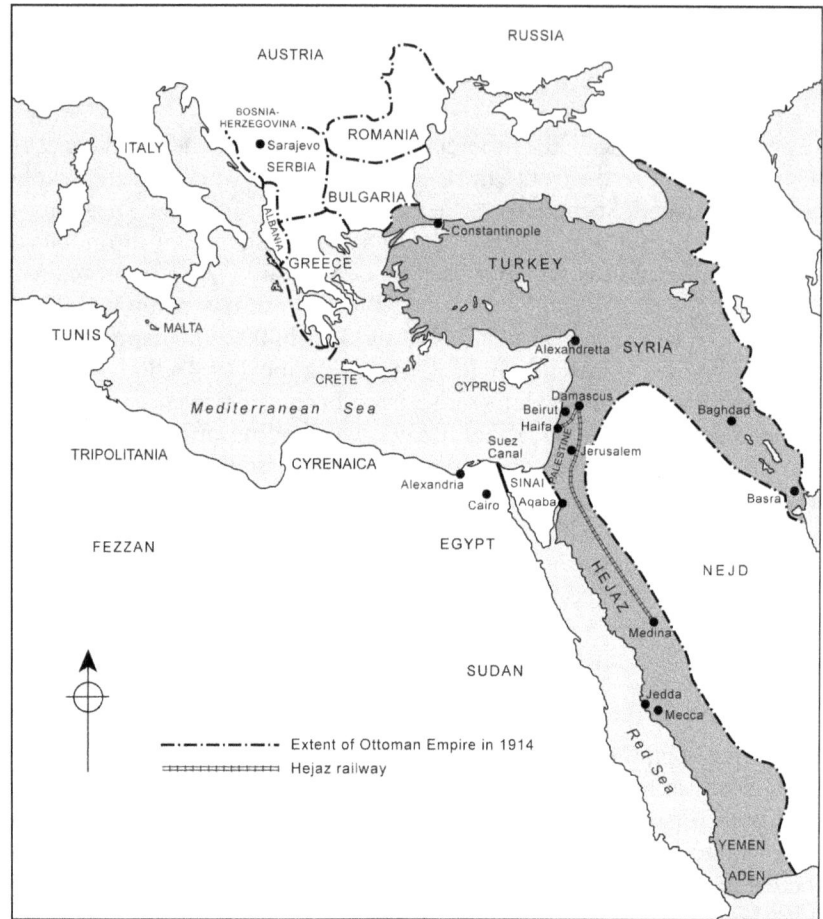

MAP 4 *The Ottoman Empire in 1914.*

Crusading past. The British cast apprehensive and then greedy eyes on the Mesopotamian oil wells now needed to fuel the Royal Navy. As early as 6 November 1914, British and Indian soldiers landed at the mouth of the Euphrates, to secure the pipeline from the Mesopotamian oil wells. On 22 November Basra was occupied.

And here were laid the seeds of future divisions and decisions which still underlie tensions in the region today. The Indian Office pursued one agenda, largely shaped by perceptions of how Muslim opinion in the subcontinent might be affected by developments in the Middle East. Separately, the high commissioner in Egypt, Sir Henry McMahon, and the Governor-General of the Sudan, Sir Reginald Wingate, sought to enlarge their fiefdoms and to manage public opinion there. In Britain, most members of the Cabinet had little knowledge of the Middle East, and inevitably affairs there took a back seat while attention was focused on the war nearer home. There was one key exception to this. Kitchener, the Secretary for War, had made his reputation in recapturing Khartoum from the Mahdi in 1898 and had retained his post as British Agent and Consul-General in Egypt when brought into the Cabinet. It was largely with Kitchener's approval that a 'Military Intelligence Office' under Colonel Gilbert Clayton was established in Cairo in November 1914, staffed with academics and archaeologists, to provide information on the Ottoman Empire.

The Turkish entry into the war allowed T. E. Lawrence to link his own ambitions directly with the war effort. His actions in the first few weeks of the war have been shrouded in mystery, but it is clear now that, after his initially bellicose response, practising rifle-shooting with Lewis Namier and acquiring revolvers from the United States, Lawrence had not joined up as two of his brothers did. He claimed after the war that he had wanted to enlist, but that 'the W[ar]. O[ffice]. were then glutted with men, and were only taking six-footers'.[104] Contemporary letters suggest that his gaze was actually on the Middle East. He wrote on 19 October 1914: 'Turkey seems to have made up its mind to lie down and be at peace with all the world. I'm sorry because I wanted to root them out of Syria, and now their blight will be more enduring than ever.'[105] Lawrence had by this time secured a post with the geographical division of the War Office in London.[106] According to Michael Yardley, he was gazetted on 26 October.[107] His Medal Card at the National Archive provides no date, but describes him as a 2nd Lieutenant on the 'Intelligence General List'.[108] After the Turkish declaration of war, Lawrence was posted to the Military Intelligence Office in Cairo. He wrote to his brother Will: 'I am going out to Egypt, probably at the end of the week, on special service.' Clearly feeling a need to explain why he had not enlisted as an ordinary soldier, Lawrence added: 'In Belgium there is less scope for untrained people.'[109] Lawrence left England for Marseilles on 8 December, travelling from there to Egypt, taking with him Mrs Rieder's revolvers.[110] He arrived a few days later and took up his duties in the Savoy Hotel in Cairo.

## Responses to the war

Of the eleven individuals selected for study here, seven volunteered for active service of some kind in the opening months of the war; a young woman, Kate Finzi, was the first to get to the war zone. Of the remaining four, Hubert Parry was too old to serve, but made his contribution by working with the Music in Wartime Committee. Stanley Spencer and Vera Brittain were both acutely aware of the pressure on them to do war service, but tried to continue with their former lives. Five of the group, if we include Vera Brittain as a diarist, had already made a creative effort to respond to the war. Virtually all were convinced that Britain was right to respond to German aggression and to defend Belgian neutrality. All heard tales of German atrocities, and some, notably Brooke, and the younger artists, such as Jones, Brittain and Finzi, had adopted a strongly anti-German stance. Although Parry clearly felt that the atrocity stories were exaggerated, it is significant that not one of the group advanced any kind of justification for the conduct of the Germans. Already a pattern was becoming established, where in their creative work – as in Brooke's sonnets – the enemy was simply absent. Aside from the external reasons for supporting the war, it is clear that several of this group joined up partly to resolve internal personal tensions, and, one suspects with Kate Finzi and David Jones, in a spirit of youthful adventure.

For all of these individuals, the war had already brought change. For two who had been out to the war zone, Finzi and Brooke, it had brought exhilaration, purpose and involvement in a great cause. For Lawrence, Nash and Jones, the move to military service had as yet produced little more than a sense of anticipation. For Spencer and Brittain, the war brought a deeply disconcerting uncertainty about what they should be doing. Parry and Elgar were both sufficiently old to feel at once distant from the actual fighting, but horrified at the thought of violence on such a scale. Both were also appalled by the anti-German feeling in Britain which directly affected people they knew and liked, and beyond this, already realized that the war might bring about larger, unpredictable consequences. One member of the group alone appeared determined to continue his life without making any concessions to the war, Ellis Evans. After writing his poem 'Patriotism', which now appears insincere and misjudged, he seems to have resolved to ignore the war and public sentiments about 'shirkers' and 'slackers'. Anyone who knows the mountains of North Wales may understand why one living and working there might be tempted to do this, but his stance would be tested in the years to come.

# CHAPTER FOUR

# January–June 1915

In the dying days of 1914, three senior figures in the British government composed memoranda on how to proceed with the war effort. Maurice Hankey, the Secretary to the War Council, proposed an attack on the Ottoman Empire and also suggested ingenious ways of breaking the stalemate in Flanders, one being the development of armoured and tracked vehicles which could crush barbed wire.[1] Winston Churchill was anxious to use the navy and suggested attacks on the Belgian coast or on the island of Sylt as a preliminary to a direct attack on Germany itself.[2] Lloyd George wrote 'we cannot let things drift' and suggested attacking either the Austrians or the Turks to weaken the enemy alliance.[3] Here was the genesis of the division between 'easterners' and 'westerners' which was to bedevil British strategy for most of the war. The 'westerners', led by Kitchener and the generals in Flanders, argued that the German Army had to be defeated on the Western Front, and that all available resources should be concentrated there. The 'easterners' believed that by using British sea power the enemy could be fatally weakened, somewhere away from the Western Front. In 1915, the 'easterners', led by Churchill, got their chance. On 13 January, the War Council, having received a request from the Russians for help, agreed to a plan to force the Dardanelles, the sea passage leading from the Mediterranean Sea to the Black Sea, and to attack Constantinople, with the aim of knocking Turkey out of the war.[4]

Initially, this plan was conceived of as a purely naval expedition, using old ships which were of little value in the North Sea, and it was on this understanding that it received Kitchener's reluctant blessing. Over the next few weeks, a large British and French fleet was slowly concentrated at the Greek island of Lemnos; secrecy was not maintained, and the Turks were given ample opportunity to strengthen their defences, with German assistance. The resulting setbacks need not be rehearsed in detail. Initial bombardments from ships failed to subdue the Turkish forts on either side of the Dardanelles, and efforts to clear the mines blocking the way to Constantinople were repulsed with heavy losses on 18 March 1915. After this it was agreed that it would be necessary to land troops, commanded by Sir Ian Hamilton, on the Gallipoli peninsula, to help the navy to break through. Once again, any element of surprise was forsaken, and with great difficulty, landings were made on 25 April. The Allied troops were unable to advance more than a few miles inland, and rapidly, trench warfare developed. More and more men, including large contingents from Australia and New Zealand, were diverted to Gallipoli, but were unable to break the deadlock. The British and French found themselves committed to maintaining an ever-growing army in a hot climate and in hostile terrain, dependent for food, water and supplies on replenishment from the sea. Hopes that a successful campaign would induce Balkan states such as Greece and Bulgaria to join the Allied cause were dashed.

In Flanders, the British were under pressure to help the French, who had suffered catastrophic losses in 1914, and to this end a series of offensives, small by later standards, were mounted by the BEF, which had now grown with the addition of soldiers from India and from the Territorial Army. At the village of Neuve Chapelle, south of Ypres, the first attack was led in March 1915 by General Douglas Haig, providing a model which in many ways would be repeated until November 1918. After a short 'hurricane bombardment' of the enemy positions, the infantry went over the top. Despite heavy losses they were able to occupy the front line of German trenches, but were by then exhausted and out of touch with their own artillery. By the time reserves were brought up, the defenders had regrouped, or even counter-attacked, and the momentum of the attack was dissipated. At Neuve Chapelle there were 12,000 British casualties; in similar attacks on the Aubers Ridge and at Festubert in May, 11,000 and then 16,000 men were killed and injured. In between these attacks, the fighting on the Western Front had taken a sinister turn when the Germans used chlorine gas for the first time in an attack on the Ypres Salient in April, provoking outrage in Britain and further allegations of barbarity. Ironically, the lesson derived by Haig and his commander John French from these failed assaults was simple: they blamed the lack of shells and concluded that with more guns and more ammunition it would be possible to punch a large hole in the German front line. Haig, displaying a willingness to use any new technology which might help, also wanted to use gas and took a keen interest in the preparations being made to prepare stocks in readiness.

In Britain, the expedition to the Dardanelles had left amid high hopes, nourished by associations with classical literature and mythology. Disappointment at the failures there and on the Western Front was compounded in the spring of 1915 by horror at the German use of poison gas, the sinking of the passenger liner *Lusitania* and the first bombing raids by Zeppelins on British cities. Together, these developments combined to

# JANUARY–JUNE 1915

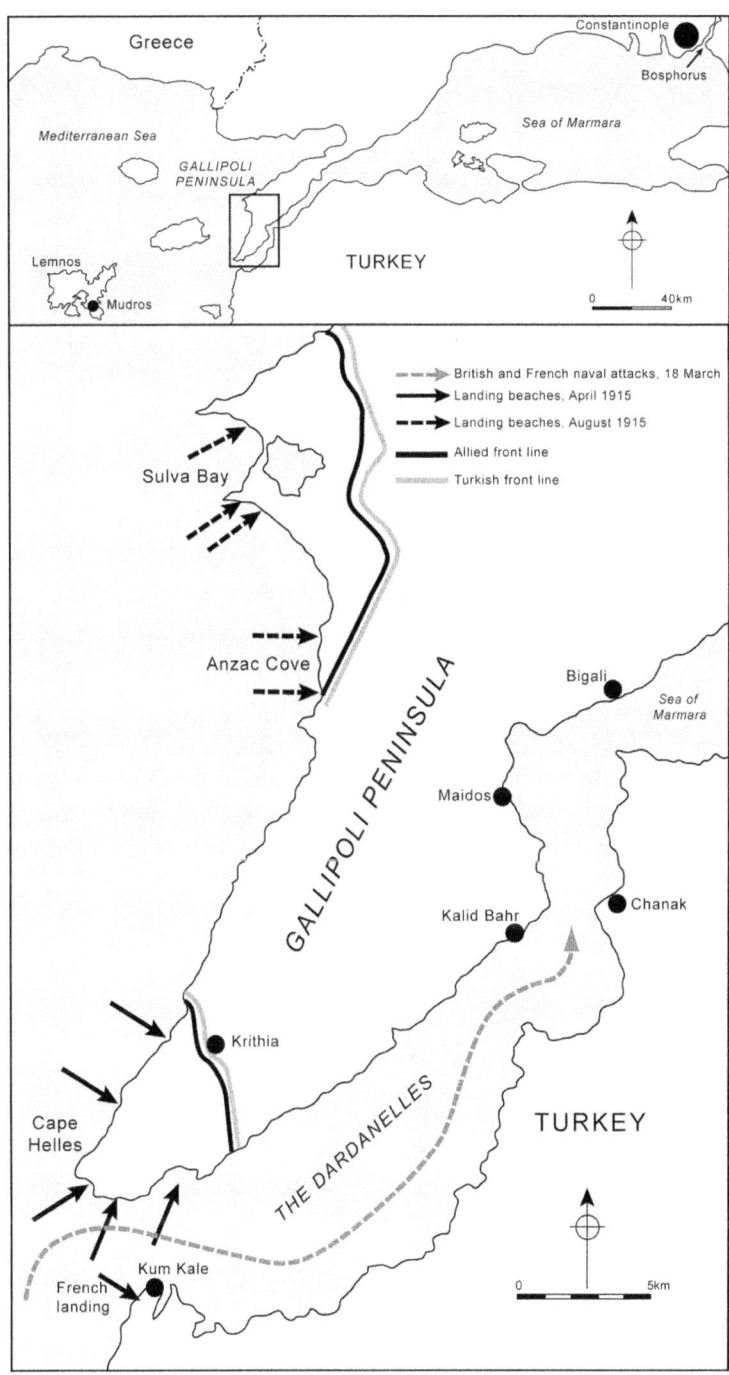

MAP 5 *The Dardanelles and Gallipoli.*

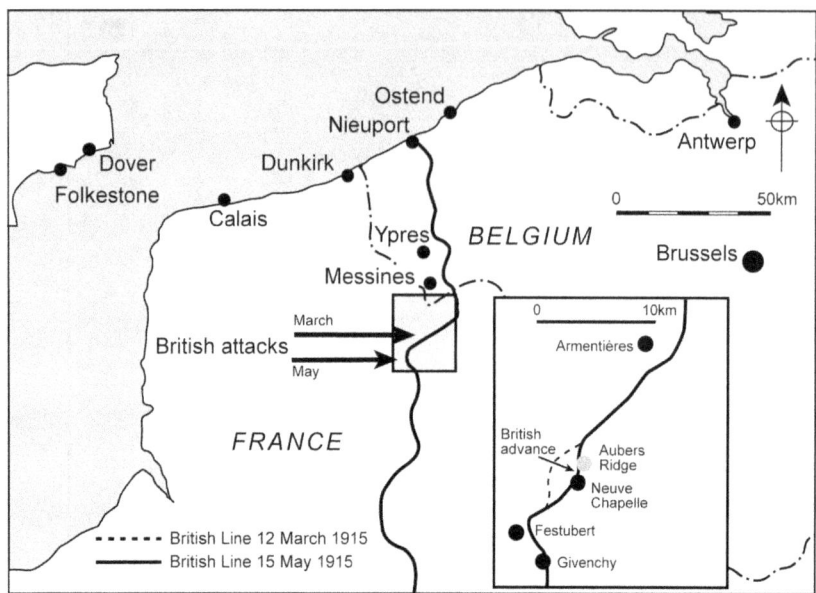

MAP 6 *Neuve Chappelle and Aubers Ridge.*

produce a mood nearing crisis, an atmosphere stoked up by Lord Northcliffe's newspapers, which blamed the government for the 'shell shortage'. Churchill, who had earlier faced criticism for the failed expedition to Antwerp, was singled out as the author of the Dardanelles expedition, and in May he was removed from his post as First Lord of the Admiralty in a wider government reshuffle. Asquith brought Conservatives, and even a Labour politician, Arthur Henderson, into a new coalition administration, and Lloyd George was given the key task of heading a new Ministry of Munitions, charged with producing the shells needed to bring victory.

## Intimations of mortality

Rupert Brooke had been transferred to the Hood Battalion of the Royal Naval Division and posted to a camp near Blandford in Dorset shortly before Christmas 1914. Here, working on his sonnets, he contemplated the likelihood of being sent to Flanders in the New Year. In a letter to his friend Dudley Ward, he realistically assessed his chances of survival: 'If it's true the war'll last two years more, there's very little chance of anyone who goes out in January 1915 returning.'[5] He was nonetheless itching to get back to the war zone. He wrote to Ka Cox early in 1915: 'I'm fixed here for God knows how bloody long: waiting till the rest of the Division gets shipshape. Till April I fear.'[6] While Brooke waited, there was a strange episode which reminded him of his past, and he turned his thoughts back to matters which had preoccupied him since the outbreak of war: marriage and children. He was given a letter written by Taatamata, with whom he had had an affair in Tahiti in 1913; the letter had been written in May 1914, posted on a ship which had sunk in the St Lawrence waterway in Canada, but had then been retrieved from the wreck and sent on to him. Brooke read the letter carefully, looking to see whether Taatamata had become pregnant by him, but he was disappointed, writing to Dudley Ward: 'And I can't decipher any reference to prospects of a baby. So that dream goes with the rest.'[7]

Convinced that he would be killed if the division was sent to Flanders, Brooke wondered whether he ought to marry first. With some arrogance, he wrote that there were several young women he could choose from who would make good partners for a while, but as he put it to Jacques Raverat, 'how dreadful to return from Berlin to a partner for Eternity whom one didn't particularly want'.[8] Brooke's musings and the monotonous routine of training in mid-winter mud were interrupted by electrifying news on 20 February, when the officers of the Naval Division were told that they were to accompany the Dardanelles expedition. Violet Asquith, the Prime Minister's daughter, has written that Churchill allowed her to tell her brother and Rupert Brooke about this in confidence, and it is possible that he heard the news first through this channel. It was more than he could have wished for. He wrote:

> Oh Violet – it's too wonderful for belief! I had not imagined Fate could be so benign. I almost suspect her. Perhaps we shall be held out of sight, on a choppy sea, for two months. . . . But I'm filled with confident and glorious hopes. I've been looking at the maps. Do you think *perhaps* the fort on the Asiatic corner will want quelling, and we'll land and come at it from behind, and they'll make a sortie and meet us on the plains of Troy? It seems to me strategically so possible. Shall we have a Hospital Base (and won't you manage it?) on Lemnos? Will Hero's Tower crumble under the 15-inch guns? Will the sea be polyphloisbic and wine-dark and unvintageable . . .? Shall I loot mosaics from St. Sophia? and Turkish delight and carpets? Shall we be a Turning Point in History? Oh God! I've never been quite so happy in my life I think.[9]

Before the Naval Division embarked for the Dardanelles, it was reviewed by the King. Churchill, his wife Clementine, Eddie Marsh and Violet Asquith were also present. Brook 'complained bitterly' to Violet that his sonnets were being spread 'amongst his mess mates', and she helped to pack up his personal belongings, which included 'futuristic curtains' before the men left their barracks.[10] On 28 February 1915 the division left Avonmouth for the Mediterranean on board the liner *Grantully Castle*. On 7 March they reached Malta, from where letters were despatched. On 11 March the *Grantully Castle* arrived at Lemnos. Brooke's letters reflect his turbulent state of mind: at points he was exalted and wrote flippantly of how he would welcome death; at other points he conceded that he was not yet ready to die. He reflected constantly on the historical parallels he saw with the expedition to the Dardanelles, calling himself 'a Crusader', and expressing approval for how the crusaders had, after slaying Turks, behaved to their 'brother Christians': They had 'very properly thwacked and trounced them, & took their money, & cut their throats, & ravished their daughters & so left them: for that they were Greeks, Jews, Slavs, Vlachs, Magyars, Czechs, & Levantines, & not gentlemen. So shall we do, I hope'.[11] To some of his friends he portrayed the expedition as a picnic; to others he expressed his concern at what would happen when the 10,000 men of the Naval Division were confronted by a quarter of a million Turkish soldiers.

In a letter dated 10 March 1915, Brooke wrote to Ka Cox:

I suppose you're about the best I can do in the way of a widow. . . .

My dear, my dear, you did me wrong: but I have done you very great wrong. Every day I see it greater.

You are the best thing I found in life. If I have memory, I shall remember. You know what I want for you. I hope you will be happy, & marry & have children.

It's a good thing I die.'[12]

On 17 March Brooke sent a letter marked 'If I die' to Dudley Ward instructing him to go through his papers and to destroy letters from two of his former lovers. 'It's odd, being dead', Brooke wrote, adding, 'Try to inform Taata of my death'. He enclosed letters to be circulated in the event of his death, to Eileen Wellesley, Cathleen Nesbitt, Jacques Raverat, Katharine Cox and Eddie Marsh.[13] This was followed by anticlimax. On 18 March the Naval Division was embarked from Mudros Bay and stood off the Dardanelles, expecting to be landed. Brooke wrote to Ka Cox that the men could see 'a dim shore', but after some hours of waiting, the division was returned to Lemnos: 'We did not see the enemy. We did not fire at them; nor they at us. It seems improbable they saw us. One of B Company – she was rolling very slightly – was sick on parade. Otherwise, no casualties. A notable battle.'[14]

As we now know, the plan to force the Dardanelles with ships alone had been abandoned; the Royal Naval Division was taken back to Egypt where all its stores and equipment were rearranged, prior to landing on Gallipoli. Although Rupert Brooke and some of his fellow officers made a brief visit to the Sphinx and other antiquities, several of them fell ill to sunstroke. Brooke was lying ill in Cairo when he was visited by the commander of the Expeditionary Force, Ian Hamilton, who wrote in his diary: 'Asked Brooke to join my personal Staff . . . enabling me to keep an eye on the most distinguished of the Georgians. Bullets are ever drawn as by a magnet towards the finer clay – vide, Sir Philip Sydney of that ilk at Zutphen. Young Brooke replied, as a *preux chevalier* would naturally reply – he realized the privileges he was foregoing, but he felt bound to do the landing shoulder to shoulder with his comrades.'[15]

Brooke had recovered sufficiently to sail with the division when it left again on 10 April aboard the *Grantully Castle*. On 17 April the vessel called at the island of Skyros, and here it became apparent that Brooke was again ill, this time very seriously. He had contracted blood poisoning, perhaps from a mosquito bite, and weakened by earlier sunstroke, declined rapidly. He was taken to a French hospital ship where he died on 23 April.[16]

Even before he died, Brooke had been elevated to fame in Britain. His sonnets, which were first published in February, were reviewed in the *Times Literary Supplement* on 11 March: 'These sonnets are personal – never were sonnets more personal since Sydney died – and yet the very blood and youth of England seem to find expression in them. They speak not for one heart only, but for all to whom her call has come in the hour of need and found instantly ready.'[17] On 4 April Dean Inge of St Paul's cathedral had read 'The Soldier' in his Easter Sunday sermon, and his words about Brooke – delivered after a man had been ejected from the cathedral after beginning 'a loud harangue protesting against the war' – were reprinted in *The Times*. Although Inge noted that 'a Christian would hardly be quite content to think of the brave man's soul as living only as "a pulse in the eternal mind"', he declared that 'the enthusiasm of a pure and elevated patriotism, free from hate, bitterness, and fear, had never found a nobler expression'.[18]

The news of Brooke's death prompted a wave of obituaries and appreciations in the press, including a famous one written by Eddie Marsh but attributed to Winston Churchill, published in *The Times* on 26 April: 'A voice had become audible, a note had been struck, more true, more thrilling, more able to do justice to the nobility of our youth in arms engaged in this present war than any other – more able to express their thoughts of self-surrender, and with a power to carry comfort to those who watch them so intently from afar.'[19] Dozens of other obituaries lamented the loss of a poet on the threshold of greatness, highlighting his talent, charm, personality, good looks and athleticism. Many newspapers printed extracts from Brooke's sonnets, and poems written in tribute to him. Walter de la Mare's comment in the *Westminster Gazette* that Brooke 'went out to die for England as naturally and instinctively as he plunged into the black icy waters of the St. Lawrence', was typical.[20] The limited print run of *New Numbers* containing Brooke's sonnets was rapidly sold out. In June, the sonnets were published in a small collection entitled *1914 and Other Poems*, which had to be issued in 10 further impressions in 1915 alone. By 1918 a dozen more reprints had been sold.[21]

In this tide of hero-worship, there was hardly a dissenting voice, and it was left to a few who had actually known Brooke to hint at other, darker sides to his character. Edward Thomas wrote in June 1915 that 'no poet of his age was so much esteemed and admired, or was watched so hopefully' and concluded: 'He did not attain the "Shelleyan altitude where words have radiance rather than meaning," but perhaps no poet has better expressed the aspiration towards it and all the unfulfilled eagerness of ambitious self-conscious youth.'[22] Privately, Thomas was less forgiving, later writing to Robert Frost in America that Brooke 'was a rhetorician, dressing things up better than they needed. And I suspect he knew too well both what he was after and what he achieved'.[23] The Cambridge musicologist Edward Dent, who had been on the receiving end of Brooke's contempt for pacifists in 1914, wrote a surprisingly kind appreciation in the *Cambridge Magazine*, noting that Brooke's 'sudden and rather factitious celebrity had been obtained by a few poems, which, beautiful as they are in technique and expression, represented him in a phase that could only have been temporary'. Dent referred also to Brooke's 'austere concentration on what was real and intellectual, which showed itself sometimes in a certain almost unsympathetic hardness'.[24]

It was intriguingly Henry Nevinson, who had met Brooke in 1912, who publicly addressed the tensions in Brooke most directly, and his appreciation offers us a clue to the basis of the public reverence for him. Nevinson had sought out the sonnets as soon as he heard of Brooke's death, writing in his diary: 'So beautiful a man & mind – dangerously beautiful to himself – & yet modest & seeking to forget his natural splendour.'[25] In *The Nation* Nevinson wrote: 'He was afraid of himself, afraid of beauty. He was driven to violent reaction against the popular idea of poetry. He was revolutionary, Futuristic, so strongly in revolt against traditional prettiness that he was ready to go hang with it, unless beauty could be extracted from hideousness and disgust.'[26] Who is Nevinson writing about here? It sounds more like his own son Richard than Rupert Brooke, and one senses that Nevinson saw in Brooke an image of Richard, just as Vera Brittain would see in him a likeness of her fiancé Roland Leighton. All over Britain, mothers, fathers and lovers saw in Brooke an idealized version of someone they loved. Few wanted to know the real person behind the heroic facade.

We must remember also that Brooke's poems became known, not at the beginning of the war, where so many popular writers place them, but at a point approaching crisis in April 1915, one identified by Adrian Gregory as seeing a culmination of anti-German feeling in Britain.[27] The setbacks in Flanders and at the Dardanelles, the German use of poison gas, the sinking of the *Lusitania* and the ever-growing casualty lists provided a unique context for the poetry of one who had uncannily foretold his own death. One fellow soldier poet, Charles Sorley, expressed privately a view of Brooke's poetry which would become more widely shared later in the war and afterwards: 'He is far too obsessed with his own sacrifice, regarding the going to war of himself (and others) by the turn of circumstances, where non-compliance with this demand would have made life intolerable.'[28]

## Boredom and bereavement

One might imagine that the attack on the Dardanelles would have captured the imagination of T. E. Lawrence, but for various reasons it did not. Since arriving in Cairo in December 1914 Lawrence had found himself effectively working as a bureaucrat. Although some of his biographers have portrayed him during 1915 involved in cloak and dagger espionage, running spies and interrogating prisoners, in fact he was largely occupied with preparing maps and writing reports. He worked very long hours and avoided the usual social diversions of British officers in Egypt. In many letters from this period he expressed his frustration and boredom. In one he wrote: 'I'm fed up, and fed up, and fed up.'[29] Furthermore, he loathed Cairo and the Egyptians, to the extent of not speaking Arabic lest his vocabulary become corrupted with Egyptian terms. The Dardanelles expedition was a conventional military venture, which did not demand specialist knowledge of the Arab world, and the arrival of the Mediterranean Expeditionary Force threatened to swamp Lawrence's homely intelligence unit with a much larger military organization in which he could only play a small part. At no point did Lawrence seek a direct involvement in the Dardanelles or the Gallipoli campaign, although his office was required to produce maps of the area.

Even as the Dardanelles expedition slowly gathered in the Eastern Mediterranean in early 1915, Lawrence, bored with his everyday work, was dreaming of an ambitious scheme to undermine the Ottoman Empire, which he thought was 'crumbling fast',[30] by supporting Arab nationalist aspirations. In February he told Hogarth that the port of Alexandretta in northern Syria was 'the key of the whole place' and urged him to emphasize to Kitchener and to Churchill the importance of a British landing there to secure the harbour.[31] In June 1915 Lawrence returned to this scheme, trying to engage the services of a British resident there whom he had met before the war.[32] The government in London did indeed consider this idea early in 1915, but decided against it. Lawrence was already toying with a larger idea. Three days before the Anglo-French fleet made its most serious assault on the Dardanelles on 18 March, Lawrence outlined a plan to assist the Arabs in 'another uncensored letter' to Hogarth, which has since become famous: 'I want to pull them all together, & to roll up Syria by way of the Hedjaz in the name of the Sherif. . . . we can rush right up to Damascus, & biff the French right out of Syria. It's a big game, and at last one worth playing.'[33]

The Sherif was Husein Ibn Ali, an Arab leader who claimed direct descent from the prophet Mohammed and had been appointed Emir of Mecca by the Turkish Sultan in 1908. Lawrence's plan appealed to his own romantic conception of the Arabs and to his vision of a fruitful British cooperation with them. But even if the practical difficulties of 'rushing' from Mecca through the Hejaz and Palestine up to Damascus could be overcome, Lawrence knew that there would be other objections to his scheme. The French had their own hopes for Syria and did not wish to encourage Arab nationalism, given that they presided over substantial Arab colonies in North Africa. The Indian Office of the British government was already supporting its own protégé in Arabia, as Lawrence knew, and did not want to see Muslim opinion in India offended by British colonialism in Arabia.

Lawrence's famous letter to Hogarth also contained a fatal ambiguity, in the phrase 'in the name of the Sherif'. Was Lawrence suggesting genuine support for Arab nationalism, or merely an exploitation of that sentiment in pursuit of British interests?

The same ambiguity was reflected in official British dealings with Sherif Husein. In the spring of 1915, the Foreign Office, concerned with the danger of Turkish mobilization of Muslim sentiment against Britain, reconsidered the idea of supporting Arab nationalist aspirations in the Hejaz. On 14 April the Foreign Office informed the high commissioner in Egypt that it was 'an essential condition of the terms of peace that the Arabian Peninsula and its Mohammedan Holy Places should remain in the hands of an independent Sovereign State'. This information was printed in a leaflet which was distributed in Egypt, Sudan and in Arabia in June to bolster Arab support for Britain. The telegram, and the leaflet, did not specify either who would head this state or where its geographical boundaries would lie.[34]

Husein, the most likely candidate to take advantage of this declaration, was in a difficult position. He was being pressured by the Turks to provide soldiers for the Ottoman Army and for their *jihad* against the British. The Arab tribesmen he could rally to his cause had few rifles, and no heavy weapons or modern equipment. It would be difficult for them to face up to, let alone to defeat, Turkish forces armed with machine guns and artillery. The Turks in Arabia depended for their supplies on the single line Hejaz railway, which traversed hundreds of miles of inhospitable desert from Damascus, far to the north, but Husein's tribesmen, with nothing more than their bare hands, could not tear the railway up. The difficulty of Husein's position was highlighted by the danger to his son, Feisal, who was in Constantinople, and exposed to Turkish intimidation. Not surprisingly, Husein temporized, wanting to be sure before he acted against the Turks.

While he waited on the sidelines, Lawrence also had to deal with the death of a close relative. He heard in June 1915 that his younger brother Frank had been killed in France. His reaction to this news was clothed in patriotic rhetoric, but was almost brutal. To his brother Will, Lawrence wrote: 'Frank's death was as you say a shock, because it was so unexpected. I don't think one can regret it overmuch, because it is a very good way to take, after all.'[35] Lawrence wrote to his parents in similar vein, appearing almost to mimic Rupert Brooke: 'and I hope that when I die there will be nothing more to regret'. He was concerned about their public display of grief, writing, 'there was no need surely to go into mourning for him? I cannot see any cause at all – in any case to die for one's country is a sort of privilege. Mother, you will find it more painful & harder to live for it, than he did to die'.[36] Separately, Lawrence chided his mother, saying 'In a time of such fearful stress it is one's duty to watch very carefully lest one of the weaker ones be offended.' He added: 'I didn't go to say goodbye to Frank because he would rather I didn't, & I knew there was little chance of my seeing him again, in which case we were better without a parting.'[37]

## Social divisions emerge

While Hankey, Lloyd George and Churchill were thinking of ways to break the military deadlock, Vera Brittain was falling in love. In the last days of 1914 she met with Roland Leighton in London while he was on leave, and a few days later they contrived to meet without a chaperone on the train taking Brittain back to Oxford for the spring term. Only now was Vera Brittain able to confide to her diary the hope that she and Leighton might be in love with one another.[38] She signalled a distinct change in the nature of this previously platonic relationship by noting on 24 January 1915 that after tea with a fellow student at Somerville, that she had 'again discussed genius with her – also sex questions'.[39]

Vera Brittain's whole world was shifting. She had tried hard to immerse herself in university life and to insulate herself from the war, but now, consumed by love, she saw the war through Roland Leighton's eyes. In March she met him briefly before he left for France, and wrote: 'For the time being all people, all ideas, all interests, have set, and sunk below the horizon of my mind. He alone I can contemplate.'[40] She marked a further departure from her pre-war life when she wrote, a few days later, 'I really don't think I can stand church much more.'[41] In her imagination, and through Leighton's letters, Brittain followed every stage of his journey to the front. Over the next few weeks, she struggled to concentrate on her work in Oxford, finding university life increasingly remote from the war. She avidly followed the war reporting in *The Times*, replicating its patriotic tone in her diary, but now she read the casualty lists with intensified concern. She wrote with horror about 'the dearly bought victory' at Neuve Chapelle,[42] and more realistically about 'an unsuccessful attack' on the Aubers Ridge, 'resulting in great loss of life'.[43] She railed at the new outrages reported, such as the 'unsporting & diabolical' German use of gas at Ypres, and the sinking of the *Lusitania* in May 1915.[44] From Leighton's letters she was learning the vocabulary of trench warfare – of shrapnel, dugouts, listening posts and snipers – and in an effort to parallel his service, she was thinking about doing war work of some kind, particularly about nursing.

During the Easter vacation, Brittain took her first steps away from academic study, doing voluntary work at the Devonshire Hospital in Buxton. Just as her perception of the war was focused through the prism of Roland Leighton's front-line experience, so her view of nursing was channelled through the idea of looking after him if he was wounded.[45] Wounded soldiers were indeed becoming an everyday sight in Britain by this time. Brittain and her fellow women students were moved to Oriel College in April 1915, when Somerville was turned into a convalescent hospital for the duration of the war. Brittain went back to Somerville in May in a party giving a concert to the soldiers now housed there. Observing the wounded men, she wrote: 'I could imagine *him* with a wrecked and broken body struggling to walk with the help of a padded stick.'[46] She nonetheless preserved an extraordinarily romanticized view of war, one heightened by hearing Rupert Brooke's sonnets in May 1915.[47] Brooke's impassioned idealism and his willingness to embrace death struck a deep chord with Vera Brittain, not least because she fondly imagined that Brooke 'must have been rather like Roland'. She wrote to Leighton to tell him this, quoting from four of the sonnets.[48] Over the next few years, Brittain would frequently refer to Brooke's sonnets, quote from them and use similar images in her own writing.

Oxford, with its arcane ceremonies – Responsions, Pass Moderations and organ recitals at New College – was becoming ever more difficult for Brittain to reconcile with her anxious daily perusal of the casualty lists, and the news of young men from Buxton or who had been at school with Roland and Edward who were now being killed. In June 1915 she watched the College 'Going-Down Play' and spent a final afternoon punting on the river before returning to Buxton.[49] On 27 June she started work as a voluntary nurse at the nearby Devonshire Hospital.[50]

Kate Finzi did not know Vera Brittain, but she would thoroughly have approved of her decision. By January 1915 the early chaos in Boulogne had been largely resolved, and the last Red Cross volunteer nurses had been dismissed from the improvised hospital on the quay there. Finzi was able to turn to work which demonstrates how much more permanent the British presence in northern France had become, and how the need for more extensive support systems for the troops there had been recognized. She was involved, together with 'YMCA secretaries, nonconformist Ministers, and volunteer ladies'[51] in setting up a hut which served as a canteen, library, meeting place, theatre and concert hall for convalescent soldiers and the thousands of others passing through Boulogne. From March 1915 she helped to establish a hostel where relatives of the most seriously wounded soldiers could stay for brief visits.

Finzi was an unquestioning patriot, liable to criticize the government for what she – reading the Northcliffe press – saw as its irresolute conduct of the war. She returned to England on leave briefly in January 1915, and for a longer period in the early summer, and experienced keenly the sense of separation between those actually in 'the great vortex of war'[52] and those at home which later became such a marked feature of post-war soldiers' memoirs. She was incensed by strikers and shirkers at home, and singled out for condemnation the feminists 'prating recently of the forthcoming Peace Conference at The Hague'.[53] She noted how the British voluntary system produced appalling contrasts, for example between farmers and businessmen in England who worried selfishly about their profits, and young men out in Boulogne condemned to death by courts-martial for cowardice or desertion. Many of her comments reproduce conventional notions of the time, and some are alarming. She wrote of her 'infinite relief' at being back in France in January 1915, and revealed her belief in the eugenicist ideas which were to gain wider acceptance across Europe after 1918: 'Why, after all, should our beautiful island be left with the unfit, the loafers, the "funks" as fathers for future generations? In every other country the army is representative, not of the pick of the land, but of the average male population. We, however, seem bent on committing race suicide.'[54] More perceptively, during her leave in June 1915, she noted that the war was also causing a generational problem. She had met the American novelist Henry James at a reception, and she now enlarged on his view that this was a 'Young People's War'. 'It may be an ironical fate that designs the younger generation to lay down their lives for the political blunders of the older – but the true tragedy is not in the youths cut down in the flower of their manhood, nor the girls broken in health by the magnitude of the task they have tackled; the true tragedy is in the derelict "dugouts" vainly hunting for jobs, the aged women wringing their hands, with the cry "We are too old to help!"'[55]

Finzi's diary for 1915 also reflects how the war was coming to be seen as permanent. In a passage which reflected her strengthened belief in the righteousness of the Allied cause, she wrote in June 1915: 'Since the German introduction of methods that would shame a savage – the poison gas, the sinking of the Lusitania – the whole attitude of our men towards the enemy has changed, and one can safely predict that next Christmas there will be no exchange of civilities and cigarettes with the Huns as there was last.'[56]

Finzi's contempt for 'loafers' and 'funks' was widely shared in Britain, and Stanley Spencer experienced this directly. His brother Gilbert applied to join the Royal Army Medical Corps in April 1915, and Stanley felt compelled to do the same. His emotional turmoil can best be judged from his letters. He wrote to the Raverats on 4 April about Rupert Brooke, referring presumably to his new found fame, but added cryptically: 'I wish those journalists knew how to behave themselves.'[57] A few weeks later Spencer was involved in a painful scene at the barber's in Cookham, when he was publicly taken to task by an older man, who told him directly: 'Now Master Spencer, you ought to be in the army.' Spencer described the incident in detail, and it is clear that he was deeply humiliated. He related how he stood looking at the man, 'feeling like an idiot and a lout'; when he left the barber's shop, Spencer felt he 'had made a thorough mess of myself' and confessed that 'My walk seemed guilty.' Trying nonetheless to make light of the whole episode, Spencer added 'these things are only unpleasant, while they last, & after that, often amusing'.[58]

Clearly this was not an isolated incident. Spencer was still trying to focus on his painting, but failing. Nor were the informal drilling sessions he had been attending a satisfactory sop to his conscience. In July he told Henry Lamb that, 'Cookham having become completely stripped of its youth', he had decided to follow Gilbert into the RAMC and to prepare by taking a St John Ambulance exam. He continued: 'It seems such rotten luck that Gil and I had to do this instead of being Tommies. I would have rather enjoyed being a private in the Berkshires. I mean I would have liked the training. Mar has got an idea that the RAMC is not dangerous & that one does not go to the front & I shall let her think that.'[59] Spencer's inner turmoil is

FIGURE 12 *The Beaufort War Hospital in Bristol, where Stanley Spencer worked as a medical orderly between July 1915 and May 1916.*

perhaps revealed by a cryptic comment added to another letter, suggesting that while he still saw his beloved village as the setting for biblical scenes, some of these associations were now infinitely painful: 'Christ being mocked is like Cookham.'[60]

In June 1915, Gilbert Spencer left Cookham, to serve as a medical orderly in the Beaufort War Hospital in Bristol. This was a former lunatic asylum, now used also for war wounded. Stanley Spencer's confusion was not assuaged by the letters the family now received from Gilbert, describing the appallingly harsh regime he had to endure in Bristol. Stanley wrote, again at length, to the Raverats about this. Gilbert had apparently to wake at 5.00 a.m. every day and was kept hard at work until 8.00 p.m. Almost wildly, Stanley wrote: 'they mean to kill him if they possibly can'. He then added a postscript: 'I shall *not* go to Bristol.'[61] On 19 July 1915, he passed his St John examination, and within a few days he received his first posting as a private in the RAMC, to the Beaufort Hospital.

## First challenges of representation

While Spencer agonized about his future, Nevinson was seizing the artistic opportunity offered by his experience of the front in Flanders. As soon as he returned from Dunkirk in January 1915, he threw himself into preparations for two exhibitions in London which were radically to change his public standing. On 6 February four of Nevinson's paintings and a bust of a driver were included in a Friday Club exhibition. The bust and two of the paintings were pre-war works, and the other two paintings had been completed before

Nevinson left for Flanders in November 1914. One, which is now lost, was entitled *Declaration of War*, and was presumably a representation of the 'spirit of August 1914'. It is difficult to judge now how this work reflected Nevinson's own reaction to the declaration of war, but *The Observer* certainly interpreted it as a celebration, one which demonstrated the potential of a Futurist idiom, containing 'a suggestion of the enthusiasm, the excitement, the patriotic impulse which swayed the crowds in the streets of London on that memorable August night. No method of exact representation, not even a clear snapshot photograph, could ever have reproduced so happily the spirit of that scene'.[62] Another painting, *First Searchlights at Charing Cross*, depicted beams of light quartering a night sky above a modernist urban landscape, generating fields of force around them. Although London had not yet been bombed, Nevinson was here using a Futurist technique to represent what would become one of the defining features of twentieth-century warfare.

The Friday Club exhibition was not universally well received, but it brought publicity. *The Times* carried a stinging criticism of the group, alleging that they continued to amuse themselves 'in spite of the war'; Nevinson was singled out as being 'not even . . . modish'; his works were 'merely rigid and diagrammatic'.[63] This understandably infuriated Nevinson, and he dashed off a letter to the newspaper, stating: 'I have spent the last three months at the Front in France & Belgium amongst wounds, Blood, Stench, Typhoid, agony & death, and as a member of the Friday Club I resent your critic writing "about the sowing of wild oats & managing to amuse myself in spite of the war".'[64] Nevinson was working hard on paintings for another exhibition, and he was given valuable advance publicity by an interview published in the *Daily Express*, accompanied by photographs of some of the paintings and one of Nevinson himself in uniform. In the interview Nevinson explicitly distanced himself from Marinetti, stating: 'Here our ways part. Unlike my Italian Futurist friends I do not glory in war for its own sake, nor can I accept the doctrine that war is the only healthgiver.' Nonetheless, he asserted: 'Our Futurist technique is the only possible medium to express the crudeness, violence, and brutality of the emotions seen and felt on the present battlefields of Europe.'[65] When the paintings were exhibited at the Goupil Gallery in early March, there was a mixed reaction from the press and public. Many critics were scathing about the exhibition as a whole, *The Times* calling the paintings 'Prussian in spirit'.[66]

Two of Nevinson's paintings, *Returning to the Trenches* and *A Taube Pursued by Commander Samson*, were though singled out for praise. Aviation, flight and the heroics of Commander Samson were obviously suited to a Futurist treatment, and Nevinson successfully captured in this painting aspects of war which were entirely new in 1914.[67] *Returning to the Trenches* depicted a column of French soldiers marching, seemingly fused together into a single machine. Nevinson's embodiment of a sense of grim determination and anonymity similarly appeared to express something new but essential about the conflict in Flanders. Michael Walsh has noted how, by depicting French rather than British soldiers, Nevinson distanced himself from either crude patriotism or anti-war feeling.[68]

Nevinson was also romanticizing his own part in the war. In a letter to the *Manchester Guardian* in February 1915 he defended the value of ambulance men at the front and emphasized the danger they were exposed to, stating 'I myself have had my motor ambulance destroyed by shrapnel.'[69] In what now appears an insincere act of self-promotion, one of Nevinson's paintings at the Goupil Gallery was entitled *My Arrival at Dunkirk*. This was actually his pre-war painting of an ocean liner arriving in port and had nothing to do with Nevinson's own rather gloomy journey to Dunkirk in November 1914.[70] Nevinson was paradoxically making life very difficult for himself by romanticizing his war experience, as he had no wish at this point to return to the front. His father wrote on 15 March: 'Heard with bitter disappointment that Rich refuses to return to Quaker unit'.[71]

In the tense atmosphere of the spring of 1915 Nevinson could not avoid this issue. In late May his father recorded that there were still 'difficulties about Rich's return to the Quakers',[72] but he appeared after this to find a way out. On 1 June Henry Nevinson took his son to the 3rd London General Hospital in Wandsworth, where he was sworn in as a private in the RAMC. Critically, the captain who enlisted Richard Nevinson promised 'that he sh. remain in this unit & not go on foreign service'.[73] As we have seen with Gilbert Spencer, service in a war hospital in Britain in 1915 was not a pleasant or an easy option. Nevinson evidently struggled terribly to adjust, his father noting: 'Very bad account of his life in Wandsworth Hospital from Rich, who seems unutterably miserable among the men, nurses, & officers.'[74] Although subsequent diary entries suggest that Nevinson's mood improved temporarily, the combination of hard, demeaning physical work and of close contact with physical injury and mental illness was to prove very difficult for him.

We have virtually no contemporary record of David Jones' experience in the first half of 1915, but what we do know tells us much about Kitchener's 'New Army'. After enlisting in the London Welsh Battalion in January, Jones was sent to Llandudno in North Wales, where the Battalion joined the 1st Division, Welsh Army Corps. The grand scheme of forming a Welsh Army Corps was soon abandoned, and the 1st Division was renamed the 38th (Welsh) Division; it was under this name that it served later on the Western Front. A division in the British Army was intended to be self-sufficient in the field and therefore included, as well as infantry battalions, artillery batteries, engineers, field ambulances, signals units, various transport units, cyclists and headquarters staff. Later in the war machine gun and trench mortar companies were added. The infantry battalions were grouped in fours, to form infantry brigades, and in the 'New Army' these typically came from distinctive geographical areas of Britain.

The London Welsh Battalion formed a brigade with two battalions of North Wales 'Pals' and with a battalion recruited from Carnarvon and Anglesey. The other brigades of the Welsh Division had battalions from the Rhondda, Carmarthenshire, Swansea, Gwent and Cardiff. Initially the Division also included a squadron from the Royal Wiltshire Yeomanry. David Jones found himself training in Llandudno therefore with a mix of recruits from North Wales – many Welsh-speaking – and from London. Demonstrating just how difficult it was to equip the 'New Army', Jones' battalion was not issued with rifles until August 1915. According to the divisional history, the men 'were clothed in Brethyn Llwyd, the Welsh cloth, until supplies of Khaki were received'. The artillery batteries had no guns or horses, and gun drills had to be carried out with improvised weapons such as a pair of 'old 'bus wheels fitted with a pole and hook'.[75]

In the meantime, Jones and his fellow recruits did physical training, drill and guard duty on the seafront. They were billeted around the town. We do not know if Jones was homesick, but it does appear that he enjoyed the comradeship of his Cockney and Welsh fellow recruits. On St David's Day, 1 March 1915, his brigade was paraded for inspection before Lloyd George. The day's events included a speech by the Chancellor, and an *eisteddfod* in the Pier Pavilion, with singing and adjudications of an *englyn* – a Welsh-language poetic form. David Jones wrote on his copy of the programme 'very wet and very cold', a comment anyone familiar with the Welsh coastline in early spring will understand.[76] These raw recruits were still far from being ready for active service.

## Memory and mourning

Since the start of the war various people had badgered Elgar about writing war music of one kind or another, but early in 1915 a suggestion was made which caught his imagination. His old friend Sidney Colvin, in an afterthought, wrote: 'Why don't you do a wonderful Requiem for the slain – something in the spirit of Binyon's "For the Fallen," or of that splendid passage of Ruskin which I quoted in the Times Supplement of Decr 31. – Or of both together?'[77] Laurence Binyon worked at the British Museum, and 2 weeks later Elgar visited him there. We do not know what they discussed, but it is likely that the idea of Elgar setting some of Binyon's war poems was high on the agenda. Binyon had published a series of poems since August 1914 in *The Times*, and they had been issued together as *The Winnowing Fan* in December 1914. Elgar, ever sensitive to words, saw here the potential for a large-scale work which might speak to both his own concerns and the feelings of a larger public, and three of the poems were chosen. Rachel Cowgill has argued persuasively that Elgar saw here the possibility of composing a war requiem, one which would though not be obviously Roman Catholic, and therefore invite confrontation with Anglican sensibilities.[78] Elgar was totally committed to two of Binyon's poems, 'To Women' and 'For the Fallen', but he was from the start ambivalent about the first, 'August 1914', and it is possible that he may – against his better judgement – have yielded to pressure from Binyon to set this.

This poem was published in *The Times* a week after the outbreak of the war and was a typical expression of the 'spirit of 1914'. It celebrated the war as an end to 'days of sour division', and called on the 'spirit of England, ardent eyed', which 'recalls its heritage' to fight against 'the barren creed of blood and iron'. One stanza depicted the Germans as the 'Vampire of Europe's wasted will'.[79] On 20 August 1914, Binyon eulogized the women of England:

> For you, you too to battle go
> Not with the marching drums and cheers
> But in the watch of solitude
> And in the boundless night of fears.

Binyon ended this poem with a statement of faith in the power of women to endure:

> To bleed
> To bear; to break, but not to fail![80]

A month later, as news arrived of British losses in France and at sea, he contributed a poem which has become one of the best known of the war:

> They shall grow not old, as we that are left grow old
> Age shall not weary them, nor the years condemn
> At the going down of the sun, and in the morning
> We shall remember them.[81]

After meeting with Binyon, Elgar threw himself into setting these words to music; Alice Elgar noted on 9 February 1915 that he 'composed violently'[82]; he sketched out much of the music for *To Women* and *For the Fallen* in the next six weeks. But difficulties intervened which threatened the whole project. Elgar heard that another composer, the now unknown Cyril Rootham, had already set *For the Fallen* for Novello, his own publisher, and felt compelled to withdraw his own work. Over the next few weeks, several of Elgar's friends appealed to his sense of duty, arguing fiercely that he should continue with the work. Binyon himself wrote: 'but think of England, of the English-speaking peoples, in whom the common blood stirs now as it never did before; think of the awful casualty lists that are coming, & the losses in more & more homes'.[83] As these discussions developed, Elgar introduced, characteristically, another reason for his reluctance, that the public would not understand his work. He had planned a work which was not jingoistic or aggressive, but reflective and sombre – effectively a requiem for the dead, and all his old fears about the British public's insensitivity were reawakened. He wrote to Sidney Colvin: 'they [the British public] do not want me & never did. If I work at all it is not for them'.[84] On 13 April, Sidney Colvin replied to Elgar with real passion: 'You put it on the indifference of our race & public to art: but what has the poor British public done now which it had not a month ago, when you were full of the project and raised all our hearts with anticipation of a great and worthy expression & commemoration of the emotions of the hour, such as you alone are capable of giving them? ... Do the work you had promised and begun – do it for those who love you – do it for the thousands for whom it will express what is deepest & most sacred in their souls, do it for your country & the future & to honour and justify the gift which has been given to you.'[85]

Colvin's entreaties evidently had impact, and on 14 April, Alice Elgar recorded: 'E. turned to his beautiful music again, loved it himself'.[86] Colvin himself wrote diplomatically to Elgar that he was delighted to hear that 'it is possible your inspiration may return', adding: '(We won't dispute about the blessed B. P.).'[87] Through April and May 1915 Elgar worked intensively on the Binyon settings, planning a large-scale work for choir and orchestra, with a solo tenor or soprano. On several occasions he played parts of the composition to visitors, including the conductor Landon Ronald, who perceptively reacted by saying that 'there had been nothing like it since the 2nd Symphony'.[88]

While Elgar grappled with his new composition, the war was coming closer. The first Zeppelin raids on Britain had begun in January 1915, and since then had continued intermittently, becoming a frequent phenomenon. These giant airships, flying from northern Germany, were initially able to attack Britain with near impunity, as they could fly higher than the fragile aeroplanes sent to attack them, and above the range of early anti-aircraft guns. The attacks in 1915 caused a huge wave of public anger in Britain, forcing the government to divert considerable resources to defences against them, and provoking calls for reprisal attacks on German cities. The Zeppelins actually faced great difficulty in navigating to Britain and back, particularly in bad weather, and were prone to mechanical problems. Even if they did reach Britain, it was difficult for them to identify exactly where they were or to drop bombs with any precision. Frequently, failing to reach their targets, they dropped their bombs on other places along their line of flight. Although they were often despatched in groups of up to a dozen airships, they usually became separated, and would arrive individually over Britain. The course of a single airship might be reported over several towns and counties, and its bombs might fall in widely separated places. Although London was most often the target for Zeppelin attacks, many bombs fell on towns in eastern England, from Kent, through East Anglia, and up to Yorkshire. The sound of Zeppelin engines at night, coming and going with the wind, became a familiar one in these areas. If by chance bombs landed

FIGURE 13 *Edward Elgar, his wife Alice and their daughter Carice were among the thousands of spectators who went to see the damage caused by the first Zeppelin raid on London in May 1915. Alice Elgar wrote: 'Horrid sight'.*

on crowded buildings, they had enormous destructive impact, killing and wounding people with shards of flying glass and collapsing masonry. The shrapnel from exploding anti-aircraft shells was also destructive and could cause injuries. On 31 May 1915, a single Zeppelin crossed the coast near Margate and reached London for the first time, dropping bombs which killed seven people and injured another 35.[89] Alice Elgar noted this raid, and a few days later recorded how she, her husband and their daughter Carice took a taxi to go and see the 'houses wrecked by the Zeppelin raid'. It was, she wrote, a 'Horrid sight'. She then added one word, underlined: '*Brutes*'.[90]

Hubert Parry was similarly horrified by German behaviour in the spring of 1915. He wrote in his diary on 8 May: 'Depressed all day by the news of the torpedoing of the Lusitania'. Like many, he read the report of the Bryce Commission on 'German atrocities'; he was 'was utterly sickened by it'.[91] This report, written by James Bryce, lawyer and former Liberal Cabinet Minister, had been commissioned by the British government in December 1914, and it was based largely on depositions made by Belgian refugees and by British soldiers. It has frequently been condemned as 'propaganda' and charged with making false allegations. The recent careful analysis of the Bryce Report by Horne and Kramer suggests that many of the gruesome stories it rehearsed were accurate, but that others were exaggerated or were fantastical.[92] Lengthy extracts from the report were published in the British press and were given wide credulity.[93]

Parry was more oppressed by blows to individual friends. On 30 April he heard 'the dreadful news' that the only son of his friend Frank Pownall had been killed in France.[94] Then on 3 May, as his students gathered to hear his address at the start of the new term, he was interrupted by the Registrar at the College, George Aveling, who gave him 'the distressing news that his nephew had died in hospital after being severely wounded in recent fighting'. Parry continued in his diary: 'It depressed me so much that I was quite upset about it, & could hardly get through the address without breaking down. So it was a very bad one'.[95] Parry's address, written before he spoke with Aveling, started with a tribute to the students who had already enlisted, and who, Parry conceded, 'may never come back to us'.[96] Over the next few weeks, he saw more and more of his students join up, including a particularly talented working-class boy from Gloucester whom Parry had taken under his wing, Ivor Gurney.[97] In January, Parry had written to another, Ralph Vaughan-Williams, to dissuade him from enlisting.[98] We can only imagine how torn he was when, as in June 1915, he was requested to write references for one of his students who was applying for officer training.[99]

The British experience of the First World War was marked by many points of particular tension, when we can perceive distinct changes in the public mood. There had been an initial shock at the news of the retreat from Mons in August 1914, and another at the fall of Antwerp. The spring and early summer of 1915 produced a sense of gravity and horror which went far deeper. The first offensives on the Western Front had been costly failures; the brave expedition to the Dardanelles had faltered; the casualty lists had grown; and the sense of being ranged against a diabolical opponent had been heightened by the terrible stories in the Bryce Report, the Zeppelin raids, the use of poison gas and the sinking of the *Lusitania*. While sensitive spirits like Parry internalized his emotions, and Elgar turned to commemoration, others in the population were impelled to more direct action. Recruiting was still strong, as initially hesitant volunteers such as Spencer, Nevinson and Brittain took the plunge. After the sinking of the *Lusitania*, there was rioting, and around the country, people and shops identified as German were subject to violent intimidation, on a huge scale. On the same day that it commented on 'German Barbarism in War', *The Times* reported without irony that in London more than 150 German shops were attacked, noting: 'Hundreds of thousands of people took part in the raids or were sympathetic spectators'.[100]

# CHAPTER FIVE

# July–December 1915

On 27 July 1915, Asquith informed the House of Commons that total British casualties since the start of the war now stood at 340,000, a figure which dwarfed that of any previous conflict.¹ The British were under pressure to support the planned French offensive in Artois and Champagne and had agreed to mount an offensive against the German lines near the small town of Loos.² Out on the Gallipoli peninsula, Ian Hamilton's multinational army was still entrenched in two small, separate beachheads, struggling merely to survive in the heat and under Turkish shellfire. In London, there was real concern that the Russians, who had by this time suffered catastrophic losses, were on the verge of collapse. One ray of light in this dismal situation was that Kitchener's 'New Army' was now coming on stream. Perhaps with the deployment of fresh men progress, somewhere, could be made.

In June 1915, the War Council, now renamed the Dardanelles Committee, had decided to send substantial reinforcements to try to force a decision on the Gallipoli peninsula.³ Hamilton developed an ambitious plan to deploy these partly to strengthen the existing Anzac beachhead, and partly in a new night landing in Suvla Bay, on the north of the peninsula. From here he hoped that it would be possible to cut the Turkish troops off in the tip of the peninsula. Without supplies they would have to surrender or to break out; either way, the Allied fleet could then proceed through the Dardanelles and threaten Constantinople. On 6 August, the new landings were made at Suvla Bay, but opportunities to seize the vital high ground were not taken, and within days it became apparent that these men too were pinned down in a small beachhead. Churchill called desperately for more soldiers to be sent out, and for the navy to renew the assault on the Dardanelles, but to no avail.⁴

This effectively ended the British effort to pursue the original objectives of the Gallipoli campaign, and the situation there was complicated in

September by the request of the Greek premier Venizelos for help against the Bulgarians, who had now opted to fight with the Central Powers. On 25 September Kitchener ordered three of Ian Hamilton's divisions to be landed at Salonica to help a French force despatched there, and thus another 'side show' was opened. After an initial sally against the Bulgarians, the French and the British had to fall back into what was called an 'entrenched camp' around the port of Salonica, where they would stay until the final weeks of the war.

In October, Ian Hamilton was replaced as commander of the Mediterranean Expeditionary Force by Charles Monro, who recommended an immediate evacuation of the Gallipoli peninsula. Although there were fears that this would be catastrophic, with careful planning the Allied troops were taken off the beachheads in December 1915 and in January 1916. It was the most successful aspect of the whole campaign, but there was no disguising that the expedition had been, in military and diplomatic terms, a complete failure. The Gallipoli campaign cast a long shadow, not just over Churchill's reputation, but over any subsequent idea put forward in Britain to win the war away from the Western Front.

On 25 September 1915, the BEF attacked, as planned, at Loos. By this time the British Army in France had grown to 900,000 men, including the first of the 'New Army' divisions, and the offensive was much larger than those in spring. It was also accompanied by the first British use of chlorine gas, released from cylinders brought up to the front-line trenches by night. The attack was an unmitigated disaster. There was virtually no wind, and in places the gas lingered close to the British trenches, and even fell back into them. General Haig, commanding the attacking forces, mistakenly believed that he had opened a gap in the German lines and ordered two untested 'New Army' divisions to exploit this. They arrived exhausted at the front lines and were quickly driven back by artillery and machine-gun fire, suffering heavy casualties. Haig maintained the offensive into November but little was gained, and by the time it was called off the British had suffered 50,000 casualties.

The public perception of Loos was not helped by the initial reports. *The Times* printed a brief but ludicrously optimistic summary from John French on 27 September which spoke of 'trenches carried on a five mile front' and of guns and prisoners taken.[5] The *Sheffield Daily Telegraph* showed a photograph of 1,100 German prisoners taken at Loos being marched through Southampton with the heading 'Captured during the British Advance',[6] and as late as 12 October, the newspapers were still speaking of further advances and of another 'very severe reverse' for the Germans.[7] None of the descriptions of the initial attack mentioned the use of gas, and it was not until mid-October that *The Times* slipped in a discreet reference to the British troops' 'use of gas and smoke' in a renewed attack.[8] *The Graphic* reported on 23 October: 'It is now officially admitted that we are using gas against the Germans.'[9] The geographical details also

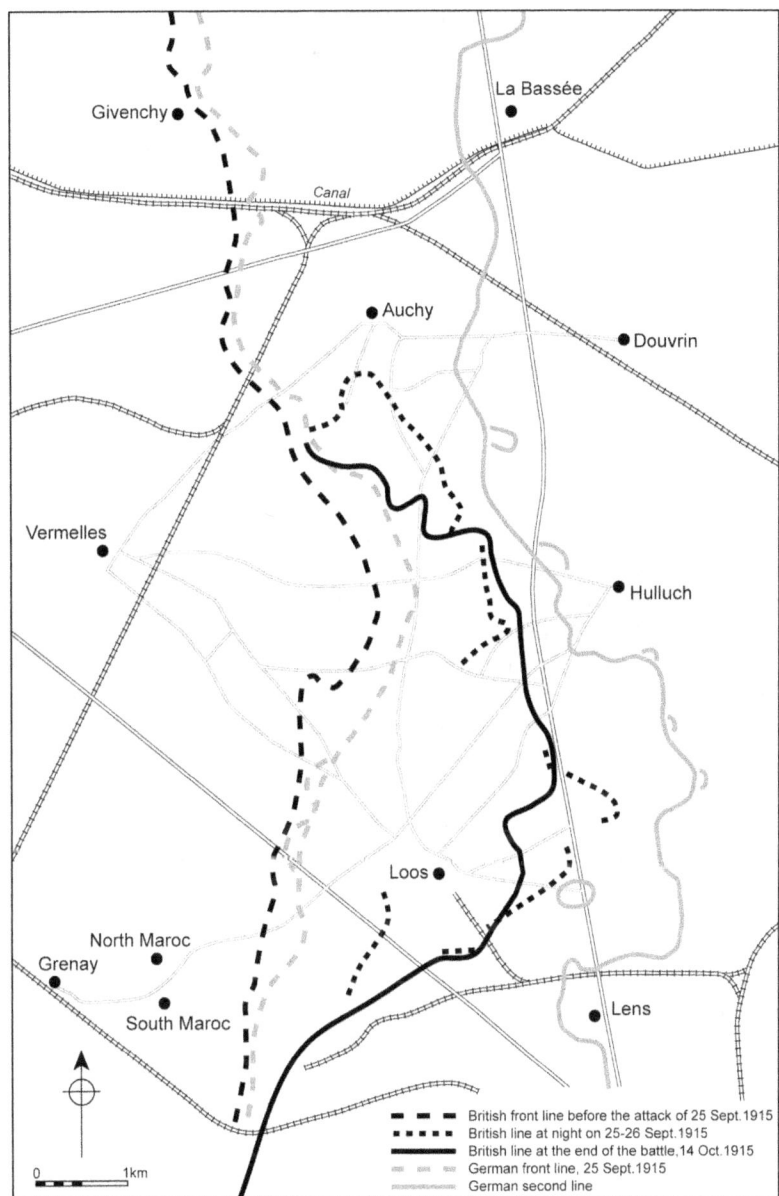

MAP 7 *The Battle of Loos.*

provided by the newspapers were nonetheless largely accurate. It slowly became clear to any intelligent reader and to the government that for all the brave talk, there had been appallingly high casualties, and that virtually no ground had been gained. From the King down to Asquith, Kitchener and other senior commanders, there was now a lack of confidence in French, and in December he was forced to resign. On 19 December Douglas Haig was appointed to replace him as commander-in-chief of the BEF, a position he would hold until the end of the war. Another former cavalry officer, Sir William Robertson, was appointed Chief of the Imperial General Staff, the key position in London acting as the conduit between the civilian government and General Headquarters in France.

There was another significant shift in the British conduct of the war at the end of 1915. After 18 months, the steady flow of volunteers had largely dried up, and Asquith's government had found it impossible to resist the growing calls for compulsory military service. Right across society, from prominent public figures to housewives, people had railed against the voluntary principle which, they claimed, allowed 'shirkers' and 'slackers' to avoid their national duty while more honourable men died in action. On 10 March 1916, the Military Service Act came into force, requiring all unmarried men born between 1887 and 1895 to present themselves for enlistment by 17 March.[10]

We can understand better the awful failure of the 'New Army' divisions at Loos by returning to the experience of David Jones. His own division, the 38th (Welsh), had continued its training in Llandudno through the summer of 1915. In August a choir from the 17th Battalion, Royal Welch Fusiliers, won a prize at the National Eisteddfod in nearby Bangor.[11] The division was moved in August to Winnall Down near Winchester, where its infantry battalions were concentrated with their supporting units. The artillery batteries now had guns and horses, and the men were dressed in regulation khaki. In October the infantry began musketry training, learning about the 63 parts of the standard Lee-Enfield Short rifle, but it was not until November that all the men were issued with their own weapon. A photograph of Jones' company taken at this time shows how young many of these recruits were, many still looking like boys.[12] The divisional history admits that there was 'very little training in trench warfare as it was thought there would be no difficulty in learning that in France', and on 29 November the whole unit was reviewed by the Queen and Princess Mary before being sent out.[13] The next morning Jones' battalion was marched out through country lanes towards Southampton, where they embarked on a troopship which carried them to Le Havre. Jones arrived in France on 2 December, nearly a year after he had enlisted.[14]

According to his later recollections, Jones found the year spent training very boring, and, like most recruits, he hated the fatigues and drill.[15] His ardour for the British cause was though undiminished, and we can gain a sense of this from a drawing he did while on leave shortly before leaving England, in answer to a request from his former art teacher A. S. Hartrick. The resulting 'cartoon', which was published in the illustrated magazine *The Graphic* in December 1915, displayed a medieval knight calmly holding his sword in protection over a recumbent soldier, against a chaotic imagined scene of trench warfare. The knight's shield bears the words *Pro Patria*, ironically the start of the Latin motto which Wilfred Owen was later to make the subject of one of his most powerful anti-war poems. *The Graphic* presented a resolutely optimistic and patriotic view of the war, and regularly included paintings and drawings by men on active service. Clearly David Jones still saw the war in chivalrous terms and cherished a romantic vision of knightly service and comradeship.[16]

Out in Cairo, T. E. Lawrence was similarly detached from the violence of war. As the Gallipoli campaign dragged out to an unsatisfactory conclusion, he watched on, perhaps with a certain degree of satisfaction. He told his parents that he was still 'very bored' with the routine of desk work,[17] and he undoubtedly felt even more uncomfortable about the relative security of his position after hearing that his brother Will was reported missing in action in October 1915. Lawrence assumed that Will had been killed, although this was not confirmed until May 1916, and reacted, as he had to the earlier death of his brother Frank, with cold detachment, writing to an acquaintance in Oxford: 'Of course, I've been away a lot from them, and so it doesn't come on one like a shock at all.'[18] In fact, while Lawrence was occupied with compiling dull reports, significant developments were taking place which would affect him in the near future.

Rumours reaching Cairo in the autumn of 1915 suggested that Arab nationalists in the Ottoman Empire might, as McMahon, the high commissioner in Egypt, telegrammed to Edward Grey, 'throw themselves into the hands of Germany'. This prompted Grey to tell McMahon to 'give assurance of Arab independence' to Sherif Husein in Mecca. On 24 October McMahon wrote to Husein that the British government was prepared 'to recognize and support the independence of the Arabs in all the regions within the limits demanded by the Sherif', hoping that this would induce an Arab uprising.[19] McMahon was deliberately vague; a later summary of British policy stated that it 'reserved the question of precise boundaries, refusing in particular to commit itself to any part of Western Syria or Lower Mesopotamia, or about the forms of Arab Government which should be established in various parts of the independent area'.[20] This studious vagueness was partly in recognition of French hopes for influence in Syria, but it also reflected British concern to secure the oil supplies of Mesopotamia for the future. Lawrence undoubtedly knew of the McMahon assurances and hoped fervently that they would stimulate an Arab uprising. For the time being, he had to wait.

## Love in wartime

From June to September 1915 Vera Brittain worked at the Devonshire Hospital in Buxton and gained much satisfaction from this. She felt at last that she was meaningfully engaged with the war effort, and was pleased to discover that she could stand up to the drudgery of hospital work and exposure to tales of physical horror. Although the Devonshire was at this point only a convalescent hospital, on her first day she had seen a number of men half-dressed and was evidently glad not to have been too shocked by discovering more about male anatomy than she had previously known.[21] Here she spent the summer months 'bed-making, dusting, washing floors, preparing meals', and 'bandaging and treating basic wounds'.[22] Shortly before the attack at Loos, Roland Leighton came back to England on leave, and the two young lovers spent 4 days together. After months of separation, they found it very difficult to communicate with one another. Leighton eventually suggested that they should get engaged, but although Brittain was thrilled by the thought of this, her unwillingness to be seen to enter a conventional relationship of dependence on a man and her deep-seated inability to reveal her inner feelings held her back. Eventually the pair agreed to consider themselves engaged but not to announce this formally. Brittain's parents were predictably unimpressed by this arrangement, but Vera pronounced this 'the sweetest hour of my life'.[23] It is painful to read now how inhibited these young people were as they tried to come to terms with and to express their feelings. When they parted at St Pancras Station in London, she wrote, 'I kissed him, which I had never done before, and just managed to make myself whisper "Goodbye." He said nothing at all but turned quickly from me and began to walk rapidly down the platform ... he never turned again. What I could see of his face was set and pale. It was over. . .'.[24]

It was not merely in her sense of social proprieties that Vera Brittain still displayed some profoundly conventional attitudes. Although horrified by the brutality of the war, she still revealed in writing many of the attitudes then commonplace among civilians. Shortly before meeting Leighton in August, she was horrified to see many soldiers drunk at Buxton railway station when they left for the front. In September she recorded an incident with a complacency which is still alarming: 'Three soldiers from the Devonshire smashed up the shop belonging to the son of Wenzel the hairdresser to-day, because he was foolish enough to say he was German and proud of it. I and everyone else sympathized very much with the soldiers, who are spending the night in the lock-up! The Wenzels, father & son, are enemy aliens, and as such ought to have been interned long ago. They would have been but for the slackness of the authorities here.'[25]

As news of the British offensive at Loos arrived, Brittain worried terribly that Leighton might have been involved, but accepted, apparently without question, the official line that the attack had been a great success. Although she was relieved to discover that Leighton was actually in a quiet part of the line, a shadow was creeping across their relationship. She wrote constantly and effusively to him, still using the heroic and lyrical idioms of Rupert Brooke; Leighton, in contrast, wrote only occasionally, and when he did, betrayed a growing coarseness and contempt for the public's view of the war. On 7 September he wrote to her: 'It is a pity to kill people on a day like

FIGURE 14 *A German shop attacked by crowds in London. Throughout the war, and particularly at moments of crisis, German shops in Britain were the targets of violent popular protest. This bakery in London was attacked by angry crowds after a Zeppelin raid in 1915.*

this. It is a pity on any kind of day, but opinions – even my own – differ on this subject.'[26] A few days later he brutally repudiated her view of the war, mocking Brooke's language: 'The dug-outs have been nearly all blown in, the wire entanglements are a wreck, and in among this chaos of twisted iron and splintered timber and shapeless earth are the fleshless, blackened bones of simple men who poured out their red, sweet wine of youth unknowing, for nothing more tangible than Honour or their Country's Glory or another's Lust [for] Power.'[27]

A fortnight later, with a cynicism which he must have known would upset her, he wrote: 'After all I do agree that it is rather a pity to kill people in any weather really; though there are some who deserve it.'[28] The distance between the two became greater after Brittain moved in mid-October to start work as a Voluntary Aid Detachment nurse at the 1st London General Hospital in Camberwell. Here, working in a surgical ward, she was exposed to appalling sights, which she again took in her stride. She was far more upset by the absence of letters from Leighton, who after a gap of 3 weeks wrote to tell her that he had undergone a 'metamorphosis'. He felt himself now to be 'a barbarian, a wild man of the woods, stiff, narrowed, practical, an incipient martinet perhaps – not at all the kind of person who would be associated with prizes on Speech Day, or poetry, or dilettante classicism'.[29] Brittain, who was struggling to cope with gruelling work in a strange and often bleak environment, was deeply hurt by this and replied with a stinging rebuke: 'I suppose I ought to thank you for your letter, since one apparently has to be grateful now-a-days for being allowed to know you are alive. But all the same, my first impulse was to tear that letter into small shreds. . .'. She finished by asking whether he was likely to get any leave, asking 'But perhaps you are not keen to leave even for a few days a sensible business-like life where one doesn't have to bother about little things like Poetry or Art or dilettante classicism?'[30]

Leighton did not get to read this letter for nearly a fortnight, and when he did he was moved to apologize and to try to write back more sensitively. Over the next few weeks, while Brittain did night duty at the hospital in Camberwell, and Leighton moved back into the trenches near Hébuterne, the two managed to renew their relationship in writing, buoyed up by the hope that Leighton might get leave soon. Both Brittain's and Leighton's parents had moved temporarily to the south coast of Britain, and on 16 December Vera was 'wildly thrilled' to receive a short note stating that Leighton would be returning on leave on Christmas Day.[31] She arranged time off from the hospital and travelled down to Brighton on Boxing Day to meet him there. The next morning she was called to the telephone, where she heard from Leighton's sister that Roland had died from wounds sustained on 23 December.[32]

Vera Brittain's response to this blow was in ways similar to that of the bereaved mothers at the centre of Michael Roper's recent study of 'emotional survival', not least in her obsessive desire to find out all she could of the circumstances of his death.[33] Within a few days she had to return to 'hateful night-duty' of nursing in London,[34] but from there, writing to her mother, she tried to find refuge in conventional rhetoric, deploying virtually the same formula which T. E. Lawrence had used with his mother. Brittain wrote that Leighton had 'at least achieved something, if only a little, in the cause for which he died'.[35] She was back with Leighton's family 'at a very opportune though very awful moment' when a package arrived containing Leighton's mud and blood soaked tunic and a few personal effects. Continuing her reporting of alleged German atrocities, Brittain noted that from the entry and exit holes in Leighton's tunic 'we discovered that the bullet was an expanding one'.[36] Although Brittain had already, with Leighton's family, carefully analysed the letters of condolence they had received from fellow officers and from a chaplain at the hospital where he died, she wanted to know more. She struck up a relationship with one of Leighton's school friends, Victor Richardson, who helped her with this, strengthening her conviction that the war had a purpose. Brittain's biographers quote from a letter she sent to her brother Edward stating how Richardson told her that Leighton 'always used to say that our one hope of salvation as a nation lay in a Great War, and if He had said this to me I should certainly have agreed strongly ... when the War in question is a War *on* War, all the usual objections are changed into the opposite commendations'.[37] Several things about this are striking. One is Leighton's canonization by the reference to

'He'; another is the harking back to the ideals of August 1914, and the notion that somehow the country had been drifting into a state of decline which could only be remedied by war; another is the idea – which was to gain popularity – that this was a 'war against war'; finally, the fact that Leighton had not mentioned this idea to Vera Brittain suggests how far apart they had grown.

For all of her painfully recorded efforts to give Leighton's death a heroic cast, it became clear that in fact his death had been unnecessary, even pointless. He had been shot by a sniper while trying to repair the wire in front of the trenches on a moonlit night. Other emerging details heightened the sense of distance which had been apparent between Brittain and Leighton before his death. Brittain learnt only now that Leighton had been received into the Roman Catholic Church back in the summer of 1915, but she was more troubled by having gradually to accept that, in his dying hours and moments, he had not spoken of her or left a message for her.

Although claiming to resent the attention she received from people around her, Brittain also made a public show of her situation. She wore mourning clothes, and a mourning ring, even though she had refused to wear an engagement ring when Leighton was alive. And, although she clearly found nursing work almost impossibly difficult during the initial months of bereavement, the rigorously structured environment of a military hospital probably helped her to survive this difficult period. She considered abandoning nursing and thought about other kinds of war service, but these plans came to nothing. Although almost numbed with grief, she also wrote a great deal, trying to come to terms with her conflicting emotions. She continued writing to her mother and to Leighton's mother; her diary entries for this period are regular and often quite lengthy. She started a 'little story about him & me'[38] and also wrote poems, both about Leighton and about her nursing work. Intriguingly, at a point when bitterness might well have crept into her writing, it is almost entirely absent. Instead, Brittain clung to the archaic and heroic idiom which Leighton himself had specifically denounced. In a sonnet which echoed those of Rupert Brooke, she described Leighton as a 'Roland of Roncesvalles in modern days'.[39] In another poem, she wrote about the 1st London General Hospital:

> A mass of human wreckage, drifting in
>   Borne on a blood-red tide
> Some never more to brave the stormy sea
>   Laid reverently aside,
> And some with love restored to sail again
>   For regions far and wide[40]

Vera Brittain was also aware that she was not alone. Her brother Edward, whose efforts to enlist at the start of the war had caused such discord in the family, had since then – to his disgust – been kept in Britain while fellow officers from his regiment had been sent to Flanders. In February 1916 he too finally made the passage to France to join the growing mass of men in Haig's army. He was apparently now the only one of his cohort of Uppingham schoolboys who had not yet suffered from the war.[41] In March 1916 Vera Brittain went to Fishmonger's Hall Hospital to visit one of this group, Geoffrey Thurlow, who had been wounded by shellfire.[42] Neither Leighton's death, nor her own direct contact with wounded men had made Brittain want to retreat from the war. She went back to Oxford to see her former Somerville tutors and told them that she had decided 'definitely not to come back till the War is over'.[43] A few days later, she signed up for voluntary nursing service overseas.[44]

## Not danger but drudgery

Stanley Spencer started work as a medical orderly in Bristol on 23 July 1915. For a young man who had spent almost every day of his life at home, this was an enormous wrench, and he wrote later about his journey from the family home to Cookham railway station and from there to Beaufort Hospital in great detail.[45] Unlike Vera Brittain, who endured the drudgery and tedium of hospital work with reasonable equanimity, Spencer found hospital work gruelling and numbing. He was as unfitted for army life as it is possible to imagine. The camaraderie, the coarseness, the joshing and

FIGURE 15 *Stanley Spencer later recreated a scene like this, of wounded soldiers arriving at the Beaufort War Hospital, as the first of his paintings at the Sandham Memorial Chapel, Burghclere.*

bullying which made up the daily currency of male interaction in the army, even in a hospital, were all totally foreign to Spencer. He found himself completely isolated, his brother Gilbert working in a different ward – which might have been a foreign country – and surrounded by people with whom he had no kinship whatsoever. The routine of an orderly at Beaufort was long and demanding, perhaps summed up by the attitude of a nursing sister with whom Spencer clearly had an argument in his early days there. He wrote to his older sister Florence that she 'told me that she would never allow an orderly to rest once during the day'.[46] More deeply upsetting was what Spencer perceived as the unkindness of his fellow orderlies, many of whom who fell into the habit of treating the hospital patients with a casual insensitivity.[47]

For the next 6 months, Spencer had to live and work in what he called 'a most blighting atmosphere'.[48] He longed to escape, and in October 1915 he wrote to Eddie Marsh in London: 'Nothing but drudgery and patients and lunatics'. He described his life in the hospital as 'all very loathsome' and asked Marsh if he could help him to get a transfer to some other unit.[49] Even in February 1916, towards the end of his time at Beaufort, he described the hospital as 'this vile place'.[50] In this oppressive atmosphere, Spencer seems almost to have forgotten that he was a painter. He had virtually no spare time and experienced an almost complete sense of atrophy. He was rescued from this dismal situation by a series of unrelated events. In December 1915, he was approached in the hospital by a soldier who had lost a leg in the Dardanelles campaign, who brusquely showed him a copy of *The Times*, and asked if he was the painter spoken of there. The Dardanelles veteran was referring to a small article reviewing an exhibition by the New English Art Club, which singled out Spencer's painting *The Centurion's Servant* for special praise, declaring: 'He [Spencer] is not trying to be artistic after any fashion, but to say what he has to say; and he does succeed in saying it with great simplicity and vividness.'[51] Spencer was completely surprised, unaware that one of his paintings was being exhibited in London, but soon the news spread. A matron next appeared, with other newspapers, asking the same question and, more significantly, Spencer was approached by a young visitor from outside the hospital, also wanting to know if he was the painter now attracting favourable criticism.

This was Desmond Chute, a sensitive Roman Catholic living nearby. Chute and Spencer immediately struck up a relationship which was to prove highly significant. Chute shared with Spencer a love of art, literature and music, and he urged him to read St Augustine's *Confessions*. This reading, and numerous conversations and letters with Chute nourished in Spencer an idea which offered a way of reconciling himself to the exacting daily routine of the hospital, and of finding a new direction as an artist. It was, put simply, the idea that a sacramental quality could be seen and found in the most prosaic tasks, what George Herbert in 1633 had called making 'drudgery divine'.[52] Neither Spencer's new found notoriety in the hospital,

FIGURE 16 *A cheery group of convalescent soldiers and orderlies at Beaufort War Hospital. Stanley Spencer did not find it easy to socialize with either group while he worked there.*

nor his wish to find spirituality in everyday work was enough to keep him there though, and in December he volunteered for overseas service.[53] Gilbert had already escaped from Beaufort by doing this and had been posted in November 1915 to Salonica. Stanley Spencer had no idea where overseas service might take him, but by now anything seemed preferable to Beaufort, and he was prepared to disregard his mother's desire that he should stay in England. He wrote excitedly in December 1915 to the Raverats that of 41 volunteers for overseas service, only 14 had been accepted, and that 'I am among that 14'.[54]

Richard Nevinson, like Brittain and Spencer, spent the second half of 1915 working as a medical orderly, in his case at the 3rd London General Hospital in Wandsworth. His situation was in one respect different from theirs. One reason Nevinson's father had helped him to get the posting in Wandsworth was to avoid him being sent abroad; another was because several other artists were employed there and were encouraged to use their work to help the patients. The hospital published its own *Gazette* and assembled an exhibition in one of its recreational huts in September 1915, which attracted much favourable press attention.[55] Richard Nevinson did find time to draw and to paint, and as well as contributing to these hospital activities, he exhibited four more paintings and a sculpture with the London Group in November. Three of the paintings were specifically related to his war experience. *La Guerre de Trous* recalled in spirit his earlier *Returning to the Trenches*, showing a number of French soldiers, all portrayed anonymously beneath a bank of mud topped with barbed wire. *Bursting Shell*, now in the Tate Gallery, was one of Nevinson's most successful applications of Futurist technique to a war subject. The explosion of a shell, with its huge release of energy, was a natural subject for a Futurist, and Nevinson combined a colourful, almost delicate representation of the energy at the centre of this vortex with a highly abstract, Cubist vision of the buildings and pavements momentarily illuminated by it. Finally, in *Deserted Trench*, Nevinson made an important contribution to an emerging British vision of the war. This painting showed the unmistakeable landscape to the north of the Ypres Salient, known to Nevinson from his time there in the winter of 1914–15. The land is absolutely flat, much of it inundated. The trench of the title is shown as a ditch filled with water. There are no human beings in this desolate landscape, and what appears as constant, heavy rain pours down in steely straight 'force lines'. In all three paintings, Nevinson represented aspects of the war without commenting on its morality or political wisdom.

Nevinson's paintings were attracting favourable comment from a number of important critics, who now praised his use of Futurist and Cubist techniques to avoid sentimentality and to portray the war more powerfully than more traditional modes allowed. One was Paul Konody, who wrote in *The Observer*: 'Mr. Nevinson's steadfastness of purpose must surely remove any doubts as to his sincerity. He is a firm believer in the theories of Futurism as expounded by Boccioni and his Italian followers: the displacement and interpretation of objects, the search for "force lines" dynamism and the cutting of the very atmosphere into geometric planes – a meeting point of cubism and Futurism. But unlike the Italians, who are getting ever more abstract and incomprehensible, Mr. Nevinson applies himself to finding a compromise between the Futurist ideal and the normal vision.'[56]

If these paintings had a sense of detached impartiality, some of Nevinson's drawings from this period were moving towards a more critical stance. One, *In the Observation Ward*, depicted a patient suffering from the phenomenon Kate Finzi had observed in 1914, and was by late 1915 horribly familiar to any who worked with the wounded. Konody wrote of this drawing: 'It is like a page from a medical book describing the symptoms of an illness. The disturbed features; the frightened, half-imbecile look; the saliva dribbling from the opened lips – everything spells: shell shock.'[57]

Although Konody spoke in this context of Nevinson's 'cruel objectivity', other evidence suggests that in fact Nevinson was deeply disturbed by working with traumatized men and feared that – as he later put it – he was 'catching their complaint'. He was oppressed by the 'dullness and squalor' of the work and found the army nurses 'with very great exceptions the most repulsive bosses'.[58] He was haunted by fear of being drafted overseas, and his health began to deteriorate. Nevinson's father, who looked after his son so carefully during the war, was away reporting on the Gallipoli campaign, and it was left to his mother to help to arrange a medical board which finally recommended his discharge in January 1916, on grounds of 'acute rheumatic fever'.[59] It was also during this difficult period, in December

1915, that Nevinson was married, an apparently impulsive step. We know little about his relationship with Kathleen Knowlman, except that it appears to have been a happy and successful one. She was, according to Nevinson's father, a 'sweet draper's daughter from Islington'.[60] His mother wrote later 'My son informed me, suddenly, one evening that, though not engaged, he meant to get married before he was killed,' adding: 'We had known his bride, Kathleen Knowlman, a very beautiful girl, for some two years or more.'[61] Nevinson himself wrote: 'I felt tremendously proud of marrying such a beautiful girl.'[62] After a brief honeymoon in Ramsgate, the newly-wed couple moved into the Nevinson family home in Hampstead. Any sense of marital bliss or relief Nevinson felt at his discharge was tempered by his knowledge of the introduction of conscription and a growing fear that he might be sent to the front.

It is striking how, in comparison with the fear and loathing which Spencer and Nevinson felt for hospital work, both Vera Brittain and Kate Finzi put up with the same kind of work in a spirit of patient good humour. In the summer of 1915 Finzi returned to Boulogne from leave in Britain, and if her diary is to be believed, quickly settled back into the doggedly cheerful mood which she had sustained since arriving there at the start of the war. She was now working for the YMCA, providing food, drink and entertainment for convalescent soldiers, and appears to have derived great satisfaction from providing home comforts for them. In August she was sent a copy of Rupert Brooke's poems: 'it may be imagined how we acclaimed him forerunner of

FIGURE 17 *The 'convalescent depot' at Boulogne soon became, according to Kate Finzi, 'a miniature village of asbestos and corrugated iron huts, interspersed with tents and planted with trim little gardens of bright flowers and evergreens'* (Finzi, Eighteen Months, *29 June 1915, p. 157*).

FIGURE 18 *Richard Nevinson,* In the Observation Ward, *1916: 'It is like a page from a medical book describing the symptoms of an illness. The disturbed features; the frightened, half-imbecile look; the saliva dribbling from the opened lips – everything spells: shell shock.'*

the poets who shall sing the greatest tragedy of history.'[63] More ominously, she noted the anticipation in Boulogne before the British offensive at Loos, and in a spirit of patriotic naivety she reported on the attack in September: 'rumour has it we have advanced five miles along the whole line, with a magnificent cavalry charge; and the 3,000 prisoners brought down to-day clearly point to a crushing victory'. The 'crushing victory' brought in its train a return for Finzi to nursing work, as the thousands of wounded men from the offensive were brought back to Boulogne, turning Finzi's extempore library into 'a sea of beds' full of 'weary bandaged forms'.[64]

Among the patriotic commonplaces, there are disturbing details in Finzi's diary. In October 1915, she commented sympathetically on the issue of men brought before courts martial for serious crimes, recording how one 'blue-eyed, fair-haired boy' was taken away, presumably to be shot, because his wounds were self-inflicted.[65] Even Kate Finzi's cheery resolve was tested as the winter drew on, and fondly anticipated victories failed to materialize. Earlier in the year, she had written enthusiastically of how success at the Dardanelles might end the war in a few months, but now she had to record the withdrawal from the Gallipoli beachheads. She even confessed that, along with others, she was becoming a little pessimistic and 'war worn'.[66] Nonetheless, Christmas provided her with an opportunity to deploy her energy in organizing concerts for the men and to celebrate their love of music. Again she contrasted the pleasures of wartime service favourably with the idle dissipation of pre-war years: 'as one who has heard most of the great music in the most of the great capitals, I should like to state that there is no more impressive thing in the world than an old barn or outhouse "somewhere in Flanders," filled with men whose voices threaten to bring down what remains of the roof for very lustiness'.[67]

Unlike Spencer and Nevinson, the young artist Paul Nash had a relatively congenial time after enlisting in the Artists' Rifles early in the war. He too had decided to marry and had celebrated his wedding to Margaret Odeh on 17 December 1914.[68] After this he had to live in barracks in Roehampton, but in contrast to the grim conditions in military hospitals, he had an easy time. The barracks was actually 'a large mansion', with 'most lovely' grounds, and he was given regular time off.[69] He was on guard duty at the Tower of London in May 1915 on the night of the first Zeppelin raid, but neither this nor any other aspect of his service appears to have provoked an artistic response from him.[70] Through the summer of 1915 he was under canvas in Richmond Park, and he appears not to have found soldiering as numbingly unpleasant as some other recruits, perhaps because he was quite good at it. He was evidently a little bored, telling Margaret that he would like something better to do, but not going into the Artillery 'if it means the Dardanelles'.[71] Although Nash had originally enlisted as a private, he found that there was now an opportunity to become an officer. In fact, the Artists' Rifles, because its recruits were typically well educated, soon became an officer training school, turning out many thousands of junior officers as the war went on. Nash applied for a commission in June 1915, hoping to get into the Ordnance Corps, according to his biographer, 'because the pay was high and the work less suicidal than in the Infantry'. He was still in London at the end of the year, on duty at the Tower of London, where, apparently, his wife Margaret 'did contrive to join him with mince pies'.[72]

## The demand for conscription

For Edward Elgar, the second half of 1915 brought an unhappy mixture of creative work, public acclaim and deteriorating health. Frequent performances of his work, particularly his wartime compositions, in London and the provinces, seemed to bring him little joy. In addition to his *Carillon*, Elgar had written a short orchestral piece called *Polonia* in June 1915 in aid of the Polish Relief Fund, and in July he wrote another setting of Cammaerts' poetry, *Une Voix dans le Désert*. These pieces, with their overt support for countries occupied by the Germans, were very popular, and Elgar conducted many performances himself. After the first performance of

*Polonia* on 6 July, Alice Elgar wrote: 'A splendid performance of the work magnificent & enormous enthusiasm, the real roar there is for E. his own roar I always calls it & recalled again & again.'[73] Between 2 and 14 August Elgar conducted two performances a day of *Carillon* at the Coliseum; in October he alternated performances of *Carillon* with *Polonia* at the Queen's Hall, where 'E. had a great reception when he appeared & a *great* ovation afterwards.'[74] He was still working on his settings of the Binyon poems, and it is striking how long this was now taking him. Elgar was frequently unwell during these months. He suffered from colds, headaches and a sore throat, as well as having problems with his teeth.

In August, Elgar added his name publicly to the campaign for conscription. He was one of a number of 'notables', including politicians, admirals, generals, bishops and industrialists, who signed a manifesto in *The Times* demanding that 'every fit man, whatever his position in life, must be made available, as and when his country calls for him, for the fighting line, or, if specially qualified, for National Service at home'.[75] Shortly after this Elgar was caught up in the intensification of the Zeppelin raids, when London was attacked for the second time on 17 August. Alice Elgar recorded that she and her husband went 'for long omnibus drive to Leyton & saw the damaged houses where the Zeppelin dropped bombs & the sweet old Almshouses damaged'.[76] Elgar was away in the Lake District when his wife saw a Zeppelin from her windows on 8 September;[77] five nights later 59 people were killed in the most damaging raid to date. Clearly going to see the areas attacked was quite a spectator sport. On 14 October Alice noted that Elgar had again gone to see the damage from a raid: 'Most interested crowd as if out for a show.'[78] *The Times* reported that 'a fleet of hostile airships' had attacked London, killing 56 people and injuring 114, prompting agitated calls for the construction of aircraft to deliver reprisal raids on Germany.[79]

In November, Elgar was inspired to write the music for a light-hearted Christmas play, *The Starlight Express*, adapted from a novel by Algernon Blackwood. As the days got shorter and colder, he worked intensively on this project, but when it opened on 29 December, he refused to attend. There had been a difference of opinion with the designer for the sets and costumes, and Alice Elgar wrote: 'E. wd not conduct as the mise en scene was so repulsive – & was not even present – Music wonderful'.[80] Alice herself had an accident in the streets shortly before this, and Elgar's spirits were low. If *Starlight Express* was an effort at escapism, it had failed. He wrote to Alice Stuart-Wortley: 'What an awful year. . . . I am very sad and nothing goes right. We have had people here – but I was not here – I am somewhere else and am not happy.'[81]

If Elgar was a supporter of conscription, Parry was not. Through his family and friends he was drawn into the campaign to oppose the whole idea of resolving international disputes with violence. Parry's son-in-law Arthur Ponsonby had formed the Union of Democratic Control (UDC) in the early days of the war, but the group had initially found it difficult to gain headway because support for the war was so widespread. By 1915 the Union was gaining in confidence, holding public meetings, printing pamphlets and collecting subscriptions. Local branches had been formed, and the Union had settled upon a four-point programme, demanding that there should be democratic control of foreign policy, no transfer of territory from one country to another without the consent of the population involved, the establishment of an International Council to regulate disputes between nations, and widespread disarmament. Inevitably, the UDC was accused of being pro-German, and anyone associated with it was exposed to great public hostility. Its public meetings were often attended by violent confrontations. Parry recorded in his diary that when he visited Ponsonby in July 1915, his son-in-law's face was still swollen after being punched at a meeting.[82]

Perhaps it was the visibly diminishing numbers of students at the Royal College of Music, or the news in October that virtually 'all remaining hands of military age' working on the estate at Highnam were now expecting to be drafted which pushed Parry closer to support for the UDC.[83] He was also undoubtedly driven by a sense of loyalty to his family. On 25 November 1915, he and his wife accompanied Arthur Ponsonby to a UDC meeting at the Memorial Hall in Farringdon Street in London. All three were members of the platform party. Parry recorded, with commendable equanimity, how upon arrival, they found 'a surging mob' outside the building and had difficulty getting in through a side door. Once the meeting got under way, 'a large body of soldiers' forced their way through the audience and stormed the platform. Parry struggled to get his wife to the safety of a small room, and the meeting was effectively prevented from continuing. Although Maude Parry 'was very frightened & as pale as parchment', we may gain some sense of her own spirit from her behaviour in the following days, when she entertained a party of soldiers to tea and visited a local hospital for war wounded.[84] The government subsequently denied that it had played any part in organizing the soldiers who disrupted the meeting.[85] It is unfortunate that Parry has left no record of his precise attitude to the UDC at this point; his diary only records the events described above. We do know that he had publically supported the war as a just crusade, and there is evidence that he was sceptical about the position of the UDC. Arthur Ponsonby recorded in April 1915, after conversations with Parry at Schulbrede Priory, that 'contempt . . . was not entirely absent from CHHP'.[86] The UDC was in fact a loose coalition, and although its official programme was restricted to demands for parliamentary control of foreign policy, and for a fair and negotiated settlement to the war, various members of the group had other, more radical views. All opposed the introduction of conscription, and some were closer to outright pacifism. From Parry's recorded statements, it appears that he supported the official programme of the UDC, but he was not a pacifist. He may well have taken issue with Ponsonby in April

1915 about the likely response of Germany to proposals for a negotiated settlement. The UDC based its hope for peace on German willingness to negotiate and to renounce territories it had forcibly occupied, and this was not something the German government was prepared to do until late in 1918. Parry's willingness to appear on a UDC platform in November 1915 indicates, I think, his moral support for his son-in-law, his commitment to ideals of free debate and his support for the UDC's official programme. He must have known that Ponsonby had been howled down when he tried to speak in parliament and that he was slandered in the press as being in the pay of the Germans. The whole experience of seeing a UDC meeting broken up by uniformed soldiers can have brought him no joy.

Parry was also composing in these difficult months. Like Elgar, he had been asked since August 1914 to produce patriotic music to support the war effort, but mistrusting any jingoism, he had resisted this. On just one occasion, he had yielded to the entreaties of the singer Clara Butt and written a 'Hymn to Aviators' which had been performed in May 1915 at the Albert Hall. Parry was uncomfortable and described the rehearsal as 'a perfect orgy of vulgarity'. Of the actual performance he wrote: 'My Aviators Song quite out of place'.[87] For the rest of 1915, unsurprisingly, Parry used his own composition to turn away from the horrors of war. His diary for these months records how he was frequently working on a set of Chorale Preludes for the organ and on a group of unaccompanied motets. These drew consciously on the models of the great sixteenth-century composers Tallis and Byrd. As the memory of peacetime musical life receded, and more and more musicians disappeared for the fighting, Parry was fortunate to find that Hugh Allen, the director of the Bach Choir in Oxford, was keen to see his motets completed and performed. On 2 December 1915 Parry recorded: 'Sent off the proofs of the 2nd set of Chorale Preludes in the course of the day'.[88]

For all his concern about people he knew, and for his students, the issue of conscription was to Parry an abstract one, insofar as he was too old for military service, and he had no sons. For Ellis Evans in North Wales, the coming of conscription had an altogether different significance. It is clear that recruitment in rural Wales had been slow and that recruiting agents in some places had been met with hostility by farmers. This was acknowledged in a substantial book titled *The War and Wales*, published by John Morgan in 1916, which argued that the war had brought about a huge and enduring change in Wales, drawing it from parochial insularity into broader, and, Morgan argued, higher streams of modern consciousness. At the start of his book, Morgan addressed the problem of recruitment in the countryside, writing: 'Welsh agriculturists have played a very ignoble part in this war. Very many farmers have made the most strenuous, and in many instances, unjustifiable efforts, to secure exemptions for their sons and their menservants who are of military age, not on religious grounds, but because, as they allege, they are absolutely indispensable.' He accepted that some Welsh farmers were benefiting from the war, admitting that 'it is not an uncommon thing to hear Welsh farmers express the hope that the war will last a long time because of the profits they are able to make out of it'. Nonetheless, he argued, 'That Wales as a whole has responded nobly in this war is fully conceded'.[89] By the end of 1915, even nonconformist Wales had been largely won over to the need for conscription. Describing compulsory service as 'a necessary evil' in December, the *Welsh Outlook* sadly accepted this 'as the surest and quickest way of ending this horror and nightmare'.[90]

Ellis Evans was one of those 'agriculturists' who did not join up through 1915, although he was undoubtedly pressured to do so. He continued to work on the family farm, and insofar as his poetry did comment on the war, it was still to express conventional sentiments. He wrote a poem for Christmas 1915, 'Plant Trawsfynydd' ('The Children of Trawsfynydd'), which lamented the disappearance from the village of many of the young men, and imagined them surrounded by 'the unceasing sound of many cannons',[91] but he was more focused on the pastoral idiom which he was working hard to master. He entered a poem on the mountains of Merionedd for the National Eisteddfod at Bangor in September 1915, encouraged by winning chairs at local events in Pontardawe and in Llanuwchllyn. His entry was unsuccessful. The National Eisteddfod itself was not unaffected by the war: although soldiers' choirs sang there, the usual male voice choir competition was one of several events which had to be cancelled.[92]

## Deepening problems

The year 1915 had been a difficult year for the British people, marked by military failures and a slow realization that the nation was involved in a conflict of unprecedented dimensions. It is a realization perhaps captured in a despatch from Hamilton to Kitchener on the Gallipoli landings. Hamilton, we know, was a literary man, who – before the landings – had seen in Rupert Brooke an embodiment of the 'preux chevalier', a reincarnation of Philip Sydney. As the fighting on the peninsula took on the grim characteristics of trench warfare, he noted that machine guns and barbed wire 'suit the Turkish character and tactics to perfection'.[93]

This growing apprehension of the brutality of the war is reflected in the experience of the artists examined here, but their individual trajectories highlight also how dangerous it is to generalize about that experience. One of them – Rupert Brooke – had died on active service; Nevinson had been discharged on health grounds; Vera Brittain had seen her hopes of study at Oxford postponed, and her dreams of love shattered; Parry, who had associated most closely with the opposition to the war, had seen his best students leave the Royal College and witnessed at first hand the ugliness of nationalistic mob violence. Spencer had, after long soul-searching, joined up, but had found service in the RAMC hard, tedious and utterly demeaning. Conversely, Kate Finzi had found a new way of life in the 'war zone' and had carved out a role for herself in the infrastructure supporting the BEF. Ironically, the earliest of the men in the group to enlist, Paul Nash, was still in Britain and had seen virtually nothing of the war yet. Lawrence, for all his ambition, had found himself doing office work in Cairo. The youngest man in the group, David Jones, had finally arrived in the war zone and was now confronting the reality of being a private soldier in the waterlogged trenches of Flanders, an experience which would mark the rest of his life.

The creative response of individuals had also varied greatly. Several, including Lawrence, Brittain, Finzi, Jones and Nash were too occupied to do much more than write letters and diaries, although Jones had produced a patriotic picture for *The Graphic*, and Brittain had produced a couple of small poems. Ellis Evans clearly did not want to write poetry about the war, while Spencer was simply atrophied by military service. Parry, pulled in different directions by his intellect, his conscience and his family, had not written any significant music relating to the war. Elgar, after writing various minor pieces, had thrown himself into the composition of a major work, clearly intended as a requiem for the dead, but although he had completed in outline two out of three movements of what turned out to be his last great choral work, he had experienced numerous difficulties along the way. He had, as ever, worried about how the public would respond to a work which, although patriotic, would speak of sorrow and loss rather than of triumph or aggression. He had found himself unable to give musical expression to Binyon's lines which depicted the Germans as the 'Vampire of Europe's wasted will', and beset by personal doubts and ill health, he had, at the end of what he called 'an awful year', left the work unfinished.

Two artists had been energized by the war and had reflected this in their creative response. Rupert Brooke had found in active service a resolution to his personal conflicts and had fused an exhilaration of purpose with pastoral lyricism to produce a group of poems which had become extraordinarily well known and influential. Although perceptive critics in 1915 had questioned their sincerity, and later generations have marvelled at the distance between these sonnets and the reality of war in 1914 and 1915, Brooke had caught the mood of the nation, giving voice to lofty hopes, and a sense of nobility with which to confront loss and bereavement, a sense which was heightened enormously by his own death.

Richard Nevinson alone had sought to represent the quintessential reality of the war for the British soldier: the trenches in Flanders. Critics will point out that he was not himself a front-line soldier, like David Jones, but he had served in conditions of danger close up to the lines in the Ypres Salient as the front was hardening there and seen for himself the flat landscape of Flanders under dreary December skies. He had worked closely, both in Dunkirk and then in London, with men whose bodies had been mutilated by bullets and shrapnel, and whose minds had been scarred by violence and horror. He had tried to represent his experience in his paintings and drawings, and in so doing had put before the British public a view of the war which they would not see in Brooke's sonnets or hear in Elgar's music. Predictably, he had been both praised and vilified for this.

One thing was abundantly clear to all of these individuals at the end of 1915, whether, like Ellis Evans, they were far from the sound and fury of war, or like David Jones, struggling to stay awake while on sentry duty in a sodden ditch in Flanders: the war would not be over soon.

# CHAPTER SIX

# January–September 1916

Early in December 1915, representatives from France, Britain, Russia and Italy met at Chantilly near Paris. They agreed that to defeat Germany and its allies they should coordinate their offensives in the summer of 1916, with the French and British attacking together to drive the Germans out of France. When Douglas Haig took over the command of the BEF a fortnight later, he was thus already committed in broad outline; he was also under pressure from the French Commander, General Joffre, for the British Army to take over more of the line, running south into Picardy and down to the River Somme.

The BEF in 1916 was an entirely different creature from that which had confronted the German Army earlier in the war. It had grown into a 'vast host' of 38 divisions, including formations from every part of the British Isles and substantial contingents from India, Canada, Australia, New Zealand and South Africa.[1] It was supported by a huge infrastructure stretching back from the front lines to the Channel coast and was developing increasingly specialized branches to deal with artillery, aviation and communications, and new weapons designed for trench warfare. Haig, with a headquarters staff of some 300 men based in a former French military college at Montreuil, presided over the whole organization from a nearby chateau. Here he received a constant stream of politicians, soldiers, newspaper owners and journalists of different nationalities, all of whom discovered that he was hospitable, but a man of few words. Haig was commanding the largest British army ever put in the field; it had in 1916 numbers of guns and shells unimaginable in 1914, but he was keenly aware of its limitations. He wrote on 29 March: 'I have not got an Army in France really, but a collection of divisions untrained for the field.'[2] Nonetheless, he believed that correctly handled, they might be used to deliver 'a decisive attack' against the Germans.[3]

Before Haig and Joffre had hammered out any detailed plan for a summer offensive, the Germans attacked at Verdun on 21 February. Here the French had held a salient around the fortress town since the autumn of 1914, and the Germans correctly calculated that it would be defended at all costs. Over the spring, summer, and into the autumn of 1916 both sides fed hundreds of thousands of their soldiers into the fighting around Verdun, which reached a concentration and ferocity hitherto unknown. As virtually every French Army formation was pushed into Verdun, to fight and suffer for a brief period before being rested and reinforced, it became clear that the French contribution to a shared summer offensive would be smaller than previously envisaged. It also became increasingly apparent that the French needed the British to draw the weight of the German Army away from Verdun. Haig agreed that the BEF would mount a full scale attack on the Somme, commencing on 1 July. It would be supported by the available French forces.

Other developments brought little comfort as plans for the offensive matured. On Easter Monday armed republicans stormed the post office and other public buildings in Dublin, proclaiming an Irish Republic. British troops quickly suppressed this uprising, and 15 of the leaders, including the former civil servant Roger Casement, were subsequently executed. It was a stark reminder that the demand for Irish independence, which had been put on the back burner at the start of the war, could not be indefinitely ignored. Only days after the Easter Rising, news reached Britain of the surrender of General Townshend's forces which had been besieged at Kut-el-Amara in Mesopotamia since December 1915. The British public, which had throughout the siege been told that Townshend's force was well supplied and safe, now heard that he had surrendered, along with 4 generals, 551 other officers and 13,300 men, mostly from the Indian Army.[4] Bizarrely, T. E. Lawrence and two fellow officers from Cairo were sent on an abortive mission to Basra in March 1916 to try to induce the Turks to call off the siege of Kut in return for gold. They arrived too late and were reduced to bargaining for the release of wounded prisoners. It was an appropriate start to a very unusual career as a soldier.[5]

Even more shocking to British pride was the news on 2 June that there had been a 'great naval battle' in the North Sea in which the Grand Fleet had suffered heavy losses. Although there is a consensus now that the Battle of Jutland, fought out in haze and gloom in the late afternoon of 31 May, was a British strategic victory, effectively confining the German High Seas Fleet to its harbours for the rest of the war, this was not apparent at the time to a public which expected to hear of another Trafalgar. The newspapers in Britain reported the British losses very accurately, but could only speculate about how many German ships had been sunk or damaged, giving an impression that the Germans had 'won'. Henry Nevinson, accurately recording the British losses, wrote: 'Terrible news of naval battle off Jutland. . . . Next to Gallipoli the worst blow in the war'.[6] Edward Elgar, who very rarely made a direct comment on the war, expressed a sense of near paralysis after hearing about Jutland, writing: 'but this awful naval news – it's killing to the spirit'.[7]

As the public struggled to comprehend what had happened at Jutland, the news broke that Lord Kitchener had been drowned when the cruiser taking him on a mission to Russia was sunk off the Scottish coast. Although Kitchener by this time had lost influence within the government, he had been the visible personification of the British military spirit, and his death was widely felt. Henry Nevinson described Kitchener's death as 'the greatest blow of the war for the people in general'.[8] Hubert Parry was about to attend a concert at the Royal College of Music when he was told of 'the Kitchener disaster'. He wrote: 'It stupefied me so much I could take little interest in the Concert.'[9]

Neither Jutland nor Kitchener's death impeded the planned offensive in France. The Somme was not Haig's choice, but, under pressure from Joffre, the BEF had moved into old French positions in this rolling countryside early in 1916. The Germans, who occupied a line of small fortified villages along the high ground, had been there for 18 months and had ample time to develop their defences. All along their line they had dug deep into the chalk, excavating underground chambers where their men could shelter from bombardments. Dense entanglements of barbed wire protected successive lines of trenches, all covered by carefully sited machine guns. In addition to villages which had been turned into redoubts with subterranean galleries, the defences used the cover provided by small woods which stood among the arable fields. These villages and woods – Thiepval, Pozières, Fricourt, La Boisselle, Beaumont-Hamel, Mametz Wood, Delville Wood and High Wood – would become the focal points of the largest battle in British history.

Haig's plan was optimistic. He intended with an artillery bombardment of unprecedented weight to destroy the barbed wire and the German trenches on a broad front astride the old Roman road between Albert, on the British side of the line, and Bapaume, on the German side. Five huge mines full of explosives would be detonated at key points under the German line to obliterate strong points. Haig's divisions – now made up largely of men who had volunteered since August 1914 – would simply occupy what remained of the German trenches. The cavalry held in reserve would proceed through the front lines and move into the open countryside beyond. Haig then visualized the British rolling up the German front to the north. The French would turn south and do likewise. In his most optimistic moments, Haig imagined that he might inflict a decisive defeat on the Germans and, as he said to King George V on 7 June, end the war that year.[10]

All the evidence suggests that Haig's optimism was widely, if not universally, shared, among the forces gathering for the onslaught. For many of the men who had not yet been in action, this was the moment they had joined up for; the vast scale of the artillery preparations they encountered as they moved up to their attack positions in June bolstered their confidence. There were more experienced eyes, notably those of some of the corps and divisional commanders opposite the Germans on the Somme, who realized with growing apprehension in the last week of June 1916, as the bombardment grew in intensity and zero hour approached, that as far as they could tell through periscopes and binoculars, many of the German wire entanglements were still undestroyed and that the German artillery was still active. Their communications to this effect did not apparently register with Haig, who wrote on the eve of the attack: 'With God's help I feel hopeful. The men are in splendid spirits. Several have said that they have never before been so instructed and informed of the nature of the operation before them. The wire has never been so well cut, nor the artillery preparation so thorough.'[11]

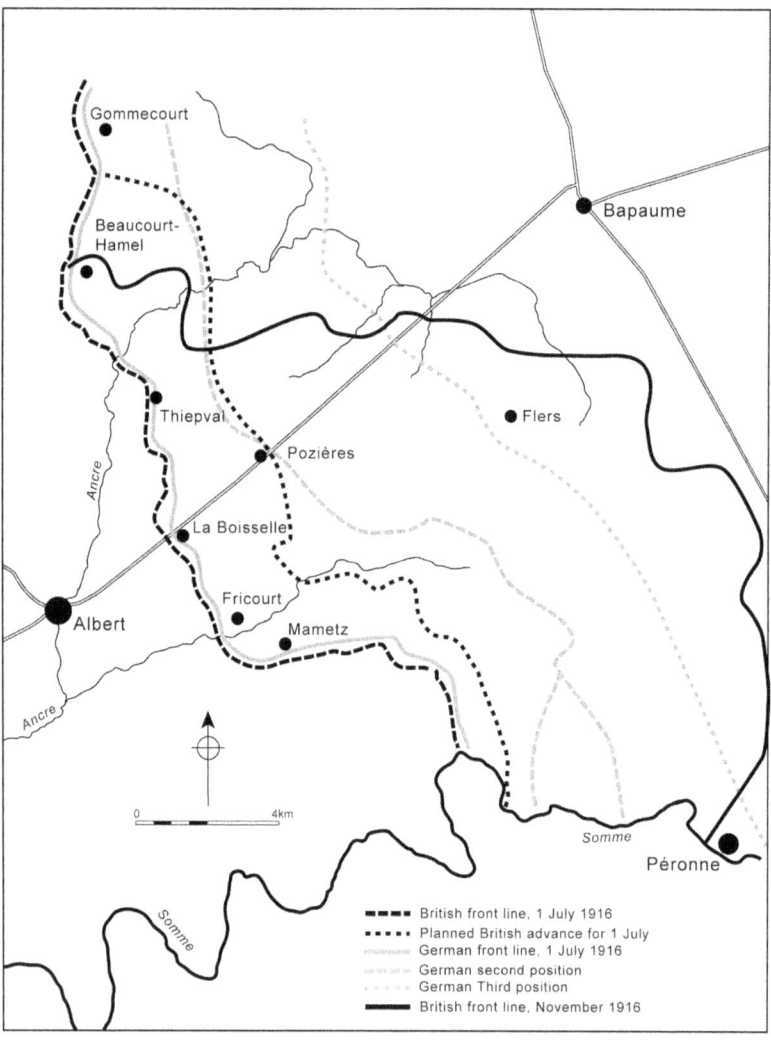

MAP 8 *The Battle of the Somme.*

The terrible story of the catastrophe on the first day on the Somme has been often told. At 7.30 a.m., on a clear summer's morning, the British bombardment ceased, and on a front of 13 miles, the soldiers climbed out of their trenches. As they crossed No Man's Land, typically struggling uphill with heavy loads, they met a hail of concentrated machine gun and shellfire. Those that reached the German wire found that it was still impenetrable, and as successive waves struggled forward, bunches of men formed at the few points where they imagined there was an opening. Few of the British troops reached the German front lines, and within a couple of hours, the survivors were for the most part back in their own trenches, from where they could hear the cries of the wounded left out between the lines. In total, 57,470 men were killed, wounded and missing. If Haig was at all disappointed, he kept this to himself. It appears from his diary that he simply did not grasp the enormity of the failure. Haig had also intended, whatever happened, 'a battle of "durée prolongée"',[12] so there was no possibility that he might now call off the attack.

He turned next to Trônes Wood and Mametz Wood, hoping by concentrating on individual strong points to unlock the whole German defence. On 14 July Haig's optimism was reinforced by a more successful night attack on Bazentin-le-Petit, at the southern end of the battlefield, which succeeded in taking a stretch of German front-line trenches after only a short bombardment. The cavalry was even sent in, and briefly the hope of restoring a war of movement was rekindled. After this, Haig used fresh units to attack different parts of the battlefield, as it became clear that in fact, the battle was turning into one of attrition. The 16th (Irish) Division had been thrown in at Guillemont, and the Welsh to take Mametz Wood. The Australians experienced a horrific baptism of fire on the Western Front first at Fromelles, and then a 'long drawn out agony' at Pozières in the centre of the battlefield. The South Africans endured 'an unimaginable agony' at Delville Wood.[13] Units representing every corner of Britain, Ireland and the British Empire were fed into the carnage. The German policy of always counter-attacking to recapture any lost ground meant that the smallest gains had to be fought over again and again.

What did the British public know of the Battle of the Somme? The newspapers maintained an optimistic tone, speaking always of 'advances' and 'gains'. They reprinted dispatches from General Headquarters in France which embellished these broad claims with details of prisoners captured and guns taken. *The Times* reported on the first day of the offensive under the heading 'Forward in the West', stating 'our leaders in the field . . . are directing a methodical and well-planned advance, not marred by any vain and headlong rushes'.[14] The *Evening Standard and St. James Gazette* had already, quoting Haig as its source, reported on the 'Enemy's heavy loss in dead' and on 'trenches taken'.[15] *The Graphic* was particularly optimistic, stating that: 'The end of the Great War is not yet; but a splendid beginning in the long-expected Push was made on July the First.'[16]

The newspapers also published maps of the battlefield, often in a large scale which made the 'advances' appear superficially impressive, but any astute reader could have seen that, measured against the larger objective of driving the Germans out of France and Belgium, they were insignificant. In many newspapers, the accurate geographical detail given flatly contradicted the constant reporting of 'gains' and 'advances'. Many individual tales of heroism and daring were published, and in a striking new development, the first important silent film of the war was shown in Britain. *The Battle of the Somme* was an assembly of different passages of film taken behind and from the British lines before and during the initial stages of the offensive. The resulting 73-minute film actually showed very little fighting; scenes purporting to show the troops going 'over the top' on 1 July were actually reconstructed behind the lines. Nonetheless, there were scenes in the film which are still shocking today and which challenge the idea that it was merely a propaganda exercise. Great numbers of wounded men – British and German – were shown, as well as corpses littering the battlefield. A funeral service at a mass burial was shown. Above all, alongside the scenes showing men relaxing, eating and bathing in the French countryside behind the lines, viewers were given a clear visual image of the actual trenches, and they could see the shell-scarred wasteland of the actual battlefield. Huge numbers – by some estimates as many as a million in London alone – flocked to cinemas when it opened at the end of August. A reissue by the Imperial War Museum in 1999 claimed on the sleeve that 'almost half Britain's population' saw the film.[17] Many were apparently shocked by the images of British dead and wounded soldiers, but others did not want to be sheltered. Henry Nevinson saw the film in London on 21 August and wrote: 'Very fine. Not horrible enough'.[18]

Nonetheless, reading contemporary diaries, letters and newspapers, it is striking how removed people in Britain were from the carnage on the Somme. The extent of the catastrophe on the first day was successfully concealed, and only gradually did the scale of the losses during the campaign become apparent. There were even optimistic rumours during August 1916 that Germany might sue for peace before Christmas, an optimism reinforced when Romania joined the Allies at the end of the month, enticed by promises of territorial gains in Transylvania and Bukovina.

## New hope in the Middle East: the Arab Revolt

The awful failure of the Gallipoli expedition and the disaster at Kut did not end British hopes of undermining the Ottoman Empire. Negotiations had been conducted by the British diplomat Mark Sykes and his French counterpart, Georges Picot, early in 1916, and their 'Agreement', broadly giving post-war control of Syria and Lebanon to the French, and Palestine and Mesopotamia to the British, was ratified in May. There was a potential contradiction, in what has been called 'a shocking document',[19] with the vague assurances of Arab independence previously given to Sherif Husein, but for the British government, the need to maintain harmony with the French was the overriding priority. When Sykes made this clear to Gilbert Clayton, the Chief of Intelligence in Egypt, in December 1915, he also reaffirmed the government's intention to continue 'to back the Arab movement'.[20]

Husein's position in Mecca had become increasingly difficult during 1915, and in February 1916 – unaware of the negotiations between the British and the French – he again appealed to the British for money and weapons. He promised now that he could raise a revolt not only in the Hejaz, but also in Syria. After Gallipoli, and with an expeditionary force still in Salonica, there was little stomach in Britain for another diversion from the Western Front, but an Arab uprising which might draw off many thousands of regular Turkish soldiers was considered by some to be worth supporting. In May 1916 the British took the fatal step of supplying Husein with a consignment of old Japanese rifles and ammunition. Spurred on by Turkish arrests of Arab nationalists in Syria, and by threats to his son Feisal in Constantinople, Husein finally decided to act. Feisal managed to get away from Constantinople, pleading that he was needed in Medina to help raise Arab forces to attack the British in Suez.

On 5 June 1916, Arab tribesmen led by Husein attacked and overwhelmed the Turkish garrison in Mecca. In nearby Medina, the terminus of the Hejaz railway, they were unable to subdue the garrison, armed with machine guns and artillery, but they were able to confine them to the city itself. The initial success of Husein's revolt initiated months of wrangling over the best way for the British to respond. Reginald Wingate, the commander of the Egyptian Army and Governor General of the Sudan, was keen to support Husein with regular troops landed on the Red Sea coast of the Arabian peninsula; the Viceroy of India was totally opposed to this, fearing that the intervention of non-Muslim troops in the Hejaz would inflame anti-British feeling among the Muslim population of India. In London, the Chief of the Imperial General Staff, Robertson, was a convinced 'westerner', and he resolutely opposed involvement in yet another 'side show'.

Lawrence, back at his desk in Cairo after his mission to Basra, was delighted by Husein's revolt and believed that the support of the British in Egypt had been vital. He wrote to his parents, asking if they had seen the article about the revolt in *The Times*: 'It has taken a year and a half to do, but now is going very well. It is so good to have helped a bit in making a new nation – and I hate the Turks so much that to see their own people turning on them is very grateful. I hope the movement increases, as it promises to do. . . . This revolt, if it succeeds, will be the biggest thing in the Near East since 1550.'[21] Lawrence was still only a Staff Captain, with little influence on grand strategy, and his enthusiasm for the Arab cause was not universally shared. It was also very difficult for the British to get reliable information about the situation in different parts of the Ottoman Empire. Was Husein a capable leader and dependable ally? Was there, as was rumoured, also an Arab Revolt developing in Syria, far to the north of the Hejaz? Would the Turks respond to Husein's revolt by despatching troops and modern weapons to the Hejaz? A vital role as the situation developed was played by British command of the seas. Admiral Rosslyn Wemyss, commanding the Egyptian Squadron of the Royal Navy, had at his disposal only antiquated warships and requisitioned merchantmen, but there were no Turkish or German vessels in the Red Sea or the Arabian Sea to oppose them. Wemyss' ships were able to move freely, if slowly, between Egypt and Arabia, to land men and stores where they wished, and to communicate by radio with senior officers and diplomats in Cairo, Khartoum and London. On 17 June 1916, the elderly light cruiser HMS *Fox* telegrammed confirmation to Cairo that the Turkish garrison in the port of Jeddah, close to Mecca and Medina, had surrendered,[22] and within a fortnight, supplies were landed there, accompanied by a diplomat, Cyril Wilson, to report on the situation and liaise with Husein.

Over the next four months, the British vacillated, but gradually the interventionist camp in Cairo gained the upper hand. The commander of the British Army in Egypt, Archibald Murray, wrote to London on 29 June: 'We are in for a long, costly, and difficult business there with increasing demands ... should the Sherif, who is fighting for his life, be successful, our task in the East will be much lightened, and the Turks' position rendered extremely difficult'.[23] Although Husein's demands for money, weapons and food grew and grew as Murray had predicted, they were still trivial in comparison with the huge requirements of the larger British war effort, and providing enough to maintain his forces did not carry the risks entailed in landing regular forces in the Hejaz.

A sign of the growing ascendancy of Clayton's Intelligence unit was the formation in June 1916 of an 'Arab Bureau' in Cairo, to produce summaries of intelligence material on the Arab world for the British government. Lawrence, who had first suggested the idea of a digest for wider circulation,[24] compiled the first issue of the Bureau's *Arab Bulletin*, but it was another demand which involved him directly with the Arab Revolt. Ronald Storrs, the Secretary to the High Commissioner, had hit on the idea of printing postage stamps for the Hejaz, which could be used to advertise Husein's revolt, and he asked Lawrence for help with this. They went together to the Arab Museum in Cairo, 'in search of arabesque motives', and soon had a set of stamps printed which Lawrence was rather pleased with.[25] He was shortly to be involved in more warlike activities.

In September 1916 a French military mission arrived in Egypt, and its head, Colonel Brémond, quickly declared a willingness to support Husein. The French had long-standing ambitions to wrest Syria from Ottoman control and were concerned to limit Husein's claims only to the Hejaz.

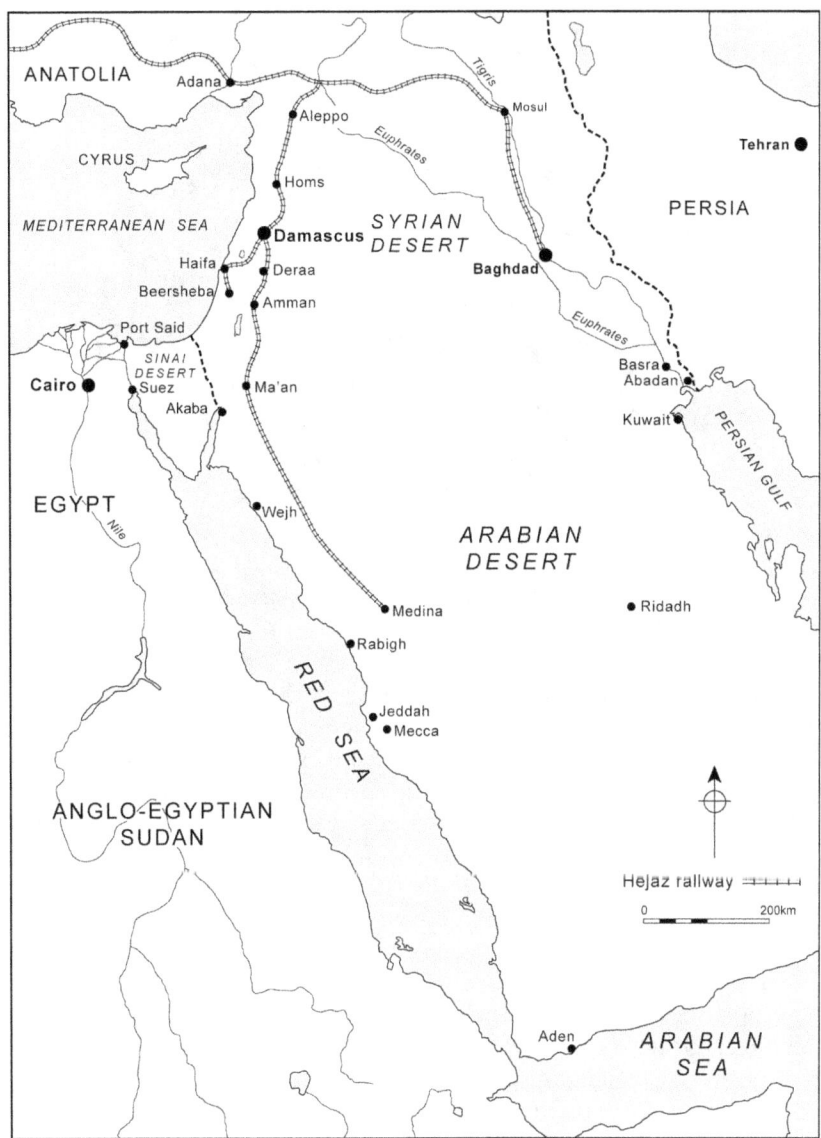

MAP 9 *The Arab Revolt.*

Nonetheless, Brémond's negotiations with Husein spurred the British to greater activity, and in October, Lawrence was despatched to Jeddah with Ronald Storrs to report on the situation there. Lawrence and Storrs landed at Jeddah on 16 October, but had immediately to disappoint Husein's second son Abdullah, who represented him there, and was hoping that troops and aeroplanes were about to be landed.[26] Lawrence now displayed the initiative and energy which were to mark his involvement with the Arab Revolt.

FIGURE 19 *T. E. Lawrence was thrilled to discover in Feisal (here sitting in the armchair), the third son of Sherif Husein, a man who might lead the Arab Revolt to victory. He wrote that Feisal 'Looks like a European, and very like the monument of Richard I, at Fontevraud.'*

He undertook to travel inland to meet Husein's third son Feisal, to see if he, appropriately financed and supported, might be a more dynamic leader of the revolt. On 19 October Lawrence was taken by ship up the coast to Rabigh. From there, on a camel, and 'dressed up in an Arab headscarf and cloak . . . to disguise his uniform', he was taken inland towards Feisal's encampment at Wadi Safra.[27] It took two days of uncomfortable riding before Lawrence arrived, but when he was taken to Feisal's quarters, he sensed immediately that this was a moment of destiny. He wrote in romantic vein later, in *Seven Pillars of Wisdom*, 'I felt at first glance that this was the man I had come to Arabia to seek – the leader who would bring the Arab Revolt to full glory'.[28] In a report soon printed in the *Arab Bulletin* – and therefore, circulated to the Foreign Office – Lawrence wrote that Feisal 'Looks like a European, and very like the monument of Richard I, at Fontevraud'. He was 'full of dreams and the capacity to realize them'.[29] To a fellow officer Lawrence wrote more simply that Feisal was 'an absolute ripper'.[30]

## Modernist representations; and the prosaic reality

There was one artist in Britain who actually benefited from the intensification of the war in 1916. Richard Nevinson's star had been rising in 1915, and during 1916 he exhibited a series of works which sealed his reputation as the most successful painter of the war to date. After his discharge from the RAMC early in the year he was free to concentrate on painting, living comfortably with his wife in his parents' house. His father returned from Egypt in March to find 'Rich established in 3 rooms and the whole house hung with his Futurisms – some new pictures very fine.'[31]

In March 1916 Richard Nevinson showed the painting which, more than any other, made his name. *La Mitrailleuse* was a brutally unsentimental representation of a French machine-gun crew, dominated by their weapon and devoted to its deathly service. The influential critic and painter Walter Sickert wrote that *La Mitrailleuse* 'will probably remain the most concentrated utterance on the war in the history of painting' and declared: 'this must be for the nation'.[32] Nevinson produced more pictures for exhibitions with the Friday Club in March and with the New England Art Club in May. In June he was involved in a show with the London Group, but this was only in preparation for a large exhibition devoted to his own work at the Leicester Galleries in London which opened in September. For this, Nevinson gathered together 35 of his paintings and 18 drawings from the beginning of the war, borrowing some from people who had bought them earlier, and including some new works. His father, solicitous as ever, arranged for an old friend, Sir Ian Hamilton, the former commander of the Gallipoli expedition, to write an introduction to the exhibition catalogue, which was decorated with a photograph of Nevinson in uniform, wearing goggles and a leather trenchcoat.

The exhibition opened on 26 September 1916 and was a huge success. A stream of politicians and society figures came to see the pictures, and critical reaction was highly favourable. A commonly taken line was that Nevinson had found a way of using modernist techniques while making his pictures realistic, uncompromising and comprehensible. Nevinson himself claimed that he had freed himself 'from all pedantic and academic theories',[33] and this was picked up by the *Daily Chronicle*, which called him 'a fighting artist, who has rampaged like a "Tank" through all the modern movements; he has bustled through Impressionism, Post impressionism, Cubism, Vorticism; and out of Cubism he has brought to birth a curious geometrical formula, sharp and glittering, which is admirably suited to his vision of this scientific, mechanical war'.[34] Referring to Nevinson's earlier military service, *The Graphic* declared: 'He has, therefore, seen what he paints.'[35] A book of reproductions was commissioned, with the title *Modern War*, containing a glowing tribute from the *Observer*'s art critic Paul Konody. Even the highbrow *Athenaum*, which had previously been constantly critical, conceded that 'All deductions made, however, we must register an extraordinary advance in Mr. Nevinson's art.'[36] *The Saturday Review*, which compared his work to 'some dexterous makeshift turn at a music hall', struck a note of rare dissent.[37]

For all the acclaim, and the critics' talk of 'convincing realism',[38] no one appears to have noticed something which may have been troubling the artist himself, that Nevinson was still drawing on the vision of the war which he had gained during his relatively brief time at the front in Flanders in the winter of 1914–15. Apart from a few drawings from the Wandsworth hospital in 1915, most of the works exhibited in September 1916, and certainly those which attracted the most attention – then and since – were not contemporary views of the war. One, *La Patrie*, which grimly displayed doctors at work among wounded French soldiers, clearly drew on Nevinson's memory of the 'Shambles' in Dunkirk, and did not reflect the much more organized reality of military hospitals in 1916. Another, *Motor Ambulance Driver*, was an implied self-portrait of Nevinson in this role in the early months of the war. Several explicitly showed scenes from the invasion of Belgium in 1914. *Pursuing a Taube* depicted aircraft which were obsolete by 1916. None showed any of the new weapons introduced since Nevinson's time at the front, such as poison gas, flamethrowers, trench mortars or tanks.

Consciousness of this distance may have contributed to Nevinson's disillusionment. That most of the works exhibited in the Leicester Galleries were sold was little consolation, and he interpreted this as a manifestation of people's fascination with war rather than appreciation of his artistry. In October he was quoted in the *Daily Mirror* as saying 'I have painted everything I saw in France and there will be no more.'[39] To another artist he wrote 'I intend to paint no more war pictures for some time.'[40] He was increasingly worried about being conscripted and sent to the front which he was representing to the British public. During 1916 there were repeated debates in parliament about re-enlisting soldiers who had been previously discharged, and Nevinson's father recorded his son's fears about this. In September Richard was 'again in terrible distress and agony'.[41] On 15 November, Henry Nevinson wrote bluntly: 'Extreme misery at night owing to Richard's terror at being called up again.'[42] Clearly overwrought, Richard Nevinson, with his father's help, started planning to escape to a neutral country to avoid being called up.

Stanley Spencer, for much of 1916, was strangely remote both from the war and from the London art scene which had been impressed by his work in November 1915. He was finally transferred from Beaufort Hospital to prepare for service abroad on 12 May 1916, being sent first to Devonport Military Hospital.[43] He summed up his experience here in two words to his friend James Wood: 'Horrible Hospital'.[44] After this he was moved to Tweseldown Camp, near Farnham, where, for 3 months, while the British Army fought on the Somme, he was trained for service in a Field Ambulance unit. The routine was much easier than that in a hospital and included long route marches through the countryside. He had plenty of time to write letters, to read and to think. He was still reflecting on St Augustine's emphasis on the spirituality of everyday tasks, and this helped him to see his experience at Beaufort as something which might be transfigured, if it could be painted. Writing to his sister Florence, he explained: 'Every thought I had dried up as soon as it realized where it was. But I did get ideas there. When I used to have a very full day, full of every kind of job you can think of, I felt very deeply the stimulating influence "doing" had upon me. Every act so perfect in its necessity seemed like anointing oil on my head. It was wonderful sometimes to wash up, to scrub, and then to dress nearly every wound in the ward. Such simple work and then such thoughtful work, all done in the same spirit.' He thanked Florence for the Bible she had sent him, which he apparently carried on every route march.[45]

He wrote again to James Wood, saying 'I think doing the dressings when you are allowed to do the things, in peace and quiet, is quite inspiring. The act of "doing" things to men is wonderful.' Spencer mentioned that he was thinking about painting scenes from his experience at Beaufort, adding: 'But why I should want to do so I could not say.'[46] Groping towards an explanation, he wrote to the Raverats: 'I will not do a picture till I can do it in the unity of the Spirit.'[47] To Henry Lamb he wrote: 'I think I would rather be here than at the hospital though of course hospital work was infinitely greater than this, which is just waste of time. I only like this better because I am out of doors & go for long route marches. . . . I wish I could do a painting of each different thing I had to do in the hospital so wonderful in their difference.'[48]

Spencer still found army life incredibly alienating. In July he poured out his feelings to James Wood: 'There is something that riles me and that is watching men play cards.' He was also offended by the men's constant smoking: 'I never say a word to these creatures. I have smoked a cigarette sometimes, but no, it is wrong, God hates it that is why. I cannot see or feel and smoke at the same time. And that ought to be the same with everyone else.'[49] Spencer was annoyed by having to attend Church of England parades and turned instead to Roman Catholic services in search of a deeper spirituality. As consignments of tropical clothing arrived during the summer, he speculated on whether he might be sent to India, or to Mesopotamia.

On 23 August, Spencer was with a group which marched out of camp, not knowing their ultimate destination. After two days on a ship in the Port of London, they sailed for the Mediterranean.[50] Spencer, who had never been abroad, wrote again to the Raverats from the ship: 'Opposite is the African coast towards the East the sea is bright & a delicate green, & it is bright against an opaque crimson horizon, which is darker than the sea. It looks very foreign.'[51] A few days later the men were disembarked at Salonica, where Spencer was assigned to the 66th Field Ambulance, and marched inland towards the line held against the Bulgarians in the Vardar valley.

## The war spreads

Vera Brittain similarly had to wait months for an overseas posting. In the meantime she had to face her mother's confusion over her willingness to continue at the Camberwell hospital, 'when I hate it so much', but she had decided that she could not leave.[52] Reflecting on this in April 1916, she wrote how she could still at least read Roland Leighton's poems, or the

'War Sonnets of Rupert Brooke', without feeling 'bitterly unworthy'.[53] It was in this mood of resigned self-abnegation that Brittain saw at first hand some of the consequences of the offensive on the Somme. She knew from her brother Edward early in June 1916 that the army was preparing for a 'Big Push', 'somewhere in the region of Albert',[54] and on 1 July she wrote in her diary how the papers were full of the news of the offensive.[55] On 4 July, convoys of wounded started to arrive at the hospital in Camberwell, and the next day she discovered that Edward was in one of these.[56] He had been injured in the arm and the thigh in an attack which epitomized, in its confusion and futility, the first day on the Somme. Although badly shaken, Edward was not in fact seriously injured. By the end of the month there were 3,000 wounded in the hospital, and the nurses were worked off their feet.[57]

Despite Roland's death, Brittain was still writing about the war in heroic terms. She fondly imagined that the offensive had opened 'very successfully',[58] and wrote uncritically in her diary about Edward's part in the attack on the first day. When she heard that he had been awarded the Military Cross for his gallantry on 1 July, she wrote to her mother 'How unspeakably splendid!'[59] After weeks of intensive work, Brittain was granted leave in September and then posted to Malta. She had a week to prepare before she was recalled on 21 September, excited to hear that she was sailing out on the *Brittanic* – a sister of the ill-fated *Titanic*, now converted for use as a hospital ship. She wrote: 'I felt no especial pang when I saw England disappear; it was all part of the hard path which I have assigned to myself to tread.'[60]

As thousands of volunteers and recruits left Britain in 1916 for various theatres of war, others were coming home, many injured, physically and mentally. Kate Finzi, who had served overseas almost without interruption since the beginning of the war, was one of these. By the time she presided over New Year's celebrations in the YMCA hut at Boulogne in January 1916, she was 'in failing health'. From her published diary, it is not clear exactly what was wrong with her, nor whether she retired from the 'war zone' voluntarily, or was asked to leave. At one point she permitted herself a note of cynicism, speaking of how people were now discarded, or 'scrapped' like an old car, 'to return home a derelict', but she quickly qualified this by saying: 'We are all fatalists now, like the men in the trenches.'[61] Finzi left Boulogne on 10 February 1916, after a nostalgic last look at the places where she had worked, the old sugar shed which had been turned into a hospital, and the improvised mortuary which was now a Censor's office. A final glimpse of the military cemetery, 'that City of Little White Crosses', provoked her to think of Rupert Brooke's phrase 'for ever England'. She concluded her diary with her thoughts as the boat left the quayside: 'Broken in body, I am to leave the work I love, and with it youth and vitality – and this whilst the fighting wages hardest in the West.'[62]

Finzi was clearly not quite as broken as she suggested here. On arrival in England she rejoined her family, which had now moved to Harrogate on the Yorkshire coast, and set about preparing her diary for publication. Within only weeks the manuscript was ready, and she wrote an interesting epilogue, dated May 1916, before sending it to the publishers. She wrote: 'It is an odd coincidence that the last words of this War Diary should be penned by candlelight in a darkened northern town, to the sound of bombs falling on an entirely defenceless city.' She was referring to a Zeppelin raid, and described how, 'with the truly sporting instinct of Britons', 'everyone has turned out to see what they may of the "fuss" by which our humane foe hopes to terrorise us'. She went on to offer an apology to her fellow citizens who were suffering these raids, realizing that in earlier passages of her diary she had been critical of those back in England, away from the 'war zone'.[63]

The Zeppelin campaign had indeed intensified in 1916. On the night of 31 January Zeppelins left a trail of destruction from Suffolk through to Staffordshire and Derbyshire, killing 54 people and injuring 67.[64] On 7 March, the *Sheffield Daily Telegraph* reported on attacks over eight counties in the north of England two nights previously, killing 12 and injuring 33 people. *The Times*, reporting on the same raid, published a table showing that, to date, 255 people in Britain had been killed and 534 injured by Zeppelin attacks.[65] Kate Finzi, living on the north-east coast of Britain in 1916, might well have seen or heard Zeppelins on several occasions. It is most probable that the raid she experienced while finishing her diary was on 2 May, when attacks on the north-east coast of Britain by five Zeppelins were reported, and 'a few bombs were dropped in Yorkshire'.[66] She was certainly struck by the way that these attacks blurred the distinction between combatants and non-combatants, and effectively brought citizens in much of Britain into the 'war zone'.

## Mametz Wood

David Jones' experience as a private in the 'New Army' in 1916 provides a fascinating counterpoint to the strategic deliberations of Haig and the politicians. Arriving in France with the 38th (Welsh) Division in December 1915, Jones' battalion, the 15th London Welsh, had its first experience of the trenches in the British line near La Gorgue just before Christmas. It spent the next six months in rotation between the front line and rest billets in the sector from Laventie, through Neuve Chapelle and Festubert to Givenchy. It was a particularly wet winter, and much of the soldiers' time and energy was devoted to trying to maintain the positions they occupied in this flat, low and marshy terrain. Although Jones was not involved in any major actions, he and his comrades had to suffer artillery and mortar bombardments – often prolonged – and the caprice of underground mines detonated near them. Wetness, cold, discomfort, fatigue and thirst were their constant companions. The battalion suffered a number of casualties, typically inflicted in a seemingly arbitrary way when a shell happened to land in a dugout or trench.

Jones also experienced at first hand the consequences of the British Army's desire to 'maintain ascendancy in No Man's land'. This oft-repeated phrase meant sending out small patrols at night to creep towards the German line, to throw bombs into their trenches and to try to take prisoners. This was incredibly hazardous and added to the flow of casualties. There is virtually no surviving written record of this period of Jones' war service, but he did make several drawings, for the most part only recently published, and they provide some clues as to how he reacted to life in the trenches.[67] It is fascinating to compare these with the pictures by Nevinson, drawn at exactly the same time, which were attracting such attention back in England. Jones was not drawing with any polemical intent or to make larger statements about the nature of the war.

His drawings do not show fighting, shells exploding, dead or mutilated bodies, or men in scenes of suffering. Although they do show the ruined buildings and desolate landscape which framed the experience of British soldiers in Flanders, they, more surprisingly, do not picture flooded trenches or rain. They are, for the most part, scenes of everyday routine and domesticity in the trenches, or behind the line. Soldiers and junior officers are depicted on sentry duty, standing ready, warming themselves at braziers or just sitting. This may simply reflect when Jones had the opportunity for sketching, that is to say when there was no action, when he was free for a few moments and when it was relatively dry. It probably also reflects something of the sense of security he gained from the routinized nature of front-line service. Jones's drawings are for the most part kind, and these portrayals of people – clearly represented as individuals, not the anonymous stereotypes who populate Nevinson's pictures – tell us much about his experience of humour and comradeship.[68]

We have a moving contemporary testimony to this spirit in a poem by Ivor Gurney. It was customary for British units which were new to the front to be taught the lore and accumulated wisdom of trench warfare by more experienced troops. Jones' battalion had been instructed by the Coldstream Guards when they first arrived, and by May 1916 it was judged ready to take on the role of instruction. Ivor Gurney, serving as a private with the Gloucestershire Regiment, arrived in the trenches near Laventie for the first time at this point, like most of these young men, fearful and apprehensive. He wrote a poem about the 'strangely beautiful entry to war's rout' which the Glosters received from Jones' battalion, which he described as 'a Welsh colony/Hiding in sandbag ditches, whispering consolatory/Soft foreign things'. The 'Welsh pit boys' shared candles and rations with the Glosters, and sang 'Welsh things' which Gurney found 'never more beautiful than there under the guns' noise'.[69]

On 10 June the Welsh Division was ordered south, to join the huge movement of men and material towards the Somme. In the next three weeks, pausing to practise 'a trench to trench attack in all its varieties', the division marched 50 miles, arriving at Mametz on 5 July.[70] The Welsh Division was not part of the fateful offensive on 1 July, but it was to be involved in one of the smaller battles which the Somme campaign turned into, one hardly mentioned in many larger histories, even though its bulks large in Welsh memory today. After the failure on 1 July, Haig's attention turned to a renewed assault on the Bazentin ridge, and in preparation for this he ordered the capture of Mametz Wood. One of the few successes on the first day of the Somme had been in taking Mametz, but this had not been exploited by capturing the small area of woodland north of the village. Now the Welsh Division, commanded by Major General Ivor Phillips, was given this job. Mametz Wood was strongly held by the Germans; it could only be approached across open ground which sloped up towards the dense undergrowth, and machine guns were positioned on both flanks of this open ground.

The first attempt, on 7 July, was a terrible failure. The Cardiff City Battalion and 10th South Wales Borderers suffered many casualties in separate attacks, 'which in both cases failed to reach the wood'.[71] Jones' battalion was held in reserve at this stage. Haig, misinformed by his staff officers, was furious with what he perceived as insufficient resolve, writing: 'although the wood had been most adequately bombarded the division

FIGURE 20 *The Royal Welch Fusiliers resting before the attack on Mametz Wood in July 1916. David Jones later wrote of this moment: 'They talked of ordinary things. Of each other's friends at home; those friends unknown to the other two. Of the possible duration of the war. Of how they would meet and in what good places afterwards' (Jones,* In Parenthesis, *p. 139).*

never entered the wood, and in the whole division the casualties for the 24 hours are under 150! A few bold men entered the wood and found little opposition'.[72] Phillips was immediately removed from command of the Welsh Division.[73] On the night after Haig wrote these comments, David Jones' battalion was moved forward to renew the attack. Waiting through the night, crouching in packed trenches, he watched as the British bombardment started at 3.30 a.m. on 10 July, alerting the Germans to an imminent assault. In the breaking light of dawn the 13th, 14th and 16th Battalions headed out across the open ground towards the wood, through a hail of machine-gun and artillery fire.

Jones' battalion was soon ordered to follow, and under intense fire, he and his comrades went over the top. Jones was one of those who made it into the wood, where they found an utter confusion of dead bodies, debris and surviving British soldiers still making their way forward. Through the morning, afternoon and into the evening the Welsh Division pushed through the increasingly shattered woodland, finally taking what shelter they could in hastily dug trenches and shell holes. In the confusion many British shells fell among them. Sometime around midnight Jones was hit by a bullet in his left leg. With great difficulty, and reluctantly discarding his rifle, he crawled back through the wood; after some time he was recovered by stretcher bearers and taken back to a casualty clearing station, where he lost consciousness.

While Jones lay, with hundreds of other wounded men, the battalions which had been so badly mauled in the first attack on Mametz Wood were brought forward to relieve the shattered remnants of the division there. In the afternoon of 11 July they 'cleared out the Germans on the northern edge of the wood', before being relieved by the 21st Division.[74] What was left of the Welsh Division marched away from the line and took no more part in the fighting on the Somme. It had lost some 4,000 men killed and wounded in taking Mametz Wood. Jones' battalion had lost 12 officers and 250 men killed and wounded.[75] Haig never changed his opinion about the initial attack on Mametz Wood, although he noted late on 10 July that 'Progress in Mametz Wood is satisfactory.'[76] In 1919, writing an introduction to the official history of the Welsh Division, Haig conspicuously omitted to mention Mametz Wood.[77]

## Love, gratitude, resignation and chastening

The year 1916 started badly for Elgar. Although the first performance of *Une Voix dans le Désert* on 29 January had – according to Alice Elgar – an 'immense reception', *The Starlight Express* was called off the next day, to Elgar's great disappointment.[78] Elgar was a composer with many different voices, and he now turned back to his more serious work on the Binyon poems, started nearly a year before. He was preparing his settings of the second and third of the poems for performance, and during February he worked hard on the orchestration of both pieces. On 29 February Alice took the finished parts to Novello. The winter weather accentuated Elgar's ill health and in April, travelling to the countryside, he collapsed and had to be taken briefly to a nursing home in Oxford. The prospect of forthcoming performances of *For the Fallen*, the title given to the two completed Binyon settings, was sufficient to restore him, if only temporarily, and in May he travelled to Leeds to conduct the work's premiere. Alice wrote: 'The Concert was magnificent. Enormous audience & orch. very good & chorus perfect. E. conducted superbly.'[79] Given that previous premieres of his important works had been ruined by insufficient rehearsal, this must have been a huge relief to Elgar.

The first performances of *For the Fallen* were followed by something which could only have taken place in wartime Britain, and challenge any idea that musical life there was in abeyance. For a whole week in May 1916, audiences in London were treated to a programme consisting of Elgar's *The Dream of Gerontius* and *For the Fallen*. Full houses turned out every night, generating large sums for the Red Cross from their ticket money. On 10 May, the King and Queen attended, but apparently over 2 hours of music of such gravity was too much for the King, who 'seemed fidgety'.[80] It is difficult to imagine these two works on the same programme today, but they clearly spoke to wartime need. Ernest Newman, reviewing 'For the Fallen' in *The Musical Times*, noted how Elgar had not abased himself to write a 'Hymn of Hate', but had expressed 'love and gratitude and pride and sorrow'. He concluded: 'The glory of our pride in the fallen swells and then subsides: in the last quiet bars the composer wisely sounds the note not of vociferous rapture, but of resignation and chastening.'[81]

Newman also compared Elgar's work with that of Rupert Brooke, and indeed there are similarities between them. But *For the Fallen* lacks entirely the naïve embrace of war and of death which Brooke had expressed. Those who seek in it a representation of the war itself will be disappointed. Binyon had not experienced the war, which had indeed hardly started, when he wrote his poems. Elgar had not been anywhere near the trenches, and although he knew that tens of thousands of young men – and animals – were being slaughtered in ever more hideous ways, he was not trying to depict this. Nor was he seeking to find a new musical idiom with which to represent a new kind of warfare. In *For the Fallen* Elgar reverted to the language of his *The Dream of Gerontius* and of his 2nd Symphony. Like *The Dream of Gerontius*, this was music dealing directly with life and death, and with transcendence. From letters surviving today in the archive at Elgar's birthplace in Worcestershire it is clear that many members of the public were deeply moved by this music.

Elgar's public success brought him no joy, and he reacted by seeking solitude. In his most intimate letters from this period he expressed a deep sense of discontent, even though he spent much of his time away from London, and the whirl of social life. Undoubtedly the continuation of the war – now seemingly without end – dismayed him terribly. His earlier desire to engage with the war effort was also waning. In early July, while he and his wife were staying at the home of Frank Schuster in Bray, Alice recorded that she entertained four soldiers, including an Ulsterman 'recently arrived from France, Tiepval [sic] & c – E. rather tired & cd. not bear talking, did not come in to tea'.[82] Why could Elgar 'not bear' to meet these men, who appear to have come straight from the central sector of Haig's assault on the Somme? The 36th (Ulster) Division had suffered 'truly catastrophic' casualties on the first day of the offensive, trying to take Thiepval.[83] Was Elgar aware of the chasm between men (and women) from the front and citizens at home, which so often reduced those on leave to silence? Was he too sensitive to take part in polite conversation which he knew must be painful to these soldiers? Or was he really just 'rather tired'? We will never know, but it is interesting to note also that – as far as we know – Elgar did not go to see the film of the *Battle of the Somme*, although his wife and daughter did.[84] Still suffering from throat problems, Elgar's doctor Sir Maurice Anderson had recommended that he undergo 'electric cautery' to cure this. Elgar underwent the first such treatment on 29 August;[85] on 31 August he wrote despairingly to Alice Stuart-Wortley that he was still 'not well': 'I feel that everything has come to an end & am very unhappy.'[86]

Parry was similarly caught between a desire still to engage publicly with the war effort, and simply to retreat from it. On 10 March 1916,

FIGURE 21 *The first page of Hubert Parry's manuscript of his setting of 'Stanzas by William Blake', written for the Fight for Right movement in 1916, but later re-dedicated to the cause of 'Women Voters'.*

he wrote in his diary: 'Wrote a tune for some words of Blakes Bridges sent me'.[87] Robert Bridges was the Poet Laureate, and he had become involved with a movement calling itself Fight for Right. The movement, which was led by clergymen, politicians and trade unionists, intended to convince the British public that they were fighting 'for the best interests of humanity', to resist a 'premature peace' and 'to accept with cheerfulness all the sacrifices necessary to bring the war to a successful conclusion'.[88] The words of Blake which Bridges had sent Parry were from the preface to an epic written in the early nineteenth century, telling how Jesus as a child had been brought to England's green and pleasant land, and expressing a mystical desire to see Jerusalem 'builded here'. Parry's tune, which soon acquired the title 'Jerusalem', was quickly printed and was sung at the Fight for Right meeting at the Mansion House in London on 13 March. It was immediately popular, was sung again on 23 March at another Fight for Right meeting at Westminster Cathedral Hall and then again on 28 March at Queen's Hall.[89] 'Jerusalem' is so well known today that it needs little comment here. Suffice to say that Parry had produced a tune which was at once uplifting and patriotic, without being vulgar or jingoistic. It was broad and extended, reaching a climax in its seventh line, before moving to a solemn but confident close. Married to Blake's words it conveyed a fervent love of country with a deep, if fairly unspecific religious sentiment. It was particularly suited to being sung in unison by large congregations, accompanied by a powerful organ. It was an instant hit, but Parry was immediately disquieted by its association with Fight for Right. Ironically, the day after he wrote the tune, he recorded that his wife Maude was in a 'violently anti-English' mood.[90] He was troubled by the tone of speeches at the Fight for Right meetings,[91] and it was with some relief that he turned away to another compositional project, the choral motets he had been working on in 1915.

On 22 May Parry heard his motets, collectively titled *Songs of Farewell*, performed at the Royal College of Music by a choir directed by Hugh Allen. He was deeply touched by the expressive rendering of his work and by the evident pleasure of the choir in singing the motets. These works appear remote from the reality of the world around Parry in 1916. Written for unaccompanied voices, they hark back unashamedly to the English music and poetry of an earlier age. The best known of this group today, 'My Soul, There is a Country', uses a text by the metaphysical poet Henry Vaughan, written after the English Civil War, and expressing a desire for a world 'above noise and danger', where 'grows the Flower of Peace'. Inevitably, given their title, these motets suggest an elderly man turning away from a contemporary world which had fallen far short of the lofty ideals once held for it. Parry was in fact still working on his large philosophical book, but with an increasing awareness of the gulf between the positive evolutionary ideals he sought to expound in it, and the mechanized slaughter still going on in Europe.

This awareness was heightened when, in October 1916, he went, like so many others, to see the 'cinematograph' of the *Battle of the Somme*. He recorded his impressions in his diary: 'Dreadfully vivid. The varieties of artillery most interesting. The trenches sometimes sickening. Advances. Dead bodies. Operating stations. Vast numbers of prisoners. Running in with hands up & under guard. Nightmare altogether. Yet the British soldier always cheery!'[92]

## The fading romance of war

During 1916 the scope of the war had broadened, drawing more and more people into its seemingly insatiable grasp. Along with the wounded, early volunteers like Kate Finzi were coming home exhausted, and later recruits such as Vera Brittain and Stanley Spencer were being sent out to take their places. In France, the largest British Army ever assembled – composed entirely of men who had volunteered – had been involved in a huge offensive, which, despite early hopes for a breakthrough, had turned into a grinding battle of attrition, a 'wearing out battle'. Undaunted by casualties on an unprecedented scale, Haig was still continuing the offensive, determined to break the German will to resist. The Germans, for their part, were still attacking at Verdun. The three major combatants were locked in struggles so huge, so violent, and yet so static as almost to defy comprehension. In Kate Finzi's words, it was 'almost untellable'.[93]

In Britain, the imagined unity of August 1914, with its appeal to voluntarism, had been replaced by a far more coordinated and directed commitment to the war effort. Haig's armies were being supplied with guns and ammunition on an industrial scale, and in a reversal of cherished liberal tradition, conscription had been introduced. Young men who had previously resisted all public pressures on them to enlist, such as Ellis Evans in North Wales, were now being called before tribunals to explain why they should be exempt from service. The violent confrontations between supporters of the Union of Democratic Control and patriotic opponents, and the bitter denunciations by volunteers such as Kate Finzi of 'shirkers' and 'strikers' were revealing fractures within British society which challenged facile ideals of a nation united in war. The terror felt by Richard Nevinson at the looming prospect of conscription may serve as a counterpoint to popular images of the cheery British volunteer waving goodbye to family and friends as he goes to war. Nevinson was not alone. Tens of thousands of young men appealed against the notices ordering them to report for duty. Adrian Gregory, who has studied the response to conscription, argues persuasively that 'the usual response to conscription was not passive acceptance, but an appeal'.[94]

In terms of representation, the very different images of the war being produced in Britain in 1916 reflect these social divisions. On the one hand, there was a continued outpouring of traditional, heroic representations. Kate Finzi's *Record of a Woman's Work on the Western Front* may serve as an example. Her diary was published in October 1916 with an Introduction by the retired Major General Alfred Turner, which rehearsed familiar tropes of 'barbarous Teutons', 'the bestial and brutish enemy' with 'savage instincts of murder and lust', who had been halted by the 'officers and men of the glorious "first seven divisions" which left these shores in August 1914', and whose sufferings had been ameliorated by 'our British nurses', 'heroic women who face all dangers and hardships for the sake of doing good to others'.[95] Perceptive reviewers noted, however, that Finzi's diary was not solely heroic, *The New Statesman* commenting that 'the romance of war fades before tetanus and gangrene'.[96] Parry's 'Jerusalem', while far more abstract than Finzi's record, presented a similar narrative of good triumphing over evil and of national unity of purpose. This imagery should though be balanced with the far more challenging visions put before the British public in 1916 by Richard Nevinson, which as we have seen, attracted great attention. By representing empty landscapes, humans dominated by machines, and, when representing individuals, choosing French soldiers, Nevinson stepped away from the tropes of British righteousness and German iniquity. His shocking representations of suffering and squalor were not, as in Finzi's narrative, counterbalanced with images of heroism and glory. The year 1916 had also seen the first, partial performances of Elgar's requiem for the dead, a work which can lay claim to being the most significant work of art produced in Britain during the war, and which while rehearsing the narrative of crusade, did so more in sorrow than in rejoicing. Anyone familiar with Nevinson's paintings, or with Elgar's *Spirit of England* will have found it impossible to agree with Robert Wohl's assertion that 'For two and a half years the war was represented as exciting, fulfilling, glorious, holy, noble, beautiful, gay, and, all in all, great fun.'[97]

Notably, all of these diverse representations were becoming anachronistic and inadequate to the scale of warfare at Verdun and on the Somme. By 1916 it was becoming apparent that there was a growing cleft between the reality of the war and the ways in which it was being represented to the British public, one which was not bridged by the as yet clumsy medium of film. The newspapers were still reporting on the war with an enthusiasm which seems almost incredible today, and which could only generate disillusionment when high hopes were subsequently dashed. Let us take as an example a leading article on the opening stages of the Somme offensive from *The South Wales Daily News*, with the reassuring title 'All Goes Well', which proclaimed: 'The fact that it is now possible, even on a limited scale, to employ cavalry again is a sure sign that at such points we are nearing the end of trench warfare and driving the enemy into the open.'[98] Two months later, Haig's army was still attacking on the Somme, and the battlefield was turning to mud.

# CHAPTER SEVEN

# September 1916–July 1917

On 15 September 1916, Haig threw in a new weapon on the Somme, the 'tanks'. Although he has been strongly criticized for using the tanks before they were ready in great numbers, in reality the tanks were not yet sufficiently developed to break the deadlock on the Western Front. The first models deployed were prone to mechanical breakdown, they moved no faster than walking pace, and once they were in action, it was almost impossible to communicate with them or to refuel them. The crews, if they survived the attentions of the Germans, were poisoned by carbon monoxide fumes and deafened by the engines, and after a few hours inside the vehicle were typically too ill to carry on. The tanks could effectively only be used to assist a first assault. The attack on 15 September did succeed to the extent of taking a few more battered French villages. After this, the offensive on the Somme continued, increasingly without clear direction or purpose. Through October Haig appears to have believed, as Travers puts it, 'that the general who held on the longest would win'.[1] Finally, in November, the last attack was made on the village of Beaumont-Hamel, at the north of the battlefield; it had been one of the first day's objectives back in July. The 51st (Highland) division finally took Beaumont-Hamel, and the Royal Naval Division, now serving in the trenches like any other infantry formation, took the village of Beaucourt. 'And so', wrote John Terraine, 'under the leaden, snow-filled skies of Picardy, the most terrible experience in the British Army's history came slowly to an end'.[2] Since 1 July, the British armies had sustained 480,000 casualties and gained a few square miles of territory of no strategic significance.

The public reporting of the campaign on the Somme in Britain maintained the unreal tone of confidence with which it had started back in July. The tanks certainly gave British journalists something new to write about. Images of the tanks, appearing to move much more quickly than they actually did, featured prominently in the silent film about the final stages of the offensive which was shown in Britain in early 1917, and called *The Battle of the Ancre and the Advance of the Tanks*. Even at the very end of the campaign, *The Times* was printing absurdly optimistic assessments. On 1 December its correspondent reported: 'I am not sure that history will not regard the achievement of these last two months as the most glorious of all the battle.'[3] This kind of bombast could not conceal from the public the awful truth that the gains made on the Somme were insignificant. Nor was it possible to hide the huge scale of human suffering. By this time, the British press had abandoned the practice of printing of regular casualty figures, but nonetheless, periodically figures were released, which must have given readers – even those who heard nothing directly from relatives or friends in the armed forces – pause for thought. The *Daily Telegraph* published a small article in September 1916 giving a misleading figure of 59,072 British casualties for the whole of July, but a staggering figure of 123,097 for August.[4] And even if they were not reading the newspapers, there were literally hundreds of thousands of British people – from the Prime Minister down – who received the news during the offensive that a relative had been killed, or injured, or was missing in action. Asquith's son Raymond was killed leading a company of the Grenadier Guards on 15 September, the day the tanks were first used.[5]

By the end of the campaign, it was clear that Haig's earlier vision of ending the war in 1916 was hopelessly misplaced. The French had not broken at Verdun, but neither had the Germans on the Somme, and elsewhere they had clear achievements to show. In a brief but effective campaign in the final months of the year the German Army overran most of Romania, gaining access to that country's agricultural resources. Although a Russian offensive almost destroyed the Austrian Army in the summer of 1916, it had been immensely costly and left the Russian Army utterly demoralized.

Back in Britain, there was dismay but not despondency. Much of the public concern was displaced into criticism of Asquith's government for failing to prosecute the war with sufficient resolve. Asquith's dignity, poise and scholarly bearing had seemed entirely appropriate as Prime Minister before 1914, but his pre-war slogan of 'Wait and see' now appeared hopelessly inadequate, and his most vehement critics had long accused him of being too pro-German. Lord Riddell expressed something about Asquith's ill-suitedness for wartime leadership when he observed that the Prime Minister would be more troubled by the thought that he had used a split infinitive in a speech to the Commons than by a German victory on the battlefield. After the death of his son Raymond, Asquith was withdrawn and appeared to have lost his concentration on political affairs.

In December 1916, after considerable political manoeuvring, Asquith resigned and was replaced as Prime Minister by David Lloyd George, leading a coalition with Conservative support. Although Lloyd George was publicly committed to a more vigorous prosecution of the war, he had been horrified by the huge losses on the Somme and was deeply critical of Haig's leadership. Since writing his New Year's Day memorandum on strategy in 1915 Lloyd George had argued for a strategy of 'knocking the props away', that is by defeating Germany's allies to leave her isolated and fatally weakened. Over the next two years, as Prime Minister, his fertile mind would constantly seek for ways to deploy British military strength away from the barbed wire and machine guns on the Western Front. Haig for his part was suspicious of Lloyd George, seeing him as a glib-tongued and devious politician. The contrast in temperament and personality between the two men could hardly have been greater. This tension between the Prime Minister and Britain's most senior officer in the field would come to a height in the difficult months ahead.

Lloyd George was almost immediately confronted, not with a military problem, but with a so-called German 'peace offensive'. In a note delivered through the American ambassador to the British government on 18 December, Chancellor Bethmann-Hollweg of Germany, speaking also on behalf of the Austrians, Bulgarians and Turks, proposed to open 'peace negotiations', since Germany and her allies had demonstrated 'their indestructible strength'. Lloyd George treated the German note with contempt, stating in the House of Commons: 'we shall put our trust in an unbroken army rather than a broken faith'. The American president, Woodrow Wilson, then asked all the belligerent countries to formulate the terms on which they would be prepared to enter negotiations. The British and French governments declared that they would demand the restoration of Belgium, Serbia and Montenegro; the evacuation of German armies from France, Russia and Romania; 'the liberation of Italians, Slavs, Roumanians, Czechs, and Slovaks from foreign domination', the 'liberation of the peoples who now lie beneath the murderous tyranny of the Turks', the payment of compensation for damages caused; and 'the rescue of Europe from the brutal encroachments of Prussian militarism'. A month later, the Germans replied. They were not prepared 'to publish any peace terms at present, because our enemies have published such terms which aim at the dishonour and destruction of Germany and her Allies'.[6] The two sides were miles apart, and both felt that they had more to gain from continuing the war than from ending it on unfavourable terms. A sense of how hostile British views of Germany were by this time may be gained from an article in *The Graphic* on 'The Disturbers of the World's Peace': 'From China to Canada, from Persia to Peru, there is not one country where the vile and servile Hun has not shown up in one of his many roles – as spy, assassin, perjurer, forger, or agent provocateur. His slimy trail is everywhere, the unclean thing pollutes the world.'[7]

Further international developments in 1917 had an important bearing on the British conduct of the war. In March a revolution in Russia led to the abdication of the Tsar and the establishment of a provisional government led by Kerensky. Tsarist despotism had not been popular in Britain, and there were initially widespread hopes, not confined to Radical circles, that Kerensky's government might reinvigorate the Russian war effort. The *Welsh Outlook* noted that 'even from a military point of view the Russian revolution should be welcomed. From the point of view of civilization it is the first fruits of the war and its value is inestimable'.[8] There was Allied relief when finally the Americans declared war against Germany in April 1917, provoked largely by the unrestricted submarine warfare which the Germans had waged since February. America had though no army to fight on the Western Front, and it would not be until well into 1918 that significant numbers of American troops would be deployed in France.[9]

At the start of the year, both Lloyd George and Haig were won over by the new French commander in the field, Georges Nivelle, who had been appointed to replace Joffre. Nivelle, who spoke perfect English, used all his charm and persuasion to convince the British that his plan for a renewed offensive, based on a greater element of surprise, had a real chance of achieving a decisive success.[10] Haig agreed to support Nivelle's offensive with a British attack near Arras in April, although he was still thinking of a larger British offensive in Flanders later in the year. Relations between Haig and Lloyd George were nonetheless terribly strained as the two men wrangled over grand strategy. The relationship with the French was also difficult to manage. At a conference in Calais at the end of February, Nivelle made an ill-judged attempt to subordinate Haig entirely to his command, and it was only with difficulty that Haig maintained operational control of his own force. Finally, in March it was agreed that the British would mount an offensive in Flanders 'to clear the Belgian coast' later in the summer if the Nivelle offensive, now only a few weeks away, did not break the German front.[11]

These negotiations were preceded by an unprecedented development, when British troops on the Somme realized that the trenches opposite them were unoccupied. It quickly became clear that the Germans were withdrawing on a front of over 50 miles to a prepared position, known to the British as the Hindenburg Line. This had been built with extensive fortifications, and by giving the Germans a shorter line, allowed them to take several divisions into their reserve. Setting a precedent for similar behaviour on a larger scale in the Soviet Union in 1943 and 1944, the Germans left behind them a devastated landscape, with railways torn up, villages in flames, bridges demolished, orchards cut down and wells poisoned. As many as 125,000 inhabitants were deported, some with no notice.[12] The British and French soldiers who cautiously advanced into this wasteland were appalled by this new evidence of German 'barbarity'. Newspapers showed photographs of the 'wanton destruction'. The German withdrawal, at its deepest some 30 miles, made a mockery of the infinitely painful advance of the British in the same area only a few months previously.

Despite the huge losses on the Somme in 1916, Haig's army was still growing. He now had 56 infantry and five cavalry divisions at his disposal. When they attacked near Arras on 9 April 1917, they were supported by no fewer than 2,817 guns which laid down a bombardment greater than that before the Somme offensive.[13] For once, *The Times*' report of 'Great Gains on Wide Front' was not entirely misleading.[14] In appalling weather, Haig's forces overran several miles of the German front-line trenches, notably on the Vimy Ridge, and captured an unprecedented 10,000 prisoners. Haig was intoxicated[15] and urged his commanders to follow up with more attacks. The long-awaited Nivelle offensive started on 16 April, but after limited initial successes, it quickly turned into a disaster. Haig was slow to realize the extent of the calamity, and he maintained his Arras offensive until early May, incurring huge losses for little gain. While the British offensive petered out, widespread disaffection in the French Army turned to mutiny. Many front-line units refused to leave their trenches, and thousands of men on leave refused to return. Marshal Pétain, the 'hero of Verdun', was brought in

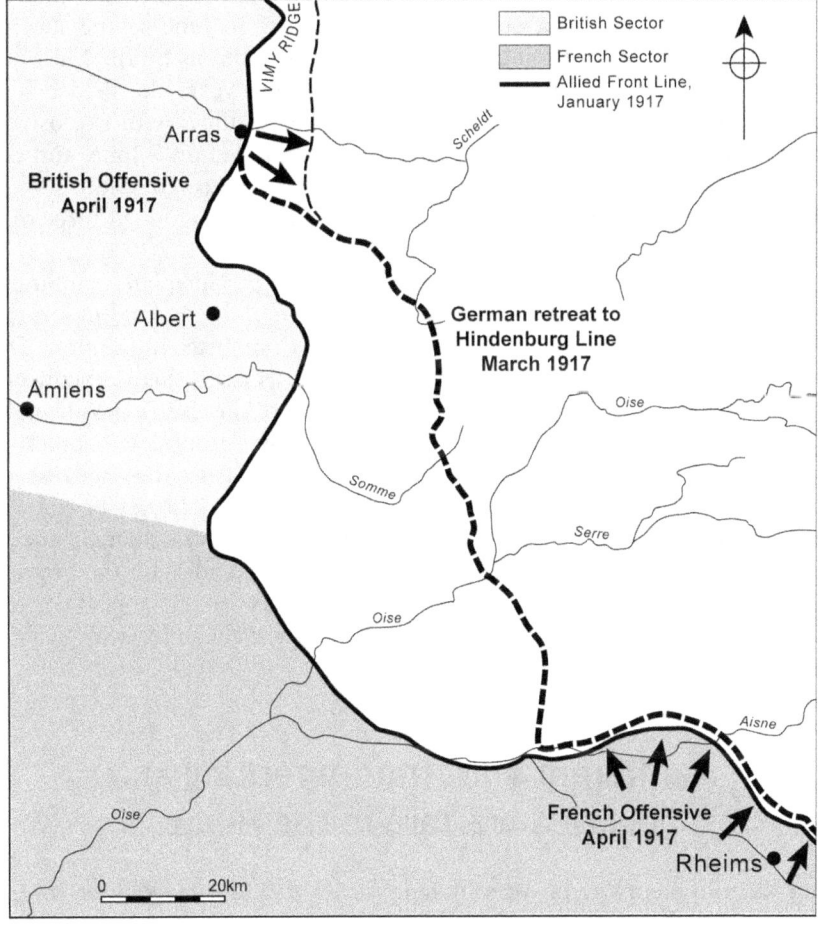

MAP 10 *The Battle of Arras and the Nivelle offensive.*

to replace Nivelle and sought with a combination of harsh punishments and inducements to restore discipline and order.

For several months the French Army was effectively paralysed, and in June Pétain told the British that his men could not contribute to any further large-scale offensives that year. Astonishingly the Germans were not fully aware of the crisis in the French Army and did not attempt to take advantage of it. The French mutinies nonetheless became an important factor in Haig's planning and a major justification for his determination to mount an offensive.[16] He was convinced that the British Army was now the single most powerful offensive force left fighting. He believed that the Germans were demoralized and could be defeated in 1917 by an assault from the Ypres Salient. From May through to the end of July, Haig tirelessly argued his case with Lloyd George, the War Cabinet and with the French. Lloyd George was deeply opposed to another costly offensive in Flanders and pressed instead for British forces to be diverted to Palestine and to support the Italians. Haig's case was strengthened in June by the success of a long-planned operation against the German positions on the Messines Ridge, to the south of the Ypres Salient. For two years the British had tunnelled underneath the ridge, digging deep mines filled with explosives. After a huge artillery barrage, 19 mines were exploded on 7 June, and the British occupied much of the ridge. Thousands of German soldiers were literally blown to pieces by explosions which had the combined force of a small earthquake.

Haig was delighted, and on 19 and 20 June he put his plan, combining a huge attack from the Ypres Salient with an amphibious landing on the Belgian coast, to the newly formed War Policy Committee in London. The Germans would be thrown back to the Dutch frontier, their submarines denied the use of Zeebrugge and Ostend, and the BEF's position in Flanders secured. At the second of these meetings Admiral Jellicoe, now the First Sea Lord, strengthened Haig's hand by stating that because of the shipping losses to German submarines, Britain would not be able to continue the war in 1918.[17] Still the government procrastinated, and it was not until 20 July that Haig was allowed to proceed, with the proviso that the offensive would be called off if unsuccessful. By this time, the preliminary artillery bombardment was already well under way. It was hardly an auspicious start.

## A different war: train-wrecking and guerilla warfare in the Hejaz

One development in the second half of 1916 had run counter to the setbacks of the year and gave Lloyd George's 'eastern' strategy new strength in 1917 – the Arab Revolt. T. E. Lawrence, by representing Feisal to the Arab Bureau in October 1916 as a charismatic leader who could lead the revolt to success, placed himself at the centre of this. The respect was mutual. Feisal gave token of his trust for Lawrence by providing him, on their second encounter, with a splendid set of white robes to wear. In January 1917 Feisal asked his father to request formally that he was 'most anxious' Lawrence should stay with him, 'as he has given such very great assistance'.[18] Lawrence quickly shook off efforts to confine him to managing supplies being landed in the Hejaz, and during 1917 he carved out a role which went far beyond that of a liaison officer. After nearly two years of tedious office work in Cairo, his special relationship with Feisal provided him with a unique opportunity to shape the Arab Revolt, and the British involvement with it. He wrote excitedly to a colleague in Cairo: 'I want to rub off my British habits & go off with Feisal for a bit. Amusing job, and all new country.'[19] He wrote to his parents with some pride in January 1917: 'the position I hold is such a queer one – I do not suppose that any Englishman before had such a place'.[20]

Lawrence's new importance was confirmed in a summary sent from the Arab Bureau to the Foreign Office in November 1916, which described him as 'an officer of great experience and knowledge of Arabs', and used his views to argue against sending British regular troops to the Hejaz.[21] Lloyd George later wrote that Lawrence, after meeting Feisal, 'had considerable influence on our subsequent action'.[22] In reports despatched from Jeddah after his first visit to Feisal, Lawrence suggested a new approach to the Arab Revolt. In the *Arab Bulletin*, he stated: 'The Hejaz war is one of dervishes against regular troops – and we are on the side of the dervishes. Our text books do not apply to its conditions at all.'[23] The 'real sphere' of the Arabs, he reported to Cairo, was 'guerrilla warfare', and the British should support this.[24] Lawrence quickly gained support for this view, and other British officers with knowledge of explosives were sent to help the Arabs to cut the Hejaz railway. Lawrence also wanted to turn the focus of the revolt north towards Syria, where the activities of guerrilla forces could support a British advance from the Sinai into Palestine.

There has been endless debate about when Lawrence learned about the British commitments to the French in the Sykes-Picot Agreement, and therefore, about the extent to which he was consciously deceiving Feisal and his followers in encouraging them to dream of a future Arab nation which would include Syria and other areas earmarked for British, French or international control. Lawrence's superior, Bertie Clayton, had certainly known about the negotiations between Sykes and Picot since December 1915,[25] and it seems improbable to this author that someone of Lawrence's acuity and perception, working with Clayton, and after May 1916 in the Arab Bureau, did not know about the British undertakings to the French. Lawrence, more than most, understood the emotional and historic importance of Syria in the French imagination. Lawrence certainly believed that if Feisal and the Arabs liberated Damascus and other parts of Syria, they might pre-empt French claims, and at the very least strengthen their claims to autonomy there. On 30 October 1916, after meeting Feisal, he reported that the Sherif and his sons 'are definitely looking north, towards Syria and Baghdad', and argued that 'they are vindicating the rights of all Arabs to a national political existence'.[26] Early in January 1917, Lawrence requested a map of Syria.[27] To his parents in February 1917, Lawrence wrote a revealing passage: 'It is indiscreet only to ask what Arabia is. It has an East and a West and a South border – but where or what it is on the top no man knoweth. I fancy myself it is for the Arabs to find out!'[28]

The success of the Arab Revolt was in any case not assured. Despite the flow of British money to the Hejaz, it was notoriously difficult to keep Arab tribesmen away from their families for long periods, and after 6 months of the revolt Sherif Husein still had nothing resembling a trained army. Disputes between tribes were liable to break out at any time and threaten the precarious unity thus far achieved. The Turks were managing to repair damage to the Hejaz railway. Lawrence reported in December 1916 that there were still 'two trains of ten trucks each' travelling down it every day.[29] The garrison of Medina was well provisioned and not likely to surrender unless subjected to a determined assault. It appeared in December 1916, even to the most enthusiastic supporters, that the revolt might easily be crushed by the arrival of Turkish reinforcements. Lloyd George's new administration, although unwilling to deploy regular troops in the Hejaz, nonetheless determined that the revolt should not fail, and new impetus was given to supporting Husein and Feisal. Reginald Wingate had replaced McMahon as high commissioner in Egypt in October, and early in 1917 he recommended to the new Foreign Secretary, Arthur Balfour, that priority should be given to helping the Arabs to cut the Hejaz railway.[30] In January 1917, a joint operation between the British Navy, carrying a force of Arabs, and Feisal, advancing along the coast, was mounted to capture the small port of Wejh, well to the north of the ports already held by the Arabs on the Red Sea coast. Wejh was a good base for operations against the railway, and soon, under the direction of Herbert Garland, groups of Arabs were being trained in the use of explosives. Garland himself led raids on the railway in February.

There was now a new tempo to operations in the Middle East. The expeditionary force in Mesopotamia was at last achieving greater success, and on 11 March entered Baghdad.[31] A fortnight later a British force from Egypt attacked Gaza on the Mediterranean coast. Lawrence had already unfolded an ambitious plan to cut the Hejaz railway at several points. He wrote to Colonel Wilson in Jeddah: 'I think the weak part of the Turk plan lies in the trains of water & food. If we can cut the line on such a scale that they cannot repair it, or smash the locomotives, the force will come to standstill. . . . I am taking some Garland mines with me, if I can find instantaneous fuse, & if there is time, will set them as near Medina as possible.'[32] On 26 March Lawrence set out on the first of his expeditions as a guerrilla, travelling with a small band of Arabs, traversing huge areas of desert, attacking small groups of Turkish soldiers and destroying sections of the railway.[33]

Lawrence's exploits have been romanticized, but it is easy to underestimate both the danger he was exposed to, and the hardships, emotional and physical, he had to endure. Particularly at the start of his career as a guerrilla, he suffered terribly from fever, from sunstroke, and from sores and boils caused by long hours riding a camel. When he and Arab fighters attacked Turkish outposts, they had to be very brutal; the Arabs were reluctant to take prisoners and could not help opponents wounded in battle. Lawrence also had to act as judge, jury and sometimes as executioner when there were disputes among the Arabs; on this first expedition he had to shoot one man who had killed another after an argument. He and his fighters faced attacks from other Arabs, and knew that if they were captured by the Turks they could expect little mercy. Lawrence was undoubtedly helped by his own ascetic habits; he did not smoke or drink, and he cultivated an indifference to physical suffering. Even when resting during an expedition, or in pauses between expeditions, he wrote long reports, often accompanied by sketch maps, giving precise topographical details, identifying water supplies, possible landing grounds for aircraft and analysing the military potential of different Arab groups.

On 9 May 1917, Lawrence set off from Wejh on his most ambitious venture so far. There is some mystery about precisely where he went, but his intentions were clear. Lawrence and Feisal had conceived a bold plan to march north to Syria, using camels and supplies already gathered along the way to make such a long move possible. Lawrence's expedition in May was to prepare for this, and to sound out Arab opinion in Syria, with a view to spreading the revolt there. Over the next six weeks, Lawrence appears to have travelled north beyond Jerusalem, Amman and Damascus, reaching the Bekka valley (in present-day Lebanon) where he demolished 'a small plate girder bridge' at Ras Baalbek. He made other raids on the railway, but discovered that although many Syrian tribes were well disposed towards Feisal, they were unwilling to rise up independently and risk Turkish reprisals. By mid-June, when Lawrence had returned to the relative safety of Feisal's encampment at Wadi Sirhan, the revolt was again stalled. All the attacks on the railway had only prevented the Turks from using it for short periods.[34]

It was at this point that Lawrence and the Arabs achieved the dramatic success which had so far eluded them. They developed an ambitious plan to attack the small port of Akaba, at the most northerly point of the Arabian Red Sea coast, not from the sea, where its defences were concentrated, but from the land. Akaba had long attracted the attention of the Arabs, the British and the French because of its strategic position, close to the Hejaz railway, and sufficiently far north to supply the revolt if its focus moved towards Palestine and Syria, but an attack upon it had been considered too risky.[35] At the end of June, Lawrence, accompanied by Howeitat tribesmen, began a march towards Akaba from Bair, more than 150 miles to the north-east. Successfully defeating small groups of Turks on their way, the Arabs finally stormed into Akaba on 6 July. Displaying extraordinary energy and resource, Lawrence then immediately rode over the Sinai desert for 3 days to reach Cairo, where, still in Arab clothing, he appeared in Clayton's office at the Savoy Hotel to announce his success.[36] Wingate was able to telegraph the imperial general staff in London that 'Captain Lawrence arrived Cairo today by land from Aqaba. Turkish posts between Tafilah, Maan and Aqaba in Arab hands. Total Turkish losses 700 killed, 600 prisoners, including 20 officers.'[37]

## Service in Macedonia and Malta

Stanley Spencer's initial experience in another of the war's 'side shows' was less dramatic. After arriving in Macedonia in September 1916, he had to acclimatize himself to working with a Field Ambulance in an entirely unfamiliar environment. There was little actual fighting in the 15 miles of the line held by the British opposite Bulgarian forces in the Vardar valley, and although Spencer did no painting at this time, he experienced

FIGURE 22 *A British Army dressing station near Salonica. Stanley Spencer later recreated scenes from his service as a medical orderly in Macedonia in the Sandham Memorial Chapel at Burghclere.*

MAP 11 *Salonica*.

a deepening sense of spirituality. He was entranced by the landscape and developed a strong affinity with the mules he worked with. Here at Camp Corsica Spencer saw horse-drawn travoys bringing wounded men in to a casualty clearing station, imparting in his imagination God-like qualities to the surgeons who worked there.

His sister Florence sent him books through the post, and he spent much time reading. Illness was rife among the troops in Macedonia and from December 1916 through into January 1917 Spencer was confined to hospital in Salonica with malaria. Here he enjoyed drawing his fellow patients. Transferred out to the 68th Field Ambulance when recovered, Spencer was now thinking about how he might resume his career as an artist. He was storing up impressions, all the while dwelling on his present surroundings, his memories of Cookham, and learning from Shakespeare, Dickens, Dostoyevsky and the other writers he was immersed in. In March Spencer was again hospitalized with bronchitis and malaria. He was then assigned to the 143rd Field Ambulance near Todorova, and it was here that he experienced offensive action from behind the lines. The French commander of the multinational Allied force in Salonica, General Sarrail, mounted an attack against the Bulgarians in April, but it was entirely unsuccessful. After this brief interlude Spencer spent much of the summer of 1917 working on outwardly prosaic duties; as a non-drinker he was entrusted with fetching and distributing the men's beer ration.

In his letters Spencer said virtually nothing about the war, not wanting to offend the censor, and wrote instead about his impressions of the landscape and wildlife around him, about his reading and about his fellow soldiers. He told his sister Florence in March 1917, while in hospital, that although he had not really painted for 16 months that 'I have improved in my work more than if I had actually been at my work all the time.'[38] Over the next few weeks he wrote to her about the books she was sending him, notably Milton, Shakespeare, Blake and Andrew Marvell. These English writers spurred him to patriotic feeling, and in April he wrote to Florence that although war was horrible, he liked the heroism it brought out in individuals.[39] He returned to this theme again, not without irony, after reading more Shakespeare: 'Cry God for Harry! England & St. George! This is how I have been feeling all day. Oh! I wish I was a 'ero.'[40]

Spencer also dreamt of home. He wrote long letters to Desmond Chute, reconstructing scenes from his pre-war life in Cookham,[41] and, missing music, he thought back to hearing his older brother Will playing from Bach's 48 Preludes and Fugues after breakfast in Fernlea. He wrote to Will and his wife about this: 'They [the 48] used to give me such a desire to paint a great picture. That is just what great music or great pictures make me feel.... I feel when I return home, I shall be fresh for work.'[42] Spencer was though clearly still dissatisfied as a medical orderly. In August he saw a notice inviting volunteers to transfer from the RAMC to the infantry, and knowing that the 7th Battalion, Royal Berkshire Regiment was stationed nearby, Spencer put his name on the list. Since the start of the war he had wanted to serve in the infantry, but he knew that this was contrary to his parents' wishes. He wrote defensively to the Raverats: 'I do not care a rap what happens to me & you ought to follow my example and not care a rap either.... Try & reconcile my parents to what I have done; they will think it very wrong of me I fear.'[43] In October Spencer was posted for infantry training with the Royal Berkshire Regiment at No. 3 Base Infantry Depot in Salonica.[44]

The war also took Vera Brittain to new places. Leaving Southampton on the huge liner *Britannic* in September 1916, she travelled via Naples to the British base on the island of Lemnos, where, like so many of the expeditionary forces, she was taken ill. Inevitably she thought of Rupert Brooke, who had died nearby, but she also reflected on how female nurses who had died out in the Mediterranean were ignored, and wrote a short poem about them.[45] She was keenly aware of the danger to British ships and later confessed to her mother that she was 'in terror' aboard the *Britannic*.[46] Her fears were not misplaced. The *Brittanic* was sunk 6 weeks later near Lemnos. On 7 October, Brittain disembarked at Malta, now a collecting point for the many wounded and sick soldiers serving in the Mediterranean theatre.

For the next eight months Brittain worked at St George's Hospital near Valletta, and although still grieving for Roland Leighton, she clearly experienced here a degree of psychic recovery. She responded to the Mediterranean light and to Malta's warm climate. She was immensely refreshed to find that the VAD nurses there were treated far better than in London, with less emphasis on petty rules. The nursing work was not so gruelling. Brittain was growing up and was no longer the naïve but precocious individual who had left Buxton in October 1914. Her letters to her mother from this period display growing maturity and self-confidence, but also show how conservative she was in many ways. She wrote home in December 1916, suggesting that the war might go on for another 5 years, but that when it finished she would go back to Oxford. She was excited to hear about the fall of the Asquith government, and echoing the newspapers, she hoped that there would now be a more vigorous 'prosecution' of the war. Reflecting on her own age group whose lives had been wrenched from their ordinary course, she wrote: 'it is very hard that we should be the generation to suffer the war, though I suppose it is very splendid too, & is making us better & wiser & deeper men and women (at any rate some of us.) . . . It seems to me that the war will make a big division of "before" and "after" in the history of the world'.[47]

These reflections were partly prompted by the sense of distance from the war which she experienced on Malta. News from Britain reached the island only slowly, and increasing German submarine activity in the Mediterranean contributed to the isolation. Nonetheless, Brittain followed events as closely as she could, and in the spring of 1917 her fragile equanimity was shattered by news from home. On 18 April she heard that Victor Richardson had been seriously injured in the Arras offensive, and on 1 May news arrived that Geoffrey Thurlow had been killed.[48] Since Roland Leighton's death, Brittain had focused much of her concern on his two former school friends, particularly on Thurlow, and she now decided to try to help Richardson, who had lost his sight. Her 6-month contract had expired, fortuitously leaving her free, and on 22 May 1917 she left Malta.

It took 6 days for Brittain to return to England, and travelling by train she passed through the 'war zone' in northern France behind the front. Once in London, 'she spent the next ten days in constant attendance' on Richardson in hospital. In an access of romantic feeling, she undertook to stay with him for life, but after a sudden deterioration in his condition, he died on 9 June. Edward Brittain came home on leave shortly afterwards and shared his sister's grief. According to her biographers he was 'distant and withdrawn, solemnly and repeatedly playing Elgar's "Lament for the Fallen" at the piano'.[49] Vera Brittain had, after nearly 3 years, stopped writing her 'Great War Diary', and we have no record of her private feelings at this time.

## Conscripts arrive at the front

A grim sign of the intensification of the war in 1916 was the establishment across Britain of some 1,800 Military Service Tribunals to assess whether men claiming exemption from conscription should be called up.[50] There was a distinct turn in the poetry of Ellis Evans at this time, brought about partly by hearing of the death of local men, and perhaps also by the awareness that he would be forced to enlist. He wrote two of his most enduring poems in 1916, one of them an *englyn* (a condensed four-line lament)

'In Memoriam' for D. O. Evans from Blaenau Ffestiniog, another titled 'Rhyfel' or, in translation, 'War'. The *englyn*, translated, runs thus:

> His sacrifice will never fade – his beloved
> countenance will not be forgotten
> though Germany stained
> her steel fist in his blood.

Evans expressed here his antipathy to the war in conventionally patriotic rhetoric, but in 'Rhyfel', he was more outspoken. In the first two stanzas of the poem he lamented God's absence from the world, and the prevalence of violence, which, he noted, was visited above all on the poor. The third and final stanza has become well known in Wales:

> The harps that once could help our pain
>   Hang silent, to the willows pinned.
>   The cry of battle fills the wind
> And the blood of the lads – it falls like rain.[51]

Unfortunately the records of the Military Service Tribunals in Wales have almost entirely disappeared, so it is difficult to reconstruct more than the outlines of Evans' experience before them. We know that, in common with most men called up, he appealed for exemption, in his case on grounds of vital agricultural work, and we know that this appeal was rejected.[52] The Evans family was told that one of its two sons of military age was to be conscripted, and as the older, Ellis accepted this as his fate. In January 1917 he reported to Litherland Camp near Liverpool as a private in the 15th (London Welsh) Battalion of the Royal Welch Fusiliers.[53] We may judge quite how little known he was as a poet from the fact that none of the other famous writers coincidentally grouped in this unit – including Robert Graves, Siegfried Sassoon, Frank Richards and David Jones – appear ever to have been aware of his existence. Sassoon was at Litherland Camp only weeks before Evans arrived and left a gloomy account of his experience.[54] The life of a new private there in the harsh winter of 1917 must have been, for the most part, a mixture of discomfort, boredom and tiredness. One letter originally written in Welsh from Ellis Evans survives, and in it he said: 'There is little poetry here but plenty of poets for most of the men and officers are Welshmen. . . . I get little news from Trawsfynydd. The folk of Yr Ysgwrn [the Evans family home] are very bad with things like that. They only ask about my shirts and socks in every letter.'[55]

Evans actually did little training, as he was one of the recruits from farming families allowed 7 weeks' leave to help with the spring ploughing. Evans spent most of this time at home working on an epic poem, to be entitled, without irony, 'Yr Arwr' ('The Hero'), for the National Eisteddfod, due to be held in Birkenhead in September that year. On 9 June Evans arrived with other recruits at Rouen in France, just one of tens of thousands being concentrated for Haig's planned offensive. He wrote to a friend: 'Heavy weather, heavy soul, heavy heart. That is an uncomfortable trinity, isn't it? I never saw a land more beautiful in spite of the curse that has landed upon it. The dreams are as beautiful as the dreams of old kings.'[56] After several weeks Evans and others were moved to Fléchin. Here he finished his poem for the *eisteddfod*; it was posted, bearing the nom-de-plume of 'Fleur-de-Lis', on 15 July.

The external story of David Jones' war after his injury on the Somme in July 1916 is quickly told. He was taken back to England, first to Birmingham, but as his was only a flesh wound which quickly healed, he was sent on to a convalescent hospital in Warwickshire, at Shipston-on-Stour. Here he fell in love with a VAD nurse, Elsie Hancock, but she already had a fiancé at the front. Although she obviously liked him, their relationship remained strictly platonic. Jones' release from hospital was hastened by the outrage of a doctor who discovered that he had visited her for strawberries and cream. After a couple of weeks' leave with his family, Jones was sent back out to the London Welsh Battalion, now in trenches to the north of Ypres. He spent much of the next ten months in this increasingly desolate area, where the battalion was frequently exposed to concentrated shell fire. Fortunately for Jones, a series of assignments kept him away from the front for much of the hard winter of 1916/17. He was employed drawing maps at Battalion headquarters, then posted to a Field Survey Unit and to an Observation Group to plot flashes of enemy guns for counter-battery fire. Jones' training as an artist was partly responsible for these postings, but given that he was not particularly successful in any of these roles, it would appear that as an old hand, previously wounded, he was deliberately kept away from the front line, where conscripts were now taking the place of those killed and injured in earlier actions.

Jones spent time in March 1917 behind the line in Rouen and in Etaples, where he had to undergo training at the notorious 'Bull Ring'. After this he returned, with the London Welsh, to Ypres, in preparation for Haig's planned offensive. The Welsh Division was still at the northern end of the Salient, opposite the Pilckem Ridge. The Division History states that this was 'a comparatively quiet time', but emphasis needs to be placed on the word 'comparatively'. As well as shelling and mortaring, there were frequent raids, both German and British, which resulted in brief but nightmarish incursions into the front-line trenches. In one of these 'some fifty Germans' were killed 'with the bayonet'.[57]

David Jones made a number of drawings at this time, not dissimilar in character to those he made before Mametz Wood. He had time as an artillery observer to take note of his surroundings, and he also drew the instruments he used. He drew fellow soldiers and officers, and a German prisoner, perhaps taken in a raid. This is a rare portrayal of a living individual enemy, not in allegorical or symbolic form. The German is shown in profile, his cropped hair emphasizing the angular squareness of his head. He does indeed appear gaunt and potentially menacing, but Jones rendered him sympathetic and human by showing him eating a biscuit.[58] Three of Jones' pictures from this period were drawn for a wider audience. While on convalescent leave, Jones was asked by his old teacher Hartrick to depict his experience at Mametz Wood for *The Graphic*. The resulting image, published on 9 September 1916, entitled *Close Quarters*, was a conventional representation of British soldiers, with bayonets fixed, advancing through dense woodland, one falling backwards, dead or wounded. In a poignant detail, one, with the face of a boy, is shown looking back towards his comrades after falling to the ground. He has lost his helmet and possibly his rifle. The picture was accompanied by a text arguing that elements of 'old-time warfare' still prevailed, notably when men were engaged in hand-to-hand fighting. The caption drew comparisons with the fighting in 'Napoleon's day', noting how the men portrayed were 'helmeted like their ancestors at Agincourt'. It added that the artist himself had been wounded in the action depicted.[59]

In the other two drawings, Jones reverted to allegory, harking back to an imagined chivalric world. He drew a New Year's card for his father to print, entitled, in Welsh, *A oes heddwch?* This is the question 'Is there Peace?' traditionally asked three times by the Archdruid at an *eisteddfod*, who sheathes his sword when the congregation answers 'Heddwch' (Peace) three times. The card showed a damsel in white, accompanied by a tonsured monk anxiously watching two knights in armour who were locked in combat. In another picture published in *The Graphic* in January 1917, entitled *Germany and Peace*, Jones again used the gendered imagery which had dominated reporting from Belgium at the start of the war. Clearly alluding to the German 'peace offensive', Jones again portrayed a damsel in distress kneeling in a graveyard, with a ruined church behind her. White doves of peace flutter about her. She looks fearfully at an armoured knight with a huge drawn sword in one hand, his shield decorated with a Teutonic eagle. With his other hand he makes a gesture of appeasement.[60] Thomas Dilworth notes how the damsels in both drawings resemble Elsie Hancock, the nurse Jones had met in Shipston-on-Stour.

While on leave in September 1916 Jones had also written an essay entitled 'A French Vision'. If Jones' drawing of *Germany and Peace* was equivocal, representing Germany as militaristic and threatening, but seeming to concede that its peace offer might be sincere, this essay is not. It is structured around a repetition of the question 'Is it worth it?', and pictures soldiers and officers in a typical trench, cold and muddy, reflecting on the misery and danger they now face. Reverting to the imagery of medieval warfare, the men entertain the idea that 'in the old days', when 'war was so different' it might have been 'fine' and 'grand', but now it is now more than 'wholesale butchery'. But, Jones concludes, if these men had not gone to war, 'Europe to-day might lie prostrate 'neath the iron heel of the Teuton terror'. So, the soldier 'goes to his post to watch for marauding Huns – goes with the smile of contentment. The trench is still cold and wet; eyes still ache, and hands freeze. But it's worth it!' Jones' father, evidently impressed, corrected his son's spelling and punctuation, and sent a copy of the essay to Lloyd George.[61]

The experience of the Ypres Salient did not change Jones' view of the war as a conflict between good and evil. He wrote a long letter to his vicar, which was then published in *The Christian Herald* on 17 May 1917, at a point when the French Army was paralysed with mutinies and when cynicism was spreading among the British troops after the Arras offensive. In this letter Jones reflected on his military service, and, like Kate Finzi, he marvelled at the way northern France had become 'like an English Colony'. He reported a conversation with 'a fairly well-educated French woman' which confirmed the accuracy of the 'press accounts of Hun barbarities' in 1914 and asked himself whether the 'Bosch prisoners' he saw were put to work in places they had earlier occupied, 'when, with vandal joy, they gloated over a prostrate and stricken Belgium'. If Jones' use of language was conventional, his front-line service had at least made him doubtful that the war might end soon. He concluded 'Like yourselves at home, we have to live in hope that 1917 may see the end of the struggle – but of course to discuss the "duration of the war" is worse than futile.'[62]

In May 1917, the Welsh Division was ordered to dig assembly trenches close to the front line on the northern edge of the Ypres Salient. This was difficult and dangerous work, which had to be carried out at night under shell fire. After this the Division, strengthened by the arrival of new conscripts like Ellis Evans, trained behind the lines at St Hilaire on 'a replica of the trenches and strong points to be attacked'.[63] On 19 and 20 July the Division moved back into the Salient, to Camp Dublin on the banks of the Yser Canal. By this time the British artillery barrage was strengthening, and the Germans were responding in kind. On 23 July the first shells carrying mustard gas exploded among the Welsh soldiers. The Diary of the London Welsh Battalion, in which Jones and Evans were serving, recorded on 24 July: 'Several of Bn. officers & men suffering from effects of gas shells sent over the night before. Nearly all these were eye cases, the gas having got in & blinded the majority of the men.'[64]

On 27 July patrols sent to probe the German defences confirmed that the enemy's front line had been evacuated, but that the second line was strongly held. This allowed the Welsh Division to move well forward into the previously prepared assembly trenches on the night of 30 July. The British barrage and the German counter barrage had now intensified to an unprecedented level. We can only try to imagine how utterly hellish this must have been for the young men crouching in the assembly trenches, some, like Ellis Evans, complete novices, all facing the prospect of going 'over the top' in the grey light of dawn. Some broke under the strain. A private in the Welsh Division recorded: 'One person he broke down, he started screeching like a pig, well he screeched like a stuck pig. He was sent back. It was no fault of his; it wasn't cowardice. We knew the fellow, he wasn't the type of boy who played football or roughed it up a bit. He was temperamental, a brilliant pianist and in fact he shouldn't have been in the army at all.'65

## Official War Artists

Paul Nash was training in England right through 1916, while others who had joined up later were gaining direct experience of the war. In the spring he was posted for officer training, and to work as a 'map instructor' at Hare Hall Camp, near Romford, but he still managed to enjoy life. We have several testimonies to Nash's ability – even in the army – to arrange things to his own benefit, and it seems that training at Romford was fairly congenial. He met there the writer Edward Thomas, who had hesitated for a full year since August 1914 before volunteering. They shared a love for the countryside which they indulged in off-duty hours. Thomas wrote to Robert Frost in May 1916: 'I was with a young artist named Paul Nash who has just joined us as a map reader. . . . He is wonderful at finding birds' nests.'66

Their friendship was to be ended, like so many, by the war and by the need for junior officers to replace those lost on the Somme. Thomas was drafted out as an artillery officer in January 1917 and was killed during the Arras offensive in April. Nash wrote to his wife that he 'didn't consider' signing up for the tanks, and decided against the Machine Gun Corps as 'it is spoken of as a suicide club'.67 He was gazetted as a 2nd Lieutenant in the Hampshire Regiment in December 1916 and left England on 22 February 1917.

In early March, two-and-a-half years after joining up, he reached the trenches, near St Eloi, to the south of Ypres. His first letters back to his wife reveal something of the conflicting emotions he experienced there. Like many British soldiers, he was struck by the natural beauty of France and by the tension between the recuperative powers of nature and the destructive impact of war: 'Flowers bloom everywhere . . . and where I sit now in the reserve line the place is just joyous, the dandelions are bright gold over the parapet, and nearby a lilac bush is breaking into bloom; in a wood passed through on our way up, a place with an evil name, pitted and pocked with shells the trees torn to shreds, often reeking with poison gas – a most ruinous desolate place two months back, to-day it was a vivid green.' He was also moved to draw: 'yesterday I sent off six finished sketches to you which after much labour I have managed to work up to a pitch of presentability'. It is noteworthy how an intelligent young man, who understood what might be in store for him – he had just read of Thomas' death – was still positive and enthusiastic: 'I feel very happy these days, in fact, I believe I am happier in the trenches than anywhere out here. It sounds absurd, but life has a greater meaning here and a new zest, and beauty is more poignant.'68

For the next two months Nash experienced the life of a British junior officer in the Ypres Salient; fortunately it was a relatively quiet period there, and he spent much of this time behind the front lines and on training courses. He was fascinated by the appearance of the landscape, writing: 'Oh, these wonderful trenches at night, at dawn, at sundown! Shall I ever lose the picture they have made in my mind. Imagine a wide landscape flat and scantily wooded and what trees remain blasted and torn, naked and scarred and riddled. The ground for miles around furrowed into trenches, pitted with yawning holes in which the water lies still and cold or heaped with mounds of earth, tangles of rusty wire, tin plates, sandbags and all the refuse of war.'[69] During these weeks Nash sent many drawings home to his wife. He got on well with his fellow officers, writing: 'I confess to you this thing that brings men to fight and suffer together, no matter from what original or subsequent motives, is a very great and healthy force.'[70] Soon though, Nash was back in England, at the Swedish Hospital in Marylebone. On a dark night, going out to observe 'the result of a short bombardment over the enemy lines', he had fallen into a trench and dislocated a rib.[71]

While Nash was remarkably cheerful about being sent to Flanders, Richard Nevinson was not. His desperate efforts to escape conscription in 1916 had failed, and his father turned next to the idea of getting him appointed as an Official War Artist. This was a possibility because of a scheme developed within the Foreign Office by Charles Masterman, a Liberal politician tasked in August 1914 with coordinating government propaganda. Working from Wellingon House, Masterman was persuaded in 1916 to employ the illustrator Muirhead Bone to record the activities of the BEF in Flanders, and to provide material for propaganda. Bone was a talented illustrator and draughtsman, and after visiting the 'war zone' in August 1916, he produced some two hundred drawings which were reproduced for sale in monthly editions. Following this, eventually more than 20 artists would be commissioned by the British Government to provide a visual record of the war.

Henry Nevinson was a good friend of Charles Masterman, and over several months, he lobbied hard on behalf of his son. Masterman visited Nevinson's enormously successful exhibition of war paintings in September 1916. Henry Nevinson exploited other contacts to promote the notion that his son could contribute to the war effort; in October 1916 he sought permission for his son to visit some munitions factories.[72] Father and son together also explored the possibility of Richard Nevinson doing camouflage painting for the armed forces; and in April 1917 he went to the depot of the Machine Gun Corps at Grantham to enquire about map work.[73] Henry Nevinson finally managed to get Muirhead Bone to support his son's candidacy as an official artist, and on 29 June, Richard Nevinson was issued with a contract to work in this role. For the increasingly anxious young Futurist, this was an extraordinary piece of luck, as the House of Commons had just passed an

Act reviewing exemptions from military service which made him once again eligible for conscription.[74]

Mightily relieved, Richard Nevinson now readied himself for his new job, taking aeroplane and balloon flights at Hendon to prepare for pictures of aerial warfare. He wrote to Masterman: 'I hope I shall be able to make a fine record & that my pictures will give the civilian public some insight as to the marvellous endurance of our soldiers & the real meaning of the hardships they are called upon to face.'[75] On 5 July he departed for France.

## Fight for Right?

Through the winter of 1916 and into early 1917 Elgar struggled with his health. The painful 'electric cautery' of his throat which he had undergone in August 1916 brought no relief and was repeated in January 1917.[76] His fascination with the Zeppelins continued, and in October 1916 he went with his wife – and a 'great crowd' to see the wreckage of one which had been brought down at Bunning Hill. They followed this up with a visit to the Nevinson pictures at the Leicester Galleries. Alice Elgar wrote: 'rather vivid but not art – or to live except as pictures of war'.[77] Anxiously they followed the political crisis, Alice writing on 4 December: 'We are longing for Asquith to go.' Like Vera Brittain, she shared the widespread assumption that Lloyd George would prosecute the war with more energy. On 12 December she wrote: 'D. G. Asquith gone and Lloyd George Prime Minister'.[78] We do not know if her husband shared her confidence. Three compositional projects occupied Elgar in the New Year. One, the music for a ballet called *The Sanguine Fan*, had nothing to do with the war. The second was a setting of Kipling poems celebrating the merchant navy, and Elgar threw himself into this in March 1917. He planned to stage these settings with singers dressed as sailors and to get 'a broad, saltwater style' to the production.[79] The show, titled *The Fringes of the Fleet* and fronted by the young baritone Charles Mott, was ready to run at the Coliseum in June. It was a huge success, attracting sell-out crowds, including many servicemen on leave. Elgar thoroughly enjoyed directing the performances, and he also made recordings of the songs.

Once again, his contribution to the war effort was to be undermined. Charles Mott had been conscripted into the Artists' Rifles, and although he was, with Elgar's help, able to postpone his call-up, at the end of July he had to go. More seriously, Rudyard Kipling was unhappy with Elgar's use of his poems. In August 1917 he asked Elgar to stop further performances.[80]

The third project was Elgar's as yet incomplete setting of the Binyon poems. The first of these, 'August 1914', had depicted Germany as the 'vampire of Europe's wasted will', and Elgar struggled with this. He was deeply indebted to German musical culture, and many of his best friends and artistic collaborators were German, or of German descent. Several,

lost monstrous.'[85] A month later, Parry wrote again, having heard that
or Gurney was due to return to the front: 'Poor Gurney. It is horrible to
think that he has to go back so soon into the vortex of barbarism. We have
just heard that one of the nicest boys we ever had at the college, young
Goodwin, has been killed. Our anxieties are neverending.'[86]

## A crisis of representation?

Parry's anxieties were symptomatic of a wider crisis. Across Europe the continuation of the war and the hugely increased toll of casualties was causing unprecedented strains at all levels. At a strategic level it was not yet clear how the German conquest of Romania, the Russian Revolution and the American declaration of war would play out. The failure of the peace feelers put out by Germany in December 1916 had demonstrated how deeply entrenched both sides were, not just in the mud and clay of the battlefields, but in the imaginations of politicians, soldiers and civilians. Having suffered so greatly, it was, at this stage, impossible for any of the combatants to contemplate relinquishing, in the German case, their existing gains, and in the Allied case, their lofty ideals for the liberation of Belgium, Serbia and Montenegro. The British had also added a whole dimension to the war against German aggression which had been entered into in August 1914. Lloyd George's government was now demanding the 'liberation of the peoples' under 'the murderous tyranny of the Turks'. Given that the Asquith government had entered into secret agreement with the French and the Russians to divide the Middle East between them after driving out the Turks, this was not merely a huge extension of British war aims, but potentially a betrayal of the understandings of a just crusade to uphold international law which the British people had responded to in 1914.

There was also a crisis of representation in Britain. Although traditional views of war anchored in historical imagination, like those of David Jones in *The Graphic* or Lawrence's presentation of Feisal in the *Arab Bulletin*, and still tapping into discourses of chivalry, heroism and sacrifice were still being produced, there was a growing awareness that they corresponded less and less with the reality of war which the public was glimpsing in film and in photographs from the front. It is no coincidence that both Elgar and Parry found themselves in 1917 turning away from 'war music' and that Nevinson produced no significant work in the first half of 1917. Paul Nash was turning to Vorticism as a way of representing his first impressions of the Western Front, while Spencer was only groping towards a way of representing the horrible drudgery he had endured at Beaufort Hospital. Vera Brittain, bowed under the weight of personal loss, had ceased writing the 'Great War Diary' in which she had recorded her earlier enthusiasm. Ellis Evans, who clearly had no wish to be a soldier, was writing escapist poetry which had nothing to do with his new experience as a conscript. Kate Finzi, now removed from the 'war zone', had seen her diary published, but it appears that she too had stopped any further representation of the war. There is no clear record of her carrying out any further war work. As a young woman from a comfortable background who had completed her voluntary service, Finzi was in a privileged position where she could choose to opt out, having done her bit. The other subjects of this study were perhaps less fortunate.

For the next two months Nash experienced the life of a British junior officer in the Ypres Salient; fortunately it was a relatively quiet period there, and he spent much of this time behind the front lines and on training courses. He was fascinated by the appearance of the landscape, writing: 'Oh, these wonderful trenches at night, at dawn, at sundown! Shall I ever lose the picture they have made in my mind. Imagine a wide landscape flat and scantily wooded and what trees remain blasted and torn, naked and scarred and riddled. The ground for miles around furrowed into trenches, pitted with yawning holes in which the water lies still and cold or heaped with mounds of earth, tangles of rusty wire, tin plates, sandbags and all the refuse of war.'[69] During these weeks Nash sent many drawings home to his wife. He got on well with his fellow officers, writing: 'I confess to you this thing that brings men to fight and suffer together, no matter from what original or subsequent motives, is a very great and healthy force.'[70] Soon though, Nash was back in England, at the Swedish Hospital in Marylebone. On a dark night, going out to observe 'the result of a short bombardment over the enemy lines', he had fallen into a trench and dislocated a rib.[71]

While Nash was remarkably cheerful about being sent to Flanders, Richard Nevinson was not. His desperate efforts to escape conscription in 1916 had failed, and his father turned next to the idea of getting him appointed as an Official War Artist. This was a possibility because of a scheme developed within the Foreign Office by Charles Masterman, a Liberal politician tasked in August 1914 with coordinating government propaganda. Working from Wellingon House, Masterman was persuaded in 1916 to employ the illustrator Muirhead Bone to record the activities of the BEF in Flanders, and to provide material for propaganda. Bone was a talented illustrator and draughtsman, and after visiting the 'war zone' in August 1916, he produced some two hundred drawings which were reproduced for sale in monthly editions. Following this, eventually more than 20 artists would be commissioned by the British Government to provide a visual record of the war.

Henry Nevinson was a good friend of Charles Masterman, and over several months, he lobbied hard on behalf of his son. Masterman visited Nevinson's enormously successful exhibition of war paintings in September 1916. Henry Nevinson exploited other contacts to promote the notion that his son could contribute to the war effort; in October 1916 he sought permission for his son to visit some munitions factories.[72] Father and son together also explored the possibility of Richard Nevinson doing camouflage painting for the armed forces; and in April 1917 he went to the depot of the Machine Gun Corps at Grantham to enquire about map work.[73] Henry Nevinson finally managed to get Muirhead Bone to support his son's candidacy as an official artist, and on 29 June, Richard Nevinson was issued with a contract to work in this role. For the increasingly anxious young Futurist, this was an extraordinary piece of luck, as the House of Commons had just passed an

Act reviewing exemptions from military service which made him once again eligible for conscription.[74]

Mightily relieved, Richard Nevinson now readied himself for his new job, taking aeroplane and balloon flights at Hendon to prepare for pictures of aerial warfare. He wrote to Masterman: 'I hope I shall be able to make a fine record & that my pictures will give the civilian public some insight as to the marvellous endurance of our soldiers & the real meaning of the hardships they are called upon to face.'[75] On 5 July he departed for France.

## Fight for Right?

Through the winter of 1916 and into early 1917 Elgar struggled with his health. The painful 'electric cautery' of his throat which he had undergone in August 1916 brought no relief and was repeated in January 1917.[76] His fascination with the Zeppelins continued, and in October 1916 he went with his wife – and a 'great crowd' to see the wreckage of one which had been brought down at Bunning Hill. They followed this up with a visit to the Nevinson pictures at the Leicester Galleries. Alice Elgar wrote: 'rather vivid but not art – or to live except as pictures of war'.[77] Anxiously they followed the political crisis, Alice writing on 4 December: 'We are longing for Asquith to go.' Like Vera Brittain, she shared the widespread assumption that Lloyd George would prosecute the war with more energy. On 12 December she wrote: 'D. G. Asquith gone and Lloyd George Prime Minister'.[78] We do not know if her husband shared her confidence. Three compositional projects occupied Elgar in the New Year. One, the music for a ballet called *The Sanguine Fan*, had nothing to do with the war. The second was a setting of Kipling poems celebrating the merchant navy, and Elgar threw himself into this in March 1917. He planned to stage these settings with singers dressed as sailors and to get 'a broad, saltwater style' to the production.[79] The show, titled *The Fringes of the Fleet* and fronted by the young baritone Charles Mott, was ready to run at the Coliseum in June. It was a huge success, attracting sell-out crowds, including many servicemen on leave. Elgar thoroughly enjoyed directing the performances, and he also made recordings of the songs.

Once again, his contribution to the war effort was to be undermined. Charles Mott had been conscripted into the Artists' Rifles, and although he was, with Elgar's help, able to postpone his call-up, at the end of July he had to go. More seriously, Rudyard Kipling was unhappy with Elgar's use of his poems. In August 1917 he asked Elgar to stop further performances.[80]

The third project was Elgar's as yet incomplete setting of the Binyon poems. The first of these, 'August 1914', had depicted Germany as the 'vampire of Europe's wasted will', and Elgar struggled with this. He was deeply indebted to German musical culture, and many of his best friends and artistic collaborators were German, or of German descent. Several, such as the financier Edgar Speyer, had been publicly vilified. The conductor Hans Richter, who had championed Elgar's work before 1914, had returned to Germany and severed his contacts with Britain. The widow of Elgar's late friend and publisher August Jaeger – the 'Nimrod' of the *Enigma Variations* – had changed her name to Hunter. All this pained Elgar deeply, and he was reluctant to join in a blanket condemnation of the Germans, although friends urged him to complete the Binyon settings. In March 1917, with some reluctance, Elgar set *August 1914*, using his music from the 'Demon's Chorus' in *The Dream of Gerontius* to depict the Germans. He explained this decision to Ernest Newman, his discomfort apparent:

> two years ago I held over that section hoping that some trace of manly spirit would shew itself in the direction of German affairs: that hope is gone for ever & the Hun is branded a less than a beast for very many generations: so I wd. not invent anything low & bestial enough to illustrate the one stanza; the Cardinal [Newman] invented . . . the particular hell in Gerontius where the great intellects gibber & snarl knowing they have fallen: this is exactly the case with the Germans now: – the music was to hand & I have sparingly used it.
>
> And this ends, as far as I can see, my contribution to war music.[81]

Parry's most significant contribution to 'war music', his anthem 'Jerusalem', was growing in popularity, but he was increasingly unhappy with the song's link to the Fight for Right movement, and in May 1917, he formally withdrew his support from the group.[82] Curiously, the song had also been taken up by others. On 17 March, Parry conducted the Ladies Choir of the Albert Hall singing 'Jerusalem' at a meeting calling for National Service for Women. Although he found the speeches that evening rather tedious, he was much happier to see his music associated with this campaign than with Fight for Right.[83]

Parry was also oppressed by the fate of some his most talented individual students. By early 1917 the Royal College of Music, like other institutions of higher education, was seriously depleted and struggling to maintain anything like its peacetime routine. Parry heard in February that Douglas Fox, a brilliant organist, had lost an arm and wrote to Fox's father: 'Thank you for your letter about this truly horrible tragedy. I don't think that anything that has happened in this atrocious war has so impressed me with the very malignity of cruelty as the utter destruction of that dear boy's gifts.'[84] Parry shared his anxiety with Herbert Howells, a former student who had been exempted from service on health grounds. He wrote to him in April 1917: 'The thought of so many very gifted boys being in danger, such as Gurney and Fox and Benjamin and even Vaughan-Williams, is always present with me. This is what horrible, senseless war means – and we can do nothing. . . . Gurney's case I feel to be quite a special martyrdom. His mind is so full of thoughts and feeling far removed from crude barbarities that is seems almost monstrous.'[85] A month later, Parry wrote again, having heard that Ivor Gurney was due to return to the front: 'Poor Gurney. It is horrible to think that he has to go back so soon into the vortex of barbarism. We have just heard that one of the nicest boys we ever had at the college, young Goodwin, has been killed. Our anxieties are neverending.'[86]

## A crisis of representation?

Parry's anxieties were symptomatic of a wider crisis. Across Europe the continuation of the war and the hugely increased toll of casualties was causing unprecedented strains at all levels. At a strategic level it was not yet clear how the German conquest of Romania, the Russian Revolution and the American declaration of war would play out. The failure of the peace feelers put out by Germany in December 1916 had demonstrated how deeply entrenched both sides were, not just in the mud and clay of the battlefields, but in the imaginations of politicians, soldiers and civilians. Having suffered so greatly, it was, at this stage, impossible for any of the combatants to contemplate relinquishing, in the German case, their existing gains, and in the Allied case, their lofty ideals for the liberation of Belgium, Serbia and Montenegro. The British had also added a whole dimension to the war against German aggression which had been entered into in August 1914. Lloyd George's government was now demanding the 'liberation of the peoples' under 'the murderous tyranny of the Turks'. Given that the Asquith government had entered into secret agreement with the French and the Russians to divide the Middle East between them after driving out the Turks, this was not merely a huge extension of British war aims, but potentially a betrayal of the understandings of a just crusade to uphold international law which the British people had responded to in 1914.

There was also a crisis of representation in Britain. Although traditional views of war anchored in historical imagination, like those of David Jones in *The Graphic* or Lawrence's presentation of Feisal in the *Arab Bulletin*, and still tapping into discourses of chivalry, heroism and sacrifice were still being produced, there was a growing awareness that they corresponded less and less with the reality of war which the public was glimpsing in film and in photographs from the front. It is no coincidence that both Elgar and Parry found themselves in 1917 turning away from 'war music' and that Nevinson produced no significant work in the first half of 1917. Paul Nash was turning to Vorticism as a way of representing his first impressions of the Western Front, while Spencer was only groping towards a way of representing the horrible drudgery he had endured at Beaufort Hospital. Vera Brittain, bowed under the weight of personal loss, had ceased writing the 'Great War Diary' in which she had recorded her earlier enthusiasm. Ellis Evans, who clearly had no wish to be a soldier, was writing escapist poetry which had nothing to do with his new experience as a conscript. Kate Finzi, now

removed from the 'war zone', had seen her diary published, but it appears that she too had stopped any further representation of the war. There is no clear record of her carrying out any further war work. As a young woman from a comfortable background who had completed her voluntary service, Finzi was in a privileged position where she could choose to opt out, having done her bit. The other subjects of this study were perhaps less fortunate.

# CHAPTER EIGHT

# August–December 1917

The Third Battle of Ypres, or Passchendaele as it has become known, started on 31 July 1917. For months men and munitions had been concentrated in the Ypres Salient, where they faced the most heavily fortified positions the Germans had yet developed. This defence was based on thousands of concrete pillboxes sunk into the marshy ground, presenting only a low profile to any attackers. Behind their lines, the Germans had massed over 1,000 guns, and from the higher ground, they were able to sweep the whole area with machine guns and shells. In July 1917, they added a new weapon to their arsenal: mustard gas. The Ypres Salient had been fought over again and again since October 1914, and the whole landscape was already cratered with shell holes. Its fragile drainage system was finally shattered by the intense British barrage preceding the attack on 31 July.

Haig's attack started at 3.50 a.m., and on the left and the centre many of its initial objectives were gained. Nonetheless, Haig's army suffered 27,000 casualties, and in counter-attacks later in the day the Germans regained some of their lost ground. It also started to rain heavily in the afternoon, making aerial observation impossible; over the next days and weeks this rain continued, turning the ground into a sea of mud. Renewed artillery bombardment made the ground more and more impassable. Further assaults in August brought heavy casualties and only tiny gains. As the battle raged, conditions became more and more horrible for both sides. Neither could maintain a continuous line of trenches in the wasted landscape, and soldiers on both sides were reduced to crouching in shell holes, or if they could, finding sanctuary in a pillbox. Haig drove his men on, encouraged during September by drier weather which allowed tiny advances. The apparent success of the attack on 26 September, which alone incurred 15,000 British casualties,[1] reinforced Haig's belief in a decisive victory by December and made it difficult for Lloyd George to call the offensive off. Although his

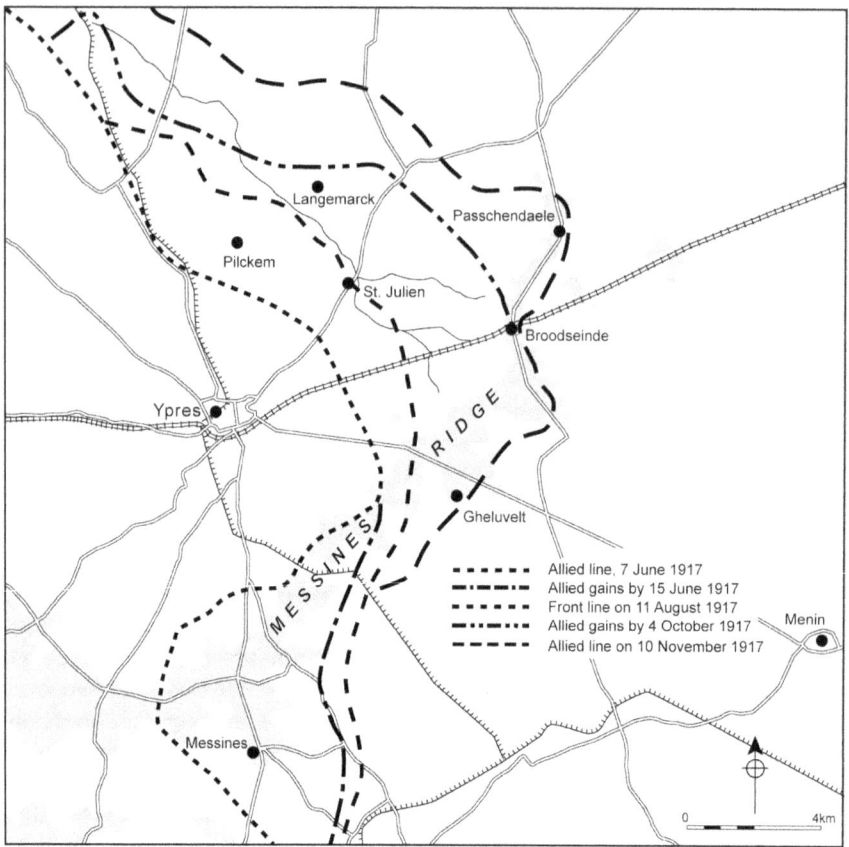

MAP 12 *Passchendaele*.

misgivings remained, he and the War Cabinet made no further attempt to review the campaign. Through October, the offensive was constantly renewed, even though the weather had turned again, and by now it was incredibly difficult even to move in the salient, let alone to fight. Men and animals could only walk on tracks made of duckboards, and these were swept by shellfire. Tanks were useless, and many were abandoned in the mud. Even after the Canadian Corps captured the pulverized ruins of the village of Passchendaele on 6 November, Haig continued his attacks. Only on 12 November was the offensive abandoned.

It is difficult to reconcile historical accounts of this battle, with their descriptions of intended attacks and counter-attacks, with eyewitness accounts by participants. Typically these could see no further than a few yards at any point as they struggled through the mud, cowered in shell holes or found sanctuary in a pillbox surrounded by corpses. Only rarely did they see a living enemy soldier, and frequently they had no idea where other units were in relation their own position. The idea of a breakthrough from the salient had been utterly illusory. The necessary preconditions for amphibious landings behind the German lines had not been fulfilled. The attackers had at the most advanced point gained only a few thousand yards of shattered ground, enlarging a salient which was still surrounded on three sides by strong German defences. The British had sustained some 200,000 casualties, and the surviving officers and soldiers had witnessed scenes of horror that would scar them for ever. Shocking scenes of men struggling in the mud which have since been frequently reprinted were published in Britain. The *Daily Mirror* published William Rider-Rider's photograph of Canadian soldiers in shell holes, and *The Times* carried a horrifying photograph of stretcher-bearers knee deep in mud bringing in a wounded man from the battlefield.[2] *The Graphic* published a double-page photograph of a grim German blockhouse surrounded by a wasteland of water-filled shell holes, as well as aerial photographs of the area, calling them 'studies in sludge'.[3] The very word Passchendaele, fortuitously combining to the English speaker the idea of Christ's passion and a slough of despond, came to sum up the futility and horror of trench warfare.

While the British Army struggled in the mud of the Salient, the larger situation was deteriorating sharply. On 26 October the British public was told of the huge Italian defeat at Caporetto, and shortly after this of the arrival of British troops there to prop up their failing ally.[4] On 9 November news reached Britain that Kerensky's government in Russia had collapsed and that the Bolsheviks, led by the 'pacifist agitator Lenin', had taken power.[5] This ended the Russian war effort, releasing great numbers of German troops to be transferred to the Western Front. In this depressing situation, news of a 'Great Victory' of 'a grand fleet of tanks led by an "Admiral"' near Cambrai in November was received with frenzied relief.[6] Even this rejoicing turned sour, when, within days, a German counter-attack regained virtually all the ground taken.

The 38th (Welsh) Division, which included the London Welsh Battalion, in which Ellis Evans and David Jones were now serving, was on the left wing of Haig's assault from the Ypres Salient on 31 July. It was tasked with taking the shattered village of Pilckem, which lay on a low ridge, and then proceeding beyond this to cross a small stream, the Steenbeck, and securing positions there. A complicated plan was developed to allow the Welsh Division to get past the 280 concrete pillboxes and bunkers facing them in this area alone. This called for different units of the division to 'leapfrog' one another as they advanced, theoretically allowing fresh troops to form the spearhead of each phase of the attack. David Jones, as an old hand, was put into the battalion's reserve – to be used to replenish companies which might suffer severe losses – and thus spared the horror of going over the top. His battalion, now including many conscripts, like Ellis Evans, was not in the first wave which attacked on 31 July, but was in the second. The first wave secured its objective – the German front line – without too much difficulty, as the Germans had already abandoned this under the hurricane of British artillery fire. The London Welsh, struggling forward towards the German second line, met concentrated machine gun and shellfire from what was known as Iron Cross Ridge.

Ellis Evans was hit in the back by shrapnel and was taken back to a first-aid post, where he died at 11.00 a.m. His reported last words, 'I am very happy',[7] may be ascribed to the influence of morphine. He was not alone. According to the divisional history, 'in a short time only a few officers were left' from the London Welsh. Fresh battalions of the South Wales Borderers and Royal Welch Fusiliers then continued the attack. For the next five days the Welsh Division held the new front line in almost constant rain and shellfire. On 6 August the survivors were relieved and marched back to Proven.[8]

A month later, the National Eisteddfod was held in Birkenhead. Lloyd George attended and delivered an upbeat speech in which he declared: 'I believe intense love for Wales conduces to the most fervent British patriotism.'[9] The mood of the event was brutally depressed by two events. First a decoration was presented to the conductor of the choir from the 17th Battalion, Royal Welch Fusiliers, which had won a prize at the Bangor Eisteddfod in 1915. The conductor, the audience was told, was now the sole survivor from the choir.[10] Second, the winner of the poetry competition was then announced, and 'Fleur-de-Lis' was invited to step forward to occupy the bardic chair, which had been specially carved for the occasion by a Flemish refugee, Eugeen Vanfleteren. After a silence, it became clear that the winner – Ellis Evans, or Hedd Wyn – was not present, and that he had died at the front six weeks previously. The bardic chair was draped in black cloth and later carried in solemn procession back to the poet's home near Trawysfynydd.[11]

Very quickly, the news of the 'Dead Soldier Bard' and of the 'Black Chair' spread in Wales.[12] The *Welsh Outlook* reported on the Eisteddfod in October 1917 and carried a page of poems in tribute to Hedd Wyn, the first of many to be written. In its commentary the *Welsh Outlook*, which had supported the introduction of conscription, blamed the Germans for his death, stating that he 'had been sacrificed to the madness of the miscreants who pretend to govern Europe. He was one of the most lovable of men, a quiet mystic dreamer who loved to tend his sheep on the mountains of Merioneth, to read his books and to dream his dreams'.[13] One of the poems in the journal's Welsh-language tribute put a patriotic gloss on Evans' death, saying (in translation) that 'for truth so that the people are not violated, Hedd Wyn gave his blood plentifully'. Again the Germans were blamed, this time for 'deceitful massacre' and for 'trickery on foreign land'. A more careful poem by Evans' friend Williams Parry, considered by some today to be among the best Welsh-language poems ever written, avoided blaming the Germans directly and also avoided the temptation to cast Evans as a heroic champion of the rights of small nations. Instead it described with lyrical beauty the sorrowful circumstances of his death and burial far from Wales:

> A sin it was to drive this soul – so gentle, so
> Reclusive, from his solitary toil;
> Still worse, to drop him down a hole
> To waste in dust; but worst, on distant soil.[14]

Just as Rupert Brooke's death had coincided with the spread of his poetry, and gave impetus to the development of a mythology, so the news of Evans' death served to throw into bitter relief his growing reputation as Hedd Wyn, the bard. Further tributes were paid to him in Welsh-language newspapers, and committees were formed to publish his poems and to erect a memorial to him. Vincent Evans, the Secretary of the National Eisteddfod, and Hedd Wyn's mentor Silyn Roberts played a key role in raising money across Wales for the memorial. J. J. Williams agreed to collect and edit material for the publication.[15]

Although Evans' death, within only hours of going into action, seems to symbolize the waste and futility of the First World War, the attack on the Pilckem Ridge was considered a great success by Haig and has been similarly viewed by historians. In Haig's eyes the Welsh Division had redeemed its reputation after what he had perceived as its poor showing at Mametz Wood in 1916. It had now, he wrote in 1919, 'achieved the highest level of soldierly achievement'.[16] As well as overwhelming numerous pill boxes, the division had captured many soldiers, as well as artillery pieces and machine guns. David Jones, who heard about the assault from friends in the battalion fortunate enough to survive, drew sketches of two of these, a howitzer and a machine gun, and one can imagine his fascination with these weapons, the two most deadly of the war. His drawings, although calm and unemotional, also reflect the huge pride a unit felt in capturing such trophies.

Jones' drawing of the howitzer shows a stubby weapon on a wheeled carriage, its barrel pointing almost vertically into the sky, allowing its gunners to throw shells onto unseen opponents. His drawing of a 'Boche Machine gun' makes an interesting comparison with Nevinson's much better known painting *La Mitrailleuse*. Nevinson wanted to make a statement about the subordination of man to machine, and about the dehumanization of the individual, but Jones' sketch appears more objectively, almost as an exercise in technical drawing. The details of the gun and its supporting sledge are carefully and accurately portrayed; no individuals are shown, and the gun is not in action. Now triumphantly captured, its danger has been neutralized.[17] After a further spell in the front line near Pilckem, the Welsh Division was mercifully withdrawn from the Ypres Salient and redeployed to a 'quieter' sector of the British front near Armentières.

While the Passchendaele campaign dragged on to its awful end, Jones was able to spend more time drawing and writing. He produced another sketch

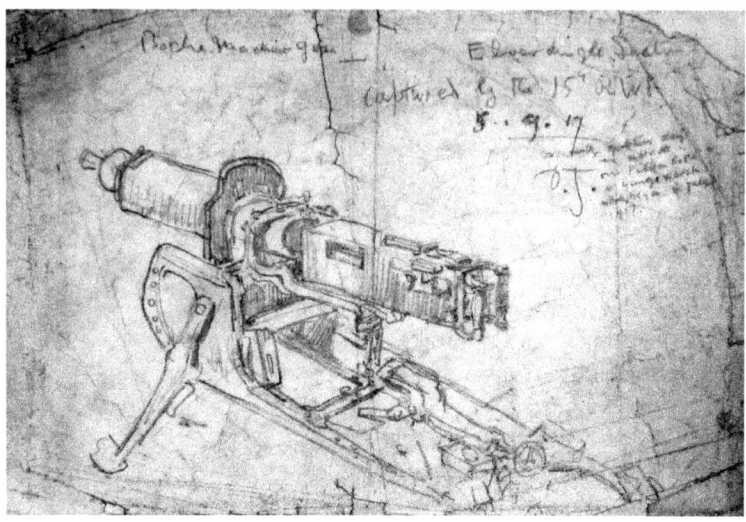

FIGURE 23 *While serving in the trenches, David Jones made pencil drawings in his field notebook. This sober representation of a captured 'Boche machine gun', drawn in September 1917, makes an interesting comparison with Nevinson's much better known, and more polemical* La Mitrailleuse.

which was published in *The Graphic* in December 1917, entitled *The Wrack of War*. It portrayed a young man and a young woman, in medieval garb, leaving a scene with a ruined church and factory chimneys behind them. They are followed by two leopards. There is an accompanying caption, from Shakespeare's *Julius Caesar*: 'O judgment! thou art fled to brutish beast,/ And men have lost their reason'.[18] Jones' message seems to be that modern industrial civilization, and its offshoot, war, have driven out the arts. Jones also produced a New Year's card for his father to reproduce, as he had done in 1916. On this occasion the card's drawing was accompanied by an allegorical story, and the whole was entitled *The Quest*. The reference to war here was much clearer: a group composed of 'a Knight, a Lady, a Minstrel, and a Man of Letters' is portrayed looking over an expanse of water to a beautiful castle, the object of their quest. The story, written in self-consciously archaic English, enjoins the group only to use their talents 'in the cause of liberty' and to further 'that which is pure and faultless true'. The British war effort is implicitly identified with these lofty ideals, the German war effort with the reverse. The Knight – the British soldier – is told: 'Thou shalt e'en esteem thy life well hazarded in such a cause'.

This is an astonishingly idealized and, by late 1917, old-fashioned view of the war, rehearsing chivalric imagery which had been commonplace in 1914 and 1915. It portrays a view of gender roles and relations which much of Britain had already left behind, and which the war was making even more distant. The bare-shouldered girl in the picture is advised: 'O thou, whose beauty doth destroy the hearts of men, when thou art filled with the wild emotion of desire, see that thou use thy matchless love to help thy lover live the better.'[19] We should bear in mind that Jones was still very young, and that since his nineteenth birthday, with the exception of short periods of leave, he had been sequestered in the army. One recipient of the card had no difficulty in interpreting its message, writing back to Jones: 'Many thanks for your admirable New Year's Card which breathes the Spirit which makes for victory. I hope that victory will come in 1918 and set you free again for your art.'[20]

## Objectivity, realism or propaganda?

Richard Nevinson arrived in France as an Official War Artist in early July 1917 and was there for just over a month, during the battle of Messines Ridge and the preparations for the Passchendaele campaign. His position was an unusual one in many senses. He did not have an officer's commission or rank, and spent most of his time well behind the lines. The BEF was at this stage not experienced in handling war artists. In his later autobiography Nevinson wrote a lively account of this period, which makes it sound much longer than it was and relates how he was able finally to get to the Ypres Salient. This, he relates, was interpreted as 'Rank insubordination', and he implies that as a result he was sent back to England.[21] On returning to London in August 1917, Nevinson produced a series of pictures from impressions gained and sketches made during his visit. Several of these have been lost, and the surviving works have been criticized for being relatively bland and conventional. Art historians have typically framed this criticism in terms of how far Nevinson deployed – or failed to deploy – 'modernist' technique in these works, taking their cue from contemporary critics who felt that Nevinson was being too cautious, and not allowing his nonconformist instincts free rein as he had done earlier in the war.[22]

It is not just the technique in this group of paintings which was conservative. Most showed scenes from behind the lines, and Nevinson avoided the shocking subjects which had given his earlier paintings of the 'Shambles' such impact. Although he was not told by Masterman what he should paint, or what representational idioms he should adopt, we know that after his return Richard Nevinson was again obsessed with fears that he would be re-enlisted, and it may well be that he exercised a degree of self-censorship in these paintings. We can hardly consider him as an objective observer of the war. He was in a fragile state, 'still nervous and miserable',[23] and desperate not to jeopardize his precarious status as an 'artist chap' (as he was apparently described in France). One of the paintings arising directly from his stay in France stands out: *Shell Holes*, sometimes known as *After a Push*, clearly depicts the landscape of the Ypres Salient, and in his autobiography Nevinson stated that it was drawn from impressions gained in his brief visit there. The painting, now in the Imperial War Museum, is a naturalistic representation of a largely flat landscape stripped of vegetation, pocked with water-filled shell holes. The ground, the water and the sky are all depicted with desolate brown and grey tones. The landscape is almost totally empty; there are no human beings, living, dead or wounded, in it. A few stakes with barbed wire on them are visible, and in the distance exploding shells can be seen. This could well be a sector where the British had attacked on 31 July 1917, possibly near the Pilckem Ridge. The shell holes full of water suggest that Nevinson saw this landscape 2 or 3 days later, after heavy rain. The painting has a strong sense of calm after a storm – both natural and man-made – but lacks polemical intent or impact.

This raises questions about Nevinson's position as an Official War Artist. What did the government expect of him, and how did he see this role? Sue Malvern argues that in 1917 the government hoped to use artists – as opposed to photographers, who were expected to portray the war 'realistically' – not only to contribute to a documentary record, but also to make more profound statements about the nature of the conflict and the British part in it. It imagined that artists might communicate better with an educated audience than photographers, who were expected to appeal more to the apparently insatiable demand for war pictures from the mass of the population. The key figures at Wellington House, John Buchan, Charles Masterman and Campbell Dodgson, recognized that crude efforts to manipulate these artists, to censor their work or to tell them what to produce were likely to invite unfavourable comparisons with imagined 'Prussian' regimentation, and that, conversely, there was much to be gained from appearing to support the work of young, challenging artists who were working as free agents. By the same token, they could hardly be expected to support Official War Artists who produced images which might spread disillusionment or despondency, and above all which questioned the righteousness of the British cause.[24]

Richard Nevinson had made his name as an iconoclast; his successful earlier paintings had been lauded for using new idioms which captured something distinctive about the war, and for reflecting his own direct experience of the conflict. In 1917 Nevinson was hugely relieved to be a war artist rather than a private soldier, and he did not want to jeopardize this position. He also stood to gain great publicity from government patronage. These contradictory impulses appear to have shaped the work which he now pursued. Bizarrely, officials from the Department of Information were disappointed with his work, one feeling that he was restraining his 'savage self' partly 'with the intention of gaining official approval'. The Department was preparing a glossy magazine entitled *British Artists at the Front*, intending to focus on Nevinson for the first issue, and Edward Hudson, who was producing this, complained that there was 'an approach to the pavement artist touch' in his work.[25] It was an extraordinary situation for the young radical who had delighted in castigating the British establishment, and it is hardly surprising that his work for a forthcoming officially sponsored exhibition should now take a more controversial direction.

Unlike Nevinson, Paul Nash was not well known to the public in the middle of 1917. Apart from a handful of critics, friends and fellow artists who were aware of the extraordinary sensitivity he brought to drawings of trees and landscapes, he had little reputation. All this was to change. Recovering from his dislocated rib in London in June 1917, he was able to work on the sketches he had sent back from Flanders in the spring, and exhibited 20 of them at the Goupil Gallery in June. These sketches displayed the influence of Richard Nevinson; we know from Nash's letters that he had been struck by how Nevinson's Vorticist technique was suited to representing the 'weird beauty' of the trenches, and he now applied this to own his work. In depicting slanting steel-like rods of rain, contrasting these with the flat stillness of the landscape around Ypres, Nash encapsulated the Vorticist ideal of an equilibrium between movement and stillness, and this vision clearly struck several of the visitors to the exhibition. One was Laurence Binyon – no modernist as we know from his poetry – who noted that Nash, previously unknown to him, was 'seeking for . . . a reality behind the external, perhaps a little painfully, but with a persuading sincerity'. He continued: 'the ruined country – dirty trenches, shattered walls, maimed trees – the starkness of it all, is seized in a way not vivid to the eye but curiously intense to the imagination. It is a kind of brooding vision, with a sense of hurt in the landscape – even the sky in one of these drawings has a bruised and livid tinge – which impresses by its felt quality more than any amount of accomplishment'.[26] Jan Gordon, writing under the name John Salis, was similarly struck by Nash's view of the landscape, writing: 'Mr. Nevinson, responsive to humanity, has reproduced the war human, what the war has stamped on humanity. Mr. Nash, with less brutal logic, but perhaps with a more prolific sensibility, has gathered what war has stamped on Nature.'[27] Nash's successful show was followed by an exhibition in Birmingham, and it was apparently Richard Nevinson who suggested to Nash that he seek appointment as an Official War Artist.[28]

In July and August Nash solicited references from friends and critics, and had these sent to John Buchan at the Department of Information. Nash was well aware that as soon as he recovered he would be sent back on active service, but he wanted to secure the post as an artist not only to avoid this. He had developed a fascination with the landscape of the Ypres Salient and wanted to represent it. He asked Will Rothenstein, then professor of civic art at Sheffield University, to stress in his reference 'my particular vision in regard to "records"'. He wanted Buchan to have no fears that 'my drawings might be fantastic or unreal'.[29] Buchan evidently had reservations about Nash, but was convinced by the weight of testimony in his favour, and in September Nash was made an Official War Artist. By this time he was back at his regimental depot in Gosport and was on the verge of being sent to Egypt. He wrote to Will Rothenstein that, having been accepted as an official artist, he did not want to miss the 'great chance' of going out to France.[30] When confirmation arrived he wrote to his wife Margaret: 'I cannot but rejoice, for it must mean that the War Office will let me be sent to France to do the drawings.'[31] In comparison with Nevinson, Nash appears to have had a much clearer sense of what he wanted to paint: the landscape of the Ypres Salient.

In early November, Nash arrived in the 'war zone', but he was sent to 'Intelligence HQ' and expected to work from there. He was given a car and a driver, but found it difficult to get close to the front line. We should not attribute this merely to a clumsy desire to censor his work. By this time the Passchendaele offensive had ground on for over 3 months, at tremendous cost. Appalling photographs – now used in textbooks to illustrate the awful conditions in the Salient – had been published in the British press, and people at home following the news were aware that the wet conditions were making any advance almost impossibly difficult. Looking after artists was not a priority at Headquarters. Nash also had a personal agenda: he wanted to see his younger brother John, who had been with the Artists' Rifles in Flanders since November 1916 and was now in the battalion reserve behind the Salient, or as he put it, 'left behind to form a nucleus in the event of the Battn. being cut up'. On 4 November, Paul Nash was able to track his brother down and the two men met for the first time in a year.[32]

Over the next few weeks, Nash was able to get closer to the front, and finally, in mid-November, right into the Salient, and to see the conditions

FIGURE 24 *The desolate, sodden landscape of the Ypres Salient has become established through both photography and painting as the quintessential British vision of the First World War.*

at the conclusion of the Passchendaele campaign for himself. He saw some of the places which have since become synonymous with the most horrible experiences of the war for the British Army: Zillebeeke; Sanctuary Wood; Gheluvelt; Passchendaele; and the Menin Road. He was profoundly affected. Since 31 July, when Ellis Evans and others had gone 'over the top' near Pilckem, half a million men had been killed and injured in this small area, and millions of shells had exploded there. The ground was littered with the debris of war, with unburied corpses and body parts, and constant rain had filled the shell holes with contaminated water. Nash was appalled, particularly after staying at a brigade headquarters overnight, and getting up to the front line at Inverness Copse for sunrise. Writing home to Margaret, he released his pent-up feeling in a letter which has become one of the most oft-quoted of the war:

> I have seen the most frightful nightmare of a country more conceived by Dante or Poe than by nature, unspeakable, utterly indescribable. In the fifteen drawings I have made I may give you some vague idea of its horror, but only being in it . . . but no pen or drawing can convey this country – the normal setting of the battles taking place day and night, month after month. Evil and the incarnate fiend alone can be master of this war, and no glimmer of God's hand is seen anywhere.

Trying to describe what he had seen, Nash also revealed how his work had taken on a new purpose:

> The rain drives on, the stinking mud becomes more evilly yellow, the shell-holes fill up with green-white water, the roads and tracks are covered in inches of slime, the black dying trees ooze and sweat and the shells never cease. They alone plunge overhead, tearing away the rotting tree stumps, breaking the plank roads, striking down horses and mules, annihilating, maiming, maddening, they plunge into the grave which is this land; one huge grave, and cast up on it the poor dead. It is unspeakable, godless, hopeless. I am no longer an artist interested and curious. I am a messenger who will bring back word from the men who are fighting to those who want the war to go on for ever. Feeble, inarticulate, will be my message, but it will have a bitter truth, and may it burn their lousy souls.[33]

Sue Malvern has observed how this letter is frequently cited without context as an anti-war statement, and her reservations about this can be supported by other evidence.[34] From this letter, it would appear that Nash had turned against his employers, seeing them now as among those 'who want the war to go on for ever'. In fact, like Nevinson, he was keener than ever to preserve his position as an Official War Artist. On the same day that he wrote about the 'bitter truth' to Margaret, he wrote to 'My dear Mr. Masterman' in a quite different vein:

> Many thanks for your reassuring letter. I am delighted to hear of the new scheme.... As far as I am concerned, nothing could be better, but I think when I have carried out these later drawings you will not want to use the old ones. I have now 40, and I think all good ones, many of which will make paintings. Do try to get me a good long time to work at them when I return, for I found the only way to work here was in rapid sketches and I have used nothing but brown paper and chalks.

Like the ordinary soldiers in the Salient, he was exposed to danger. 'Yesterday I was damn nearly killed. The bosche seemed to have got wind of my coming and shelled me most rudely every time I opened my book.'[35]

Nash had also decided to canvass for his brother's appointment as an Official War Artist to get him out of the trenches, and applied himself to this as soon as he returned to England in December. He found a studio in Iver Heath, and in January 1918 he was working his sketches into oil paintings there. He was preoccupied with the likelihood that he would be returned to the Hampshire Regiment, and as he was now unpaid, he was struggling to get enough food. He wrote on 22 January to Masterman to express these fears, asking for more time to complete his paintings, and recommending his brother's employment. He finished by saying 'Altogether I'm very miserable.'[36]

## Consolation in Palestine?

Even before news of Lawrence's astonishing journey behind Turkish lines and of the capture of Akaba reached London in July 1917, 'easterners' there were arguing that an offensive from Egypt offered the best hope of attacking the Ottoman Empire. On 5 June, General Edmund Allenby replaced General Murray as commander of the Egyptian Expeditionary Force, and Lloyd George personally impressed on him the importance he attached to a 'determined attack to be pushed against the Turks, with the object of driving them out of Palestine'.[37] Lloyd George and Allenby were up against the formidable figure of William Robertson, who, as Chief of the Imperial General Staff, had the difficult job of balancing the demands of politicians and generals in different theatres of war and was a convinced 'westerner'. One can imagine his annoyance when Wingate in Egypt desperately urged him in June 1917 to support 'an aggressive military policy in Palestine and Syria'.[38] Fortunately for the British, the Turks also underestimated the importance of the Palestine front.

The capture of Akaba provided new impetus for the 'easterners'. Lawrence now developed an ambitious plan to use Arab tribes in Palestine and Syria to support a British offensive from the Sinai by attacking the Turks on their exposed flanks, presenting this in person to Allenby on 12 July. Allenby agreed, subject to Lawrence and Feisal being placed under his command. It was an inauspicious time to propose such a grand scheme. Robertson was largely preoccupied with the wrangling over Haig's planned offensive in Flanders and was trying to resist sending more troops or guns to Italy or to Palestine. Allenby faced great difficulties supplying his troops across the Sinai desert. Lawrence's plan for Arab support was attractive on paper, but there was concern that if Allenby's forces were not able to advance quickly, tribes which rose up against the Turks might face terrible reprisals. Allenby was told to delay until the autumn, and Lawrence was sent back to prepare Akaba as a supply base for Feisal.

There, Lawrence was able to write letters to his parents and to old colleagues back in England, and he found time to formulate 'Twenty Seven Articles', a set of guidelines for other British officers working with the Arabs. One part of his complex nature was understandably buoyant after his recent successes. The personal congratulations of William Robertson had been communicated to him. He had been promoted to the rank of Major; and Wilson in Jeddah had recommended him for the Distinguished Service Order, on account of his 'personality, gallantry, and grit'.[39] Wingate recommended him for a Victoria Cross, but because no other British officers had witnessed his accomplishments, Lawrence was only made a Companion of the Bath (CB).[40] His advocacy of guerrilla warfare had been widely accepted, and his hopes for Feisal in Syria appeared to be gaining favour. He wrote to his parents: 'However it is the maddest campaign ever run, . . . and if it works out to a conclusion will be imperishable fun to look back upon.'[41]

Lawrence was also concerned that the Turks would try to retake Akaba and decided to frustrate them with some new weapons. He set out on 7 September with a small party of Arabs, part of a personal retinue he was now cultivating, and two sergeants, one Australian and one British, who had been sent to train Arabs in using two of the staple British weapons of the war, the Lewis gun and Stokes mortar. Lawrence planned to attack a station at Mudowarra on the Hejaz railway where the locomotives took on water, and after several days' travelling, he was able to lay an electrical mine under a small bridge nearby, doing his best to cover the tracks in the sand which might alert a Turkish patrol to his activities. Although the station's garrison spotted Lawrence's Arab companions, they were not able to stop a train from driving over the mine.

The electrical detonator worked perfectly, blowing one of the train's two locomotives completely off the line. Lawrence's two sergeants opened up machine gun and mortar fire on the hapless passengers who tried to escape from the wrecked carriages. Lawrence rushed down to investigate and discovered a gruesome scene. The train was carrying wounded soldiers and sick refugees from Medina, and the front carriage had been derailed, throwing its unfortunate passengers into a heap at one end. While his Arab companions indulged in a frenzy of looting, weeping women pleaded with Lawrence for mercy; a group of Austrian officers and NCOs also begged him for help, but in the confusion they were gunned down by the Arabs. Finally, Lawrence's party made off with 90 prisoners, leaving more than this dead behind them, to be feted as heroes when they got back to Akaba. A week later, Lawrence mined another train, with similarly destructive results.[42] After this he was flown back to Cairo to speak again with Allenby.

As he moved into the period of his wartime career which forever made his reputation, Lawrence moved between exaltation and despair. One side of his nature rejoiced in the daring, and destructive, business of 'train-wrecking'. Another was sickened by the brutality he was now directing. He wrote to a fellow officer about his the attack near Mudowarra: 'The last stunt has been a few days on the Hejaz Railway, in which I potted a train with two engines (oh, the Gods were kind) and we killed superior numbers, and I got a good Baluch prayer-rug and lost all my kit, and nearly my little self.' Then, in a rare moment of revelation, he continued: 'On a show so narrow and voracious as this one loses one's past and one's balance, and becomes hopelessly self-centred. . . . I hope that when this nightmare ends that I will wake up and become alive again. This killing and killing of Turks is horrible. When you charge in at the finish and find them all over the place in bits, and still alive many of them, and know that you have done hundreds in the same way before and must do hundreds more if you can.'[43] Three days later, Lawrence was off again, with 150 Arabs, all enthusiastic at the prospect of booty which mining trains now offered. They managed, after some difficulties, to blow up a train with 12 wagons. In his report, Lawrence wrote: 'The Turkish killed amount to about fifteen. Some civilians were released, and four officers were taken prisoner.'[44]

Although Lawrence, and others, were now seriously disrupting the Hejaz railway, alarming reports were reaching Cairo that Feisal was becoming depressed, concerned that his tenuous grip on the loyalty of disparate tribes was slipping away.[45] Lawrence was also aware of this, and unfolded to Allenby an ambitious scheme to cooperate with the long-awaited British offensive into Palestine. Lawrence had identified a stretch of the railway near Deraa in Syria which passed over several large viaducts spanning the Yarmuk valley. He argued that if one of these could be demolished, the Turkish Army in Palestine would be deprived of its most important supply route, and unable to escape if it was forced to fall back in Palestine. Lawrence was dreaming of the Arabs taking Damascus before Christmas, but Allenby had more limited objectives. On 2 November, Lawrence set off from Akaba again; as his party moved through the open spaces of the desert they were able to hear Allenby's guns herald the start of the offensive.

Instead of attacking Gaza frontally, Allenby had concentrated his attack on the Turkish flank at Beersheba. After several days' resistance, the Turks fell back; Gaza fell to the British on 5 November, and a few days later, Jaffa fell, and the Turks retreated, leaving the road to Jerusalem open. Lawrence's expedition was not greeted with the same success. His party made it to the Yarmuk valley, but his attempt to demolish a viaduct there failed ignominiously. Lawrence was forced to retreat into the desert, and although he succeeded in mining a troop train a few days later, it was a harrowing experience. He had to detonate the mine from only 60 yards' distance and only narrowly escaped from the resulting explosion, writing 'I was knocked backwards and boiler plates flew about in all directions.' He had 'then to run up a steep hill for 400 yards under fire'. As well as destroying two locomotives, Lawrence noted that 'Turkish losses were obviously quite heavy.'[46]

By the time Lawrence returned to Akaba on 26 November, Allenby's troops had realized that the Turks had abandoned Jerusalem. On 11 December Allenby entered the city on foot in a deliberate show of humility. Lawrence accompanied him wearing the uniform of a British staff officer, but his pleasure at this great success was tempered by his growing sense of disillusionment. The strain of constant mental and physical exertion was beginning to tell on him. It is clear that Lawrence was thinking beyond

FIGURE 25 *T. E. Lawrence was allowed to accompany General Allenby when he entered Jerusalem on foot on December 1917. Lawrence later wrote that 'this for me was the supreme moment of the war'* (*Lawrence,* Seven Pillars of Wisdom, *p. 358*).

the war; he had in conversations and letters earlier in the year alluded to his intention to write a book about the Arab Revolt. Now he wrote to a friend at the Ashmolean Museum in Oxford about returning to archaeological work at Carcemish in Syria after the war, but even as he expressed the idea, he conceded that it might not be easy for him to recapture the past. 'After being a sort of king-maker,' he wrote, 'one will not be allowed to go on digging quietly again.'[47]

The capture of Jerusalem appeared on the surface as a great triumph, but Lawrence had hoped for more. Allenby was at the limit of his supply columns and felt unable to press on; with the benefit of hindsight it is apparent that the Turks might have been more relentlessly pursued, and Beirut and Damascus taken from them. There were further political complications which also threatened Lawrence's dream of Arab independence. The Bolsheviks in Russia had published the hitherto secret provisions of the Sykes-Picot Agreement, and in November 1917 the British, in a gesture intended to rally Jewish support around the world, had published a Declaration signed by the Foreign Secretary, Arthur Balfour. Using the studiously vague language which had marked earlier communications with the Arabs and with the French, Balfour declared that the British government 'views with favour the establishment in Palestine of a national home for the Jewish people'.[48] Lawrence was well aware of the presence of Jewish settlers in parts of Palestine, and of the Zionist programme to turn Palestine into a Jewish state. Although Sherif Husein had assured the British that Arabs and Jews in Palestine could live together in his future Arab confederation, Lawrence feared that Jews in Palestine might reduce Arabs there to the status of 'a day labourer class'.[49] He would not have been entirely reassured by *The Times*' editorial on the capture of Jerusalem, which reported that 'the yoke of the Turk is broken for ever. The SULTAN will dominate the Holy Places no more; the scattered Jews will have a prospect of returning to their national home, and a new order will be established, founded upon the ideals of righteousness and justice'.[50]

## Between celebration and regret: the challenge to representation grows

Despite steadily worsening health, Elgar maintained a demanding schedule through the summer and autumn of 1917. After the success of his *Fringes of the Fleet* in London in July, he went with the singers on a series of provincial tours, to Leicester in August, to Chiswick and to Chatham in September, and for another week at the Coliseum in London in October. One admirer wrote to him: 'I cannot describe to you the delight and gratitude of the six or seven hundred soldiers who heard it. It would have pleased you to see their intent, delighted faces – and to hear their shouts of applause.'[51] Elgar was hugely dismayed that Kipling wanted these performances stopped, but finally acceded to his wishes.

Elgar's completed version of the three Binyon poems, now called *Spirit of England*, was finally premiered in Birmingham Town Hall on 4 October, more than 2 years after Elgar started work on it. He conducted performances in Leeds and Huddersfield, and on 24 November he conducted the London premiere. Large audiences attended all these performances, and several reviewers realized that Elgar had produced an enduring work of art, one 'definitely born of the war, worthy of the war, to survive the war'.[52] Elgar himself seemed curiously detached from the work. He did not – for reasons which are still unclear – even attend the premier in Birmingham, although he was staying nearby at the time. At the final rehearsal for the Leeds performance, Alice Elgar noted that although the 'Chorus rehearsal' was 'very very fine', Elgar himself was 'most dreadfully bored'.[53] After the London premiere, Elgar directed the final run of *Fringes of the Fleet* at the Coliseum and seemed more concerned with what he called its 'funeral' than with *Spirit of England*.[54] In December he cancelled his engagement to conduct the work with the Hallé Orchestra in Manchester. One researcher notes that this was 'only the second time he had ever had to pull out of a concert engagement'.[55]

After years of declining health, Elgar was now seriously unwell. He spent much of December 1917 in bed and wrote sorrowfully to Alice Stuart-Wortley of his loneliness.[56] His regular doctor, Maurice Abbott, having tried numerous different treatments over the last few years, brought a specialist from Guys Hospital, Dr Hale White, to examine Elgar after Christmas. White was equally baffled, recommending nothing more sensible than 'smoking, golf, change &c &c'.[57] Although Elgar had done a lot of conducting, he had not written any music since March 1916.

Two events in the difficult winter of 1917 ended Parry's involvement with 'war music'. He was now 69 years old, and, like Elgar, beset with health problems. He had seen his daughter and son-in-law vilified and abused as pro-Germans, their friends and associates hounded and in one case imprisoned for anti-war activities.[58] He had fought long and weary battles to protect his German servant George Schlichtmeyer from internment. He had seen some of his best students killed, and others, like Ivor Gurney, horribly wounded. Musical life at the Royal College had been reduced to a pale shadow of its pre-war glory, and he had fallen out with colleagues there. His estate at Highnam was increasingly neglected, and he was facing demands from the government to cut down many of the trees there. He was still working on his philosophical project, but it seemed ever more out of place in wartime, and he was not sure it would ever be published.

Parry was still writing music and had composed a 'Naval Ode', *The Chivalry of the Sea*, which was given its first performance at the Albert Hall on 24 November, in the same programme as Elgar's *Spirit of England*. With an uncharacteristic lack of generosity, Parry wrote after the concert that

Elgar's work was 'Very poor stuff for the most part'. Although he thought the choir sang his ode 'splendidly', he added: 'I don't think the audience liked it.'[59] Three weeks later, Parry was again at the Albert Hall to see a work of his performed, this time in a memorial event dedicated to 'The Seven Divisions' which had gone out to France in the first months of the war. This was attended by an impressive roll-call of dignitaries and was intended to combine music with speeches and ceremonial readings of the Order of Battle of units from the seven divisions. Wives and mothers of the soldiers involved had embroidered flags which decorated the hall. One of Parry's *Songs of Farewell*, the motet titled 'There Is An Old Belief,' was to be included. According to *The Times*, it had been written 'for the years 1914–1916'.[60] Parry found the whole event 'misconceived'. Although intended 'in a mournful key of respect', he recorded that there were great numbers of uniformed soldiers in the audience who 'were in an exuberant state ready for triumphant exhilaration'. The choir he thought sang well, especially his motet, but 'naturally there was no enthusiasm for such things. It would have been better in church'.[61]

In the very last entry in Vera Brittain's 'Great War Diary', made after her return to London on 27 May 1917, she wrote of how, when she and other nurses travelled through the 'enormous & very dusty camp' at Etaples, they were cheered by the British soldiers there: '[it] made me very glad that I had elected to be a nurse & remain one, instead of doing something else'.[62] After Victor Richardson's death on 9 June, she decided to resume this role. She signed on again, applied to go to France, and on 5 August she arrived back in Etaples. By this time, the medical services supporting the BEF had developed enormously since the early days of improvisation in Boulogne which Kate Finzi had experienced, and Brittain found herself part of a huge organization, dealing with tens of thousands of injured men. Supply dumps, training areas and tented encampments housing hospitals and quarters for soldiers covered a large area along the coast around Boulogne and Etaples, and a stay there was becoming part of the experience of the hundreds of thousands of men and women of the BEF. Brittain arrived just when nurses were particularly needed, as thousands of casualties from the huge offensive in the Ypres Salient started to flow into the hospitals there.

Etaples was only 45 miles from the front line at Ypres, and this was the closest Brittain had come to the war. She was assigned to a 'German Acute Surgical Ward', where, as she wrote to her uncle, 'anything up to 18 or 20 to operations a day' were carried out: 'mostly amputations, chests, abdominals & heads'.[63] As the offensive continued, in terrible weather, Brittain was kept continually busy, apprehensive all the while about whether her brother Edward was involved in the battle. She wrote to her mother in mid-September: 'Here there has been the usual restless atmosphere of a great push – trains going backwards & forwards all day long bringing wounded from the line or taking reinforcements to it; convoys arriving in all night, evacuations to England & bugles going all the time; busy wards and a great moving of the Staff from one ward to another.' Patriotically she added: 'Our prisoners have of course made the German ward very busy.'[64]

For most of the First World War, the dreaded enemy – imagined as 'the Hun', the 'Boche' or known to the front-line troops as 'him', was largely unseen.[65] There are remarkably few images of the Germans in British artistic representations of the war. A woman serving close to the front, as Brittain did in 1917 and 1918, might actually see more German soldiers than a man serving in the trenches. Vera Brittain's reaction was typically humane and sympathetic. She confessed to her uncle that whatever hostility she felt theoretically towards the wounded Germans, it was 'hardly possible to feel antipathy to one's patients in practice'.[66] She wrote a poem, where, as Kate Finzi had done back in 1914, she contrasted the viciousness of the Germans with the kindness they now received: 'And those who slew our dearest, when their lamps were burning low/Found help and pity 'ere they came to die'.[67] Brittain had now written enough poems to think about publication, and it was at this time that Roland Leighton's mother Marie approached Erskine Macdonald in London on Brittain's behalf to see if this was possible.[68] Brittain was relieved in November to hear that her brother, after several spells as a company commander near Ypres, had been posted to Italy. She wrote to her mother: 'no one who has not been out here has any idea how fed up everyone is with France & with the same few miles of ground that have been solidly fought over for three years'. Although there was now a new directness and brusqueness in Brittain's letters, she was still using the public school vocabulary she had learnt earlier, continuing: 'There is a more sporting chance anywhere than here.'[69]

Brittain's view of the war was changing, affected both by her experience of bereavement, and of tending to the wounded. On 5 December she wrote to her mother: 'I wish those people who write so glibly about this being a holy war & the orators who talk so much about going on no matter how long the war lasts & what it may mean, could see a case – to say nothing of 10 cases – of mustard gas in its early stages – could see the poor things burnt & blistered all over with great mustard coloured suppurating blisters, with blinded eyes – sometimes temporarily, sometimes permanently – all sticky and stuck together, & always fighting for breath, with voices a mere whisper, saying that their throats are closing & they know they will choke.'[70]

## Disillusion

There was a striking shift in 1917, which reflected a wider change in public perception, and which I have earlier labelled a crisis of representation. This was not overcome by the end of the year, by which time Elgar's *Spirit of England* had finally been put before the public in its finished form. By December 1917, Elgar had effectively stopped writing music, and Parry's brief return to 'war music' with his 'Naval Ode' had been, in his own eyes, unsuccessful. For others, even their continued small efforts at representation were marked now by a sense of weariness, frequently combined with uncertainty about how long the war would continue, and how it would end. We see this even in the patriotic representations by the young David Jones, still expressing confidence in the justice of the British cause, but unwilling to pronounce on how long the war would last. The weariness is present in Vera Brittain's letters, not despondent, but now lacking the cheerful confidence of earlier years. It is there in Lawrence's repugnance about 'this killing and killing of Turks'. It is strongly present in *Spirit of England*, not only in the weariness with which Elgar completed the work, more than 2 years after beginning it, and in his inability or unwillingness to write new music to depict the Germans in the first movement, but in the music of the second and third movements. When Elgar started the work, the outcome of the war was unclear, but it was becoming evident that it would be a protracted conflict. This awareness had only grown during 1916 and 1917, and Elgar expressed it powerfully in the second movement of the piece, 'To Women', which has a powerful martial theme, a slow march clearly expressing that the war simply carries on. John Norris describes the work's final message as 'ambiguous' and 'uncertain'. Although the work carries a redemptive conclusion, 'an understated sense of hope and belief',[71] Elgar was far too realistic in 1915, and later, to embody in *Spirit of England* any bombastic expression of confidence of victory, as there was in *Carillon*, written at the start of the war.

Coupled with this deepening weariness was a sense of the war as a huge inhuman force, something with its own momentum and logic, seemingly beyond the control of individuals and governments. This was expressed by Parry's concern about Ivor Gurney, having to return 'into the vortex of barbarism'. The metaphor of the vortex, a force of nature which caught people and then drew them ineluctably into its concentrated and chaotic centre, had been used since the start of the war, and it is striking how frequently it appeared in different individual representations. Lloyd George, in his first speech as Prime Minister in December 1916, had spoken of how 'Europe has been plunged into this vortex of blood'.[72] It was peculiarly appropriate to the British situation, where from the homeland, the war was only a day's travel by train and boat from London, but sufficiently distant to allow a complete contrast between the image of the vortex, and the calmer, if now infinitely dangerous waters around it.[73] The contrast between the experience of those who had been sucked 'into the vortex', and those who had not, or who tried to avoid it, had, as we have seen in the writings of Kate Finzi and Rupert Brooke, been felt since 1914, but now it become stronger, producing an ever-growing chasm between them. Ellis Evans, who had been sucked in and destroyed in 1917, had expressed powerfully the sense of the war as an inhuman force in his poem 'Rhyfel'.

At its most bitter, there was emerging in Britain by the end of 1917 a perception that the war was not just a terrible accident, but something which had been malevolently willed, and that there were some who wanted it, as Paul Nash had imagined, 'to go on for ever'. There is a striking similarity here with the statement which Siegfried Sassoon wrote and had read out in the House of Commons in July 1917, in which he alleged that 'the War is being deliberately prolonged by those who have the power to end it'.[74] Like Sassoon, Nash was by the end of 1917 convinced that he had a responsibility to use his art to articulate some kind of protest about this. Nevinson too, after a period of inactivity, and despite wanting desperately to preserve his protected position as an Official War Artist, was moving towards a more outspokenly critical position. Today, even the most cynical critics would find it difficult to argue convincingly that Asquith, Grey, Lloyd George, Kitchener, Haig or even Churchill wanted to prolong the war, or that there were sinister interests, whether imagined as armaments manufacturers, 'profiteers' or Welsh 'agriculturists', who wanted this in order to boost their incomes, but there were by the end of 1917 people, particularly among front-line soldiers, who felt that way. The institutionalization of the war, the introduction of conscription and the stasis in the trenches had by 1917 produced a situation where industrial war had simply become part of life. The regular news of 'pushes', of 'gains' and 'reverses', of ships lost at sea, of civilians killed by air raids, of casualties on different fronts had become an awful, wearying constant, and there appeared to be no option but to muddle on.

# CHAPTER NINE

# January–July 1918

The protracted agony for the British of the failed offensive in Flanders in 1917 had been compounded by the unexpected success of the German counter-attack at Cambrai. Inevitably, there was a backlash. Blame was heaped on General Headquarters in France, criticized for its over-optimistic assessments of German capability and misleading the public about the situation at the Front. *The Times* declared: 'We can no longer rest satisfied with the fatuous estimates, *e.g.* of German losses in men and *moral*, which have inspired too many of the published messages from France.' It called for 'the prompt removal of every blunderer', and while it did not blame Haig directly, it attacked his 'choice of subordinates', some of whom had served him 'too long'.[1] Lloyd George clearly shared these views. During the Passchendaele campaign he was planning to get rid of Robertson, the Chief of the Imperial General Staff, whom he blamed for blocking his efforts to send support to Italy. Lloyd George also told George Riddell on 23 December that 'unduly optimistic opinions and prognostications have been disseminated' and that 'the military position . . . has been mismanaged'.[2]

There had been a serious deterioration in the strategic position. The French Army was clearly exhausted. The Italians were on their knees, dependent now on British support. On 12 February 1918, Russia's 'unconditional surrender' to the Germans was announced.[3] Already the Germans were transferring substantial forces to the Western Front. Although the first American units had arrived in France, it would be many months before they were a significant factor. And, after 3 years of continuous growth, the British Army was contracting. Conscription had 'combed out' men such as Ellis Evans in 1916 and 1917, and there were no longer sufficient new men to replace those killed, injured and traumatized in different theatres of war.

In a series of meetings, GHQ in France, the War Cabinet in London and the newly formed Supreme War Council in Versailles grappled with these problems, and with the anticipated German offensive on the Western Front. Through the winter months, Lloyd George's government considered whether Haig should be replaced; Robertson lost his post in February, and several of Haig's key subordinates were dismissed, but Haig kept his position. He had to accept that there was no imminent possibility of resuming the offensive. Haig also had to accept decisions made in London to send more troops to Palestine, and to take over more of the French line. British divisions in France were reduced from twelve battalions to nine, and Haig was left to face the growing German threat with some 70,000 fewer men than he had in early 1917.[4] Haig and Lloyd George were now engaged in a trial of strength about the best possible use of the remaining new drafts of men. Haig wanted them sent to France; Lloyd George to keep them in Britain. This was a potentially disastrous situation. The Prime Minister and the commander-in-chief of the largest British army ever deployed in the field had almost totally lost confidence in one another, both displaying contempt for one another in their private remarks.

On the morning of 21 March 1918, a five-hour German bombardment rained three million shells onto the British positions south of the Somme. The infantry attack which followed, in foggy weather, was led by elite groups of 'storm troopers' with orders to bypass islands of resistance to achieve a deep penetration. It is hardly surprising that the British front lines were largely overwhelmed, but in the days which followed a larger catastrophe loomed. As the British were forced back, many were taken prisoner, and individual units and groups of men were isolated from one another. It was apparent by 25 March that the whole Allied position was in grave danger, as German forces advanced with a speed which had not been seen since the autumn of 1914, bearing on the town of Amiens, 40 miles from their starting point, driving a wedge between the British and the French armies. This precipitated a serious crisis in Allied relations. Already Haig and his staff were blaming the French on their right for giving them 'very little assistance'.[5]

Aware that the Germans still had substantial reserves to deploy, the British were concerned that they might turn north towards the Channel ports, or in Haig's words, that 'the British will be rounded up and driven into the sea!'[6] The French feared that the Germans would turn to threaten Paris. At an emergency conference in Doullens on 26 March, it was agreed that Marshal Foch should coordinate the actions of the British and the French armies, but in practice this proved very difficult over the coming weeks. On the same day, the town of Albert, which had been *behind* the British lines on the Somme in 1916, fell to the Germans. There was an unprecedented sense of crisis as the German attack unfolded.

Lloyd George was deeply shaken and confessed to Riddell: 'I fear it means disaster'. Haig maintained his usual air of imperturbability, but reading between the lines in his diary one can sense his deep disquiet. He appealed directly to the French premier, Clemenceau, for help, but to no avail.[7] Both Haig and Lloyd George were a little calmer when they met on 3 April at Beauvais for talks with the French. Haig wrote: 'The P.M. looked as if he had been thoroughly frightened, and he seemed still in a funk. He travelled some part of the way in my car, and then he changed and Wilson (C.I.G.S.) joined me. L.G. is a fatiguing companion in a motor. He talks and argues so! And he appears to me to be a thorough impostor. . . . when I am with him I cannot resist a feeling of distrust of him and his intentions.'[8]

Their troubles were not yet ended. The next blow fell on 9 April against the British lines to the south of Ypres. Once again Ludendorff chose a weak spot, focusing his attack against two Portuguese divisions in the line with the British XI Corps. The Portuguese were poorly supported by

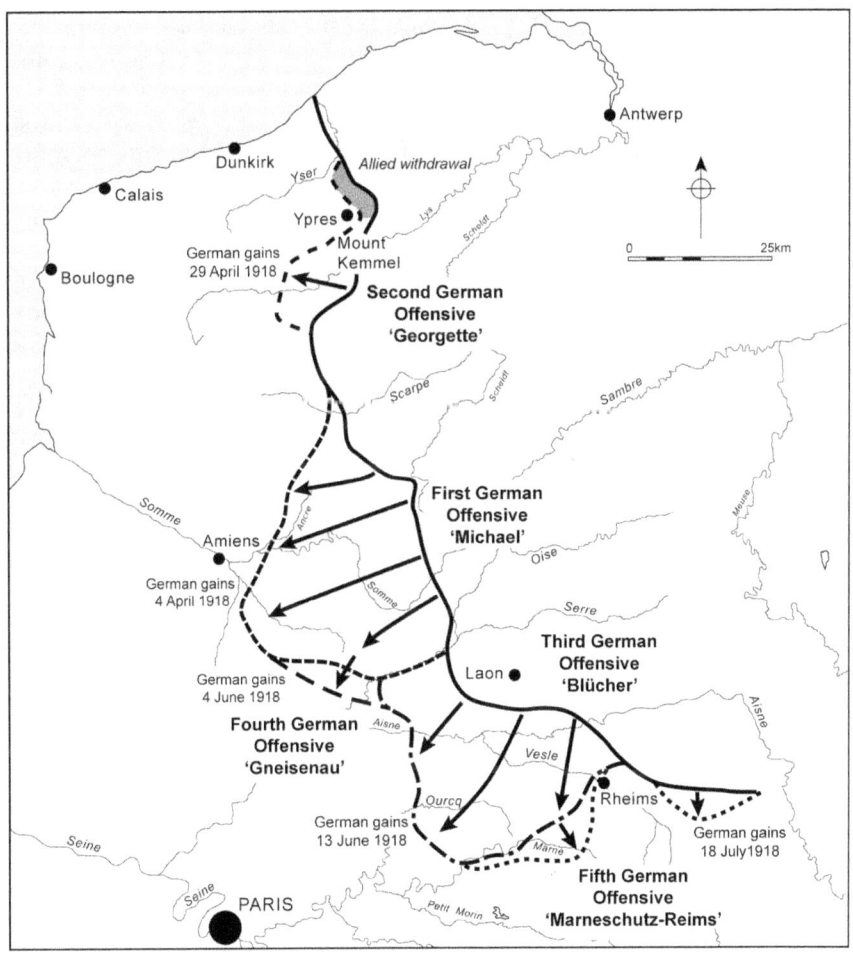

MAP 13 *The German offensives of 1918.*

British artillery, and when they were attacked with overwhelming force, they simply broke, allowing the Germans to advance 6 miles through the British line. Haig wrote dismissively that 'the Portuguese troops with their Portuguese officers are useless for this class of fighting'.[9] On 10 April the Germans forced the British out of the town of Armentières. This left the Ypres Salient threatened and exposed the fragility of the whole British position in Flanders. The Germans were less than 40 miles from Calais. On 11 April, Haig issued his now famous 'Order of the Day', in which he stated: 'There is no course open to us but to fight it out. Every position must be held to the last man. There must be no retirement. With our backs to the wall, and believing in the justice of our cause, each one of us must fight on to the end. The safety of our homes and the freedom of mankind alike depend on the conduct of each one of us at this critical moment.'[10] Despite this rhetoric, Haig was forced into carefully measured withdrawals. On 12 April, Passchendaele at the tip of the Ypres Salient was evacuated. Haig even prepared to abandon the whole salient, a move which would have been strategically justified, but, given the sacrifices which had been made there since 1914, a huge blow to morale.[11] On 25 April, British spirits were depressed still further when the French troops holding Mount Kemmel, to the south of Ypres, relinquished the hill to the Germans. Haig wrote: 'We all thought Kemmel practically impregnable, yet the place was abandoned by the French troops after two hours' fighting. . . . What Allies to fight with!'[12]

Fortunately for the Allies, the Germans were experiencing all of the problems associated with First World War offensives. As their troops moved forward, they incurred heavy casualties, they lost touch with their supporting artillery and it became more difficult to supply them. They had virtually no tanks and were constantly harassed from the air, where the Allies now had a notable superiority. In 1918 the Germans were also conscious that this was a last roll of the dice, or in their own words, that they were playing their 'last card'.[13] It was a bitter irony for many of the German soldiers, overrunning Allied trenches and supply dumps, to discover that their enemies were much better provisioned than they were; increasingly their forward movement was slowed by soldiers pausing to loot, to eat and to drink. Nonetheless, Allied fragility was still evident at a meeting of the Supreme War Council on 1 May. On this occasion, Haig's frustration and his contempt for foreigners were directed at the Americans. Haig, unsurprisingly, argued that the best use of the American soldiers was to integrate them with British and French units. General Pershing, the American commander, had orders to maintain the independence of his forces and resisted this.[14] Haig's response was to write: 'I thought Pershing was very obstinate and stupid. He did not seem to recognise the urgency of the situation.'[15]

The Germans now switched their attacks to the French, and on 27 May opened a huge offensive in Champagne. Once again they surged forward, now towards Paris. As the Germans advanced across a landscape undamaged by war, the War Cabinet met in Downing Street to consider 'the possibility of withdrawing the whole Army from France'.[16] Now it was Haig's turn to resist French demands for British support in their hour of need. He was convinced that the French were not fighting with real determination, and saw any assistance to them as 'a waste of good troops'.[17] The American troops who were rushed into the line to plug gaps left by the retreating French quickly learnt hard lessons in European warfare in their first engagements.[18] On 15 July, the Germans mounted another offensive south of the Aisne, revisiting territory they had first taken in the heady days of September 1914. They now stood again on the River Marne. From a salient near Laon they were using a huge naval gun, the *Pariskanone*, to hurl shells into Paris from a distance of 77 miles.[19]

The offensives which have been briefly sketched here were a colossal military effort, and they left the once mighty German Army exhausted. In the first half of 1918, they suffered nearly a million casualties. What became known as 'Spanish flu' was spreading across much of Europe, and German soldiers, less well fed than their Allied counterparts, were particularly susceptible to it.[20] A junior officer, Ernst Jünger, reported that by late June, 'several men a day' were reporting sick in his company, and that 'Young men in particular sometimes died overnight'.[21] The strain of conducting a war on several fronts, propping up allies who for years had been largely dependent on German help of all kinds, and above all, the cumulative impact of the British naval blockade, was apparent.

Conversely, by the middle of 1918, the British and the French, for all the crises of cooperation they had suffered earlier in the year, were still capable of offensive action. At last, thousands of American troops were coming into the line. On 4 July a carefully prepared attack at Hamel by the Australian Corps, supported by 60 tanks, was a notable local success. On 18 July the French and Americans attacked together in what became known as the Second Battle of the Marne and achieved significant successes. On 21 July, Field-Marshal Haig made this note: 'I attended Church of Scotland at 9.30 a.m. The Rev. George Duncan preached from the first chapter of Joshua, which was considered by the late Mr Stead as the most important in the Bible because it directs us to be courageous. "Only be thou strong and very courageous," and you will obtain what is promised.'[22] Two days later he wrote that he was now 'prepared to take the offensive'.[23]

## Mechanization and brutality: changing warfare in the Middle East

The war in the Middle East was changing in 1917 and 1918. In Flanders, Allenby had seen the impact of modern artillery and aviation, and he now sought to apply these to the hitherto largely unmechanized campaign in Palestine. A critical part in the offensive which ended with the capture

FIGURE 26 *Throughout 1918, Lawrence had at his disposal a number of armoured cars and Rolls-Royce tenders. The driver of one of these described how it 'had been fitted with a low, sporting body, set in streamline with her long bonnet. Thus lightened, she answered to her accelerator, when on firm going, like a shell coming out of a gun'* (Rolls, Steel Chariots in the Desert, *p. 134*).

of Jerusalem was played by the 'Palestine Brigade', a detachment of the Royal Flying Corps equipped with the most modern British aircraft. These had played a vital role in directing artillery fire, in reconnaissance, and in ending the aerial supremacy previously enjoyed by the Turkish forces. A detachment of Rolls-Royce armoured cars had been shipped to Akaba to help Lawrence, and on New Year's Day 1918, he led these in an attack on the Hejaz railway.[24] For all his fascination with the Middle Ages, and with earlier periods of history, Lawrence loved modern machines and delighted in riding at the highest speed possible over hard sand in an armoured car.

Although the Turks had virtually no modern armaments of their own, they were now getting more help from their allies. A German 'Asia Corps' comprised of infantry, artillery, signalling and aviation units had been formed in July 1917 to operate with a Turkish army in Syria, initially intended to help to retake Baghdad. After the loss of Gaza, this force, given the pompous title of the 'Lightning Group', was slowly deployed in Palestine. Liman von Sanders, who had successfully overseen the defence of Gallipoli in 1915, was appointed to command the 'Lightning Group' in February 1918.[25] German engineers were brought in to supervise the repair and operation of the Hejaz railway, and Arab guerrillas found that it was now more systematically defended. The *Arab Bulletin* reported that in a confrontation at Abu el Jurdhan in May 1918 the Turks used infantry accompanied by an 'armoured relief train' and aircraft to retake the station from Arabs, who were 'supported by two aeroplanes and armoured cars'.[26]

The fighting in the desert was changing. In January Arabs occupied the small town of Tafilah in mountainous terrain and had to fight a pitched battle against a Turkish force armed with machine guns and 'powerful Austrian mountain guns'.[27] Lawrence arrived in time to help them, but not before the Arabs had suffered serious casualties, something he had always sought to avoid.[28] The increased violence of these confrontations was also generating more cruelty. The Arabs had never been keen to take Turkish prisoners, and the Turks, enraged by the operation of guerrilla fighters, were treating Arab prisoners they captured in an equally barbarous fashion. Lawrence wrote in a later report – to which we shall return – that Arabs had seen 'the Turks swing their wounded by the hands and feet into a burning railway truck ... at Jerdun', referring presumably to one of the confrontations there earlier in 1918.[29] After a confrontation with a Turkish patrol which left one of his servants badly injured in April 1918, Lawrence felt compelled to shoot this man, lest he fall alive into the hands of the Turks.[30] That he had recently been made a colonel and awarded the Distinguished Service Order for his part in the battle at Tafilah was little consolation for this kind of horror.

The Palestine campaign lay heavily under the shadow of the German successes on the Western Front in the spring of 1918. Allenby had to send his best units back to Flanders to help to plug the gaps there, and efforts to consolidate his position to the north of Jerusalem were repulsed early in May. There was bickering between different Arab tribes, and not surprisingly, even Feisal and Husein were keeping open channels of communication with the Turks. Von Papen, the future German Chancellor, was a staff officer with the Asia Corps in 1918 and wrote bluntly that Feisal had not wanted 'to find himself on the losing side'.[31] Clayton, the Director of British Intelligence in Egypt, wrote in May 1918 about the difficulty of holding the Arabs together and expressed the British sense of priorities very clearly: 'We must get the upper hand of the Hun in the West (of course all hangs on this).'[32] At all levels the British were aware of this fragility, and none felt it more keenly than Lawrence himself.

Back in Egypt in July 1918 after a failed attempt to meet with Husein, Lawrence revealed the immense strain he was working under to a pre-war friend in Oxford. He wrote about the difficulties of living among the Arabs, never able to be one of their number, and about the dangers he faced: 'So it's a kind of foreign stage, on which one plays day and night, in fancy dress, in a strange language, with the price of failure on one's head if the part is not well filled.' He spoke of the feeling that he was living in a dream, adding 'Only the different thing about this dream is that so many people do not wake up in this life again.' Turning to the reality of fighting with the Arabs, he concluded: 'we ride like lunatics and with our Beduins pounce on unsuspecting Turks and destroy them in heaps: and it is all very gory and nasty after we close grips. I love the preparation, and the journey, and loathe the physical fighting. Disguises, and prices on one's head, and fancy exploits are all part of the pose: how to reconcile it with the Oxford pose I know not'.[33] On the same day he wrote to his parents, concealing his deeper fears and expressing his confidence that the Turks in the Hejaz were now finally cut off. 'It's very nice', he wrote, 'to have finished our part of the show.'[34]

## Infantryman or Official War Artist?

The manpower crisis which was preoccupying Lloyd George and Haig was also felt in Salonica, where Spencer was one of the new men now filling the ranks in the infantry. In February 1918 he was sent 'up the line', and he joined the 7th Battalion, Royal Berkshire Regiment facing the Bulgarians near Kalinova. Spencer had volunteered for the infantry partly in the hope that he might be posted to this area, which he associated with great spiritual feelings from his earlier service there. Although the journey to the front line was arduous and exhausting, Spencer was again uplifted by the mountain scenery and the onset of spring. He was not a natural infantryman. He still found it hard to adapt to the company of the other soldiers and struggled to master his fears when sent out on night patrols. Fortunately for him, this was the nearest he came at this stage to any action. Spencer was still thinking hard about painting, and while accepting that he could not in this situation do 'any work of an ambitious nature',[35] he wrote to his old friend James Wood, asking him to send some pencils and a sketch book. He told him that he was 'up the line again', at a place which 'has a very great spiritual significance for me', and he explained how he was trying to get through: 'I think my period of "service" is not a period of degeneration, but a period of being in the "Refiner's Fire".'[36] To his sister he portrayed soldiering as a combination of spirituality, aestheticism and improvisation: 'the only thing I do is to dig, love God, read Milton, and go on the scrounge occasionally'.[37]

In May 1918, Spencer had cause to think that his old life as an artist might be resumed more quickly than he had thought. First he received a parcel from James Wood enclosing not just pencils and a sketch book, but a 'box of colours', two brushes, a drawing block and a book of Tintoretto reproductions.[38] Then, out of the blue, on 10 May Spencer received a letter from the Ministry of Information in London, inviting him to become an Official War Artist and to contribute to a planned war memorial exhibition. The letter was confusing. Apparently he had been recommended by Muirhead Bone – who was unknown to Spencer – who thought Spencer was possibly at the front in France. Would Spencer, the letter asked, be interested to paint something 'under some such title as *A Religious Service at the Front*'?[39]

Although Spencer was hundreds of miles from France, and was not particularly keen to paint a religious service – something he now had very ambivalent feelings about – he was excited about other possibilities. He wrote: 'I am aching to paint ideas I have for men asleep in a tent, that bivouac idea I showed to you. Of men drinking water . . . 2 pack mule pictures. A picture of a lecture on Mosquitoes, 2 mule line pictures. A picture of one limber wagon bringing grub. I am as much influenced by this particular sector as I was by Cookham in peace times I do believe.'[40] To his sister he outlined a fantasy of returning to England, revisiting Beaufort Hospital, going back to Salonica, then to England again, to Ireland and to

America: 'Then I would return to Cookham & work, and I would not stop working.' He added: 'I have had no further news of my prospective job, but I expect to hear in a few days.'[41]

## Votes for women, and the Americans arrive

On 7 January 1918, Elgar was visited again by his doctor Maurice Abbott, who decided to X-ray his patient to find the root cause of his ailments.[42] After the X-rays, Elgar was subjected to further 'electric treatment', and also given a belt to wear to help with what was diagnosed as a 'dropped stomach',[43] but neither of these seemed to help. In February, still unwell, he was subjected again to the attentions of the dentist, and finally, on 6 March, Elgar was seen by a leading throat specialist, who recommended a tonsillectomy.[44] A week later he went into a nursing home in Dorset Square for an operation on his throat. Here the surgeons found and removed an abscess, and a stone the size of a pea. The operation left Elgar in agonizing pain, and he spent the next week in the nursing home.[45]

It was now a year since Elgar had written any music. He was 61 years old and was weakened by chronic illness. Elgar scholars have typically ascribed this compositional block to a combination of ill health and depression induced by the war, a sense by 1918 that an old world had disappeared for ever. It is impossible now to say how these different factors were balanced in Elgar's complex make-up, but there can be little doubt that he was deeply dismayed by what he knew of the war. He and his wife still anxiously followed the news, noted grimly the air raids by German bombers, and twice, early in 1918, visited exhibitions of war photographs in London. In January they went to an exhibition at Burlington House,[46] and, on the day his tonsils were 'condemned', Elgar noted, in the diary he had started, that they visited the 'War pictures Grafton Gallery'. This exhibition included the largest photograph yet made, 23 feet by 17 feet, showing 'tanks going into action on the Western Front'.[47] Back at Severn House after his operation, they heard of the crisis facing Haig's army in France. Alice Elgar wrote: 'Frightfully anxious for our splendid dear Army – God help us'.[48]

There was another significant development in these dark days. On the night he returned home, Elgar wrote out what he called a 'Very full, sweet and sonorous theme',[49] and clearly he developed this over the next few days. On 3 April he wrote: 'Writing E minor stuff'.[50] This 'stuff' was to come to fruition as Elgar's Cello Concerto, and this return to composing started what has been regarded as the final great creative period of his life. The tonsillectomy brought no instantaneous cure though, and for the next few weeks Elgar was still unwell. On 17 April he noted the bad news from Flanders. He appears to have been reading *The Times*, which that day carried several articles reporting further German advances in Belgium.[51] On 2 May he and Alice made the short journey by train to Fittleworth in Sussex to begin several months' stay at a cottage they had identified in 1917 as a suitable summer retreat, Brinkwells. The weather was improving, and Elgar appears to have enjoyed being reclusive. He spent his time walking, and in the workshop by the cottage, noting the flora and fauna he observed. After years of public engagements and city life, this was a huge tonic, but even in the Sussex countryside, the war was never far away.

A letter arrived in mid-May from the singer Charles Mott, who had now been in France for 'five weeks', and was facing an imminent action. The letter is a remarkable testimony to the positive spirit still animating many of the conscripts being rushed out to fill the gaps in the BEF: 'I have enjoyed the experience immensely, and look forward to heaps of "fun" (admittedly of a rather grim nature) within the next few hours! I *know* you would feel the same. There is something grand and very fascinating about a battery of big guns & a shell that can make a hole in the ground big enough to put a motor-bus in – what a vast amount of pent up energy.' Mott seems to have realized how warlike he was sounding, and went on to say how awful it was that so much human effort was being turned to destructive purpose. He continued: 'What consolation to recall your glorious Gerontius & that beloved work "To the Fallen." . . . There is one thing that "puts the wind up me" very badly & that is of my being wiped out & thus miss the dear harmonies of your wonderful works. . . . But I have a supreme confidence in my destiny & feel that I have some useful work to do in the world before I am called away. Meanwhile the roar of the guns thrills me somehow, & I only dread my comrades coming to grief & seeing them wounded. I pray they may all get through safely.'[52]

On 25 May, Elgar wrote in his diary: 'Heard Mott was wounded';[53] in fact Mott was dead, having been mortally wounded in fighting in Aveluy Wood on 20 May. One wonders whether Elgar thought back to his earlier public support for conscription. On 30 May Elgar noted: 'Bad war news this & succeeding days. Incessant gun fire (distant cannon)'.[54]

Parry similarly had to endure further bad news. Most disturbingly, in June 1918 he received a letter from his protégé Ivor Gurney, who had been hospitalized in the autumn of 1917, stating that he intended to kill himself.[55] Parry immediately tried to ascertain what was going on and it was with some relief that he later heard that Gurney had not carried out his threat. Closer to home, Parry had at last completed his cherished work of philosophy, but heard 'the depressing news' from Macmillan in June that his book had been declined, writing bleakly in his diary: '3 years and more work come to nothing'.[56] One development brought comfort to Parry in these difficult times. In March 1918, the government had finally passed the Representation of the People Act, giving the vote to women over the age of 30. This was not equality with male voters, but after more than 50 years of suffragist campaigning, it was a huge step forward. Maude Parry was understandably excited, and her husband was involved in some of the celebrations which followed. On 13 March 1918, he directed the Bach Choir at the Annual Council Meeting of the National Union of Women's Suffrage Societies, where the indomitable Millicent Fawcett announced that 'the enfranchisement of women will contribute to the true and permanent welfare of the country'.[57] Parry wrote: 'The sound of "Jerusalem" when the audience joined in was tremendous'.[58] Millicent Fawcett subsequently wrote to him to request that 'Jerusalem' become the 'Women Voters' Hymn', and Parry immediately agreed to this, writing: 'I wish indeed that it might become the Women Voters' Hymn, as you suggest. People seem to enjoy singing it. And having the vote ought to diffuse a good deal of joy too. So they would combine happily.'[59] Parry was also one of many in 1918 who took heart from the arrival of the Americans. He went to an 'entertainment in honour of Independence Day' for American soldiers in London in July, and noted approvingly: 'They joined in the singing, & were vociferous with applause & whistling. A fine sturdy lot of men & looking full of spirit.'[60]

## Visions of heroism and chivalry

By early 1918, Vera Brittain was showing signs of strain. She had been working intensively during the Passchendaele campaign and was granted a brief home leave in the new year. Her parents had moved to London, and Vera's brother Edward managed to get there for a few days in January. Vera was ill for most of her leave and was soon heading back to Etaples, after seeing Edward depart once again for Italy. After a short period when the hospitals were quieter, Vera was caught up in the turmoil which followed the German offensive on 21 March. The rapid German advances caused some disarray in the BEF's rear areas, and great numbers of wounded men flowed into Etaples. It was in this atmosphere of crisis that Brittain received a letter from her father telling her that she was needed at home to look after her mother, who had suffered a breakdown. This only exasperated Brittain, who now regarded herself as one of the BEF, and pointed out to her parents that she was under contract as a VAD nurse. She nonetheless dutifully applied to be released early.[61]

There is some confusion about the next few weeks in Brittain's life. Her biographers, following her later account in *Testament of Youth*, write that she returned to London at the end of April, but Brittain also wrote, confusingly, about her experience of suffering air raids in Etaples. There were no air raids there in April, and I have seen no documentary evidence which places her elsewhere in May 1918. In fact there was a serious air raid on Etaples on the night of 19/20 May 1918, when bombs were accidently dropped on several of the hospitals there, killing and injuring nurses, patients and soldiers. The Matron-in-Chief of the BEF, Maud McCarthy, recorded this event, noting that there were no casualties at No. 24 Hospital – where Brittain was working – but that 'this unit took in a large number of casualties' from the raid.⁶² This attack was followed by several nights of German aerial activity over Etaples and Abbeville, just as Brittain later described in *Testament of Youth*.⁶³

Brittain was greatly affected by what she called 'the great air raid' and wrote a poem 'in memory of the sisters who died', entitled 'Vengeance is Mine'. In the poem she reverted to the atrocity language of 1914, unconsciously revealing how deeply this had penetrated into the British psyche after nearly 4 years of war:

> Who shall avenge us for anguish unnameable
> Rivers of scarlet and crosses of grey
> Terror of night-time and blood lust untameable
> Hate without pity where broken we lay?⁶⁴

Shortly after the air raid in Etaples, Brittain was released from her contract and returned to London. Here she was forcibly struck – again – by the contrast between the atmosphere of crisis behind the front lines and the petty concerns of her parents, preoccupied with the difficulties of finding servants and with food shortages. Resentful at being expected to look after them, she occupied herself by starting a novel, and she toyed with the idea of joining the Women's Army Auxiliary Corps, but quickly rejected this. Writing to Edward about different possible options, it was clear that, even though VADs were always in subordinate positions in hospitals, she identified deeply, and with pride, in the role of a nurse: 'Somehow no female figure in the whole of this War has such a glamour as a hospital nurse, or such a dignity.'⁶⁵

As the anniversary of the Battle of the Somme approached, Brittain wrote a poem about her brother. This was the last time that she used what we might call the language of 1914. She began:

> Your battle-wounds are scars upon my heart
> Received when in that grand and tragic 'show'
> You played your part
> Two years ago;

and concluded:

> May you endure to lead the Last Advance
> And with your men pursue the flying foe
> As once in France
> Two years ago.⁶⁶

She sent these verses out to him, on the flyleaf of a newly published anthology of poems, but he did not read them. In July 1918 Vera Brittain read about the Austrian offensive on the Asiago Plateau, where Edward was stationed;

and on 22 July she and her father received a telegram telling them that he had been killed in action.⁶⁷

For almost four years Vera Brittain had maintained a heroic conception of the war, despite seeing the most horrendous wounds modern weapons could produce, and witnessing many deaths. She had lived through the death of her fiancé, and his two best school friends, and had experienced aerial bombardment. She had maintained her belief in the justice of the British cause and had contributed to the war effort with extraordinary courage and stoicism. The death of her brother came as a final blow, one which was almost too much to bear.

David Jones was also affected by the British Army's manpower crisis in early 1918, but in his case it may have been a fortunate turn of events. As a result of the reduction of infantry brigades from four battalions to three, the London Welsh Battalion in which Jones had served since enlisting was disbanded in February 1918. Jones was redeployed to the 13th Battalion, Royal Welch Fusiliers, then in the trenches near Armentières, but within only a few days he was invalided out with a high fever. For a young man like Jones, who had served continuously with the same battalion since leaving home for the first time early in 1915, this transfer was potentially highly disruptive, but his fever probably had more to do with the cold and wet conditions in the trenches. The cumulative psychological impact of front-line experience, with repeated shelling, may also have played a part.

Although British front-line soldiers during the war were well fed, the physical and psychical conditions they endured were testing in the extreme, and many men suffered from illnesses not caused by enemy action. David Jones was diagnosed with 'pyrexia', which only means fever, and is a symptom rather than an actual illness. Often colloquially referred to as 'trench fever', this fever was thought to be transmitted by lice, which lived in the troops' clothing, and as all war memoirs testify, thrived despite all efforts to exterminate them. 'Trench fever' sometimes lasted only days, but was often recurring. Jones clearly had a very serious attack. He was sent from France back to hospital in London, where he spent the next few months. Although he did not know it at the time, his war as a fighting soldier was over. We do not know if he heard anything about Lloyd George's speech, partly delivered in Welsh, at the Queen's Hall on St David's Day, in which the Prime Minister declared: 'The Welsh troops have been worthy of the noblest cause Britain ever fought to uphold.'⁶⁸ While convalescing, Jones produced another drawing for *The Graphic*, which was published in July. Keeping to the medieval imagery he had previously used, he depicted a crusader confronting a 'Black Knight of Prussia' who was standing over a half-dressed and bound young woman. The symbolism was clear: the crusader is an Allied soldier, defending the virtue of a defenceless female from the brutality of the Prussians.⁶⁹

While Jones lay in hospital, the Welsh Division was marched south to help stem the great German advance which started on 21 March. Eventually the division was used to plug a gap in the now improvised front line at Aveluy Wood, a few miles behind the Somme battlegrounds of 1916. In the two weeks before Charles Mott was killed there, the Welsh Division fought to improve the British position by gaining the high ground in the wood. David Jones was well off out of it. His new battalion suffered 271 casualties pushing the line forward by 250 yards. The divisional history notes that 'some of the attacking companies were reduced to a strength of thirty men'.[70]

## Censorship

As the Passchendaele campaign dragged on Nevinson was still working for the Department of Information, but if he had initially felt constrained in this role, he soon recovered his anti-establishment spirit, producing several pictures which were increasingly controversial in subject matter if not in technique. Nevinson was preparing for an edition of the series called *British Artists at the Front*, and for a major exhibition in London, and produced many works between August 1917 and March 1918. If the title of the proposed publication suggested images of the front line, for the exhibition Nevinson took a much wider view, also depicting civilians at home, reflecting changed social conditions in Britain after 3 years of war. In several works he was deliberately provocative, producing images with ambivalent meanings, and in some cases adding titles which posed disturbing questions to his audience. Inevitably this brought him into conflict with the Department of Information, whose officials several times visited his studio in Robert Street to assess his work.

Although these officials were troubled by three paintings of civilians Nevinson produced late in 1917, they were not sufficiently offended to try to prevent them being shown. The first of the three, a pastel called *The Food Queue*, showed a crowd of civilians, mostly women, outside some shops. Several of the people appear ground down and anxious, and one working-class woman in the centre of the picture stares out at the viewer with hands on hips, openly confrontational. Food rationing was introduced in Britain in February 1918, and people of all classes were by now complaining about food shortages. The crowd in Nevinson's picture, while not on the verge of revolution, presents a variety of emotions, suggestive of barely concealed social tensions. In an oil painting, Nevinson tackled the controversial theme of *War Profiteers*. If the 'spirit of 1914' had been lauded as an end to days of 'sour division', Nevinson's painting suggested that the war had produced new divisions. It showed two well-dressed women – presumably the female relatives of businessmen, or prostitutes – against the background of a city street with beams of light, suggesting either the searchlights which swept the skies for Zeppelins, or the lights of a night club. Both women appear to be enjoying themselves, but their ugliness gives the picture a strong sense of misogyny, prefiguring the strikingly similar images of prostitutes and pampered women produced in Germany between 1919 and 1932 by artists such as Otto Dix and George Gross.

A third painting, *He Gained a Fortune but he Gave a Son*, revisited the theme of profiteering, depicting a well-fed businessman who sits in his living room with, behind him, a framed photograph of a young man in uniform. The expression on the man's face is almost schizophrenic, an impression heightened by the difference between his two eyes. On the one hand he appears complacently self-satisfied; on the other almost broken with sorrow. The picture conveys class tension – this man is clearly a bourgeois – and generational tension. Too old to be called up himself, it is clearly his son who has paid the ultimate price. To judge quite how controversial and offensive an image like this was, we should perhaps refer to an actual example who in some ways resembled Nevinson's subject. Vera Brittain's father Arthur was a prosperous businessman, who before 1914 ran a successful company producing high-quality paper. During the war Brittains Ltd. started making cigarette papers, the normal supply from Germany having been cut off, and cotton cellulose paper used for aeroplane wings. Business boomed, and the company opened extensions to its mills in 1914 and again in 1917.[71] Arthur Brittain was actually opposed to the firm producing cigarette papers and retired from an active managerial role late in 1915.[72] His family continued living on profits generated by the firm. Arthur Brittain, as we know, had been strongly opposed to his son Edward joining up in 1914, but his objections had been overruled. He fell into deep depression after his son's death in June 1918, and later committed suicide. Was he a profiteer in the sense implied by Nevinson's painting? Although none of these three pictures had an explicit anti-war message, by presenting social tensions so bluntly they could only undermine the narrative of a nation united in the prosecution of the war.

Official disquiet was aroused by two of Nevinson's representations of soldiers. On 22 November 1917, Henry Nevinson wrote: 'Richard in great trouble and rage because Major Lee who was at school with him & is a mere imbecile has censored his "Old Contemptibles" as too ugly for British soldiers.'[73] This painting, later renamed more neutrally *A Group of Soldiers*, showed four infantrymen simply standing around, but looking brutish and stupid. It was not a flattering portrayal of the British soldier, and Major Lee, who had earlier supervised official war artists out in France, objected that it showed men of a type 'not worthy of the British Army'.[74] This prompted an internal debate in the Department of Information about artistic freedom and censorship; Nevinson himself sent a sarcastic letter to Masterman complaining that he was being subjected to 'aesthetic censorship' as well as 'military censorship' and stating that he would not paint British soldiers as 'castrated Lancelots' as the illustrated newspapers did.[75] Nevinson clearly had in mind exactly the sort of representation David Jones was publishing in *The Graphic*. Eventually Masterman ruled that there was no objection to the picture being shown. With another picture, Nevinson went too far. In December 1917 Major Lee aroused Nevinson to 'great fury'[76] by objecting to a small painting Nevinson had completed, entitled *Dead Men*. This showed a front-line scene, with two dead British soldiers lying face-down in the mud in front of a barbed-wire entanglement. Nevinson had here abandoned his Vorticist technique, and the work is actually reminiscent of an Impressionist painting. The predominantly brown tones of the mud and of the soldiers' uniforms are flecked with blue, reflecting the sky in the background, and the whole scene is laced with strands of barbed wire glinting in the sun. The delicacy of the representation contrasts strikingly with grim horror of the subject.

Major Lee, having been rebuffed over *A Group of Soldiers*, took care to object to *Dead Men* on grounds of policy, arguing that as newspapers were now prevented from showing photographs of dead British soldiers, Nevinson's picture should not be shown. Despite Nevinson's protests, he was informed on 20 December that this ruling was final.[77] Two days later, rumours that discharged soldiers would be compelled to register for re-enlistment plunged him again into despair. His father wrote: 'The torture of life is hardly bearable.'[78] But in January Henry Nevinson met with John Buchan at the Foreign Office, and was assured that 'Richard need have no fear of going back in the army.' If necessary the Department of Information 'would take him for the whole war'. It was an 'unspeakable relief'.[79] It may have been this assurance which encouraged the painter's truculence in his exhibition at the Leicester Galleries in March. He decided to show his painting of *Dead Men*, now given the deliberately sarcastic title *Paths of Glory*, and when he was told that this was not acceptable, he covered the painting with a strip of brown paper bearing the word 'Censored'.

Nevinson's exhibition must rank as one of the strangest propaganda exercises of the twentieth century. The show was given huge publicity by posters with one of Nevinson's most striking Vorticist designs, the word 'War' in large type standing out against serried upward thrusting bayonets. It was opened by the new Minister of Information, Lord Beaverbrook, who claimed in a speech that 'as an instrument of propaganda' the paintings displayed were 'most effective'. Presumably Beaverbrook knew that one of the paintings he referred to was covered with the word 'Censored'. The newspapers certainly did, and their descriptions of this added a *frisson* of excitement to the proceedings.[80] If the paintings were deeply ambivalent in the messages they communicated, Nevinson's own preface to the exhibition catalogue was, as even his father conceded, 'terribly provocative'.[81] It started with a reasoned exposition of his theme, which was not 'the horrors of war', as it had been in 1916, but an attempt 'to synthesize all the human activity and to record the prodigious organization of our Army'. But, as it proceeded, Nevinson's statement degenerated into a rant. With a scattergun approach he attacked the 'loathsome tradition-loving Public Schools', 'Intellectuals', the 'Press' and 'our antiquity-stinking Universities', appealing instead to 'the largest possible general public'.[82]

If Nevinson wanted publicity, he was successful. The exhibition attracted many visitors and widespread press comment. Inevitably, some were offended. *The Times* again hinted that Nevinson was stifled by his official position, stating that the exhibition contained 'too many pieces of effective commonplace, mere task-work no doubt imposed on the artist, and the penalty of success'.[83] The *Saturday Review* was outraged by 'Mr. Nevinson's self-righteous, bumptious preface' and particularly by the purchase of several of his pictures for the Imperial War Museum. It questioned the judgement of the museum's trustees if they could not see that in *A Group of Soldiers*, 'the best of British manhood is lyingly represented and typified by a gang of brutish cretins'.[84] Conversely, several newspapers pointed out that other images of dead soldiers were in the public domain and argued that the censorship of *Paths of Glory* – which was soon taken down and replaced by a painting of a tank – was unnecessary.[85] A junior officer from the Warwickshire Regiment wrote to the *Saturday Review* to refute its criticism, arguing that front soldiers saw their own experience reflected accurately in Nevinson's work.[86] Most bizarrely, no fewer than eight of Nevinson's pictures were bought by the Imperial War Museum, including *A Group of Soldiers* and *Paths of Glory*.

It appears that Beaverbrook himself, perhaps thinking that any publicity was good publicity, had become Nevinson's greatest fan. Henry Nevinson recorded his son's fear that Beaverbrook wanted 'to see him enshrined as an official war artist without any freedom', and 'to run him "as a circus" & buy him up to paint only war pictures'.[87] Over the next few weeks, as the terrible news of the German offensives reached Britain, Richard Nevinson was again haunted by fears of conscription. Henry Nevinson wrote on 8 April that there was 'a black cloud of war & fear for Richard hanging over me'. Once again Masterman came to the rescue, assuring him that the Ministry of Information would continue to employ his son, and to 'buy all his pictures at a fair rate'.[88] Early in June, as the war news improved, Henry Nevinson recorded a scene at his house in Hampstead which hints at the strange, frayed atmosphere in London after 4 years of war: 'Richard & Kathleen gave a great party at home: about 80–100 people came: dancing to a gramophone in one room.'[89]

## Nash's vision of a new world

Paul Nash's progress towards canonization as one of the twentieth century's great war artists was more sedate. Although he started 1918 in great anxiety – about his own future and that of his brother – he was quickly relieved on both these scores. John Nash was released from active service at the end of January, and from March Paul Nash was paid a small allowance while he prepared his sketches from the front.[90] By May he had produced 56 works for an exhibition called 'The Void of War' at the Leicester Galleries. To accompany this, the Ministry of Information published the third of its series *British Artists at the Front* with 15 reproductions of Nash's work, a biographical essay on him written by Jan Gordon, and a commentary on his work by C. E. Montague, an Intelligence officer at GHQ.

Nash's work appeared at a pivotal moment, when weariness and disillusionment were spreading. Millions of people had now suffered bereavement and loss, and hundreds of thousands of wounded and traumatized men were back in Britain after active service. Air raids and rationing had further depressed the population. The 'Maurice Debate' in parliament, widely seen as tantamount to a vote of confidence in the government, although ending with a resounding majority for Lloyd George, had indicated deep disquiet in the government's integrity. The German spring offensives had rocked public confidence, and it was not yet clear that the tide had been turned. Although no one could see any alternative to fighting on, it was in an increasingly grim spirit that this was contemplated. Samuel Hynes has expressed this by saying 'England had lost its direction before it had won its war, and it had no course but to struggle on to the end, in increasing bitterness of spirit.'[91] Nash's pictures of the Ypres Salient, that tiny area which had encompassed so much human misery, spoke directly to this feeling, expressing horror, dismay and an incomprehension bordering on despair. As sensitive critics have observed, they did not simply express anti-war feeling. The poster advertising the exhibition set the tone, using a Vorticist idiom to portray a barren trench scene, with a duckboard path snaking through dead trees and a wasteland of shell holes.

Above all in his now famous paintings *We Are Making a New World* and *Void* Nash represented the Ypres Salient as a place of utter destruction, the flat landscape disfigured by shell holes and the debris of war, the trees shorn of branches, and the sky blood red. The only human presence in these pictures is of bodies which are rotting into the mud. The titles of these pictures indict the perpetrators of the war and express a deep pessimism. Nash's own comment that he meant 'to rob war of the last shred of glory the last shine of glamour' does not, however, indicate that he thought the British should immediately sue for peace.[92]

It is fascinating to see what contrary views these pictures, now reproduced to evoke 'the pity of war', provoked at the time. In the exhibition catalogue, Arnold Bennett, emphasizing that the painter had served at the front, wrote: 'Lieutenant Nash has seen the Front simply and largely. He has found the essentials of it – that is to say, disfigurement, danger, desolation, ruin, chaos – the little figures of men creeping devotedly and tragically over the waste.... They seem to me to have been done in a kind of rational and dignified rage.... Their supreme achievement is that in their sombre and dreadful savagery they are beautiful.'[93] The *Westminster Gazette* wrote that Nash had presented his vision of the war 'with a beauty of colour and design, and with an innocence of perception'.[94] Others were less impressed. The *Saturday Review* stated that future students might think Nash a 'talented amateur, unusually perceptive and with a charming sense of colour, but obviously a person who had never learnt to draw', and spoke disdainfully of 'his poverty of form and childish figures'.[95] One wonders whether this and the scathing criticism in the *Liverpool Post* were actually motivated by concern about the potential cynicism these pictures might engender: 'It is also impossible to arouse any enthusiasm for Mr. Paul Nash's pictures from the front. They are mostly cryptic studies of mud holes, and his object appears to be to make a landscape look as little like a landscape as possible. His draftsmanship is appalling.'[96]

## Britain's darkest hour

The crisis which came to a head in Britain in the spring of 1918 was the most serious of the war. Although with hindsight it is possible to argue that the Germans did not have the strength to exploit the huge initial gains they made in their spring offensives, this was not so apparent to the British war leaders at the time. The extraordinary confidence which had carried Britain into war and sustained it through the setbacks of 1915 and the battles of attrition in 1916 and 1917 was exposed to searching examination. At home, the narratives of national unity and equality of sacrifice which had saturated public discourse for years were similarly challenged.

These tensions were reflected in, and heightened by the images produced by Nevinson and Nash, now articulating visions of the war which were far from the earlier representations of Rupert Brooke or Kate Finzi. This is not to argue that the 'bitter truth' being portrayed by Nash and Nevinson was now dominant, or that their cynicism was universally felt. Some people, like Vera Brittain and David Jones, were still clinging to older models, trying to imagine the war as a chivalrous crusade; others were simply silent, or like Elgar, retreating into private worlds of nostalgia and regret. The compositions he began in the spring of 1918 have some resemblance in that sense to Parry's *Songs of Farewell*. But Nevinson and Nash were still grappling with the contemporary reality of the war which they had experienced, and what they produced was not uplifting or consolatory. In his images of the Ypres Salient, Nash corroborated the photographs the public had already seen and went further in suggesting that the destruction caused by the war outweighed anything which might be gained from it. Nevinson challenged directly the idea that death in war was somehow glorious, suggesting that actually it was simply squalid and miserable. In his images of the public at home, Nevinson extended Nash's earlier comment about those 'who want the war to go on for ever', suggesting that there were businessmen, and female hangers-on who were profiting from the sufferings of others. These representations of social discord reflected the obvious divisions in the political and military conduct of the war. Notably, even these most embittered representations offered no specific sense of how the war might be ended. There was no significant movement in Britain advocating peace offers to Germany that would leave Belgium and large areas of France occupied. The Union of Democratic Control, while more and more bitterly critical of the British government, still depended for its demands for a negotiated peace on a totally unrealistic appreciation of Germany's position.[97] Having defeated Russia, the German leadership, increasingly concentrated in the hands of Ludendorff and Hindenburg, was still committed to a similar victory over the French and British in the West. In January 1918, Lloyd George, stung by criticisms and aware of the national mood, spoke to the Trades Union Congress, in what he called 'the most critical hour in this terrible conflict'. He restated the British demands: 'First, the sanctity of treaties must be re-established; secondly, a territorial settlement must be secured based on the right of self-determination or the consent of the governed; and lastly, we must seek by the creation of some international organisation to limit the burden of armaments and diminish the probability of war.'[98]

In this context, the dull despair felt by Vera Brittain after hearing of Edward's death, the mute resignation of Elgar after news of Charles Mott's injury, the exhaustion felt by Lawrence out in Egypt and David Jones' prostration by trench fever all appear symptomatic of a deeper national tragedy. There was no alternative but to go on.

# CHAPTER TEN

# August–November 1918

The British Army which attacked the German line at Hamel so successfully on 4 July 1918 was a very different one from that which attacked on the Somme two years previously. After nearly 4 years of war and 2 years of conscription this was a more professionally organized fighting machine. In the final battles on the Western Front it was to demonstrate its growing mastery of what historians have called 'the all arms battle', the combination of infantry with massed artillery using shells of different kinds, tanks and aircraft in a variety of roles. The naïve cheerfulness of Kitchener's 'Pals' preparing to go 'over the top' had indeed been replaced to a large extent by a hardened grimness, but the cynicism of British troops was still underpinned with determination and resolve. Morale had actually improved after the German offensives which started in March 1918, despite the enormous losses suffered. There was by July a marked contrast between the state of the German and British armies in France and Belgium. The British troops were much better fed, and backed up by a weight of artillery which had developed great technical proficiency, using carefully calculated combinations of shrapnel, high explosive, gas and smoke-producing shells. The tanks first used on the Somme were now available in great numbers and were more reliable. The first clumsy models had been supplemented by lighter vehicles which were also used to supply other tanks on the battlefield. Aircraft, which at the start of the war had been fragile and largely unarmed, were now organized in a Royal Air Force and deployed in thousands to support the ground forces. Above all the British had learnt to coordinate these different elements effectively, and for all the resentment felt by front-line soldiers towards staff officers who worked behind the lines, these had developed great skill in directing the diverse forces available by the summer of 1918.

On 24 July, the commanders of the French, British and American armies in France met. They agreed on a 'general plan for the next few weeks', intending 'to regain the initiative'.[1] Haig was already planning an attack near Amiens, and this was approved by Foch. A few days later, having set the date of the attack for 8 August, Haig met his army commanders and stressed the need 'to get troops out of the influence of *Trench* methods'.[2] Meanwhile, preparations for the Amiens attack were carried forward in great secrecy, hoping to achieve surprise. The result was a triumph. Instead of the prolonged bombardments which had preceded the campaigns on the Somme and at Passchendaele, the British attack commenced with an intensive 5-hour bombardment and was strengthened by 422 tanks.[3] The Germans were taken by surprise and totally overwhelmed. So great was the confusion that 33,000 of their men were recorded as 'missing' after 3 days.[4] Most of these had surrendered to the British, who also captured more than 400 guns.[5] Ludendorff, describing this as 'the black day for the German Army in the history of this war', wrote a few months later: 'The [British and French] broke deeply into our front. . . . divisional headquarters were surprised by enemy tanks.'[6] The Canadian troops who spearheaded the attack advanced 8 miles on the first day. This was – for the British Army – unprecedented and prompted Haig to reassess the broader situation. In a notable departure from his previous methods, Haig called off this attack when it stalled after 3 days, looking to renew the offensive elsewhere. He was elated. Meeting Winston Churchill, now Minister of Munitions, on 21 August, Haig told him that 'we ought to do our utmost to get a decision this autumn' and was dismayed to hear from Churchill that the General Staff in London still thought the war would be decided in 1919.[7]

Even as Haig and Churchill conferred, the British Third Army was attacking between Albert and Arras, and again achieved notable success, taking another 10,000 prisoners. Haig now told his army commanders that they were facing 'changed conditions', demanding that they advance more rapidly.[8] He had realized that the Germans were in desperate straits, and although he was still fuming about what he perceived as the ineffectual conduct of the Americans and the French, he was trying to cooperate with them in what Foch called a 'General Offensive'. Although after the success at Amiens Haig's position as commander-in-chief of the BEF was finally secure,[9] old controversies resurfaced when on 29 August he received a telegram from Wilson, the Chief of the Imperial General Staff, telling him that 'the War Cabinet would become anxious if we received heavy punishment in attacking the Hindenburg Line, without success'. Haig was enraged, writing that the politicians were allowing him to attack, and would claim credit if he succeeded, but dismiss him if he failed. In his diary, he concluded: 'What a wretched lot of weaklings we have in high places at the present time!'[10]

After this, Haig requested a meeting in London, 'to explain how greatly the situation in the field had changed to the advantage of the Allies'. It was, Haig believed, 'the beginning of the end'.[11] Haig did not see Lloyd George in London, but tried to persuade Milner, the Secretary of State for

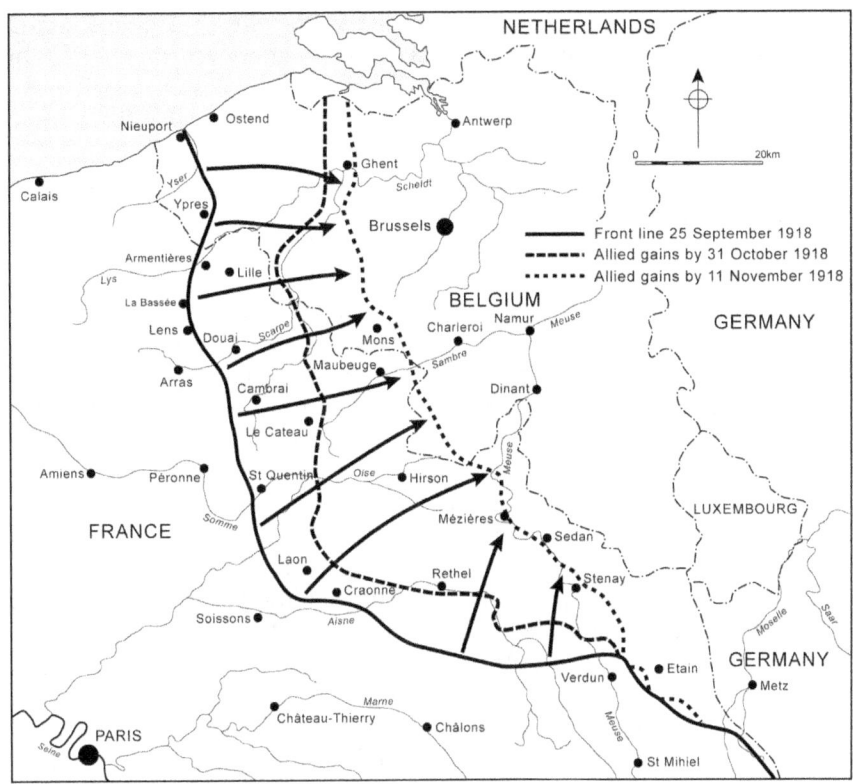

MAP 14 *The Allied offensives of 1918.*

War, that there was a real opportunity before them. Lloyd George was still profoundly sceptical, mindful of the over optimistic prognoses Haig had made in 1916 and 1917. After addressing a meeting in Manchester on 11 September, Lloyd George fell seriously ill with flu and returned to work only at the end of the month. Milner was sent to France to assess the situation and decided that Haig was 'ridiculously optimistic'.[12]

Events were to prove Haig correct. On 12 September the Americans had forced the Germans out of the St Mihiel salient which they had occupied since 1914. Over the next fortnight, the British pressed on, pushing up to the Hindenburg Line. German difficulties were not confined to the Western Front. Their allies in the 'League of Four', Austria, Turkey and Bulgaria, were all in the last stages of exhaustion. After years of inactivity, French troops at Salonica and Serbians in Albania struck against the Bulgarians on 15 September, followed a few days later by the British. The dispirited Bulgarian Army collapsed, and within days the government in Sofia appealed to the Allies for an armistice. On 19 September the British started what turned out to be a final offensive against the Turks in Palestine, advancing towards Damascus. On 25 September the French and Americans returned to the 'General Offensive', opening an attack in the Meuse-Argonne sector. This was rapidly followed by a renewal of British attacks further north. On 28 September British and Belgian troops occupied the Passchendaele ridge and in the following weeks they did what had been impossible for 4 years, advancing out of the Ypres Salient.

Lloyd George had long argued for 'knocking the props away' from the Germans, and the last days of September saw a coming together of the 'eastern' and 'western' strategies which had for years divided British politicians and soldiers. The Germans were now falling back all along the Western Front. As in 1917, their withdrawals were preceded by 'wholesale destruction of all property and forced removal of the population'.[13] On 29 September an armistice was signed with Bulgaria, and on 1 October Arab and Australian forces entered Damascus. On 6 October Haig travelled to meet General Foch again: 'He had a Paris newspaper opened out on the table in front of him in which in large type was printed a note from Austria, Germany, and Turkey, asking for an armistice on the basis of President Wilson's 14 points.'[14] It was a moment of vindication for Haig, and one can only guess at the enormous satisfaction he must have gained from it.

Over the next month, as their armies pressed forward, Allied attention turned to armistice terms with the German and Ottoman Empires. The British, French, Italians and Americans had individual national agendas, and all were concerned with public relations in the final stages of the war. There was thus some unseemly wrangling over which nation's ships should finally enter the Dardanelles and who should occupy the various forts which had defied the British and French attackers in 1915. Much more serious for the British was the worry that President Wilson would insist on the second of his 14 points, the 'freedom of the seas', being honoured in an armistice with the Germans.[15] Lloyd George was absolutely insistent that the British retain the freedom to enforce a blockade and was prepared, if necessary, to continue the war to uphold this.[16] The Admiralty and the commander of the Grand Fleet, David Beatty, wanted to insist on the complete surrender or destruction of the German High Seas Fleet. The French for their part were determined to enforce the surrender of all the German Army's heavy weapons and aircraft, and to occupy the east bank of the Rhine. After four years of grinding attrition, it was difficult for British politicians and soldiers to believe that the Germans were now defeated. Haig, confronted with continuing resistance on the Western Front, and apprehensive about having to continue the fight on German soil, favoured more moderate armistice terms.[17] Lloyd George discussed with Riddell on 27 October 'the chances of peace'. They agreed that there was 'a slight shade of odds in favour of an armistice before Christmas'.[18]

Lloyd George and Riddell also agreed that Germany's allies should be detached, one by one. This had been Lloyd George's vision, and it was realized more quickly than he imagined. On 30 October another prop was knocked away when the Turks signed an armistice on board the British battleship

*Agamemnon*; on all sides the Ottoman Empire was disintegrating. Arab and Indian cavalry units had taken Aleppo a few days before; British troops were close to Mosul in Mesopotamia and were threatening Adrianople, which the Bulgarians had taken from Turkey in 1913.[19] The Austrian Empire was by the autumn of 1918 in a state of economic collapse, its soldiers on pitifully low rations. During October it simply broke up into separate ethnic components. Croatian, Bosnian, Czech, Hungarian and Romanian soldiers deserted, and a final Italian offensive at Vittorio Veneto completed the dissolution. An armistice was signed with the Italians on 3 October, and French and Serbian troops entered Belgrade on 5 November. The last Habsburg emperor, Karl I, went into exile in Switzerland in March 1919.[20] The Austrians had indeed paid heavily for their reckless gamble in July 1914. The Serbs who had provoked them also suffered, having a greater percentage of their population killed in the war than any other combatant nation.

The Germans now stood alone. After years of unequal struggle, the combined effects of the British blockade, of the 'Spanish flu', now raging unchecked, and of military defeat abroad had brought Germany to the point of collapse. Ludendorff, whose judgement and mental stability had become increasingly doubtful during the year, resigned on 26 October and fled to Sweden to write his memoirs. Fantastic plans for some kind of 'final struggle', perhaps using a *levée en masse*, were canvassed, but outside the officer corps they found little support.[21] A mutiny in the German Navy at Kiel at the end of October turned to revolution on shore, and quickly spread to major cities. It fell to Ludendorff's replacement, General Groener, to tell Kaiser Wilhelm on 9 November that the army no longer stood behind him, upon which news the kaiser 'quietly' fled to Holland. On the same day the Social Democrat Philipp Scheidemann proclaimed a German Republic in Berlin, and civilian representatives of the new government were found to sign an armistice with the Allies.[22]

On the morning of 9 November, these German representatives, led by the Catholic Centre Party politician Matthias Erzberger, arrived at a clearing in the forest near Compiégne, to the north of Paris. They were led to a railway carriage where Marshal Foch received them coldly. When they protested that handing over the supplies and rolling stock of their armies, as demanded, would lead to starvation among German civilians living on the east side of the Rhine, Foch told them that that 'was their affair'. He had been, he subsequently told the British, 'Très propre mais sec'.[23] The armistice came into force at 11 a.m. on 11 November, and all along the line the guns fell silent.

## Into darkness

Lloyd George's hopes for an aggressive campaign in Palestine had been stalled in the spring of 1918 as all available resources were channelled to the

Western Front, but after the crisis had been weathered, Allenby was again told to press forward. He planned to strike northwards into present-day Lebanon and Syria, and, by this time fully aware of the role that the Arabs could play, he accepted a plan put forward by Lawrence to attack the vital railway junction of Deraa with an Arab force travelling through the desert to the east of the River Jordan. This last expedition of Lawrence's was on a different scale from those preceding it. He assembled a thousand men and two thousand camels, armed with 24 machine guns, four French mountain guns, two British aircraft, three armoured cars with tenders carrying supplies, and 'a demolition company of Egyptian Camel Corps'.[24] Lawrence himself travelled in an armoured car, leaving after the Arabs, and arriving at their desert base of Azraq before them. The Hejaz railway, starting in Damascus, travelled through Deraa, from where another line went westwards past Nazareth to the sea at Haifa. Lawrence and Allenby reckoned that if they could break these lines, the Turkish and German forces in Palestine would be cut off from their supplies and from any line of retreat. The Turks and Germans were by this time already starved of supplies, and the Turks were suffering from desertions.

By 12 September Lawrence's composite force was assembled at Azraq, where they prepared a landing ground for aircraft. Different groups set out and, while Allenby's offensive started near to the sea at Tulkarm, they managed, not without mishap, to cut the lines leading out of Deraa. Allenby's forces were far too strong for the now demoralized Turks, and

FIGURE 27 *A mine exploding on the Hejaz railway near Deraa in 1918. By the end of the war, Lawrence and Arab fighters were using 'tulip' mines which destroyed longer sections of railway track, making it more difficult for the Turks to repair the Hejaz railway.*

these were forced back in disorder. On 21 September Lawrence was flown to Allenby's headquarters, where Lawrence was instructed to restrain Feisal from entering Damascus before Allied forces had secured it. This was obviously contrary to Lawrence's personal intentions. Returning to Azraq, Lawrence left the desert encampment on 25 September, accompanying the 'camelry, guns, and machine guns' in his Rolls-Royce. Over the next few days, different elements of Lawrence's force had numerous encounters with groups of Turks, Austrians and Germans, now 'a confused mass of fugitives'. Unable to use the railways, these were trying desperately to escape from Allenby's regular forces, from aerial attack and from Arabs, all now sensing that the Turks were finally beaten.

It was in this confused situation that Lawrence became embroiled in a scene of appalling horror. Looking to engage a Turkish column which had been reported by British aircraft, Lawrence's group came first to the village of Turaa, where they discovered that the Turks 'had allowed themselves to rape all the women they could catch'. They then pursued the Turks to the village of Tafas where they found that the inhabitants had been massacred, including 'some twenty small children (killed with lances and rifles), and about forty women'. Lawrence provided this account, printed in the *Arab Bulletin* on 18 October 1918, of what ensued when his men caught up with the Turks:

> With Auda's help we were able to cut the enemy column into three. The third section, with German machine-gunners resisted magnificently, and got off, not cheaply, with Jemal Pasha in his car in their midst. The second and leading portions after a bitter struggle, we wiped out completely. We ordered 'no prisoners' and the men obeyed, except that the reserve company took two hundred and fifty men (including many German A. S. C.) alive. Later, however, they found one of our men with a fractured thigh, who had been afterwards pinned to the ground by two mortal thrusts with German bayonets. Then we turned out Hotchkiss on the prisoners and made an end of them, they saying nothing. The common delusion that the Turk is a clean and merciful fighter led some of the British troops to criticize Arab methods a little later – but they had not entered Turaa or Tafas, or watched the Turks swing their wounded by the hands and feet into a burning railway truck, as had been the lot of the Arab army at Jerdun.

There has been much debate about this episode. While there is agreement that the atrocities at Turaa and Tafas happened, and that the 250 Turkish and German prisoners were subsequently massacred by the Arabs, differing post-war accounts – not least by Lawrence himself – have raised doubts about whether Lawrence was actually present at the massacre of the prisoners; whether he ordered the massacre; whether he took part, or whether indeed, he tried to prevent it. Lawrence's most immediate account – which is cited above – suggests that he was there, and that if he did not order the massacre, he accepted responsibility for it, as he did for the earlier order not to take prisoners, which can only be interpreted as an order to kill any who surrendered or who were wounded. Given that the Turkish/German force was reported originally as two thousand strong, Lawrence's report suggests that more than half that number was killed. The whole episode is shocking and gruesome, recalling in its horror the worst German atrocities in Belgium and France in 1914, and presaging the far more numerous atrocities in Eastern Europe between 1939 and 1945, and in the Bosnian wars of the 1990s.

The Hague Conventions of 1889 and 1907, to which Britain and the Ottoman Empire were signatories, demanded that soldiers who surrendered or who were captured when wounded must be humanely treated, but there were numerous occasions when these conventions were breached by all sides in the conflict.[25] On the Western Front, many soldiers were resentful about prisoners who appeared to be getting a relatively soft option of captivity when they themselves had to continue fighting. Frequently, enemy soldiers who were wounded or who had surrendered were done to death on the spot, or as they were being led behind the lines. Audoin-Rouzeau and Becker note how the killing of prisoners (carried out in the French Army by *nettoyeurs de tranchées*, or 'trench cleaners') 'was a widespread practice on all fronts in the First World War'.[26] All too often, prisoners of war suffered more from neglect than malicious intent. Sometimes, when large numbers of men surrendered, there was no immediate provision of food, water, sanitation or shelter for them, and this was often the case in the Middle East. The appalling ill treatment of the British and Indian soldiers who surrendered at Kut in May 1916 is well known, but fewer people in Britain today know anything about the treatment of the tens of thousands of Turkish prisoners captured by the British between 1914 and 1918. By the middle of the war there were organized camps in Egypt for the majority of these unfortunates, but these were far from the fighting fronts, and it was not easy for prisoners to be transported there.

During the Arab Revolt, and subsequently in Palestine, Turkish soldiers often surrendered along with women and children, typically in situations where there was no provision whatsoever for them, and they suffered accordingly. A telegram from the British in Jeddah to Cairo 6 months after the start of the revolt noted that there was 'totally inadequate and most insanitary accomodation [sic] provided for Turkish prisoners, number of whom suffering from fever'. It went on to state that women and children among the prisoners were living without shelter or food, and concluded: 'Hope steamer for their removal will soon be available.'[27] It is perfectly clear from Lawrence's own reports on guerrilla raids that his men frequently killed wounded and captured Turks. Nor did he and his Arab followers expect anything other than the cruellest treatment if they were captured.

Clearly some of the British soldiers present at Tafas protested about the massacre, but Lawrence was not reprimanded or disciplined by any more senior figure for his part in it. One wonders how those who read the *Arab Bulletin*, in Cairo, in the Indian Office, the War Office or in the Foreign Office reacted to it. The copy now available for research in the National Archives has a small pencil mark next to the lines in which Lawrence reports how one of the Arabs was found pinned to the ground by German bayonets, as if to emphasize this mitigating circumstance.[28] Without seeking to excuse what was by any standard a war crime, we should be aware of how the levels of violence and cruelty in the desert since 1916 had escalated – on all sides – and of how civilians, including women and children, had been caught up in this. There is evidence that the murder of Turkish and German prisoners at Tafas was only one of numerous atrocities carried out in the last days of September 1918.[29] One of the armoured car drivers with Lawrence wrote in a later memoir that, in the final stages of the drive to Damascus, 'Half-naked, festering bodies lay in all directions, some with staring eyes and discoloured with blood'.[30] A further massacre of two hundred prisoners gathered by Lawrence's forces on the day of the Tafas massacre was only narrowly averted after he, other British officers, and the Arabs held a debate. One of the British officers appealed for clemency, arguing that he was a member of Parliament, and would have to face an electorate on his return to Britain. Apparently this caused so much mirth among the Arabs that the whole situation was defused, and the prisoners were spared.[31]

Lawrence had little time to dwell on the massacres at Tafas. He was desperate to get to Damascus, which was entered by soldiers of the Australian Light Horse on the night of 30 September. Lawrence himself was driven into the city on the morning of 1 October and found, to his dismay, that two Algerian Arabs 'had assumed possession of the provisional civil government'. He turned them out and announced 'as Feisal's representative' that Shukri el-Ayubi was the new 'Arab Military Governor'. During the day, more Australian horsemen led by Harry Chauvel arrived, surprised to find that Lawrence was already there, insisting that an Arab administration was in place. By the evening there was looting and disorder, and Lawrence had to post machine guns around the central square to try to control the situation.

The situation was still confused the next morning, and, touring the city with a fellow officer, Alec Kirkbride, Lawrence had frequently to intervene to prevent Turks from being killed by angry Arabs. He and Kirkbride were also alerted to problems at a hospital full of dead and dying Turkish soldiers, and Lawrence was incensed to find that the Australian soldiers already present refused to intervene. Lawrence – according to a letter he subsequently wrote to an American who was also there – remonstrated with them and forced the Turkish doctors (who 'were skulking in their quarters') and some Turkish prisoners to start tending to the sick and removing the dead.[32] It was a situation similar to that which had confronted Finzi in Boulogne and

Nevinson in Dunkirk in the early days of the war. If Lawrence's later account in *Seven Pillars of Wisdom* is to be believed, it was more horrible still. At midday on 2 October Chauvel marched a body of his troopers through the city, which helped to enforce some degree of calm. Lawrence returned to the hospital the next day and was accosted by an Australian doctor who was now continuing the gruesome work begun the day before. Lawrence lost his self-control when asked if he was in charge of the hospital and became hysterical, screaming at the doctor. The Australian then slapped Lawrence twice across the face, after which he calmed down. One senses that Lawrence was on the edge of total breakdown.[33]

Allenby himself arrived on 3 October, rapidly followed by Feisal, who insisted on galloping into the city on horseback. Allenby convened a meeting attended by Feisal, Chauvel and Lawrence among others and informed them that an Arab, Ali Riza Rikabi, would serve as governor of Damascus under Feisal, who would in turn be under Allenby's control, but would work alongside a French liaison officer. Allenby also announced that Lebanon, now liberated from the Turks, would be under French control. Feisal balked at this; Lawrence claimed not to have known about this arrangement, and in total frustration, asked Allenby if he could take some leave and return to England. Allenby sensibly accepted this, and dismissed him.[34] Lawrence was exhausted and overwrought, and appears to have accepted that his war was over. He would now pursue the cause of Arab independence with his pen. Two weeks later, having submitted his final report for the *Arab Bulletin*, he wrote from the Grand Continental Hotel in Cairo to a colleague:

> As we hoped we got to Damascus, and there I had to leave the Arabs – it is a pity to go, and it would have been unwise to stay. I feel like a man who has suddenly dropped a heavy load – one's back hurts when one tries to walk straight.
> 
> I'm off, out of Egypt. This old war is closing, and my use is gone. . . . We were an odd little set, and we have, I expect, changed history in the near East. I wonder how the Powers will let the Arabs get on.[35]

## Final blows

Back in England, Hubert Parry was not finding life easy. His health had deteriorated as he neared his 70th birthday, and in common with others of the British upper and middle classes, he was struggling to maintain his accustomed lifestyle. Unable to get petrol for his Rolls-Royce, he had taken to riding a bicycle. The usual difficulties rich people were now experiencing in finding domestic servants were compounded by his wife's capricious behaviour, which had alienated otherwise loyal workers. Most troubling was the effect of the war on his estate at Highnam. By 1918, Parry had

had sorrowfully to acquiesce in demands for many of the trees planted by his father to be cut down. On 23 July he took stock, writing: 'Such a scene of desolation & confusion . . . was never seen.'[36] A few days later Parry found himself in a difficult social situation. He went with his wife to tea with some of her aristocratic friends, one of whom apparently expressed the view that Germans ought to be crucified. Although Parry had apparently not previously contributed much to the conversation, he wrote: 'I now let fly.' It is difficult to imagine Parry being angry or intemperate, but we can assume that he could marshal formidable powers of rhetoric when needed. He continued: 'I said enough to shock them.'[37] One wonders how many xenophobic and anti-German views he had endured with forbearance since August 1914 before exploding on this occasion.

The last entry in Parry's diary is dated 9 September 1918. Shortly after this he fell ill, and rapidly declined. He may well have been a victim of the 'Spanish flu' which was now raging unchecked across Europe. Parry died on 7 October 1918, at Rustington. He lived long enough to see the upturn in Allied fortunes, but died when the end of the war still seemed distant. His funeral was held at St Paul's Cathedral on 16 October and was attended by a roll-call of the great and the good in British musical life. Elgar and his wife Alice were present. Assembled musicians, including the choral class from the Royal College which Parry had been so involved with, performed Croft's *Funeral Sentences*, music by Wesley, Stanford, Bach and his own *Song of Farewell*, 'There Is An Old Belief', which as we know, he had wanted to be performed in a church.[38] In an address to students at the Trinity College of Music, Frederick Bridge said: 'If anybody did his best to leave English music and English musicians better than he found them, that man was Hubert Parry.'[39] It was the end of an era.

The news from Italy in July 1918 was the final blow in a long process of maturation and change in Vera Brittain's perception of the war. Her experience of the war through the prism of participants she knew closely ended with Edward's death. She also appears to have been slightly unhinged by the cumulative impact of the death the four young men she knew best. She wrote a poem 'in memory' of Edward, titled 'That Which Remaineth', using again the archaic language of medieval chivalry which had such a hold on the English imagination, depicting 'the fitting end of a gentle knight',[40] but in actuality, finding out more about his 'end' became an obsession. Her biographers relate how she read in the newspapers that Edward's commanding officer, Lieutenant-Colonel Hudson, had been wounded, and tracked him down to try to discover from him more about the precise circumstances of Edward's death. Although Hudson agreed to see her, she was convinced that he was hiding something after he related how Edward had been shot in the head by an enemy sniper, apparently leading his men in a brave counter-attack.[41]

Her subsequent behaviour can only be described as stalking. She pursued Hudson with enquiries and even went to Buckingham Palace when he was decorated in September 1918 with the Victoria Cross for his part in the action in which Edward had been killed. According to *The Times*, Hudson had shown great gallantry in leading a counter-attack after all the 'officers on the spot were killed or wounded'.[42] Vera Brittain developed the idea that Hudson had profited from the gallantry of his fellow officers, and wrote a poem about this. Irrespective of the actual facts surrounding her brother's death and Hudson's decoration, the poem is notable for its bitterness and cynicism, entirely different from her previous writing. She wrote:

> 'Tis not your valour's meed alone you bear
> Who stand the hero of a nation's pride;
> For on that humble Cross you live to wear
> Your friends were crucified.[43]

Only months earlier, she had written of her brother's Military Cross:

> And silver in the summer morning sun
> I see the symbol of your courage glow.[44]

It was in this mood of increasing resentment that Brittain signed on again as a VAD nurse. She wrote later that 'the Army had become a habit which only the end of the war could break', but she was now told that as she had earlier not fulfilled her contract, she could not be sent abroad.[45] She worked briefly at St Thomas' Hospital in London, before transferring to Queen Alexandra's Hospital in Millbank, now coping with many cases of 'Spanish flu', where she stayed until April 1919. It was little comfort that she had, before the war ended, achieved her ambition of becoming a published writer. Her small book of poems written during the war, entitled *Verses of a V.A.D.*, was finally published in August 1918, by which time she clearly felt some distance from the largely romantic and heroic view of the war which these verses presented. On Armistice Day Brittain went in to central London with other nurses; later she wrote an account of this, presenting herself as too grief-stricken to join in the frenzied celebrations she found there. Already, she claimed, it was evident to her that a new age had begun, one in which 'people would be light-hearted and forgetful', in which 'their careers and their amusements would blot out political ideals and great national issues'.[46]

Brittain was a disapproving observer of the Armistice celebrations in London, but Nevinson, who was also there, joined in, his own behaviour typifying the day's brittle and schizophrenic mood. Again we rely on his later memoir for an account. According to this, Nevinson and his wife Kathleen went to Whitehall, and to Trafalgar Square with great crowds, and on to the Café Royal for champagne; then to various clubs, to Piccadilly, back to the Café Royal and finally to a party in Regent's Park. It was, he wrote, 'the most remarkable day of emotion in my life'.[47]

## Spencer's trial by ordeal

Through June, July and August 1918, Stanley Spencer waited to hear confirmation of his appointment as a war artist, and to be recalled from the front. In September, he had still heard nothing, writing to his sister: 'I begin to give up hopes.'[48] On 1 September the long-awaited joint offensive against the Bulgarians, led by the new French commander, General Franchet d'Esperey, had opened on a long front. On the British sector, the offensive started on 18 September; the initial attack, led by the Oxford and Bucks Light Infantry, and the South Wales Borderers, was a bloody slaughter. Advancing in gas masks up steep slopes against a resolute defence, the British suffered terrible casualties. The 7th Battalion of the South Wales Borderers was reduced to only 50 men; only one of 17 officers leading the attack was unhurt.[49] Spencer's battalion from the Royal Berkshire Regiment had been held back, but was now moved forward to renew the assault. Before this, letters were distributed and the men were told to destroy them once they had been read. One to Spencer, from Gwen Raverat, congratulated him on his new appointment, but he had little time to think about this. He spent a tense night dwelling on the prospect of going over the top, only to discover in the morning, with his comrades, that the Bulgarians had fallen back.

Although Spencer was spared the horror of a frontal attack, the next few days turned into a nightmare for this sensitive young man as his battalion pursued the fleeing Bulgarians. Spencer was detailed with a couple of other men to reconnoitre along some hills, but he had lost his water bottle, an important accessory in the dry countryside. Looking rather desperately for the lost bottle, Spencer was assumed by another unit to be malingering, threatened at pistol point, and told to move on. After this Spencer felt that he was branded as a coward and was deliberately persecuted. A few days later, as the pursuit continued, Spencer partly redeemed his reputation by going out with an officer to observe for the artillery, and staying to tend him when he was wounded. According to his Spencer's later reminiscence, when stretcher bearers arrived, he heard the wounded officer whisper to one of them, 'Understand, Spencer is not a fool; he is a damned good man.' This only confirmed Spencer's suspicion that his reputation had suffered because of the earlier incident.

As the British advanced further, Spencer saw more of the horror of war. The Royal Berks crossed the frontier into Bulgaria, passing dead men and horses. He was shocked by the cruelty of a fellow soldier who shot a dog for no apparent reason, and he had to suffer jibes from fellow-soldiers who clearly found his unworldliness amusing or contemptible. Spencer was also going down again with malaria, and near to collapse, he was taken to 'a crowded hospital, previously German'. From there he was taken by train to Salonica, where he stayed in hospital until the Armistice with Bulgaria was announced on 19 October.[50] Although Spencer reconstructed these experiences in some detail many years later,[51] we can best judge how seriously they affected him from the cryptic references to them in letters he wrote from hospital immediately afterwards.

On 6 October Spencer was sufficiently recovered to write to old friends. To Henry Lamb he wrote: 'I am in hospital for a few days with Malaria, after some trying experiences. Don't these experiences make you feel awful afterwards. I feel depressed & long for something nice: to do some fine paintings or to find some fine literature or hear grand music. . . . I have had no news at all about the Min. of Inf. job. I am afraid they have forgotten all about it. I have written twice to Yockney. It will be a cruel disappointment to me if I can't do any painting'.[52] To Jacques and Gwen Raverat he wrote: 'I have had some rather trying experiences which have rather unmanned me but during the actual time I stuck it & did well I think. I did not like seeing such things & I don't want to again.'[53] Before leaving hospital, having heard that the Bulgarians had capitulated, Spencer wrote to his sister, 'But I hope we do not release the grip we have just now on the German, before her power to retaliate is exhausted.'[54]

It was another fortnight before Spencer felt able to write to his parents, but he was still low. He told them how isolated he had been in the army, saying that since he had been split up from a friend he had made in Bristol, 'I have been silent. My conversation has been reduced to "yea" and "nay"'. Trying bravely to look ahead, he added, 'The war *is* coming to end and that very soon, I feel sure.'[55] A letter which Spencer wrote to his sister, possibly shortly after the armistice with Germany on 11 November, suggests that he was beginning to recover his equilibrium. He confessed that he had 'just had a bottle of stout', explaining that he had been 'put on' stout three times a week, needing 'strengthening'. He continued: 'Every now and then a marquee of men set up cheering à propos of nothing: we are all "tapped." But I must close this letter and do my share of the cheering, so cheerio darlin.'[56]

## The end comes

Elgar spent the summer and early autumn of 1918 at Brinkwells in the Sussex countryside. He was out of doors for much of the time, and, although there were visitors to the cottage, he was able to concentrate also on writing music. A typical entry in the diary he kept for this period reads simply: 'Music & wood'. Although he had declared in the summer of 1917 that he was finished with 'war music', Elgar did accede to a request from the Ministry of Food to write a children's song for the journal *Teacher's World*,[57] but his creative energies were focused on a group of works which he had started immediately after the operation on his throat in March 1918. These works, eventually to reach posterity as a Cello Concerto in E Minor, a String Quartet, a Violin Sonata and a Quintet for Piano and Strings, have much in common, and it appears that he worked on them interchangeably. One expert has suggested that they should be seen not as separate works but 'as a single sustained outpouring in thirteen movements'.[58] The first to be completed, in September, was the Violin Sonata.

There has been much discussion of how these works might be related to Elgar's external life. On the one hand, they mark a distinct change from all his earlier wartime compositions, in that he appears to have abandoned programme music – settings of words – and taken instead to absolute, abstract, instrumental music. Elgar himself was typically enigmatic about these works. Later, he wrote that the Cello Concerto expressed 'a man's attitude to life'; the Violin Sonata had a dedication to Marie Joshua, a long-time German friend of the Elgars who died in September 1918. Recently, Brian Trowell has argued that these works embody and express detailed aspects of Elgar's wartime experience, above all his 'sense of loss', and has supported this analysis with a close reading.[59] If these works do speak of Elgar's wartime experience and of his view of the world after 4 years of war, they are notable for the lack of any sense of celebration, rejoicing or triumphalism, being marked instead by sombre and often deeply sorrowful reflection.

At Brinkwells Elgar was aware of the upturn in Allied fortunes in the late summer, briefly noting good news from the Western Front in his diary on 5 August.[60] He also noted in early October the news that the Germans were suing for peace,[61] but unlike his wife, who expressed the hope that the Germans would be dictated to,[62] Elgar himself said nothing about a post-war settlement. Notably, he refused to write what he called 'peace music', although several old friends and collaborators pressed him to do so. Laurence Binyon, who had inspired Elgar with his early war poems, had served in an ambulance unit on the Western Front, and now published a 'Peace Ode' in the *Observer*. He asked Elgar to set this to music, but Elgar replied on 5 November: 'I think your poem beautiful exceedingly – but I do not feel drawn to write peace music somehow – I thought long months ago that I could feel that way and if anything could draw me your poem would, but the whole atmosphere is too full of complexities for me to feel music to it; not the atmosphere of the poem but of the times I mean.' Referring to the last verses of Binyon's poem, Elgar wrote: 'I regret the appeal to the Heavenly Spirit which is cruelly obtuse to the individual sorrow and sacrifice – a cruelty I resent bitterly and disappointedly.'[63] As so often with Elgar, this remark is enigmatic. Did he mean by 'individual sorrow and sacrifice' those killed in the war, or himself, or both?

Elgar's behaviour at the very end of the war is also striking. His wife Alice clearly did not share his pleasure in the rural seclusion of Brinkwells, and as the autumn drew in, she had looked forward to returning to London. Together they left Brinkwells on 11 October, and for the last few weeks of the war, Elgar stayed with various friends, travelling only briefly to London. On the day the Armistice was signed, and as vast crowds gathered in London, he managed to get to Victoria Station and left the 'busy hum of men',[64] returning to Brinkwells. There he was pursued by letters from supplicants.

Sidney Colvin, who first suggested that he set Binyon's poems in 1915, had been moved by seeing huge crowds gather outside Buckingham Palace, singing 'Land of Hope and Glory', and he wrote to Elgar on the first day of peace: 'It really must be that you shall write the great & final peace music, & Binyon or someone must be inspired to provide the words for you.'[65] A few days later, the critic Robin Legge wrote in similar vein: 'Meanwhile what do you think of Binyon's poem, enclosed, cut from today's *Observer*? Can't you persuade your real self to clinch "Carillon" & all the horrors of war with a Hymn of Peace? You are the only one to tackle a Peace Hymn – it would have stirred you – and even you, its creator, would have had a lump in the throat if you had heard about 200,000 sing "Land of Hope & Glory" in front of Buckingham Palace on Monday. Is it nothing to have done a National Anthem which already has passed into the blood?'[66]

Elgar would have none of it. He liked Sidney Colvin too much to reject his appeal brutally, and replied in a way which suggested that he was still thinking over the whole idea: 'I fear *peace* music is "off" – I am trying to gather up the broken threads but up to this present music does not go on well'.[67] Given the composition of the last few months this sounds a little disingenuous. Despite other subsequent requests, Elgar never did write any 'peace music', but we should not imagine that, as he retreated to the countryside on Armistice Day, he was entirely broken in spirit. He noted before leaving London that day: 'Armistice – ran up flag' and the next day, in Brinkwells, he wrote: '*Put up Flag*'.[68] In his letter to Colvin saying that 'peace music' was 'off', he gave a better description, writing that he had erected a '40 ft staff so our Jack floats proudly over the valley'.

It is tempting to imagine the last months of the First World War as a succession of Allied victories, of heroic engagements resulting in towns and villages liberated, and prisoners taken. It is easy to overlook how terribly costly the final offensives were, particularly – as ever – for the attackers. The British, French and American armies suffered huge casualties in the unrelenting assaults which started in July 1918 and were sustained into November. Soldiers who, like Stanley Spencer, had not previously been in combat were involved in bitter fighting; many, like Charles Mott, were killed. In France and Belgium, as the survivors advanced, the encounter with civilians who had suffered German occupation, and the spectacle of buildings, bridges and railways deliberately destroyed as the Germans fell back seemed to confirm years of hostile representation of the enemy as fiendish and diabolical. That the mild-mannered Stanley Spencer should express his desire to see the Germans thoroughly trodden down indicates how widespread the anger felt against them was. There were indeed far fewer arguing, as Parry had done with his wife's aristocratic friends, that the Germans should not all be tarred with the same brush, and that harsh punishments would only breed further discontents.

In Cardiff, as elsewhere across Britain on 11 November 1918, there was great public rejoicing. By 2.00 p.m. in the afternoon the trams had stopped running as the 'tram girls', like most other workers, abandoned work and flocked into the city centre to celebrate. A wounded officer, described in the local press as a 'legless hero', enthused the crowds outside the Queen's Hotel with an impromptu speech praising Lloyd George as 'the hero behind the guns'. Patriotic songs were sung and flags were waved. In St Mary's Street 'a life size effigy of the Kaiser was suspended by the neck on a rough-and-ready gallows'.[69]

# CHAPTER ELEVEN

# 1919-23

The First World War came to a remarkably clear-cut end on the Western Front. In other theatres fighting continued for some days after the Armistice came into force on 11 November 1918. In central Albania the war was prolonged until 21 November. In East Africa, where a small German force had escaped destruction by much greater British numbers since the start of the war, hostilities only ended on 23 November when General Lettow-Vorbeck brought his 155 surviving Germans and 4,416 African auxiliaries into the settlement of Abercorn to surrender.[1] The Turkish garrison in Medina which had been besieged by rebellious Arabs since June 1916, now weakened by influenza, finally surrendered to Husein's forces on 10 January 1919. From the Mediterranean Sea and from the Atlantic Ocean German submarines made the hazardous passage home, hearing at different times of the end of the war. A group of 11 U-boats, including one commanded by Martin Niemöller (later to be achieve fame as a Protestant priest imprisoned by the Nazis) finally returned to Kiel on 29 November, defiantly flying the war flag of the German Navy.[2] They found that most of the German fleet had already crossed the North Sea into British internment and that the remaining vessels in Kiel were largely under the control of revolutionary councils. The British had demanded in the armistice terms imposed upon the Germans that no fewer than six battlecruisers, ten battleships, eight cruisers, and 50 destroyers 'of the most modern types', and 'all existing submarines' should be handed over to the Allies within days.[3] Accordingly, on 21 November no fewer than 70 German warships had assembled off the Firth of Forth, led by the British cruiser HMS *Cardiff*. From there they were escorted to the Grand Fleet's base at Scapa Flow and anchored with skeleton crews to await the signing of a peace treaty. The German ships had been so short of lubricating oils and coal that they could only proceed to this final destination 'at funeral pace'.[4]

On the Western Front, the German Army surrendered to the Allies 5,000 artillery pieces, 25,000 machine guns, 3,000 trench mortars and

1,700 aircraft, as well as 5,000 locomotives and 150,000 carriages, and 5,000 lorries. After that its units were allowed to retire, abandoning all the territory they had occupied since August 1914, and relinquishing German territory on the west bank of the Rhine to Allied armies. British forces advanced through Belgium and reached the German frontier without opposition on 24 November. The first British troops entered Germany on 1 December, and 11 days later they crossed the Hohenzollern Bridge at Cologne to establish a bridgehead on the east bank of the Rhine. The last British occupation units did not leave the Rhineland until December 1929.[5] In the meantime the huge military machine which had been assembled by the end of the war had to be dismantled. An end to conscription was announced on the day after the Armistice,[6] and by mid-1919 most of the civilians who had been mobilized during the conflict had been released. 140,000 British soldiers, sailors and airmen who had been imprisoned in Germany were returned, many weakened and traumatized by their experiences.

In January 1919, the delegates of the victorious Allies arrived in Paris to discuss the peace terms to be enforced on Germany and the other defeated countries. After months of haggling, harsh terms, including the payment of huge reparations to France and Belgium, a more or less total disarmament, the loss of all overseas colonies and some of its own territory, were inflicted on Germany. All of these punishments were based on a formal assertion that the Germans alone had caused the war in 1914.[7] Fearing that their warships would be handed over to the victors, the crews on the German vessels interned in Scapa Flow managed to scuttle all of them as the negotiations came to a conclusion in June 1919. This act of defiance did little to incline the Allies to be more sympathetic to the Germans, who were effectively forced to accept the terms of the Treaty of Versailles on 28 June. Only after German representatives had signed the treaty was the British naval blockade relaxed, by which time many of the population were seriously affected by undernourishment and the lack of fuel. Belgian independence, which the British had gone to was to defend in 1914, was restored, something which now seemed insignificant in the greater scale of the catastrophe which had ensued. The French recovered the territories occupied by Germany during the war and, in addition, achieved their long held goal of regaining Alsace and Lorraine, taken from them by the Germans after the war of 1870, but this brought little joy to British hearts. Separate treaties were concluded by the Allies with the Austrians in October 1919, with Bulgaria in November 1919, with Hungary in June 1920 and with Turkey in August 1920. A net result of these treaties was a considerable enlargement of the British Empire, many former German and Ottoman territories being designated as 'mandates' under British control by the newly established League of Nations. Priya Satia, in her penetrating study, argues that there was a short period at the end of the war when the prospect of developing Mesopotamia within the British Empire, 'offered something of a narrative of compensation' for the disappointments arising from the war in Europe: 'for a brief moment', she writes, 'the British public glimpsed a shimmering vision of the old world rising, like a phoenix, from the ashes of total war'. This case is easily overstated. There may have been individuals, and some of these are central to her own narrative, for whom the prospect of an invigorated and enlightened empire in the Middle East was an exciting vision, but there were few in Britain for whom this prospect offered anything approaching satisfactory compensation for the losses and suffering caused by the war. As Satia herself notes, it was in any case a vision which was quickly shorn of its romantic gloss.[8]

British forces were involved in armed conflict in many parts of the world in the months and years after November 1918, in smaller struggles arising from the war. There was an ill-considered attempt to intervene in the civil war in Russia; there was fighting in Afghanistan and in parts of the Middle East and Africa. Closer to home the bitter struggle for Irish Home Rule turned into a bloody civil war only concluded in 1922 with the partition of Ireland and the establishment of the Free State of Eire. In mainland Britain there was nothing like the prolonged revolutionary struggles and sustained political violence which characterized the post-war period in much of Central and Eastern Europe, and have caused historians now to see the First World War as a conflict extending over a decade and more, from 1912 until 1923, rather than one of only 4 years' duration. For most British people, the war did end in November 1918, and after this civilians and soldiers alike had to contend with the difficulties of a transition from war to peace.

Just as in 1914 and 1915 the move to war had affected different individuals in different ways and at different speeds, so the transition to peace was experienced in very different ways by those who had survived. More than a million British people had physical wounds of varying severity, some of which healed rapidly, some of which caused lifelong disabilities. All but the very youngest had memories of the war, and literally millions carried with them experiences of bereavement, loss, separation and suffering which would now be considered as traumatic. In many cases this trauma was so apparent, and so disabling as to prevent any possibility of resuming any kind of 'normal' life.[9] In a society which prized a stoical concealment of feeling as one of its defining characteristics, millions simply tried to repress their memories and to hide the damage done. Creative artists were something of an exception to this British habit of denial, and in their work they had the possibility, if they chose to exercise it, of trying to use words, images and music to reflect upon what they and others had gone through.

## The creation of a legend

One artist alone in the group studied here attempted to combine the construction of memory with the appeasement of his personal demons, and with a pursuance of the cause he had worked for during the war. T. E. Lawrence had left Damascus in October 1918 in an emotional and overwrought state, excited by the entry of Feisal's Arabs into the city, frustrated by the tensions already arising between them, the British and the French, and sickened by the scene of neglected Turkish wounded at the city's former barracks. In a letter written in 1929, Lawrence, referring to his efforts to clean up this 'charnel house', claimed that 'Anyway, all my thought was of going home, where I meant to get transferred to the French front. The eastern business was badly on my nerves'.[10] Although this last sentence has the ring of truth, it appears that Lawrence was determined to continue working on the 'eastern business', now using the weapon of publicity.

He was clearly calmer by the time he arrived in Cairo, where on 8 October he wrote the first of four brief accounts about the Arab Revolt which contained in condensed form some of the key elements he would later develop in *Seven Pillars of Wisdom*. Through his acquaintance with Geoffrey Dawson, the editor of *The Times*, Lawrence was able to publish four articles over the next six weeks which for the first time presented to an avid British public a romanticized vision of the Arab Revolt, and which hinted at his own – typically concealed – involvement in it. In the first article, presented on 17 October 'from a correspondent in Cairo', Lawrence also subtly advanced Arab claims to inherit the mantle of Turkish authority in Syria. Describing the 'Arab March on Damascus', Lawrence called Feisal's men 'a detachment of the regular forces of King Hussein'. He described how, when attacked by German aircraft, they had camouflaged themselves in a wadi near Deraa, 'like black stones in the story of the Arabian Nights'. Echoing the discourse of German barbarity early in the war, he described how the Turks had attacked Arab villages 'with every revolting circumstance of atrocity'. He did not mention the atrocities perpetrated in revenge by Feisal's 'regular forces'. Hinting at the practical competence of Feisal's men, he stressed how the 'Arab administration' in Damascus had managed 'to restore the electric lighting system' in the city by the evening of 2 October and restored the tram service only 3 days later. Then, in lyrical tones which would characterize some of his later prose, Lawrence likened Feisal's triumphal entrance into Damascus to a series of historical precedents, ranging from the '14th century B.C.' through to 'the Amorite Arabs who returned to it in the 19th century'. Rejecting the possibility of entering the city in a motor car, Feisal had allegedly 'entered Damascus at full gallop and rode furiously through the city to the accompaniment of a *feu de joie* and shrill screams of victory'.[11]

Back in London, Lawrence was called before the Cabinet's Eastern Committee on 29 October, and on 4 November he presented a memorandum to the group. After years as an amateur strategist in the Arab Bureau and as a fighter in the desert, access to the highest levels of government was in some ways a consummation for Lawrence, who now proposed that the Sykes-Picot Agreement be abandoned. In its place he suggested giving the French control of Beirut and Lebanon, and installing Arab rulers under British protection in Syria and Mesopotamia. Feisal would rule in Syria, and his brothers Abdullah and Zeid in Lower and Upper Mesopotamia, respectively. In a hopeful attempt to reconcile British, French and Arab claims, and to bolster the Arab cause, Lawrence claimed that the Arabs would be prepared to support 'Jewish infiltration' in Palestine if this was behind 'a British, as opposed to an international façade'. They would not, however, approve 'Jewish Independence for Palestine'.[12]

Between these two visits, Lawrence made a characteristically confused gesture. Invited to Buckingham Palace to receive his CB and Distinguished Service Order on 30 October, Lawrence told King George V that he could not accept these honours because of the deception about to be practised upon the Arabs.[13] Although this might have been calculated to gain publicity for the Arab cause, his next steps laid the foundations for the later legend of 'Lawrence of Arabia'. On 26, 27 and 28 November 1918, *The Times* published three substantial articles by Lawrence presenting a stirring narrative of the Arab Revolt from its start in Mecca in June 1916 through to its coordination with Allenby's offensive in Palestine in April 1918. Although Lawrence's name was not revealed, the author was described as 'a correspondent who was in close touch with the Arabs throughout their campaign', and readers were left in no doubt that this 'correspondent' had shared in the hardships and triumphs now unfolded.

Lawrence's narrative cleverly linked the Arab Revolt with the wider British conduct of the war. The Arabs, under the Sherif of Mecca, had decided 'soon after . . . the surrender of Kut' that they could no longer bear their 'continued subjection' and had asked the British for help against 'the Young Turk Party and their German masters'. Even before this request was granted they had risen up against their oppressors, and only the Turkish possession of modern weapons had prevented them from taking the holy city of Medina. As he described the subsequent adoption of guerrilla tactics, and the Arabs' advance along the coast to Wejh, Lawrence shifted into the first person plural, suggesting his own intimate involvement with the Revolt.[14] In the second article, Lawrence praised the unity which had been brought about by Feisal: 'To-day there are no blood feuds among the Arabs from Damascus to Mecca; for the first time in the history of Arabia since the seventh century there is peace all along the pilgrim road.' He stressed how, after the capture of Akaba, their exploits had become a part of Allenby's wider offensive, 'instead of joyous ventures of our own'.[15] In his final article on the 'Arab Epic', Lawrence provided tales of heroic endurance and military daring which would become central parts of the later legend. He detailed the harsh winter of 1917/18 he and Feisal's men had endured in the mountains around Tafileh, embroidering his account with details which sound implausible today, before proceeding to stirring descriptions of attacks on the Hejaz railway. 'Unquestionably,' Lawrence wrote, 'the greatest game of all railway work is blowing up trains.'

This kind of war writing was not entirely new to the British public. They had heard plenty of tales of individual courage and daring, some as fantastic as Lawrence now told, but they had not been set in such exotic environments – for example in 'a selected position on the heights around Petra – the "rose red city half as old as time"'.[16] They had not been allied to speed, movement and initiative, and, above all, attended by such apparent success. Nor had they been told by a writer with such gifts, with a command of archaeological, historical, religious and philosophical ideas. With these articles Lawrence established in the British imagination the idea of one of their own who had accomplished legendary feats in the desert. He was also thinking about a longer book, writing to the Arabist Charles Doughty in December 1918: 'It has been a wonderful experience, and I have got quite a lot to tell.'[17]

Lawrence had first to devote his attentions to promoting the Arab cause at the forthcoming Paris Peace Conference. Feisal arrived in London at the end of November, and Lawrence accompanied him on visits to dignitaries – including the King at Buckingham Palace – and other significant figures in the forthcoming negotiations, such as Chaim Weizmann. Lawrence managed to get himself appointed as a technical adviser to the British delegation travelling to Paris, and, with rather more difficulty, Feisal was allowed to attend as a representative for the Hejaz but not Syria.[18] Although Feisal's delegation, in Arab robes, caused quite a stir at the Conference, and Lawrence, similarly attired, attracted particular attention, in truth they were marginal figures. The key figures, Lloyd George, Clemenceau, Wilson and the Italian Prime Minister Vittorio Orlando, were preoccupied with arrangements in Europe, and the complexities of the Middle East had to take a back seat. The French were absolutely determined to extend their influence in Syria and Lebanon, and in the final analysis it was more important for the British to maintain good relationships with them than with the Arabs. It was agreed in March 1919 that a joint Anglo-French-American commission would travel to Syria to investigate the situation there.[19] Lawrence heard in April that his father had died of 'Spanish flu',[20] and a few weeks later, he made an impulsive decision to hitch a lift on a British bomber flying out to Egypt. It has never been clear whether Lawrence intended merely to recover papers he had left in Cairo, or to get involved in the conflict which had broken out in the Hejaz between Ibn Saud's Wahabi tribesmen and Husein's Hashemite followers. It was a conflict which, ironically, gave the lie to Lawrence's recent statements about Arab unity.

Lawrence never made it to the fighting in the Hejaz. The aircraft he was travelling in crashed near Rome on 3 May 1919, and Lawrence was fortunate to escape alive, if badly shaken. Both pilots were killed.[21] The conflict in the Hejaz was only decided in Husein's favour when British tanks were sent to help him, and Lawrence returned to Paris in July. With the all-important questions relating to Germany settled – at least temporarily – the Conference postponed decisions about the Middle East, and Lawrence made a last effort to find a compromise which might satisfy his own conscience, if nothing else. He wrote a letter to *The Times* which was published in a redacted form on 11 September 1919, seeking to expose the conflicting wartime assurances given to the Arabs. Again Lawrence called for 'the necessary revision' of the Sykes-Picot Agreement, asking that 'weight and expression' be given to Arab views.[22] On 15 September Lawrence addressed a memorandum to the Foreign Office detailing how this might be done.[23] It seemed too late. Days later, Lloyd George and Clemenceau concluded an agreement effectively giving Syria and Lebanon to the French, and Mesopotamia to the British. In meetings with Lloyd George and the Cabinet on 19 and 23 September Lawrence was bluntly told that 'Britain had no further interest in Syrian affairs, and he was advised to go to Paris to get the best terms he could from Clemenceau.'[24] Lawrence did not take this advice, but summarized his hopes in a letter to Lord Curzon, the Foreign Secretary, writing: 'My own ambition is that the Arabs should be our first brown dominion, and not our last brown colony.'[25] The Americans, unhappy with this reassertion of imperialism, now intervened and suggested that the Arabs in Syria and in northern Mesopotamia should be given a large measure of independence, and that all these areas taken from the Turks should be described as 'mandates'.[26]

This compromise was attractive to the British government, which recognized the potential difficulty of ruling over recalcitrant Arabs in Mesopotamia, and it was accepted in October 1919. Lawrence was at last appeased, and in an excess of relief wrote a short letter to Lloyd George, which was apparently never actually sent. He thanked Lloyd George for finally keeping the promises made to the Arabs, and promised not to see Feisal again, concluding: 'My relief at getting out of the affair with clean hands is very great.'[27] Lawrence now turned back to his own writing, accepting an offer to take up a research fellowship at All Souls College, Oxford.[28] Lawrence had already, in Paris, started working intensively on his narrative of the Arab Revolt, and, once back in Oxford in late September 1919, he devoted himself to this.

If Lawrence, with one part of his complex psyche, sought anonymity behind the gates of All Souls, with another he courted publicity. While the politicians wrangled in Paris, the American journalist and film director Lowell Thomas, whom Lawrence had helped, had been presenting a 2-hour 'illustrated travelogue' entitled 'With Allenby in Palestine' to packed houses in New York. The show, which mixed 'lantern slides' and 'motion pictures' from the desert war with music and breathless descriptions of the action, opened in Covent Garden on 14 August 1919. From there it moved to the Albert Hall. Within six months Lowell Thomas' show had been seen by a million people. Its title was quickly changed to 'With Allenby in Palestine and Lawrence in Arabia'. Much of the show's success was undoubtedly, as Priya Satia has argued, attributable to its representation 'of individual heroism in the modernist shape of Lawrence of Arabia'.[29] Ironically, given the entirely marginal part played by women in Lawrence's own life, and in the Arab Revolt, the slides and film clips were preceded by the Dance of the Seven Veils, and advertised with pictures of scantily-clad Arab girls. Lawrence himself was described as 'a young man whose name will go down in history beside those of Sir Francis Drake, Sir Walter Raleigh, Lord Clive, Charles Gordon, and all the other famous heroes of Great Britain's glorious past'.[30] In such illustrious company 'Lawrence of Arabia' was born.

## Coming to terms with the new world

In contrast Vera Brittain's transition to peace was – initially at least – an almost exclusively private affair. It is clear now that, however this is labelled, she was by the end of war deeply traumatized by the cumulative effect of repeated bereavements, the strain of sustained hard work, exposure to the most ghastly physical injuries, experience of 'shell-shocked' soldiers and of aerial bombardment. There is a black hole in the literature on Brittain between her memories of armistice night and her subsequent return to Oxford as a student in April 1919. This is largely because the major sources for her early life are silent. Her diary had ceased in the middle of 1917, and her later memoir, *Testament of Youth*, provides only a broadly impressionistic account of this period.[31] We know that until April 1919, Brittain was still completing her 6-month contract at Queen Alexandra Hospital, Millbank. Much of this time was spent with flu patients and must indeed have been a grim conclusion to her earlier nursing work. She did not herself catch flu and suggested in *Testament of Youth* that she functioned almost as an automaton, detached both from the affairs of politicians at Versailles and from the behaviour of her peers in London, 'frantically dancing night after night in the Grafton Galleries, while pictures of the Canadian soldiers' wartime agony hung accusingly on the walls'.[32]

We also have two poems written by Brittain during these months. In one, written in December 1918 three years after the death of Roland Leighton, she reaffirmed their bond: 'I think you love me just the same, if you/Can see me still'. In a second, which appears to have been written as she finished her 'days in hospital', she acknowledged how nursing had provided healing as well as trauma: 'Where mending broken bodies slowly healed/My broken heart'.[33] Clearly Brittain's mind was not entirely numbed: she resolved to return to Oxford, to change her degree from English to History – in order better to understand the events which had led to the war – and she preserved her ultimate goal of becoming a writer. It seems likely that much of her mental energy went into a sustained effort to repress her wartime experience and to present some sense of composure to the outside world.

At the end of April 1919, Brittain returned to Somerville, now in its last weeks of exile in the buildings of Oriel College. She lived for the next few months in a shared house with five other female students, striking up a friendship with one in particular, Nina Ruffer. Although this first term back is painted in depressing colours in *Testament of Youth*, as a time in which Brittain felt desperately isolated and misunderstood, unable to relate meaningfully to her younger fellow students and lacking the respect given to ex-soldiers, this was not the full story. Deborah Gorham has drawn on Brittain's letters to her mother to show that she was socially active and still giving thought to matters such as clothes and furnishing, just as she had when she first went to Oxford in 1914.[34] She was also writing and made contact with a group who were starting up a new literary journal, *The Oxford Outlook*, to embody their hopes for a 'post-war university Renaissance'.[35] This gave Brittain the opportunity to articulate her resentment at how women students who had performed war service were slighted, unlike returning soldiers who were held in respect. After years in which her consciousness of gender inequality had largely been suppressed by her perceived sense of war imperatives, there was a new feminist perspective to her writing.

Brittain wrote an article on women students for the second issue of *The Oxford Outlook*. It is a strange piece of writing, couched in an impersonal third person, but clearly about herself, and reflecting her strong sense of alienation and disillusionment. She wrote: 'The returning war worker feels herself a stranger from a strange land,' adding that 'With the signing of the Armistice she passed from the all-important to the negligible.' Brittain still managed to conclude optimistically, clearly linking 'war workers' like herself with male students who had been killed. She asserted that the 'woman student' 'will find her place at last.... She will inherit that wider future which the University owes both to its living and its dead'.[36] For the fourth issue of the journal, Brittain produced an angry riposte to a recent *Times*' article which had argued against admitting women to degrees, again underlining a claim to equal treatment by reference to women's war work.[37]

Any sense of a straightforward transition from wartime nursing to a nascent literary career was though disrupted in the summer of 1919, by the sudden death of Brittain's new friend Nina Ruffer.[38] After this, Brittain started to suffer from hallucinations, imagining when she saw her face in mirrors that she was 'beginning to grow a beard, like a witch'.[39] Tense and overwrought, Brittain returned to Oxford for the Michaelmas term of 1919, and her trauma was at least partially played out in public when, in November, she proposed a motion at the newly formed Somerville Debating Society. Speaking in favour of travel as opposed to university life, Brittain delivered a bitter speech, juxtaposing the rigours of her wartime experience with the frivolous and sheltered lives of the other students. Her motion was unanimously rejected and she felt publicly humiliated, weeping bitterly alone in her room afterwards. This was a cathartic event, and, paradoxically, it brought Brittain closer to her principal opponent in the debate, a young woman called Winifred Holtby.[40] It also prompted Brittain to write a poem, 'The Lament of the Demobilised', which has a directness and sense of authenticity far removed from the artificial and elevated tone of so many of her earlier efforts. She presented here an imagined conversation between 'war workers', and others who had stayed at university. In her use of dialogue, and of a more everyday idiom, as well in its cynicism, the poem is reminiscent of Sassoon, some of whose work she knew. She concluded:

'You threw four years into the melting pot –
Did you indeed!' these others cry. 'Oh well,
The more fool you!'
And we're beginning to agree with them.[41]

Edward Elgar completed the first of the four works he had been composing during 1918 shortly before the end of the war, and after the Armistice he continued working on the other three. All these works were marked by deep introspection and reflection, appearing to look back at a vanished world rather than to anticipate a new one. In December 1918 and January 1919 Elgar completed the String Quartet and the Quintet for Piano and Strings, and the two works were premiered in May 1919. Like so many others, he was struggling to come to terms with a changing world. His wife Alice was unhappy in the isolation of the countryside, but they could no longer afford the upkeep of their large London home. The first signs of the lung disease which would kill Alice were becoming apparent. During the summer of 1919 Elgar nonetheless focused on completing the most substantial of the works begun in 1918, his Concerto for Cello in E Minor. The parts were sent to his publisher, Novello, in August 1918, and a first performance was arranged for October, with Felix Salmond playing the solo part.

The premiere, at Queen's Hall in London, 'was a disaster'. The orchestra had not rehearsed the piece sufficiently and it made little impact on an audience which was 'politely cordial'.[42] The review in *The Times* tried to find positives in the understated nature of the work, declaring: 'It is not a work to create a great sensation.'[43] Elgar, who conducted, must have thought back to the similarly ill-prepared first performance of his great religious masterpiece, *The Dream of Gerontius*, and one wonders how far he dwelt again on his conviction then that 'God was against art'.[44] Clearly the Concerto did not create a sensation in 1919; it was not even performed again until 1921. It was left to later audiences to realize the emotional depth and sensitivity of this deeply contemplative work, and to ponder over how far it was intended as a statement about the war. One does not have to follow every detail of Brian Trowell's interpretation to accept his broad contention that the concerto was originally conceived as an elegy and was 'a musical translation of the "cruelty I resent bitterly & disappointedly" of Elgar's letter to Binyon of 5 November 1918'.[45] Other insightful writers on Elgar have argued, convincingly, that 'the requiem here is not so much for the dead in Flanders fields as for the destruction of a way of life'. Elgar himself seems to have seen it as a final statement, writing in his personal catalogue of works, 'Finis. R. I. P.'[46] However we interpret it, the Concerto must be seen as one of the most important works of art to emerge in Britain from the First World War.

Shortly after the premiere, Alice Elgar fell ill again. She died in April 1920, leaving Elgar totally bereft. He had to complete the sale of their London home, and lost the ambition to compose. He wrote in August 1920 to a young musician he had met during the war, Adrian Boult: 'I am lonely now & do not see music in the old way & cannot believe I shall *complete* any new work.'[47] Shortly after this Elgar experienced another disappointment, when an abridged version of *Spirit of England* which he had arranged for military band to be played at the unveiling of the Cenotaph in Whitehall was not used. Nor was his music used in the service for the burial of the Unknown Warrior in Westminster Abbey on the same day, 11 November 1920.[48]

Elgar's resigned and sorrowful mood in the years after 1918 was clearly attributable his ageing, to his continued sense that he was misunderstood as a composer, and after 1920 to his bereavement. It is difficult to know how far a sense of the destruction and loss caused by the war contributed further, not least because just as during the war he had said little directly about it, he made few direct comments subsequently about the peace. One he did make is revealing. Shortly after the premiere of his Cello Concerto, Elgar was invited to Belgium by Lalla Vandervelde, one of the young women whose company had sustained him during the war. Elgar was dismayed by what he saw and struggled to relate his wartime enthusiasm for a heroic ideal of Belgium with the post-war reality. He wrote to a friend: 'The B's swagger & do nothing but eat and drink – have forgotten the war & seem to detest the thought of the English!'[49]

## Painting and remembrance

In a memorable phrase from his later autobiography, Paul Nash referred to the 'Struggles of a war artist without a war'.[50] This applied also to Richard Nevinson and Stanley Spencer, both of whom also entered the post-war era as 'Official War Artists'. All three were young men whose careers as aspiring artists had been interrupted at a critical point for more than 4 years, and who now faced the challenge of trying to establish lives as autonomous adults, of making ends meet financially, and as artists, of finding subjects and styles which might resonate in a changed world. Nevinson had indeed made his name as the best known and most controversial British painter of the war, but several critics had suggested that, with the gradual abandonment of his pre-war Futurist stance, he had already lost his way stylistically before the Armistice and questioned whether he now had anything more to offer than publicity seeking gestures. Nash had gained great recognition for the application of his intensely spiritual vision of landscape to the tortured wastes of the Ypres Salient, but now had to find new subjects. Spencer had hardly painted since joining the RAMC in 1915. Apart from his military service, he had never lived away from the family home. He was still a virgin and was, as a painter, little known.

Before the war ended, all three had been commissioned by the Ministry of Information to produce paintings for a national exhibition and then to be housed in a planned Hall of Remembrance.[51] This placed a huge burden on them. How were they to 'remember' the war? The elevated mood of August 1914, the conviction that Britain was acting to uphold the rule of law and the rights of small nations, to defend civilization itself, had simply disappeared during 4 years of slaughter and squalor. The restoration of Belgian sovereignty produced nothing like a comparable emotional response to the huge outrage generated by the German invasion of that country in 1914. The successful defence of France and the expulsion of foreign invaders from its soil similarly brought little joy to the British public, or even to soldiers who had fought there. The surrender of the German fleet, and the humbling of its once mighty army appeared as small consolation for the terrible loss of life, and indeed few British people appeared very interested in Germany in 1919. Triumphalism seemed hardly fitting, and not many felt there was much to celebrate after the Armistice, other than, as Gordon Bottomley put it to Paul Nash, to express relief that 'the nightmare is now over'.[52] Were the painters then to extend and develop the mood of disillusionment which had become apparent in some of the paintings of 1917 and 1918? Ought they to communicate more of the 'bitter truth' which Nash had perceived in the Salient in November 1917? Even if they felt that a sense of futility and pointless destruction was the quintessential experience of the war, was this appropriate for a national act of 'remembrance'?

Nevinson was the first of the three to conclude his artistic involvement with the war. He was working when the Armistice was declared on what he later called his 'Passchendaele picture', a huge canvas showing the Ypres Salient after an attack, clearly drawing on his brief visit there in early August 1917. Titling this *The Harvest of Battle* allowed Nevinson to make a statement which was critical of war in general rather than the specifically British involvement with the war and to combine a sense of Nash's 'bitter truth' with compassion and sorrow. Nevinson wrote later that immediately after the Armistice, he could 'not glorify war'.[53] By representing again the flat, wasted landscape of the Salient, he helped to consolidate the quintessential British imagination of the Western Front, but in *The Harvest of Battle* he abandoned altogether the elements of Futurism and Vorticism which had made his earlier war paintings so distinctive.

In his autobiography, Nevinson described these months as 'the most repulsive time in my life'.[54] His existing paranoia was heightened by negative critical responses to several of his works at the Canadian War Memorial Committee exhibition in January 1919, and he became obsessed by the idea that both conservatives and radicals in the art world were equally hostile, jealous of his wartime success and determined to do him down. He reacted with characteristic pugnacity, going out of his way to insult and offend all his perceived enemies. He visited Paris to see his old friend Severini, but the trend towards abstraction in painting which he perceived there only depressed him. By the end of February 1919 Nevinson had finished *The Harvest of Battle* and, characteristically, he managed to stir up publicity around the picture well before it was exhibited. He had been requested by the War Office not to exhibit the painting before its own planned national exhibition, despite his wish that it should be included in a Royal Academy 'peace' exhibition in May. So Nevinson invited critics and journalists to his studio to preview the work. His father was there to see the painting, along with 'a good crowd' on 2 April.[55] The tabloids developed the idea that the painting was so grim and terrible as to have been rejected by the Academy, and published lurid descriptions of it, reawakening the controversy over the censorship of *Paths of Glory* in 1918.[56]

In search of new subjects, Nevinson then made a well-publicized visit to New York in May. While he was there, searching out scenes of modern life, his wife Kathleen gave birth to a baby boy on 20 May 1919. The *Daily Sketch*'s announcement of the 'The Cubist Baby'[57] gives some indication of the celebrity status which Richard and Kathleen Nevinson had now achieved. Sadly, the baby, named Anthony Christopher Wynne, died 15 days later. It was presumably Henry Nevinson who placed a small notice of the death in *The Times*.[58] The existing literature on Richard Nevinson glosses over this episode, as does Nevinson himself in his autobiography, leaving only a number of questions. Why did Nevinson go to New York when his wife was due to give birth? Why did Nevinson write in his autobiography that 'I am glad I have not been responsible for bringing any human life into this world'?[59] How did Kathleen feel about his strange lack of concern for the baby? I can only presume that Nevinson was not pleased by her becoming pregnant, and that he did not want a child. His father recorded that when Richard departed for New York early in April he was 'in very low spirits',[60] and this may have been because of his mixed feelings about the impending birth.

He did try to look after Kathleen when he returned to London days after the baby's death, but his own mental health, already fragile, was pushed further towards breaking point. In the rest of 1919 we can trace the growing deterioration in Nevinson's condition in his father's journal. When *The Harvest of Battle* was finally exhibited in 'The Nation's War Paintings and Drawings' in November, Nevinson felt that it was hidden away from the main rooms in Burlington House, and that his earlier works were deliberately scattered to diminish their impact. Again he detected a conspiracy by establishment figures such as Muirhead Bone, and his former Slade tutor Henry Tonks, to undermine him.[61] Although there was apparently great public interest in *The Harvest of Battle*, the critical reception was hostile. Several, reviewing the exhibition, simply failed to mention it. Masterman, echoing the perception that Nevinson had lost the individuality of his early war paintings, told Henry Nevinson that his son 'paints in any one's style'.[62] The *Evening Standard* asked whether it had been a good use of money to supply Nevinson with a car to drive around the battle zone.[63] Muirhead Bone incensed Nevinson by calling the painting 'a potboiler'.[64] Nevinson was not just 'almost insane with rage' against the organizers of the exhibition. He was also aware that there was some truth in these remarks, confessing to his father that he was 'uncertain as to his future line in art'.[65] By Christmas Day 1919, according to his anxious father, Nevinson was 'in a terrible state of rage and depression against critics and artists. He is "obsessed" hardly sane, utterly wretched, incapable of reason or work'. Richard Nevinson never returned to the subject of the First World War in his painting.

Paul Nash had been working since the spring of 1918 on his large memorial commission. Like Nevinson he chose to represent again the Ypres Salient, where, like so many British soldiers, he had most intensely experienced the war. Nash took a more symbolic approach, depicting the Menin Road, which led out of Ypres into the Salient, and which had been almost literally a *via dolorosa* for tens of thousands of British soldiers. This subject also allowed him to depict again the shell-torn landscape, as he had so successfully done in paintings such as *Void* and *We Are Making a New World*, making a powerful statement about the destructive impact of war without polemicizing about exactly who was responsible for this. *The Menin Road* was finished by the end of April 1919, by which time he had already finished another set of drawings of the war which are today almost unknown.

Searching for ways to make money, Nash was already experimenting with illustrations for books, and he produced a set of drawings for a limited edition of poems, *Images of War*, published in 1919 by Richard Aldington, later to become notorious as the first to deconstruct the legend of 'Lawrence of Arabia' in 1956. Aldington was an Imagist poet who before 1914 had close links with leading lights of the avant-garde literary scene such as Ezra Pound and the philosopher T. E. Hume. During the war he had worked alongside Ford Madox Ford and D. H. Lawrence. Aldington had then served in the Royal Sussex Regiment and been wounded on the Western Front. His poems in *Images of War* anticipated many of the themes and individual scenes from his 1929 novel, *Death of a Hero*, but they contained little of the novel's excoriating bitterness. Aldington's mood in 1919, exquisitely accompanied by Nash's drawings, was one of sorrow, resignation, fear and apathy. He portrayed the soldier's alienation from former life, from women and from pastoral beauty, and expressed a powerful conviction that the front-line survivor would never be able to reconnect with those cherished memories. Although Aldington questioned in these poems the purpose of the war, he was not yet ready to dismiss out of hand the arguments which had been put forward between 1914 and 1918. It is a great shame that the illustrations for Aldington's poems of 1919 are so little known, as they constitute a remarkably concentrated distillation of Nash's experience. The drawings share short titles with individual poems, such as 'Pickets', 'In the Trenches' and 'Fatigues'. Three, titled 'Barrage', 'Bombardment' and 'Terror', stand out, conveying powerfully in a Vorticist idiom the terrible experience of being shelled.⁶⁶ If Nevinson had lost his cutting edge as a war artist by abandoning Vorticism, Nash had gained by learning from him, and by developing the technique pioneered by Nevinson in 1915.

By the time these pictures were published Nash was deep in personal difficulties which were to bring him close to breakdown. Today it is tempting to use the descriptive label of 'post-traumatic stress syndrome' to suggest that these problems were a result of Nash's war experience, but this would be largely speculative. Searching for ways to make money, Nash became involved in journalism in 1919, contributing articles to two art journals. In a bizarre episode reminiscent of more recent scandals where authors post glowing reviews of their own books under assumed names on internet sites, Nash foolishly presented favourable remarks about his own work under a pseudonym in both of these journals, but this was exposed in December 1919 by another art critic, much to his embarrassment.⁶⁷ Moving with Margaret to various places, and experimenting with different styles and techniques, Nash finally experienced a complete collapse in September 1921. He was unconscious for a week and was taken to hospital in London, where his condition was diagnosed as a reaction to his experience of the war and to subsequent emotional difficulties.⁶⁸

Stanley Spencer, discharged from hospital in Salonica shortly before the Armistice, was shipped home from the Mediterranean and disembarked at Southampton on 12 December 1918. He was given leave, and he arrived back in Cookham on 16 December. Although he only heard now that his brother Sydney had been killed in France shortly before the Armistice, Spencer's relief at being home was absolutely overwhelming. The intensity of feeling he expressed in letters is a testament to quite how awfully he had suffered, both as medical orderly and particularly as a soldier in the final offensive against the Bulgarians. Spencer had of course dreamed of Cookham throughout his exile. We know from letters written to Desmond Chute while he was in Salonica that Spencer had visualized the village and its people in minute detail, investing it and them with deep significance.⁶⁹ He later wrote that he never experienced such joy in his life as when he walked back over Cookham Moor on the evening he returned from the war.⁷⁰ On the day he arrived he wrote to his sister: 'Oh, everything is so dazzlingly beautiful that I feel like the Disciples did at the Transfiguration.'⁷¹ In his bedroom at Fernlea, Spencer found the unfinished canvas of the *Swan Upping* where he had left it in 1915, and laid his hands on the painting before resuming work on it, in a symbolic and literal act of reconnecting with his past.⁷²

Spencer was delighted to hear from the War Office that, as an Official War Artist, he was not required to rejoin his regiment, and he turned with relief to the composition of a memorial painting, something he had been thinking about since first hearing from Alfred Yockney back in May 1918. He sent a series of sketches to Yockney at the War Artists Advisory Commission and gained approval for a work with the prosaic title *Travoys with Wounded*

*Soldiers Arriving at a Dressing Station at Smol, Macedonia*.[73] For the first six months of 1919, Spencer worked on this large canvas, using a nearby stable as a studio. After the years of enforced artistic inactivity Spencer was experiencing an access of great spiritual feeling, which he connected to the reacquaintance with his pre-war life. He took enormous comfort in returning to his earlier routine of painting, and family meals at set times, this sense of normality heightened by his brother Gilbert's return from the war in March. Now, after years of contemplation, Spencer was free to represent his wartime experience in the first of a series of important works. Spencer chose not to dwell on the horror of war, or on suffering, although his painting depicted British soldiers wounded in battle. Instead he distilled his own vision of redemption through healing, one he had first developed while watching operations at Beaufort Hospital. He portrayed the wounded soldiers with immense compassion, showing them safely now in the oversize hands of medical orderlies, their stretchers (or travoys) pulled by benign horses and mules. The picture's focus was on an operating theatre where doctors, bathed in light, ministered to the wounded in an act of transfiguration. It was a painting, he later wrote, of 'spiritual ascendancy'.[74]

Although it might seem that Spencer, after years of demeaning work and danger, was at last liberated, this was not entirely so. Yockney, after seeing *Travoys* in Cookham, offered Spencer the chance to do two more memorial paintings, but Spencer, with characteristic obstinacy and individuality, resented working to order. He wrote: 'I began to feel too much as if I was cooking, and so I wrote at once to Yockney to knock me off the job.'[75] For all his joy at being back in Cookham, Spencer was irked by the restrictions of family life. He struggled to concentrate in the confined space of his bedroom, and his efforts to find a studio in some disused village building failed. He had no money of his own to buy or rent a studio. He was also unsettled at a deeper level. Throughout the war, Spencer had meditated on religion and had developed his own intensely personal spirituality. He had become increasingly dissatisfied with Anglicanism, and in his wartime letters he had frequently railed intemperately against what he perceived as the ugly materialism and utilitarianism of Protestantism. He was attracted more to Roman Catholicism, and we know that an Augustinian interpretation of everyday work had made a deep impression on him. In January 1919 he briefly visited a Catholic priory in Staffordshire on the invitation of the sculptor Eric Gill, but he did not stay there, nor did he convert to Catholicism. Later Spencer wrote that he visited the priory merely 'to discuss some building scheme'.[76] John Rothenstein writes that 'no man could have been less fitted, by temperament or intellect, to belong to any institutional religion, Catholicism least of all'.[77] For the rest of the year, Spencer attended the Anglican church in Cookham with his family every Sunday, as he had done before 1914,[78] but this may well have been another source of deep discomfort for him.

In November 1919 Spencer was invited by Henry and Margaret Slesser to visit their house in Bourne End, on the other side of the river from Cookham. He went with two others who had taken an interest in his painting, Louis and Mary Behrend. Shortly after this Spencer made another fateful meeting at the house of the Carline family. Sydney Carline had studied at the Slade before 1914, and Spencer had met his brother Richard, another painter, in 1915. In December 1919, Spencer met their sister Hilda, whom he would later marry. Later he wrote of this encounter: 'I was in the *real* presence of a woman for the first time.'[79] In April 1920 Spencer moved out of his family home to stay with the Slessers.

## Living with trauma

One artist in the group selected here emerged with his perception of the conflict apparently unchanged: ironically he was the youngest and had experienced the longest period of front-line service, David Jones. After recovering from 'trench fever' in the summer of 1918, Jones had been posted to Limerick, in south-west Ireland, and he saw out the war doing garrison duty there. After the Armistice, Jones produced two Christmas cards for his father to print for distribution among family friends. The first showed an infantryman greeting a young girl in traditional Welsh costume, over the words 'Napolig Llawen' (or 'Happy Christmas'). It also contained a verse celebrating the end of the war:

> Christmas comes round, and a fifth New Year
> But what a different story:
> Let's drink a toast to the Fusilier,
> Blighty, Home, and Glory.

In the second card Jones reverted to the chivalric idiom he had used for his wartime illustrations in *The Graphic*. This card bore the motto *Sic Semper Tyrannis*, which might be rendered ''Twas ever thus with tyrants'. It showed a German soldier with his hands up, being driven away from a young woman who holds her face in her hands by an angel holding a sword before him. It clearly identified Germany with tyranny, the Allied cause with virtue, and presented a gendered view of the conflict, which recalled descriptions of the 'rape' of Belgium at the start of the war. Inside the card was a message, addressed particularly to those 'who mourn the fallen'. Jones wrote, recalling the language of Rupert Brooke: 'They [the fallen] surely did not die vainly. Through their splendid sacrifice the brutish gods of the Teuton lie despoiled and broken. Justice and meek-eyed Compassion stand unshrouded before the eyes of the distressed people. Let us then, with cheerfulness of heart, step into the sunlight of a New Day, ever keeping in remembrance the sacred dead who preserved for us so great a heritage.'[80]

As Jones had enlisted early in the war he was quickly released from active service, being 'disembodied' or transferred to the reserve, in January 1919. He returned to London, where like many ex-soldiers, he found it difficult to replace the sense of comradeship and purpose, and the institutional structures which had surrounded him since January 1915. Briefly, he toyed with the idea of joining the British forces sent to fight the Bolsheviks in Archangel, but was dissuaded by his father. Instead, he resumed what he had been doing before the war intervened, enrolling as a student of 'Commercial Design and Illustration' at the Camberwell School of Arts and Crafts; he transferred soon to the Westminster School of Art, where he studied until 1921. Over the next few years, Jones turned away from his war experience, and towards Roman Catholicism. Like Stanley Spencer, Jones had been attracted to Catholicism during the war, and near the end of his life he recounted having been deeply moved by seeing a Catholic Mass being conducted in a barn near the front line, probably in the winter of 1916/17.[81]

Again like Spencer, Jones felt a deep correspondence between his view of art and Roman Catholicism, and in January 1921 he went to stay with Eric Gill at Ditchling Common. Gill had established a small artistic community at this village in East Sussex, seeking to live and work in harmony with the ideals of the arts and crafts movement of the late nineteenth century. Jones visited Ditchling several times during 1921, and after being received into the Roman Catholic Church in September 1921, he moved in there. Initially he tried to study carpentry, but finding this difficult, he turned instead to wood engraving, learning from Gill, and from Desmond Chute, who had earlier befriended Stanley Spencer at Beaufort Hospital in 1915. Immersed in this new life and searching for artistic direction, Jones appeared to have turned his back on the war.

All of the creative individuals examined here who survived the war were deeply affected by that experience. Some, such as Vera Brittain, T. E. Lawrence, Stanley Spencer and David Jones, would spend the next decade and longer trying to exorcise that memory through considered and reflective representations of the war. Others, such as Nevinson, Finzi, Nash and Elgar, wanted to turn away from the war, and to other personal and creative concerns. Some, notably Spencer and Nash, would successfully explore other artistic paths, but others, such as Nevinson, Jones, Finzi and Lawrence, would never find in other subjects the recognition they gained from their representations of war.

# CHAPTER TWELVE

# 'We will remember them'

The construction of memory of the First World War in Britain started soon after the outbreak of the conflict, with the publication of poems such as Binyon's 'The Fourth of August', which helped to consolidate a view of the cause of the war, its purpose, the spirit it would be fought in, and his 'For the Fallen,' which declared 'We will remember them.' Rupert Brooke's poems, published early in 1915, similarly portrayed one vision of the reaction to the conflict; as we have seen they were widely read and discussed, among both civilians and combatants, and the image of Brooke as a golden-haired Apollo who had willingly embraced death for a noble cause was further strengthened by the publication in 1918 of Eddie Marsh's memoir.[1] David Jones was sent a copy of Marsh's memoir in Ireland shortly before the Armistice, and it seems more than coincidental that in the Christmas cards discussed in the previous chapter, Jones used the high diction Brooke had employed, even specific words, such as 'heritage', which were central to Brooke's elevated conception of the British cause.

But although historians use categories such as 'social' or 'collective memory', and 'personal memory' to differentiate between shared and private views of historical events, we should be aware that these too are constructs. There are as many memories of historical events as there are individuals in a given society, and these memories are not fixed. Private understandings of the past overlap and interact with narratives in the public sphere, and all of these senses are fluid and transient.[2] They are subject to a host of changing factors, and we should not imagine that everyone in Britain shared the same memories of the conflict, or that because they read Binyon or Brooke's poems, they simply adopted their views. Well before November 1918, conflicting memories of the war were taking shape in Britain, forming part of a complex discursive play. If a 'heroic' view of the war was still widely propagated, this was balanced by the emergence, during and after 1915, of a view that the war was bleak, destructive and ultimately without purpose. By the time that Paul Nash so vividly presented this vision to the public in May 1918, there were many who already privately felt that way. The Imperial War Museum's purchase of paintings by both Nash and Nevinson gave a significant official weight to their representations of the war.

Within the larger views of the war which were emerging by 1918, we can discern currents of memory which addressed more specific and local concerns. In a St David's day issue of the Welsh-language journal *Ceninen* in March 1918, a tribute to Hedd Wyn identified the dead bard as a specifically Welsh hero, who had inherited a tradition of Welsh pacifism, and embodied this in his behaviour and in his poetry. By juxtaposing this with an image of English militarism, the journal presented a vision of Welsh nationalism which could distance itself from the conflict and lay the blame for it at the feet of, not the British, but the English.[3] The legend of Hedd Wyn was given further impetus by the publication in August 1918 of a small volume of his collected poems.[4] The first print run of a thousand copies was quickly sold out, and another thousand had to be printed.[5] Although knowledge of Hedd Wyn was confined to the Welsh-speaking community, the memory of his life and death were already making him better known than he had been in his lifetime.

Similarly, ideas about chronology and periodization of the war were already in the public domain before November 1918. Kate Finzi's memoir, published in 1916, was by no means the only book which had presented a vision of the early months of the war as somehow different from the years that followed, more disorganized perhaps, but also more spontaneous, drawing on the best of an imagined British voluntary spirit, and producing its own special comradeship. The influential writer John Masefield published *The Old Front Line* in 1917, celebrating this voluntary spirit in Kitchener's army, and suggesting that with the Battle of the Somme had come the end of an era, not just in the organization of the British Army, but in British history. Masefield also addressed the rapidly developing phenomenon of battlefield tourism, the desire of bereaved relatives to see the places where their loved ones had fought and died, and the fascination with the now abandoned landscapes of trench warfare, with what would soon be thought of as the 'Waste Land'.[6]

Early in the war, the War Office decided not to repatriate the bodies of British soldiers killed in action overseas, and in 1917 an Imperial War Graves Commission was established to oversee the burial and commemoration of the dead in theatres of war around the world. During the 1920s, this body, employing distinguished architects, garden designers and writers, developed uniform principles for this work and undertook the construction of the many cemeteries and memorials which now mark the areas where the First World War was most fiercely fought. By choosing architectural styles which blended classicism with Eastern influences, the Commission sought to avoid sectarian strife and to allow relatives and survivors of different churches and of none to bring spirituality to the memory of the dead. By landscaping the cemeteries with lawns and, where possible, with plants grown in Britain, they sought to give the cemeteries the appearance of the home country. The choice of white limestone for headstones and for monuments in the cemeteries provided an association with innocence and justice, and this portrayal of the British cause was heightened by placing in every cemetery of a 'Stone of Sacrifice' and a 'Cross of Remembrance'. Rudyard Kipling, who had lost his own son at Loos, paralleled the adoption of traditional architectural idioms with the consciously archaic phrase 'Their Name Liveth for Evermore' to be inscribed in all the cemeteries. The war graves outside Britain therefore presented a very different memory of the war from that embodied in the paintings of Nash and Nevinson in the Imperial War Museum. The calm, ordered rows of white headstones grouped around the Stone of Sacrifice and the Cross of Remembrance in military cemeteries large and small harked back to a long continuity with British landscapes and traditions. Unsurprisingly, many relatives tried to give purpose to the deaths of their loved ones by using the space on individual headstones for a family inscription for phrases such as 'He died that others might live.' Many chose phrases from Brooke's sonnets. When Ellis Evans' body was re-interred in the Artillery Wood Cemetery near Boesinghe, the words 'Y Prifardd Hedd Wyn', meaning, as Alan Llwyd explains, 'the chief poet' or 'head poet', something similar to the 'poet laureate Hedd Wyn', were added to his headstone at the request of his parents.[7]

In Britain, the construction of war memorials was less uniform, being left to local communities and to individual institutions. There was, in the 1920s, an outpouring of sentiment which found expression in the construction of thousands of memorials, in towns, villages, schools and institutions of every kind. Overwhelmingly, the committees which oversaw the construction of memorials opted for traditional rather than modernist modes of representation. This was not surprising. The disruptive, discordant idioms of modernism had shown themselves well suited to the expression of horror, of fear and of cynicism, but these were not emotions which people wanted to see in war memorials. Unsurprisingly, they wanted consolation, reassurance and a sense that the dead had not died for nothing. Nonetheless, it was not always easy to find consensus. In parts of Wales there were arguments over whether the inscriptions on local memorials should be in English, in Welsh or in both languages. There were debates about who should be named on memorials. Should those who had died in accidents in munitions factories be included? This raised the question of gender which Vera Brittain had addressed in her poem to 'Dead Sisters' in the Mediterranean. Clearly most of the dead were male, but were the women who had lost their lives in the conflict to be overlooked? The majority of First World War memorials in Britain refer exclusively to men. There are exceptions, such as the memorial in Swansea, the foundation stone of which was laid by Douglas Haig in 1922, which lists, alongside the names of soldiers killed in the war, those of munitions workers who died in industrial accidents during the war, at least nine of them female.

Although many memorials used abstract forms, following the example of the Cenotaph at Whitehall, which was unveiled in November 1920, others presented more naturalistic representations, again raising complex questions. Should soldiers be shown as older men, or so young as almost to be boys? Should they be portrayed in heroic poses, or cast sorrowfully, in mourning? Around the country today readers will see many different examples, and judge for themselves how different communities and their representatives handled these questions. As we have seen, fund-raising for a memorial to

FIGURE 28 *This memorial to the poet Hedd Wyn, portraying him in romantic and pastoral mood, was erected in his home village of Trawsfynydd in 1923.*

Hedd Wyn in Trawsfynydd had commenced shortly after his death in 1917. After the war, appeals were made for donations from Welsh emigrants to the United States, and in 1922 the sculptor L. S. Merrifield was commissioned to design a memorial statue. This was erected in Trawsfynydd and unveiled in August 1923, representing Hedd Wyn not as a soldier, but in a romantic pose as a farmer, striding forward, with one arm raised, as though about to speak.[8] The inscription, in Welsh, noted that 'he fell on Pilkem Ridge, Flanders, on 31 July 1917', but this carefully neutral statement was accompanied by his *englyn* 'In Memoriam', implying that he was a victim of German militarism.

## Heroism, justice, disillusionment and redemption

Many writers have been tempted to periodize the construction of memory, for example to suggest that an initial period of war weariness after 1918 was followed in the late 1920s by the emergence of a 'literature of disillusionment'. Later periods, such as the 1960s, can similarly be imagined as times when one or other vision of the First World War became dominant in the collective British imagination.[9] In truth, different strands of memory have been continually in play since 1918, and different individuals and institutions have always given greater weight to certain of these. Individual works of art, books, poems, paintings, pieces of music, films and television productions, have added to this constantly shifting terrain, always feeding into collective memory ideas specific to the time of their creation. It may help to isolate distinctive themes within this discursive field, to examine how these have evolved, and how the artists in this study have contributed to them. Four will be considered here: heroism, justice, disillusionment and redemption.

Heroism embraces both the notion of bravery in the face of adversity, such as might be displayed by a soldier in a particular military encounter, and the broader idea of war as ennobling. This was embraced by Rupert Brooke when he wrote that the war had brought back 'Holiness', 'Honour' and 'Nobleness'; Kate Finzi wrote similarly of discovering in nursing work 'the joy of service'.[10] Vera Brittain had written that the war was 'very splendid too, & is making us better & wiser & deeper men and women'.[11] The notion of heroism is closely linked, if not dependent upon the idea of justice, that the British cause in the war was righteous. We have seen how this was accepted by David Jones, who through the war portrayed the British as chivalric defenders of civilization and of outraged feminine virtue against German tyranny. T. E. Lawrence, at the start of the war, believed straightforwardly that British imperialism was more civilized than Ottoman despotism, and that in helping the Arabs against the Turks, the British were pursuing a just cause. The sense of justice was embodied in all British war memorials. After 1918, the belief in justice was progressively undermined, not least after the Treaty of Versailles, by a growing sympathy for the Germans. Even before the Armistice, we have seen how disillusionment had started to creep into perceptions of the war. Nevinson's paintings from 1915 had portrayed the war as cruel and impersonal, something with an uncontrollable momentum of its own. Nash had taken this further with his bitter portrayal of the 'new world' the war was creating. Even Elgar, that staunch patriot, had felt by November 1918 unable to write 'peace music'. Vera Brittain, while not yet criticizing the wider purpose of the war, had been simply overwhelmed by the weight of personal grief and left questioning whether it had all been worthwhile.

The exploration of disillusionment after 1918 would deepen fault lines in the memory of the war. One was that between the generals and the ordinary soldiers; another was generational, the idea that young people had been sacrificed by their elders. Women like Vera Brittain rapidly came to think that their war service was overlooked and undervalued, and saw this as a wider symptom of a society characterized by gender equality. The legend of Hedd Wyn was already being used in Wales to promote the idea of a small nation oppressed by its larger neighbour. For many, male and female, whose lives had been interrupted by war service, the sense of distance between those on active service and civilians at home was heightened in the post-war years, as they sought to readjust to civilian life. Perhaps one of the cruellest disillusionments of the post-war period was the visible absence of national unity. Binyon's words, set by Elgar in *Spirit of England*, had spoken of moving from 'days of sour division' to 'the grandeur of our fate'. Referring to women, he had spoken of 'hearts that are as one high heart'. Brooke had spoken of leaving a 'world grown old, and cold, and weary'. The visible divisions in British society after 1918, between social classes, age groups, genders and regions, seemed to some to mock these elevated hopes.

From the start of the war, the idea of redemption had been used to console those confronting loss. In British society this had deep Christian foundations, in the idea of the life eternal; and many during the war had turned towards religion as a way of understanding their predicament. Stanley Spencer and David Jones are obvious examples. It is striking how many people were attracted to other, less specifically Christian notions. Brooke had written 'We have built a house that is not for Time's throwing'; Elgar had set Binyon's words which imagined the 'fallen' as 'stars that shall be bright when we are dust/Moving in marches upon the heavenly plain'. Kipling's line 'Their Name Liveth for Evermore' had meaning for Christians and non-Christians alike. In a society which even before 1918 was questioning whether the enormous suffering caused by the war had been worthwhile, a concept of redemption offered a counter to disillusionment without depending on tainted visions of justice or heroism.

## Lawrence and *Seven Pillars of Wisdom*

We have seen that even during the Arab Revolt, Lawrence was thinking of writing a book about his experiences, and it appears that much of his epic *Seven Pillars of Wisdom* was written during 1919, often in marathon sessions lasting many hours. The title, a quotation from the book of Proverbs 9.1, was one he had chosen before 1914, when he envisaged a book about seven great cities of the Middle East. The book's complex genesis has been well documented: Lawrence lost the original manuscript at Reading station in December 1920 and had to rewrite the entire text from memory in 1921. Eight copies were made of the resulting '1922 Edition', which was abridged to create a limited edition for subscribers in 1926, with illustrations by several distinguished artists, including Paul Nash. Lawrence then further abridged this text to create the first widely available edition, titled *Revolt in the Desert*, published in 1927. Shortly after Lawrence's death in 1935, the 1926 edition was published as *Seven Pillars of Wisdom*. Not until 1997 was the '1922 Edition' made more publicly available. The mystique surrounding *Seven Pillars of Wisdom* was heightened by Lawrence's own search for anonymity after 1922, when he first joined the RAF as an aircraftsman, and then the Tank Corps as a private soldier. The legend of 'Lawrence of Arabia' had already been launched by Lawrence himself, and by Lowell Thomas; books published by Robert Graves in 1927 and Liddell Hart in 1934 consolidated and extended this further. Richard Aldington published his deconstruction of Lawrence as an 'imposter' in French in 1954, provoking outrage, but only spurring greater interest in him. Rumours about Lawrence's possible role as an intelligence agent or as a prospective politician were sustained by the uncertainties surrounding his death in a motorcycle crash, and ever since then, theories about his personality and his role in history have abounded. David Lean's hugely successful film *Lawrence of Arabia* in 1962 has disseminated an image of him to huge audiences worldwide, many of whom have not read Lawrence's own book.

*Seven Pillars of Wisdom* has provoked extremes of opinion, and one can only imagine how, with Lawrence's love of disguise, he would have been amused to see how, after his death, the most contrary opinions about his work have flourished alongside one another. To some, *Seven Pillars of Wisdom* is a beautifully written contribution to English literature, the finest book to have emerged from the First World War. Others find Lawrence's prose painfully overwrought. Lawrence claimed that it was, as far as his memory permitted, an accurate record of events; sceptics have seen it as 'rather a work of quasi-fiction than of history'.[12] Some readers have been struck by Lawrence's sincerity and lacerating self-revelation; others think him self-promoting and deceitful. Although Lawrence, in his Preface, admitted that his 'war-story' was 'self-regardant', he named several colleagues and officers who had campaigned alongside him, and paid tribute to the 'un-named rank and file';[13] nonetheless many have been offended by the image he presented of having almost single-handedly directed the Arab Revolt. On the critical question of his motivation for supporting the revolt, some have found him candid and open, others a fraud. The Communist writer Christopher Caudwell, writing in 1938, called him 'a might-have-been', a 'pathetic figure'.[14] Today's readers will make their own judgements.

Lawrence has undoubtedly, through the enormous popularity of his book, as well as in his mythological guise as 'Lawrence of Arabia' made a substantial, if complex contribution to British memory of the First World War. *Seven Pillars of Wisdom* is of course a tale of heroism. It is full of tales of boyish adventure and derring-do, of bravery, fortitude and endurance. Its portrayal of guerrilla warfare and of train-wrecking, crowned by the successful capture of Damascus, provided a refreshing contrast to the attrition and slaughter of the Western Front, and to the relative inactivity of the Grand Fleet during the war. Even British generals, in the idealized picture of Allenby which Lawrence presented, came out of the story well, again in contrast with the developing picture of ineptitude on the Western Front. Much of the enduring popularity of *Seven Pillars* is due to its portrayal of Lawrence as a hero.

The justice of the British cause is a far more complex issue in *Seven Pillars*. In his opening chapter, Lawrence was clear: he was 'charged by duty to lead them [the Arabs] forward and to develop to the highest any movement of theirs profitable to England in her war'.[15] We know now that the British government's wartime commitment to the conflicting assurances of the McMahon letters, the Sykes-Picot Agreement, and the Balfour Declaration, and its own interests in what Lawrence called the 'petrol royalties in Mesopotamia'[16] made any honest fulfilment of the assurances given to the Arabs quite impossible. We may agree with Lawrence that Ottoman rule over the Arabs was a bad thing, and deserved to be overthrown, but by any token, successive British governments do not come out of *Seven Pillars* with their honour intact. It is a tale of deception, of the consequences of what, in the post-war period, was called 'secret diplomacy', and in this sense it was an important contribution to the literature of disillusionment.

This perception is strengthened by the personal tragedy which lies at the heart of the book, clothed in tales of adventure and travel. Lawrence depicted in *Seven Pillars* how he gave himself 'to be a possession of aliens', and states how this 'destroyed' his 'English self'.[17] In the most controversial passage of the book, in which he related how he was captured, tortured and buggered by the Turkish commander at Deraa, he explored his own sexuality, writing that after this episode, 'the citadel of my integrity had been irrevocably lost'.[18] Whether, as has been endlessly debated, this episode actually occurred, or whether it mixes truth and fiction, is irrelevant here.[19] Lawrence's account of his downfall at Deraa is followed by his extraordinarily lurid description of the massacre at Tafas in September 1918, which went beyond the more factual account written for the *Arab Bulletin* at the time. He concluded: 'In a madness born of the horror of

Tafas we killed and killed, even blowing in the heads of the fallen and of the animals; as though their death and running blood could slake our agony.'[20] The inclusion of these humiliations and horrors makes *Seven Pillars* an account of personal corruption and ruin. In Priya Satia's words, it 'told the story of a hero's bitter disillusionment with the duplicity of his country; it is this tragic element which makes the book unmistakeably modern and yet even more of a romance'.[21]

Lawrence does not temper this narrative of political and personal fall with a sentimental notion of redemption, and here there is a striking contrast with his immediate post-war representations in *The Times*, and those of him presented in the Lowell Thomas show. Lawrence's humiliating and masochistic personal life after finishing the book is a testimony to the difficulty he had in carrying on after his involvement with the Arab Revolt. He never reconciled the contradictory impulses he felt towards obscurity and anonymity, and towards public and political engagement. Like David Jones, he avidly consumed other memoirs of the war and corresponded with their authors. Shortly before the motorcycle accident in which he was killed, Lawrence wrote about hearing of the death of one of his favourite war memorialists, Frederick Manning, the author of *Her Privates We*: 'In fact I find myself wishing all the time that my own curtain would fall. It seems as if I had finished now.'[22] Through his own writing, and through the elaboration by others of the mythology he first created, Lawrence's immortality appears guaranteed. When he died in May 1935, the front page of the *Daily Sketch* proclaimed: 'Lawrence the Soldier Dies but Lives for Ever'.[23] Nearly 80 years later, the public fascination with him is undiminished. An exhibition devoted to him at the Imperial War Museum in 2005 attracted huge numbers, and the visitors' book was full of admiring comments, many celebrating him as a hero.

## Vera Brittain's *Testament*

Vera Brittain also tried to publish her war memories soon after the Armistice. She entered her 'Great War Diary' for a competition in 1922, but, for reasons unknown, it was rejected. As we know, during the war she had tried to write stories, drawn from her own experience, with thinly disguised characters based on real people, and after graduating from Oxford in 1921 she continued with this, publishing two novels, neither specifically concerned with her wartime experience. During the 1920s Brittain developed an independent lifestyle, based closely on the supportive friendship of Winifred Holtby, whom she had met at Somerville. They both joined the feminist Six Point Group. Brittain became active as a public speaker and journalist, notably in pacifist circles, and with the League of Nations Union. In this capacity she travelled to Germany in 1924, with a deeply felt personal agenda of reconciliation. The cumulative effect of Brittain's war experience had been to make her a lifelong pacifist, rejecting violence as a means of settling international disputes, and a feminist.

In 1925 Brittain married George Catlin, a university lecturer, and in 1927 they had a son. She had gained greater prominence in 1928 with a book entitled *Women's Work in Modern England*. In 1929, noting the success of wartime memoirs by writers such as Aldington, Sassoon and Blunden, Brittain decided to try again to publish her own wartime experience, not as a novel, but as an 'autobiographical study'. Gathering up her wartime diary and correspondence, she spent the next four years, a period interrupted by pregnancy and numerous other distractions, working on the text which was published by Victor Gollancz in 1933 as *Testament of Youth*. Brittain's memoir sold very well in both Britain and America, going through 12 impressions in Britain before the Second World War.[24] It remains the pre-eminent British memoir of the First World War by a woman, and one of the most influential by any writer. Several factors contributed to the book's success: it was at once a coming of age novel, a memoir of wartime nursing and a tragic love story. In its portrayal of a young woman losing all four of her most important male contemporaries, it was a moving testimony to the idea of a 'lost generation'.

The view of the war presented in *Testament of Youth* was not unheroic. The four young men at the heart of the book were portrayed as chivalric figures: kind, gentle, sensitive and courageous. Roland Leighton is an aesthete, a scholar and a poet; Edward Brittain is a violinist and would-be composer; Geoffrey Thurlow is a quiet and peace-loving man who reads Rupert Brooke to overcome his fears; and Victor Richardson displays extraordinary sensitivity in helping Vera after Roland's death. But Brittain went beyond this, grappling also with how to come to terms with war's heroic appeal. She wrote that 'war, while it lasts, does produce heroism to a far greater extent than it brutalises'. She recognized that it 'had concrete results in stupendous patience, in superhuman endurance, in the constant re-affirmation of incredible courage'.[25]

*Testament of Youth* was, more importantly, a book about disillusionment, and it charted Vera Brittain's personal trajectory from initial enthusiasm for the war through suffering to pacifism. By the later stages of the book, it had become a bitter denunciation of the older generation and of the generals. The crowning disillusionment for Brittain came in the Treaty of Versailles, which she called 'a thoroughly nasty Peace'.[26] The bitterness with which she described the post-war period was all the more marked after her earlier idealism. The Vera Brittain who writes of 1919, 'the year did not seem to have begun very auspiciously for those who still clung to the ingenuous notion that by their sacrifices they had created a world of sweetness and light for their descendants to inhabit', is clearly a world away from the young woman who celebrates her brother's award of the Military Cross for his 'courage and splendid behaviour' on that most fateful day, 1 July 1916.[27]

Strikingly, when Brittain went on to analyse the Treaty of Versailles, she wrote that she 'was beginning to suspect that my generation had been deceived, its young courage cynically exploited, its idealism betrayed'. The British involvement in the war was presented here as a deliberate fraud, a trick played on the young by an older generation. Brittain made her own contribution to the idea that 'English propaganda' had misrepresented German behaviour during the war, relating how a German woman professor in Cologne had told her – 'quite correctly' – that it had had to be 'more malevolent' than that of France and Germany.[28] Brittain also brought a gendered dimension to her disillusionment. 'Had I been an ex-service man', she wrote, she would have been treated better on her return to Oxford.[29] In describing this period she wrote of men, particularly older military men, with a contempt which would have been unthinkable in the passages set before 1918. Reflecting again on her personal loss, she wrote: 'How futile it had all been, that superhuman gallantry!'[30]

Had Brittain written a testament to despair, it would surely never have had such enduring impact. She offered no redemption in a religious sense, but did present a message of hope. For women, she proposed autonomy, independence and political engagement. She rejected the pre-war ideal of confinement to marriage and the domestic sphere, and also counselled against retreat into private life, writing: 'I have had to learn . . . that no life is really private, or isolated, or self-sufficient.'[31] She put forward a new model of marriage and motherhood, one that 'need never tame the mind, nor swamp and undermine ability and training, nor trammel and domesticize political perception and social judgement'. Finally, in describing her own 'personal resurrection'[32] after the war, she dedicated herself to the campaign for internationalism, 'a more exultant fight than war itself . . . a fight capable of enlarging the souls of men and women with the same heightened consciousness of living and uniting them in one dedicated community whose common purpose transcends the individual'.[33]

*Testament of Youth* is also, despite the impression of directness vividly conveyed by extensive quotations from letters and from Brittain's diary, a product of the late 1920s and early 1930s. Most of it was written 15 years after the events portrayed, and it is impregnated with the spirit of pacifism and internationalism which Brittain developed only after the summer of 1918. Ironically, only weeks after its publication the new Chancellor of Germany, Adolf Hitler, took his country out of the League of Nations, the organization in which Vera Brittain had invested so much hope.

## Spencer and resurrection

Stanley Spencer similarly spent more than ten years in reflection before making his most significant creative contribution to British memory of the war. He had in 1922 painted *The Unveiling of the War Memorial in Cookham*, a celebration in microcosm of the whole process of commemoration and an exploration of theme of resurrection which preoccupied him after 1918. The War Memorial which he represented was in many ways a very typical one, a white Celtic stone cross inscribed with the names of 64 men from Cookham who had died during the war. At the centre of the painting, the white cross carries an obvious Christian symbolism, one linked to the young girls dressed in white around its base. Spencer wrote that they appeared like 'little alive parts of the Memorial'.[34] The painting is also an idealized representation of community: the whole village appears to be at the unveiling, united in a common spirit. The presence of many young people in the foreground suggests continuity despite the losses of the war. There is no hint in the picture of disunity or of whether there had been any in Cookham who were not in sympathy with the war effort.

Spencer was already working out ideas which had been with him since 1916, for 'a sort of Odyssey' of his war experiences. Early in 1923 his ambitious scheme for a series of frescoes covering three sides of a building took shape, and he wrote with excitement to his sister of how a wealthy couple, the Behrends, had decided to construct a chapel specially for these. Mary Behrend's brother had died after the war from an illness contracted during his service in Macedonia, and she and her husband were clearly taken by Spencer's vision.[35] They commissioned the architect Lionel Pearson to design a suitable building, working closely from Spencer's ideas. Spencer modelled the building, which was built in the village of Burghclere in Hampshire, on Giotto's Arena Chapel in Padua. In 1925 he married Hilda Carline, and they moved into a cottage in Burghclere with their new baby Shirin in May 1927. For the next five years, Spencer was completely involved with painting the Sandham Memorial Chapel, or the Oratory of All Souls, Burghclere, as it was formally known.

Spencer's scheme was for the two side walls of the chapel to be covered by eight arch-topped canvases, each one over a smaller predella. Above these on each wall was a larger mural, providing unity and continuity. The whole east wall of the chapel, behind the altar, was given over to a large mural representing the Day of Judgement. These three walls covered by paintings are lit by a large window above the door in the fourth wall. The side walls, with their 16 smaller paintings and two large panoramas, represent Spencer's own wartime service, starting at Beaufort Hospital, moving through Tweseldown Camp and on to Macedonia. All, excepting *The Resurrection of the Soldiers* on the east wall, were clearly drawn from Spencer's direct experience. In several of the pictures he may be identified. Spencer chose not to represent any fighting; there are no scenes here of men in battle. Instead he focused on the prosaic day-to-day activities which filled his life as a medical orderly and then as a private soldier, activities which we know he had found it very hard to endure.

There is therefore little of conventional heroism in Spencer's paintings for the Sandham Memorial Chapel, unless it is the heroism of ordinary people carrying out everyday tasks in a patient spirit. Similarly there is no direct comment on the justice of the British involvement in the war. We find no reflection of Spencer's own wartime commitment to the righteousness of the British cause, and he does not represent any enemies, German, Turkish or Bulgarian. There is a powerful and unmistakeable indirect comment in *The Resurrection of the Soldiers*, where many British soldiers are portrayed rising from their graves, struggling through coils of barbed wire. Those already resurrected extend hands of comradeship to those just awakening, and many carry the white crosses which have marked their graves towards the figure of Christ. One, in the centre of the picture, gazes with wonder on an image of Christ crucified on a white cross.

Spencer's concept of the resurrection was concerned as much with this world as the next, and he tried to explain this in a number of letters. In one, he wrote of Donne's idea that, in the journey of the soul, it 'not only will not die but will not so much as even suffer an "interruption."' He continued: 'The men looking at the crosses are meant to be expressing happiness, . . . which is the result of certainty; the certainty in this case being clearly understanding . . . the meaning of "He that loses his life for my sake shall save it."' Earlier, describing his preoccupation with the idea of Resurrection, he had written of an 'intercourse' between his experience of this life and his imagination of the resurrection: 'The contemplation of the Resurrection throws back into this life a light which licks on this life's perfection and its special meanings that I love so much.'[36]

Spencer found ennoblement in the war, not in the heroics of combat, but in the performance of everyday tasks. Several of the smaller paintings in the scheme represent the daily tasks which we know he found so gruelling at Beaufort Hospital: scrubbing floors, polishing taps, sorting out kit bags and laundry, filling tea urns and scraping frostbite from the patients' feet. Others represent aspects of military routine: the stand-to at dawn, kit inspection, filling water bottles, map-reading and pitching tents. The first painting in the whole series depicts a lorry loaded with injured soldiers arriving at the Beaufort Hospital, with huge iron gates being opened by two grim warders, suggesting the descent into a hellish underworld, and the beginning of a journey which will lead to transfiguration, what Spencer called 'the whole progress of my soul'.[37] From this terrifying introduction, many of the paintings develop a theme of restoration and redemption. One, from Beaufort Hospital, shows patients resting on their beds and others eating huge piles of bread and jam, something Spencer loved. The painting above this of soldiers resting and refreshing themselves from a water fountain in Macedonia, filling their bottles from its healing waters, is one of several in which men are shown in close kinship with horses and mules, here similarly quenching their thirst. The two panoramas which depict camp scenes in

Macedonia are replete with small details of men resting, washing clothes and engaged in homely but constructive tasks.

It was only possible for Spencer to create this broad, spiritual vision of the war years after it ended. We know that during the war he felt atrophied and blighted, isolated in the army and profoundly homesick. He was almost entirely incapable of creative work. Ten years later, having had space for reflection, opportunities for conversation with a large circle of creative friends, the support of wealthy patrons and having enjoyed for the first time – if only briefly – the fulfilment that came from a successful sexual relationship, Spencer was able to transmute his wartime experience into a personal vision which spoke to many others.[38] The Sandham Memorial Chapel is today owned by the National Trust and is open to the public. Some art historians regard Spencer's work there as the single most impressive painterly achievement to emerge from the First World War. A noticeboard inside the chapel describes him as 'the greatest British painter of the twentieth century'.

## David Jones and *In Parenthesis*

We do not know exactly why, after a decade spent working on engravings and watercolours, David Jones decided to write about his war experiences. Although he had had some success as an artist, Jones had experienced disappointment in his personal life. His engagement to Petra Gill, the daughter of Eric Gill, had been broken off, and he remained a bachelor for the rest of his life. According to anecdote, after reading a translation of Erich Maria Remarque's *All Quiet on the Western Front* in 1929, Jones said: 'Bugger it, I can do better than that' and started work on what would become *In Parenthesis*, a memoir of his service with the London Welsh Battalion from December 1915 to July 1916.[39] Jones wrote in his Preface that the title indicated both how he had written the book 'in a kind of space in between – I don't know between quite what – but as you turn aside to do something', and 'because for us amateur soldiers . . . the war itself was a parenthesis'. He added, suggesting how difficult he found it to adapt to anything outside army life after 1918, 'how glad we thought we were to step outside its brackets at the end of '18'.[40] Jones' friend René Hague argued 'that his four years in the army, the months in the trenches and the bloody battle of the Wood left him spiritually and psychologically unscarred and even invigorated'.[41] Another friend, speaking in 1978, said that 'David never really got out of the trenches.'[42]

*In Parenthesis* was completed in 1932, but after this Jones experienced a nervous breakdown, attributed by some to a delayed traumatic reaction to the war. He was seen by a 'shell-shock' specialist and made a trip to the Mediterranean to try to recuperate. In 1935, on his return, Jones returned to the work's notes and Preface, and it was published in 1937. It is a complex work, written in a modernist idiom. It moves between poetry and prose, and is densely allusive, referring constantly to a wide range of literature, in English and Welsh. To understand it, the reader needs a good familiarity with Shakespeare, the Bible, Malory's *Morte d'Arthur*, the Welsh lyric fragments of *Y Gododdin*, the Welsh medieval manuscripts known as the *Mabinogion*, the poetry of Gerard Manley Hopkins, Coleridge, Blake and other literary sources. This apparent erudition is balanced by reference to folk songs, music hall and army songs, and by use of Cockney rhyming slang. *In Parenthesis* was awarded Britain's major literary prize, the Hawthorndon, in 1938. T. S. Eliot called it 'a work of genius', and many other writers have agreed with his verdict. In 1985 Jones was included among sixteen First World War poets commemorated in Westminster Abbey. But his work has also had its detractors, notably the influential literary scholar Paul Fussell, who called *In Parenthesis* an 'honorable miscarriage', bordering at points on incoherence. Fussell argued that Jones' method of association, above all his effort to liken the experience of British soldiers in the First World War to that of soldiers throughout the ages, 'used the past not, as it often pretends to do, to shame the present, but really to ennoble it. The effect of the poem, for all its horrors, is to rationalize and even validate the war by implying that it somehow recovers many of the motifs and values of medieval chivalric romance'. Going further, Fussell argued that this tendency put *In Parenthesis* close to other writings which were 'overtly patriotic and even propagandistic'. This reading has been roundly rejected by other critics.[43]

*In Parenthesis* is such a rich and multifaceted text that it is too simplistic to see it as merely glorifying war. It actually offers a much more ambiguous view of the war – seen from the perspective of a private in the trenches – than perhaps both admirers and detractors are ready to admit. As with *Testament of Youth*, or Spencer's paintings in the Sandham Memorial Chapel, *In Parenthesis* was the product of years of reflection, a child of its time, differing radically from the naïve and youthful simplicity of Jones' wartime pictures and writings. It has been viewed as part of the literature of disillusionment, the last great memoir in a series that started with Ford Madox Ford's *Parade's End*, and included Graves' *Goodbye to All That*, Aldington's *Death of a Hero*, Sassoon's autobiographical trilogy and Brittain's *Testament of Youth*. And disillusion is indeed a strong theme in the book. Jones prefaced the work with a dedication, to, among others, 'the enemy front fighters who shared our pains against whom we found ourselves by misadventure'.[44] This view, typically deploying a literal translation of the German term *Frontkämpfer*, is entirely different from Jones' wartime representations and derived from his dissatisfaction with the Treaty of Versailles and with his developing view during the 1920s and early 1930s that the Germans had been unfairly treated. He wrote: 'I did not intend this as a "War Book" – it happened to be concerned with war. I should prefer it to be about a good kind of peace – but as Mandeville says, "Of Paradys ne can I not speken propurly I was not there".'[45] William Blissett, who became friends with Jones much later, recalls how in 1959 Jones 'made the admission (or rather tore the admission out of himself) that he had been quite pro-German in the appeasement era, out of fellow feeling for the "enemy front fighters against whom we found ourselves by misadventure," having dismissed all earlier reports of Nazi cruelty and nihilism as propaganda, like the stories of soldiers crucified on hay ricks in the Great War.'[46]

Apart from the brief reference in the dedication, the 'enemy front fighters' are a largely unseen presence in *In Parenthesis*, as in so many other First World War representations. Jones addresses the theme of disillusion elsewhere, in other ways. From the start of the book, he describes his experience as 'a life singularly inimical, hateful, to us',[47] and the many hideous and graphic details he provides of everyday life in the trenches — to say nothing of the fighting — bear this out. *In Parenthesis* comes to a climax with the attack on Mametz Wood during the Somme campaign in which Jones was wounded, and here he provides a scathing attack on the generals which must rank with any other denunciation, in any medium. One of the soldiers hears from his 'brother Charlie what was a proper crawler and had some posh job' at divisional headquarters of the plan of attack: Charlie 'reckoned he heard this torf he forgot his name came out of ther Gen'ral's and say how it was going to be a first clarst bollocks and murthering of Christian men and reckoned how he'd throw in his mit an' be no party to this so-called frontal attack never for no threat nor entreaty, for now, he says, blubbin' they reckon, is this noble fellowship wholly mischiefed'.[48] Aside from the typical features of Jones' writing in this passage, the juxtaposition of Cockney argot with the formal register and Shakespearian allusion of the 'torf', the front soldier's disdain for the 'crawler' who has a 'posh job' behind the lines, and the humour, there is a deep underlying seriousness in the whole passage. And, as Vera Brittain had done, Jones portrayed the British leadership here not just as inept, but as perpetrating a wanton deception on the men who are to be sacrificed in this attack. They have been 'wholly mischiefed'. Jones makes other powerful contributions to the theme of 'lions led by donkeys'. Has there ever been a more convincingly satirical representation of the fatuousness of official communiqués than Jones' description of the men being told of the first day's attack on the Somme? He portrays how an officer tries to read the communiqué against a backdrop of noise from the nearby road:

> Received from extract issued G.H.Q. of the 2nd to be communicated to all ranks. With transport on the paved road you missed half the good news . . . and have carried his trenches on a wide front . . . in the south subsector . . . our advanced troops have penetrated to his third system'.

Although the final parts of the communiqué were 'obliterated' by the noise of a truck changing gear, the men 'were permitted to cheer'.[49]

Intriguingly, Jones referred obliquely to his own wartime patriotism, describing how the troops passed the time in a rest break: some looked 'at illustrations in last week's limp and soiled *Graphic*, of Christmas preparations with the Fleet, and full-page portraits of the high command; to be assured that the spirit of the troops is excellent, that the nation proceeds confidently in its knowledge of victory, that Miss Ashwell would perform before all ranks, that land-girls stamp like girls in Luna'.[50] One would never know from this that Jones himself had contributed patriotic pictures to the *Graphic*.

But heroism is not absent from *In Parenthesis*. It is present in the stoical fatalism of the ordinary troops, who endure the sufferings and indignities inflicted on them with humour and tolerance. Notably, Jones provides examples of heroism among officers at different levels in the army hierarchy. There is Captain Cadwaladr who 'restores the Excellent Disciplines of the Wars' at a critical point in Mametz Wood when some of the men panic and start to run away, complaining of 'a monumental bollocks every time'.[51] Although Jones portrays the soldiers as contemptuous of all, including staff officers, who avoided the front line with its dangers, he was prepared to give credit to senior officers where it was due. In the passage quoted earlier where the Welsh Division was ordered to take Mametz Wood, it is actually one of the generals who dissents from the plan and courts retribution by arguing for a more subtle approach.[52] Jones was also struck by the personal bravery of some of his own senior officers. Memorably he portrayed Brigadier General

FIGURE 29 *The memorial to the 38th (Welsh) Division at Mametz Wood on the Somme, erected in 1985, overlooks the open ground which David Jones and his comrades had to cross to reach the wood.*

Price-Davies with his subordinates in the heat of battle, in the carnage of Mametz Wood, 'down among the dead men and: It's only right he should be with the boys the fire-eating old bastard'. Jones continues, quoting one of the officers, who appears oblivious to danger: 'I say Calthrop, have a bite of this perfectly good chocolate you can eat the stuff with your beaver up, this Jackerie knows quite well that organizing brains must be adequately nourished.'[53]

David Jones joined the Roman Catholic Church in 1921 and maintained his faith for the rest of his life, but he did not directly project this onto *In Parenthesis*. There is what John Johnston called 'an emphasis on ritual and liturgy' in the book,[54] but the soldiers are not shown as religious, and indeed there is little of redemption here. Jones portrayed the deaths of both named and anonymous individual soldiers, sometimes with a callousness and indifference which speaks of how the front-line soldiers had to equip themselves mentally to come to terms with this. If there is redemption, it is in his view of comradeship movingly portrayed both in the dedication and in the biblical quotations at the end of the text. For all its grimness and horror, *In Parenthesis* is an affectionate, even idealized portrayal of life in the 'New Army' before the Somme, what Jones called 'the intimate, continuing, domestic life of small contingents of men, within whose structure Roland could find, and for a reasonable while, enjoy, his Oliver'.[55] This echoes directly the periodization earlier used by Kate Finzi, John Masefield and others. René Hague has written convincingly: 'David enjoyed the war. He loved soldiering and comradeship. . . . His happiness in the ranks was largely due, I believe, to the absence of responsibility and of any need to make decisions.'[56]

Although *In Parenthesis* quickly gained recognition in literary circles, its complexity has prevented it from ever being read as widely as the other great memoirs of the 1920s and 1930s. It was adapted for radio broadcast, first in 1947 and then in 1959, and this brought elements of it at least to post-war audiences. The book was reissued in paperback in 1961 and reprinted in this format in 1969. Since then, and after Jones' death in 1974 a devoted circle of admirers has kept the flame alight, but sadly *In Parenthesis* becomes ever more inaccessible to successive generations less familiar with the literary references it draws upon.[57]

## Elgar and Parry

Britain was not a hotbed of musical modernism after 1918. A new generation of composers, many of whom had been taught by Parry, explored neoclassical idioms in the further development of a distinctive national tradition. Parry and Elgar both suffered from their casual identification with the generation and with the establishment which had taken Britain into war in 1914. After 1918, much of their music increasingly appeared to be out of date, representative of an era of imperial splendour and complacency. Parry's 'Jerusalem' was adopted by the Women's Institute movement in 1924, a development he would surely have welcomed, and it has retained its popularity, particularly with institutions such as schools. Even today, few know of the song's genesis with Fight for Right in 1916 or of its withdrawal from that movement in 1917. Parry's *Songs of Farewell* have kept a place in the repertoire of British choirs, but few who sing them link them with the First World War. His 'Naval Ode' and 'Aviators' Song' are unknown. Perhaps because of the musical language he used, and because his music is used at public ceremonials, Parry is imagined – if at all – as a conservative figure. His ardent radicalism, his support for women's suffrage and his appearance on public platforms with the Union of Democratic Control are virtually unknown. Perhaps with the resurgence of interest in his music in the early twenty-first century there will be an overdue reappraisal of his personal history.

Even Elgar's most passionate supporters acknowledge that he has suffered greatly from being identified with nationalism and imperialism.[58] The spectacle of 'Land of Hope and Glory' being sung badly by crowds waving Union flags at the last night of the Proms has obscured from a larger public the introspective and mystical composer of *Spirit of England*. Elgar's smaller contributions to 'war music', *Carillon*, *Une Voix dans le Désert*, *Le Drapeau Belge* and *Fringes of the Fleet* have disappeared almost without trace and are only broadcast or performed today as curiosities. In the 1920s, the 'For the Fallen' movement from *Spirit of England* was used to start the BBC's annual broadcast of the Armistice Day service of remembrance, but after 1945 it was replaced by 'Nimrod' from his *Enigma Variations*. *Spirit of England* has undoubtedly also suffered from its title, which suggests a vulgar nationalism which is not present in the actual music. Although Binyon's words are today widely known in Britain and in Commonwealth countries, few are even aware of Elgar's musical setting of them. Of the instrumental works Elgar wrote in the final months of the war, the Cello Concerto has, after, its dismal first performance, won a place in the concert repertoire and in the hearts of generations of music lovers. Its very abstraction has meant that apart from a deep sense of sorrow and regret, it has not contributed to social memory of the war.

Elgar's music has enjoyed a notable resurgence in recent years, not just in Britain. He is again being performed in Germany, and there is growing interest in his music in America. The image of the country gentleman with a military moustache is slowly yielding to a broader understanding of a composer who combined a unique sensitivity with extraordinary technical gifts. With the turn in academic musicology towards locating music in societal context there has been an expansion of Elgar scholarship, and recently, a whole book with contributions by distinguished specialists has examined his relationship with the First World War.[59] On the evening of 27 July 2012, an estimated 900 million people worldwide watched the opening ceremony for the Olympic Games in London on television. At the start of the ceremony an orchestra of 100 musicians played Elgar's 'Nimrod' from the *Enigma Variations*, and this was followed by a solo treble singing Parry's 'Jerusalem'.

## Recent developments

Each age sees the past through the prism of its own preoccupations, and this has been evident in the fate of some of the artists selected for this study. Those perceived to have articulated support for the war, like Rupert Brooke, or identified with the establishment, like Elgar and Parry, have appeared unsympathetic since the 1960s to generations suspicious of militarism and cynical about the manipulation of patriotic spirit. Conversely, the paintings by Nevinson and Nash, canonized by their prominent display at the Imperial War Museum, have maintained their popularity, and since the 1960s been in tune with the prevailing scepticism of younger British people. Nevinson's bold and simple use of colours, which offended Alice Elgar and many art critics in 1916, has appeared vibrant and challenging to generations which do not draw such a clear distinction between 'high art' and popular culture. Similarly, the Vorticist idiom employed by Nevinson and then by Nash still appears radical and edgy. To this day, books and posters about the First World War are frequently decorated by their representations.[60]

With the emergence of 'women's history' in the 1960s and 1970s, Vera Brittain, similarly, was given a new lease of life. Her *Testament of Youth* appeared to a new generation of readers not only as a passionate criticism of war, but as a pioneering text of female emancipation. Kate Finzi, who was clearly an independent and determined young woman, was not similarly taken up, as she had neither criticized the war effort nor called for significant changes in gender roles. She is absent from several of the investigations of women's writing on the First World War written in the 1980s, or if present, was scornfully dismissed. Claire Tylee wrote that Finzi's diary was 'facile war-propaganda'.[61] Only in the last ten years has she received scholarly attention in a book examining 'the ideology and language of writers who recorded the Great War in a different way and justified the sacrifices made in its name'.[62] Finzi's 'War Diary' has now been republished, one of many long-forgotten memoirs finding a new public.

The memory of Hedd Wyn displays clearly how contemporary concerns shape understandings of the past. For decades knowledge of his life and his poetry was confined to the Welsh-speaking community, a memory lovingly tended by a small circle of devotees. With the development in the 1970s and in subsequent years of a new Welsh nationalism, and a broader commitment to support the Welsh language, the legend of Hedd Wyn and the 'Black Chair' was ideally suited to contribute to a series of interlinked goals. A man who would once have been vilified as a 'shirker' or a 'slacker' could now be remembered as a poet who had abhorred war, but had been prepared to serve when this was demanded of him. His death on the first day of the most awful campaign of the war for the British could be blamed not on the Germans, but on English militarism. Generations of schoolchildren in Wales were taught his poetry and taken on pilgrimages to see the 'Black Chair' at the Evans' family home, Yr Ysgryn. In 1992 the Welsh-language television channel S4C commissioned a feature-length film about him, which won a number of awards outside Wales.[63] Although faithful to the known facts about the poet's life, the film is structured around a clear opposition between the Welsh, presented as soulful, sensitive and peace-loving, and the English, who appear as coarse, arrogant militarists.

In a more recent development, the legend of Hedd Wyn has been taken up by Flemish nationalists, who since the 1950s have achieved much greater political and cultural influence in Flemish-speaking parts of Belgium. These include, coincidentally, the area of Belgium defended by the British Army between 1914 and 1918 around Ypres, or Ieper as it is now known. The Flemings see themselves as a Celtic linguistic minority similar in many ways to the Welsh. Since the creation of the Belgian nation-state in 1837, the Flemings have felt oppressed by a French-speaking majority, but have proudly guarded a distinctive linguistic and cultural heritage. The legend of Hedd Wyn, and his posthumous award of the 'Black Chair', carved – coincidentally – by a Flemish refugee, has appealed to a specifically Flemish imagination, and this was reflected in the memorial erected to him on the wall of a café near Pilckem in 1992. The memorial is made of Welsh slate and carries an inscription celebrating him written in Welsh, English and Flemish. Since 1992, the memorial has attracted visitors, and now has a small display case next to it for newspaper articles and notices. In the last five years, local residents have held a ceremony on the first Monday of every month to commemorate the sacrifice of Welsh troops here. The traffic outside is briefly stopped, the Welsh flag is raised, and Welsh songs and the 'Last Post' are played by a local trumpeter. When this author visited the Hedd Wyn memorial, the noticeboard was displaying an article from the Welsh *Daily Post*, with a headline which quotes a local resident declaring 'We will never forget the sacrifice of Welsh soldiers who came to liberate us'.[64] While not wishing to question the sentiment underlying this, one might well doubt how far it is accurate to imagine a reluctant conscript such as Ellis Evans coming to the Pilckem Ridge to liberate the Flemish people. He ended up in fact where the British Army sent him, and might equally well have been posted to Palestine or to Macedonia. It is doubtful that he, or his fellow soldiers, had any consciousness whatsoever of Flemish nationalism or of a distinctive Flemish minority. There is no sense of this in the contemporary literature, which exclusively uses French place names. Between 1914 and 1918, comparisons between Wales and Belgium were frequently made, but ironically when the *Welsh Outlook*, a journal dedicated to fostering a distinctive Welsh identity, examined this in more detail in October 1914,

FIGURE 30 *This small memorial to Hedd Wyn, with a legend in Welsh, English and Flemish, was put on a building at Hagebos crossroads in 1992, close to the site of his death on 31 July 1917.*

it noted the similarities between the Welsh, and, not the Flemings, but the Walloons.[65]

If we turn to the broader memory of the First World War in Britain, we may be approaching a turning point. The sense of the war as futile, misconceived and destructive probably reached its apogee in the 1990s and was powerfully summed up in the hugely influential television series *Blackadder Goes Forth* (1989). This series, written by Richard Curtis and Ben Elton, rehearsed many of the paradigms which had emerged with the literature of disillusion in the 1920s, notably the idea of stupid, blundering generals. It appealed to older age groups affected by the anti-war movements of the 1960s, and through the vehicle of comedy had enormous attraction to a younger generation learning anew about the First World War. *Blackadder* presented memorable images of the central British stereotypes of the First World War: a boisterous, brainless general, who stays well away from the front line; two junior officers, one ludicrously naïve and credulous, who still imagines the war is an extension of public school sports, the other more knowing and cynical, who as a last resort will try to feign madness to escape a 'push'; and an ordinary soldier, who understands nothing of the situation he finds himself in, but cheerfully does his bit. At the end of the series, the last three, when the whistle blows, have to go 'over the top', where we know they will be killed in a pointless offensive. In one episode, when discussing how the war started and what is was for, none of the men can come up with a sensible answer.

Since then, although the cynical view of the war is still strongly rooted, deeply anchored in ignorance about how the war started, and about attitudes during the war, there have been notable developments. In separate fields of academic history more nuanced views are now strongly represented, and many post-war myths are being challenged. Among gender historians, the simplistic idea that the war emancipated women has been largely replaced by an understanding that although women's lives were clearly changed during the war, their strategic position in relationships of power in British society was not significantly altered. Attention is now shifting to changed senses of citizenship which emerged from the war, and to how this might enable us better to understand how the war affected gender roles and relations.[66] In military history, the long-established paradigm of unimaginative generals wedded to nineteenth-century ideas of warfare has yielded place to detailed investigations of the technical complexity of different branches of warfare by 1918, and of how these were welded together to produce a highly specialized military machine which finally broke the deadlock on the Western Front. Even Haig's reputation is being substantially rehabilitated. In the arts, the sense of 1914 as a watershed between traditional and modern has long been abandoned by serious scholars, and detailed studies of different art forms and of individual artists have taken the roots of modernism further and further back into the nineteenth century. This has been balanced by a recognition of the persistence of traditional forms, whether we see this as the survival of narrative in literature, of naturalistic representation in the visual arts or of melody in music.

Perhaps unsurprisingly, we are even witnessing a revalidation of the idea of heroism. Richard Aldington bitterly called his memoir *The Death of a Hero* in 1929, and Bernard Bergonzi, writing on First World War literature in 1980, echoed this with his title *Heroes' Twilight*. Since the First Gulf War of 1990, British armed forces have been more or less constantly in action somewhere in the world. The long and torturous involvements, above all in Iraq and Afghanistan, have meant that since 2003 few days pass without the announcement of another British soldier killed or injured in a distant land. The country has found itself in an Orwellian state of continuous war, the so-called war on terror, and has been deeply divided in its response to this. There has been a sustained discursive effort to validate the notion that, whatever the political or ideological conflicts in Britain over these wars, the men and women fighting for the country in them are heroes. Regardless of their individual conduct or experience, they are all portrayed in the press and mass media as heroes. A leading charity which runs many public fund-raising events is called 'Help for Heroes'. Ideas derived from the disillusionment of the First World War, of individual soldiers as cannon fodder, of generals as incompetent idiots, of war itself as futile are profoundly unhelpful to any government still using war as an instrument of policy, and public anxiety has been combated with a sustained effort to valorize the contribution of individual soldiers today and to portray the British armed forces as competent and professional. This in turn has helped to create a more receptive climate for reappraisals of the mythology of the First World War.

# Conclusion

What can the experience of this group of creative individuals, and their response to the challenge of representing the war, tell us more broadly? How have their representations affected currents of memory in Britain? In addressing these questions, we shall first advance some broad conclusions before proceeding to a more detailed examination of how far their individual experiences and representations were shaped by social differences, by gender, age, class and region, and of what it was that prompted some of them to modify their attitude to the war.

It is abundantly clear that the distinction drawn by Janet Watson between experience and memory is confirmed by study of this group.[1] There is a striking difference between most of the wartime representations of this group of artists and the representations produced by the surviving members after the war. The distinction between experience and memory is reflected also in the reception of different wartime representations after 1918. To illustrate this we might contrast the canonization of Nash's paintings of the Ypres Salient with the gradual disappearance from the repertoire of Elgar's *Spirit of England*. Overwhelmingly, the artists focused on here believed that Britain was right to go to war in 1914, and that this was a just response to German aggression and disregard for international law. To this extent, their experience supports the ideas about moral consensus advanced by Audoin-Rouzeau and Becker in their recent appraisal, and in the case of several of the group – Brooke, Finzi, Brittain, Jones, Elgar and Lawrence – would justify their use of the word 'crusade'.[2] The clear evidence that most of these artists were not hostile to Germany before August 1914 supports Adrian Gregory's contention that Britain did not go to war because of 'mass jingoism and anti-German antagonism', but rather that 'it was *the war* that massively increased anti-Germanism and popular patriotism'.[3] Further, it is clear that in common with many other British people, several of the artists in this group became increasingly disillusioned with the war and with this sense of moral purpose during the war, and after it. If we turn to what Peter Mandler has called the 'throw' of their cultural representations,[4] that is to say their wider influence on contemporaries and on succeeding generations, it is clear that it is the representations of disillusionment which have had most impact. The most literal representations of the war as a crusade, which as we have seen were strikingly widespread, have quietly disappeared, even – in the case of David Jones – been deliberately obscured, and where they have survived – as in Brooke's poetry – held up to scorn and ridicule. What Nash called in November 1917 'the bitter truth' about the war has become widely accepted as just that.

It is though important to qualify these broad outlines, and a closer analysis of these individual artistic trajectories will suggest that we need constantly to be aware of variations upon these themes. Let us examine first individual reactions to the declaration of war. We are all familiar with the stereotypical image of nationalistic crowds in Downing Street and outside Buckingham Palace singing patriotic songs, but fewer know of Asquith's comment to Venetia Stanley, just before the declaration of war, of how he loathed 'such levity'.[5] We know now that the crowds in London which so disturbed Asquith were not representative of the wider nation;[6] intriguingly, only the two young women among my subjects might be considered to have displayed anything approaching 'levity' in their response to the outbreak of war: Vera Brittain was 'thrilled' and 'excited', and Kate Finzi, who volunteered immediately, imagined that war might be 'a Great Game'. Both were clearly invigorated by what they recognized as a momentous historical development and impressed by the image of young men going to fight. It may be more than coincidental that both these young women had attended girls' boarding schools, and both had brothers who had been educated in public schools.[7] To be fair, we should note that both women were also aware that war meant violence and bloodshed and were horrified by this. T. E. Lawrence and Rupert Brooke were both more focused and serious in their embrace of war, perhaps reflecting a gendered awareness that involvement in it would bring great personal danger. Lawrence later wrote to another of the war's great memorialists, Cecil Day Lewis: 'My age made me just ripe for it'.[8] Four others, all of similar age – Spencer, Nash, Nevinson and Evans – were clearly dismayed by the outbreak of war and faced the issue of participation with very mixed feelings, torn between senses of moral obligation, reluctance to behave violently, and fear. Here there is an obvious gendered distinction. For men who were fundamentally non-violent, there was an option to be closely involved in the war in a non-violent role, as medical orderlies or ambulance drivers. Spencer and Nevinson went down this route, as did other well-known figures such as the composer Ralph Vaughan-Williams, the journalist Kingsley Martin and the poet Laurence Binyon. While this was a route open to young women, particularly those from a secure financial background, such as Finzi and Brittain, there was no corresponding possibility for them to volunteer to fight.

Strikingly, it is the two older members of the group, Elgar and Parry, who reacted with real anguish to the declaration of war. Despite their very different political views – Elgar a staunch conservative, and Parry an ardent radical – both shared a considered view that the war was just, but were completely horrified by the prospect of violence on an unprecedented scale. Here I take issue with Dan Todman, who has written that this was 'A war often entered into in a spirit of hope, enthusiasm, and willing sacrifice'.[9] Disquiet, apprehension and horror must be added to this list. There is a fascinating class dimension to those in the group who were closest to outright opposition to the war, Parry and Ellis Evans. Parry, largely through his aristocratic family connections, was brought into close contact with pacifists and with those calling for an early negotiated peace; in passing we might note that Rupert Brooke, similarly well connected, was also exposed to dialogue with pacifists, although he had no sympathy with them. The sheep farmer Ellis Evans, in contrast, although he clearly did not want to join up, and resisted this for as long as possible, did not opt to present himself as a conscientious objector. The documentation on him is so sparse that it is not clear whether he considered this, but it may well have been that he was in a social and cultural milieu in which this was simply not a viable option.

We may deepen this analysis by considering how these artists represented the enemy once the war had started. Several displayed humanity, kindness and personal empathy when representing individual Germans. Finzi and Brittain both took some pride in treating wounded German prisoners with compassion, using this also to fortify their assumption of British moral supremacy. David Jones showed similar humanity in his drawing of a captured German prisoner. Much more striking is the way in which all wartime representations of the Germans as a collective by these artists were condemnatory. David Jones used the figure of an evil Teutonic knight to represent German 'tyranny'. Even in 1918, Vera Brittain wrote of 'blood lust untameable'. Parry, Finzi and Brooke – all of whom had knowledge of Germany, German culture and the German language – adopted the idea of 'two Germanys'. The war had been caused by 'Prussian militarism' which had somehow gained sway over the rest of the population and led a cultured people into a path of violence and aggression. Elgar, who was clearly tortured by this problem, finally produced perhaps the most damning indictment of the Germans, representing them as demons, 'fallen intellects', whose misery was even greater because they knew they had fallen.[10] Interestingly Rupert Brooke, so often condemned for his alleged naivety, produced a similarly prescient view shortly after his experience at Antwerp in October 1914, writing: 'There's nothing to say, except that the tragedy of Belgium is the greatest and worst of any country for centuries. It's ghastly for anyone who liked Germany as well as I did. Their guilt can never be washed away. I'm afraid fifty years won't give them the continuity and loveliness of life back again'.[11] Brooke's estimate now appears a conservative one. Fifty years on from 1914 the German historical profession was deep in controversy over Fritz Fischer's thesis that the First World War had indeed been caused by German aggression. Even today, the wider German public is struggling to master its own twentieth-century history, to come to terms with the past.

Between 1914 and 1918, not one of this group of artists could advance the least shred of justification for the conduct of the Germans, however cynical their view of the British involvement became. In the wartime representations which might be considered the most critical of the British war effort, and of war in general – one thinks here of Nevinson's *Paths of Glory*, Nash's *We are Making a New World*, or Evans' 'Rhyfel' – the Germans were absent. This absence reflects a complete inability to sympathize with what the Germans had done or to portray them as morally in the right. Not until well after the war could survivors such as Vera Brittain and David Jones represent the Germans in a different light, as having suffered equally from misfortune, from British 'propaganda', or from 'misadventure'.

This picture is complicated if we consider the other enemies Britain became engaged with, the Austrian and Ottoman Empires, and Bulgaria. Unsurprisingly, they feature much less prominently in the British consciousness. There was little direct contact between British and Austrian forces in the war, and in Macedonia, the Bulgarians opposite the British in the Vardar valley were for the most part unseen. Stanley Spencer commented in 1929 on his awed and mysterious feelings about the Bulgarians, as 'he never saw them, and yet they were only a few yards away'.[12] He did not – as far as I know – represent them in his painting or in any detail in his wartime writings. What Parry called 'the unspeakable Turk' had suffered from a deeply prejudicial image in British consciousness since the time of the 'Bulgarian massacres' in the 1870s, and by 1914 the Turks were widely imagined as backward, despotic and corrupt. Their decision to fight on the German side only confirmed these dismal views in the eyes of many, and nothing they did in the war – not even the unquestionably successful defence of the Dardanelles and Gallipoli – could redeem them in British eyes. Lawrence, although he found the killing of Turks repugnant, shared this completely negative view and was not prepared even to credit any of them with the military virtues he ascribed to their German and Austrian allies. This perception helped Lawrence and others – one thinks of Lloyd George's romantic interpretation of the capture of the holy places in 1917 – to portray the war against the Ottoman Empire in the Middle East again as a crusade, and not as a war for British imperial gain.[13]

When and why was the sense of crusade undermined and supplanted by disillusionment, mistrust and cynicism? This is a question which has been addressed on different levels. Historians seeking to characterize a wider societal shift, the change of a national mood, are apt to single out the great battles of the war as points around which to structure their narrative. For some, the Battle of the Somme, and above all the terrible first day of that campaign, has been the decisive moment. John Keegan wrote: 'The Somme marked the end of an age of vital optimism in British life that has never been recovered.'[14] Alan Taylor, whose *Illustrated History* of the 1960s was so influential in consolidating a view of the war as pointless and futile, wrote characteristically: 'The Somme set the picture by which future generations saw the First World War: brave helpless soldiers; blundering obstinate generals; nothing achieved. After the Somme men decided that the war would go on for ever'.[15] John Terraine, who was no advocate of the 'lions led by donkeys' theory which Taylor championed, wrote in 1980 about the Somme: 'The nation never recovered.'[16] Peter Whelan's 1981 play *The Accrington Pals* dramatized the story of a group of volunteers from a closeknit working-class community which was largely wiped out on the first day of the Somme. The promotional material for a recent production of the play at Manchester's Royal Exchange Theatre rehearsed these views, stating: 'And back home amongst the women they leave behind – their mothers, wives, daughters, lovers – nothing can ever be the same again'.[17] Robert Wohl, concerned with the literary representation of the war, took a similar view. After the Somme, he wrote, 'the final illusions about the knightly character of the war began to vanish'.[18] The Passchendaele campaign, although considered by military historians to have been more taxing for the British Army, has not been so widely seen as a turning point, perhaps because it lacks the romantic lustre given to the Somme by the notion that all the soldiers participating were volunteers. As far as the army itself is concerned, J. P. Harris has recently singled out the Arras campaign of April 1917 as the point at which morale turned, an idea which might be supported by Sassoon's brief but bitter portrayal of lions and donkeys in his poem 'The General'.[19] Historians analysing the turn to disillusion after the war have focused on the Treaty of Versailles, the accompanying economic depression and on the influence of Keynes' *Economic Consequences of the Peace* as causal factors, suggesting that by 1921 the emotional tide had turned.

Where individuals are concerned, the stereotypical image has been of the young soldier or junior officer who goes to war in a blithe spirit of trust, and is changed by exposure to incompetent leadership and horrible experiences at the front line, which provoke a gradual realization that youthful enthusiasm has been cruelly exploited. This is the 'progress' put forward so powerfully by Sassoon in his three autobiographical volumes of the late 1920s and 1930s. We have seen a female parallel in Vera Brittain's post-war *Testament of Youth*. Paul Nash, whose paintings of 1918 and 1919 have made such an enduring contribution to what has been called 'the myth' of the war, fits this model well. He was sheltered from suffering and horror until 1917, and even his brief tour of duty as a junior officer in the spring of that year did not depress his spirits. It was the first-hand experience of the Passchendaele campaign which provoked a much more embittered and cynical view, and inspired his now iconic paintings. If we turn to the other individual subjects of this study and focus upon their wartime experience, we see immediately that this model is not universally applicable. Rupert Brooke's case is an interesting one. He was sent to Antwerp as part of an expedition which in many ways epitomized the notion of 'lions led by donkeys'. He and his comrades in the Royal Naval Division had virtually no training, no heavy weapons and no preparation for their mission. Hundreds were killed, wounded and captured before the remainder beat a hasty retreat to England. Yet in all of Brooke's letters and commentaries on Antwerp, there is no criticism of Churchill or reference to these problems. Brooke was then sent to the Dardanelles, where he was part of the slow and well publicized preparation for the attack; he was even involved in the abortive effort on 18 March to force the Dardanelles, and although he was ironic about how anti-climactic this was, he appears not to have been in any sense disillusioned. We do not know how he might have reacted to other experiences had he lived longer. Kate Finzi similarly experienced some of the chaos attendant upon Britain's entry into a Continental war for which it was utterly unprepared. She saw at first hand the most gruesome sights on the quayside at Boulogne as thousands of wounded were left without adequate medical provision. She then experienced, and chronicled, numerous examples of bureaucratic incompetence and intra-service bickering by her superiors. She recorded instances of sexist and ageist discrimination; she clearly thought the government was spineless and irresolute. Yet well into 1916 she maintained her optimistic spirit, and her faith in the qualities she imagined were shared by the British population as a whole. We do not know if she ever changed these views.

Even more striking is the case of David Jones, who served as a private soldier from January 1915 to January 1919, and was wounded on the Somme. The battle for Mametz Wood is now regarded – particularly in Wales – as a quintessential example of the bungled frontal assault on a strongly defended German position which resulted in needless loss of life. This image of a 'murthering of good Christian men' was of course at the narrative climax of Jones' post-war memoir *In Parenthesis*, and it was earlier given powerful expression in 1931 by another beautifully written memoir, Llewellyn Wyn Griffiths' *Up to Mametz*, which Jones had read. But right through to the conclusion of the war, David Jones maintained a straightforward view of the conflict as a contest between good and evil. Even after being wounded at Mametz Wood, he posed publicly the rhetorical question 'Is it worth it?' and answered with a resounding affirmative. In his case we need to look into the late 1920s and early 1930s to understand why his views changed, and we will need to jettison a simple concept of 'disillusion'. In my view it is mistaken to see *In Parenthesis* simply as an extension of the canon starting with Blunden, Aldington, Graves, Sassoon and Vera Brittain. It is noteworthy that in two of the most important recent works on the British memory of the First World War, by Janet Watson and Dan Todman, there is no discussion of David Jones.

Nor do these books mention Stanley Spencer, who again does not fit a simple linear progression from enthusiasm to disillusionment. We can see now that he was deeply troubled by the outbreak of war, felt compelled, almost bullied, into enlisting in the RAMC, and found military service thoroughly demeaning and depressing. He did not experience the consolations of comradeship which Jones did in the London Welsh, and he felt oppressed by the coarseness of his fellow soldiers. His final experience as an infantry soldier in Macedonia in September 1918 appears to have added layers of fear and horror to a war experience marked predominantly by spiritual oppression. His post-war representations say nothing of disillusion, but are best understood as an attempt to redeem and transcend this gruelling experience. Spencer's vision in the Sandham Chapel paintings was produced at exactly the same period of British history as those of Blunden, Graves, Sassoon and Brittain, and his voice needs to be placed alongside theirs in an analysis of the construction of memory.

Richard Nevinson provides a very different model. In his case he was an iconoclast before August 1914, already hostile to anything and anyone he considered representative of the old order. Like Spencer, Nevinson was not a hero and it appears that he needed pressure from his father to become involved in the war as a medical orderly. He was, unsurprisingly, shocked by what he saw at the 'Shambles' in Dunkirk in the winter of 1914, and his subsequent experience at a military hospital in London only confirmed these initial impressions. He appears to have been in a state of anxiety bordering on neurosis for much of the war, and this was increasingly reflected in his representations of different aspects of the conflict. In his pictures and paintings from as early as 1915 we can see several of the central tropes of the post-war vision of disillusionment: the sense of the war as mechanical and inhuman; the destruction of landscape and natural beauty; the mental trauma suffered by soldiers; random violence visited upon civilians; the transference of male resentment onto females who did not have to serve; the condemnation of an older generation of 'profiteers'; and pointless deaths in the name of glory. In this light, Nevinson, for all his self-promoting bombast, may be seen to run counter to a broader pattern of wartime consensus.

Parry and Elgar are particularly interesting. Although both appear on the surface to support a linear narrative of emerging disillusionment, there are complexities in both cases. In his response to the war Parry was never enthusiastic, or hopeful, or willing. Although at an intellectual level he accepted the war as necessary, he was far too conscious of the negative side of any equation which sought to balance sacrifice with potential gain from the war. He is the only one of my group to have clearly expressed scepticism about the more lurid examples of German atrocities he heard reported; he deplored jingoism and opposed a collective punishment of Germany after the war. He was clearly sympathetic to the ideals of the Union of Democratic Control and cherished the hope of a fair and negotiated settlement to the conflict. It is regrettable that we do not know precisely why he withdrew his support, and his song 'Jerusalem', from the Fight for Right movement in May 1917, and can only surmise that it was because of the vulgar nationalism and anti-German sentiment its speakers articulated. Parry was also, and this is abundantly clear from his diary, increasingly troubled during the war by illiberal aspects of the government's behaviour which he saw at close quarters: he fought a long and ultimately unsuccessful battle to prevent the internment of his German servant George Schlichtmeyer, which he clearly saw as totally unnecessary (unlike Vera Brittain who wanted to see 'enemy aliens' in her home town interned); he witnessed at first hand the mob violence which curtailed the efforts of the UDC to debate freely the conduct of British foreign policy; and he knew that his daughter and her husband – a Liberal member of Parliament – had to conceal UDC literature in his grandchildren's bedroom in case the police searched their home. At a different level he was dismayed by the government's intervention into the affairs of his estate, demanding that many of the trees planted by his father should be cut down for war production. I interpret this not as a selfish concern for his own material assets, but as a deeper sorrow, reminiscent of Elgar's concern for 'my horses', that the trees should be sacrificed to the quarrels of men. And Parry charted through the war the slow decline of musical life at the Royal College as the students departed for the front. One ray of light in this bleak picture was the achievement of female suffrage, but this alone could not balance the various losses the war had entailed. Speaking to his students in September 1914, Parry had declared that if 'the war-fiend' could not be 'scotched', 'life would not be worth living'. Undoubtedly, as the war progressed, he was deeply disturbed by the prospect of what sort of life would be preserved at its conclusion. His willingness to argue against the idea of collective punishment of the Germans in the summer of 1918, shortly before his death, is evidence that he had not surrendered to despair, but one senses that at points this was not far away. Like Paul Nash, he undoubtedly wondered what sort of 'new world' was in the making.

Elgar initially reacted differently. His support for the British involvement in the war was more willing, and in setting Binyon's poems he did give voice to hope that some good might come out of the spirit of sacrifice and national unity of August 1914. His growing disillusionment is so thoroughly mixed with other personal anxieties and his developing ill health that it is impossible now to pin down with great precision what it was that had reduced him to silence by December 1917. Various scholars have put forward different ideas, including the persuasive notion that it was *not only* the Germans whom Elgar viewed by 1917 as 'fallen intellects', but that he was oppressed by a wider sense of loss.[20] In this context, there is a striking contrast to be observed between his behaviour in August 1914 and November 1918. At the declaration of war, he rushed back from the Scottish highlands to be in London, at the heart of events, and to offer what service he could. At the Armistice, he left London for the seclusion of the countryside and refused to write 'peace music'. He did not want to see or hear the crowds singing 'Land of Hope and Glory' outside Buckingham Palace. His private gesture in flying the Union flag shows clearly that his disillusionment was not total, and that he still identified with the British cause, but this was more in sorrow than in rejoicing.

T. E. Lawrence, a young officer from a privileged if insecure social background, takes us back in some ways to the model represented by

Sassoon, Brittain or Nash, albeit in the very different setting of the war in the desert, but again there are critical individual deviations to note. For all his commitment to ideals of empire, Lawrence in 1914 was no starry-eyed idealist or naïve innocent. Priya Satia sees him as a disenchanted modernist, already jaded with the onset of change in British society, and seeing in the imagined boundless space of 'Arabia' the potential not just for British imperial renewal, but for personal salvation and literary fulfilment. On the surface his war was a huge success, and Satia attributes much of the popularity of the legend of 'Lawrence of Arabia' after 1918 to the public desire to identify with this. She writes: 'his cultural capital lay in another discourse of redemption – a discourse about the redeemer from the desert, which built on the image of the old imperial adventure-hero even as it envisioned a new kind of modernist prophet'.[21] But, as I have argued, and as Satia also recognizes, Lawrence's post-war memoir was a tale of disillusionment. In his case he depicted not the incompetence of generals, but the duplicity of politicians. He experienced sexual degradation and not only witnessed horror, but participated in the most shocking violence. His involvement in the Tafas massacre is central here. Just as Elgar and Brooke recognized that German brutality and depravity affected the perpetrators themselves, Lawrence knew that he had been corrupted by his own connivance in deception, and his descent into brutality. It is not irrelevant in this context to mention that Lawrence, after the war, was a passionate fan of Elgar's music, writing personally to him to express his appreciation. Characteristically he wrote: 'You have had a lifetime of achievement, and I was a flash in a pan.'[22]

Ellis Evans' fate during the war presents the historian with particular problems. There is insufficient documentary evidence to explain central aspects of the legend of Hedd Wyn and the 'Black Chair'. Why did he not enlist in 1914, or in 1915, despite writing poetry which drew on familiar tropes about German aggression and the duty of sacrifice? Why did he then very largely ignore the war in his poetry, concentrating on pastoral and historical themes? Why did he accept being conscripted in 1916 and not register as a conscientious objector? It is becoming apparent that there were many young men like Evans across Britain, who were not ready to volunteer for military service, but how far was his behaviour shaped by his social class, that of effectively an agricultural labourer? Was his identification as a member of a Welsh-speaking minority community more important? What role was played by his upbringing in a nonconformist culture? As we have seen, the mythological representation of him as a peace-loving, pastoral dreamer, hostile to the 'abomination' of English militarism, but tragically killed in action, was being constructed before the war finished and was literally set in stone by 1923. The central aspects of this mythology may well have a basis in reality, but this leaves many questions unanswered. From his conduct and his wartime poetry two things are clear: Ellis Evans did not want to go to war, and by 1917, he viewed that war as a wider calamity.

In her recent study, Janet Watson concluded: 'The story of disillusionment was a product of the late 1920s and early 1930s.' This clearly needs to be qualified. The 'story of disillusionment' became a much stronger element of the larger British memory of the war in the late 1920s and early 1930s, and Dan Todman has charted how this element then became dominant after 1945. But if we take 'disillusion' to mean scepticism about claims of German 'barbarity', and counterclaims of British moral rectitude, fear about the destructive effects of the war on the natural world, the changes it was bringing to British society, and about its corrupting influence on individuals, then it is abundantly clear that this 'story' was emerging in Britain well before 1918. We need to recognize that, just as modernist and traditional modes of representation of the war persisted after 1918, and heroic and disillusioned narratives jostled for position in the wider discursive field of memory, so they competed before November 1918. Eddie Marsh's elegiac memoir of Rupert Brooke, with his poems, was published at exactly the same time as Dyfnallt Owen presented Hedd Wyn as a principled opponent of English militarism, and Nevinson's *Paths of Glory* was displayed in London, partially covered with a strip of brown paper. Nevinson's Futurist representations of the war excited public attention at exactly the point, in March 1915, when Brooke's war sonnets were acclaimed as the genuine articulation of a British patriotism. Elgar's *Spirit of England* had its first complete performance in London in November 1917, days after Paul Nash wrote to his wife about the 'bitter truth' he had seen near Passchendaele, and while, from 'The Trenches, France', David Jones was writing: 'Thou shalt e'en esteem thy life well hazarded in such a cause'. Gertrude Bell wrote home effusively about 'the making of a new world' in the Middle East at the same time,[23] clearly unaware of the painting Nash was working on with the title *We Are Making a New World*, but with a very different meaning. In 1936, as Faber & Faber prepared to publish Jones' modernist *In Parenthesis*, and Victor Gollancz produced a ninth impression of Brittain's *Testament of Youth*, Odhams Press published *Fifty Amazing Stories of the Great War*, a collection full of 'exciting incidents' and 'thrilling moments'.[24] Clearly we must be careful before generalizing. Britain in 1914 was an extraordinarily diverse society, one which permitted, even in wartime, a huge range of opinions. If, as Catriona Pennell has argued, the kingdom was united at the start of the war, it clearly was not by the end.

It is precisely in the diversity of the experiences of this group of artists that we may find some reflection of what happened to the larger society they came from. Three of the group died, directly or indirectly as a result of the war. Others suffered physical injury and mental trauma. Some found purpose, comradeship, and discovered resources of personal courage and stamina which they had not previously been aware of. Some found exhilaration. For a significant number, including some who experienced another world war and lived into the utterly changed world of the 1960s and 1970s, the First World War remained the defining event of their lives. Nearly a century later, it is becoming ever more apparent that it was the defining event in twentieth-century European history. In many ways, in the mass mobilization of society, the application of science and technology, in the use of chemical weapons, the ill-treatment of prisoners, and the mass killing of civilians, it set a template for the greater horrors to follow. The contested memory of the First World War fundamentally shaped British attitudes to the Second, and it still exerts a powerful influence on the imagination of war in general. The Prime Minister who took Britain into war in 1914, and whose own son was killed on the Somme, was much criticized for his conduct as a war leader, and his reputation has not been enhanced by the later popular belief that the war was pointless and futile. He was though not mistaken when he wrote on 3 August 1914: 'We are on the eve of horrible things'.

# ARCHIVAL SOURCES, NEWSPAPERS, JOURNALS AND MAGAZINES

## Archival sources

British Red Cross Society Archive, London
David Jones Papers, National Library of Wales, Aberystwyth
Edward Thomas Archive, Cardiff University
Edward Elgar Birthplace Museum and Visitor Centre, Lower Broadheath
Henry Nevinson Papers, Bodleian Library, Oxford
Papers of Hubert Parry, Schulbrede Priory, Sussex
Rupert Chawner Brooke Papers, Kings College Archive Centre, Cambridge
T. E. Lawrence Papers, Bodleian Library, Oxford
Tate Gallery Archive, London
The National Archive, Kew
Vera Brittain/Paul Berry Archive, Somerville College, Oxford University

## Newspapers, journals and magazines

*Athenaum*
*Burlington Magazine*
*The Cambridge Magazine*
*The Canadian Medical Association Journal*
*Daily Chronicle*
*Daily Express*
*Daily Mail*
*Daily Mirror*
*Daily Sketch*
*Daily Telegraph*
*English Review*

*Evening Standard and St. James Gazette*
*The Graphic*
*London Gazette*
*London Hospital Gazette*
*Manchester Guardian*
*The Nation*
*New Numbers*
*The New Statesman*
*The New Witness*
*The Observer*
*Punch*
*The Saturday Review*
*Sheffield Daily Telegraph*
*South Wales Daily News*
*The Times*
*The Times Literary Supplement*
*Welsh Outlook*

## Abbreviations used in the notes

| | |
|---|---|
| AED | Diary of Lady Alice Elgar, photocopies in the Elgar Birthplace Museum, Lower Broadheath |
| *BDOW* | George Gooch and Harold Temperley (eds), *British Documents on the Origins of the War, 1898-1914* (London: His Majesty's Stationery Office, 1926–38), 11 vols. |
| BRCS | British Red Cross Society Archive, London |
| *CC III* | Martin Gilbert (ed.), *Winston S. Churchill, Vol. III, Companion* (London: Heinemann, 1972) |
| CHHPD | Diary of Charles Hubert Hastings Parry, Schulbrede Priory |
| DJP | David Jones Papers, National Library of Wales, Aberystwyth |
| EBM | Elgar Birthplace Museum, Lower Broadheath |
| EED | Diary of Sir Edward Elgar, photocopies in the Elgar Birthplace Museum, Lower Broadheath |
| *GWI* | J. A. Hammerton (ed.), *The War Illustrated Album de Luxe: The Story of the Great European War told by Camera, Pen and Pencil* (Amalgamated Press, 1915–17), 8 volumes |
| HD | Gary Sheffield and John Bourne (eds), *Douglas Haig: War Diaries and Letters 1914–1918* (London: Weidenfeld and Nicolson, 2005) |

| | |
|---|---|
| HND | Diaries of Henry Nevinson, Henry Nevinson Papers, Special Collections, Bodleian Library, Oxford |
| *LRB* | Geoffrey Keynes (ed.), *The Letters of Rupert Brooke* (London: Faber & Faber, 1968) |
| *PPDH* | Robert Blake (ed.), *The Private Papers of Douglas Haig, 1914–1919* (London: Eyre and Spottiswoode, 1952) |
| RCB | Rupert Chawner Brooke Papers, Kings College Archive Centre, Cambridge |
| *SS* | Adrian Glew (ed.), *Stanley Spencer: Letters and Writings* (London: Tate Gallery Publishing, 2001) |
| TEL | Papers of T. E. Lawrence, Special Collections, Bodleian Library, Oxford |
| TGA | Tate Gallery Archive, London |
| *THW* | *The Times History of the War* (London: Printing House Square, 1915–20) |
| TNA | The National Archive, Kew |
| VB/PBA | Vera Brittain/Paul Berry Archive, Somerville College, Oxford |
| VB GWD | Vera Brittain's 'Great War Diary', Box 7, Vera Brittain/Paul Berry Archive, Somerville College, Oxford University |

# NOTES

## Introduction

1 Priya Satia, *Spies in Arabia: The Great War and the Cultural Foundations of Britain's Covert Empire in the Middle East* (Oxford: Oxford University Press, 2008), p. 5. See for important studies of the imagination, in chronological progression, John Johnston, *English Poetry of the First World War: A Study in the Evolution of Lyric and Narrative Form* (Princeton: Princeton University Press, 1964); Paul Fussell, *The Great War and Modern Memory* (London and New York: Oxford University Press, 1975); Robert Wohl, *The Generation of 1914* (London: Weidenfeld and Nicolson, 1980); Bernard Bergonzi, *Heroes' Twilight: A Study of the Literature of the Great War* (London: Macmillan, 1980); Modris Eksteins, *Rites of Spring: The Great War and the Birth of the Modern Age* (London: Bantam, 1989); and Samuel Hynes, *A War Imagined: The First World War and English Culture* (London: Bodley Head, 1990).

2 For fuller references to the memoir literature, see 'Further Reading'.

3 See in particular Gary Sheffield, *Forgotten Victory. The First World War: Myths and Realities* (London: Review Books, 2002); and Tim Travers, *How the War Was Won: Command and Technology in the British Army on the Western Front, 1917–1918* (Barnsley: Pen and Sword, 2005).

4 See for example Adrian Gregory, *The Last Great War: British Society and the First World War* (Cambridge: Cambridge University Press, 2008).

5 See for example Nicoletta Gullace, *'The Blood of our Sons': Men, Women, and the Renegotiation of British Citizenship during the Great War* (London: Palgrave Macmillan, 2004).

6 See Dan Todman, *The Great War: Myth and Memory* (London: Hambledon and London, 2005); Janet Watson, *Fighting Different Wars: Experience, Memory, and the First World War in Britain* (Cambridge: Cambridge University Press, 2006).

7 This is one of many insights contained in Stéphane Audoin-Rouzeau and Annette Becker, *14–18, retrouver la Guerre* (Paris: Gallimard, 2000).

8 A good example is Catriona Pennell, *A Kingdom United: Popular Responses to the Outbreak of the First World War in Great Britain and Ireland* (Oxford: Oxford University Press, 2012).

9 See for example Wohl, *The Generation of 1914*, p. 94.

10 Michael Roper, *The Secret Battle: Emotional Survival in the Great War* (Manchester: Manchester University Press, 2009).

11  See Jane Potter, *Boys in Khaki, Girls in Print: Women's Literary Responses to the Great War 1914–1918* (Oxford: Oxford University Press, 2005).
12  See Richard Cork, *A Bitter Truth: Avant-garde Art and the Great War* (New Haven and London: Yale University Press, 1994); Paul Gough, *A Terrible Beauty: British Artists in the First World War I* (Bristol: Sansom, 2010); and David Boyd Haycock, *A Crisis of Brilliance: Five Young British Artists and the Great War* (London: Old Street Publishing, 2009).
13  See Lewis Foreman (ed.), *Oh, My Horses! Elgar and the Great War* (Rickmansworth: Elgar Editions, 2001).
14  Lawrence to Graves, 9 June 1927, Robert Graves and Liddell Hart (eds), *T. E. Lawrence to his Biographers* ([1938] New York: Doubleday, 1968), p. 45.
15  See Chapter 3, fn. 22.
16  Gregory, *The Last Great War*, pp. 11–13.
17  We should not neglect also the impact of memoirs published in this period by politicians and generals who had experienced the war. See 'Further Reading' for important examples.
18  'The Empire and the War', *The Times*, 3 August 1914.

# Chapter 1

1  Martin to Elgar, 24 March 1914, Elgar Birthplace Museum, Broadheath (hereafter EBM), L3893.
2  Cited in Michael Kennedy, *Portrait of Elgar* (Oxford and New York: Oxford University Press, 1987), p. 164. See pp. 105–38 for a sensitive discussion of *Gerontius*.
3  In addition to the vast correspondence at the Elgar Birthplace Museum, Broadheath, this archive holds transcripts of Alice Elgar's diary (hereafter AED), which is major source for any study of the composer. Elgar himself was not a regular diarist, although he did make very brief notes in a diary in 1918 (hereafter EED).
4  Elgar to Atkins, 2 July 1914, cited in John Allison, *Edward Elgar: The Sacred Music* (Bridgend: Poetry Wales, 1994), p. 97.
5  AED, entries from 19 to 25 July 1914.
6  Elgar to Alice Stuart-Wortley, 2 August 1914, EBM L4197.
7  Shaw to Elgar, 8 March 1920, cited in Jerrold Northrop Moore (ed.), *Edward Elgar: Letters of a Lifetime* (Oxford: Clarendon Press, 1990), p. 333.
8  Parry's diary, Schulbrede Priory (hereafter CHHPD), 18 July 1914. Schulbrede Priory in Sussex was the home of Parry's daughter Dorothea and her husband Arthur Ponsonby. The largest surviving collection of unpublished documents relating to Parry is kept there.
9  CHHPD, 31 July 1914.
10  CHHPD, 3 August 1914.

11  Cited in Keith Hale (ed.), *Friends and Apostles: The Correspondence of Rupert Brooke and James Strachey 1905–1914* (New Haven and London: Yale University Press, 1998), p. 287.
12  A large collection of unpublished manuscripts and of transcripts of letters to and from Brooke has been gathered at the Archive Centre of King's College Cambridge (hereafter KCA).
13  See the extracts from Eddie Marsh's diary for July 1914, KCA RCB/L/10/5.
14  Brooke to Jacques Raverat, 2 July 1914, Geoffrey Keynes (ed.), *The Letters of Rupert Brooke* (London: Faber & Faber, 1968) (hereafter *LRB*), pp. 596–7.
15  Brooke to Jacques and Gwen Raverat, July 1914, *LRB*, p. 595.
16  Brooke to Nesbitt, Wednesday [end of July 1914], KCA RCB/L/9/1.
17  The largest collection of unpublished material relating to Vera Brittain has been gathered at McMaster University, Texas. I have used the materials collected and reproduced at the Vera Brittain/Paul Berry Archive, Somerville College, Oxford. These include full transcripts of Brittain's 'Great War Diary' and much of her correspondence, as well as other family papers.
18  Vera Brittain, *Testament of Youth: An Autobiographical Study of the Years 1900–1925* ([1933] London: Virago, 1978), p. 42.
19  Vera Brittain's 'Great War Diary', 11 July 1914, Box 7, Vera Brittain/Paul Berry Archive, Somerville College, Oxford (hereafter VB GWD). An edited version of this document was published in 1981. Where quotations from Vera Brittain's 'Great War Diary' also appear in the published edition, I have added a page number to the reference. The page numbers refer to Alan Bishop (ed.), *Vera Brittain: Chronicle of Youth. Great War Diary 1913–1917* (London: Phoenix Press, 2000).
20  VB GWD, 25 July 1914, p. 82.
21  Richard Nevinson was not a diarist, and few of his letters from this period have survived. His father Henry Nevinson kept a journal, frequently noting the activities and the mood of his son, which is now in the Bodleian Library Oxford, Papers of H. W. Nevinson, Ms. Eng. misc. e.618-621 (hereafter HND).
22  C. R. W. Nevinson, *Paint and Prejudice* (London: Methuen, 1937), pp. 23–53. All of Nevinson's comments in this autobiography should be treated with caution. His sense of chronology was not exact, and he could not avoid a tendency to over-dramatization.
23  Cited in Annette Becker, 'Une culture de guerre, Otto Dix', in Thomas Compère-Morel (ed.), *Otto Dix: Der Krieg* (Milan: 5 Continents, 2003), pp. 25–36, p. 25.
24  See 'Futurism and English Art', *The Observer*, 7 June 1914. Nevinson later reproduced the manifesto in *Paint and Prejudice*, pp. 58–60, significantly omitting this endorsement.
25  Nevinson, *Paint and Prejudice*, pp. 61–2. If Nevinson and Marinetti meant to use Elgar as a symbol of 'passé-ism', they may have erred in using a record. The commercial recording of music was still in its infancy, and Elgar is widely regarded as the first composer of note to have taken a serious interest in this new medium.

26 'Rebels in Art', *The Times*, 16 June 1914.
27 Michael Walsh, *C. R. W. Nevinson: This Cult of Violence* (New Haven and London: Yale University Press, 2002), p. 85.
28 Nevinson, *Paint and Prejudice*, p. 67.
29 Margaret Nevinson, *Life's Fitful Fever* (London: A. C. Black, 1926), pp. 243–5.
30 Paul Nash, *Outline: An Autobiography and Other Writings* (London: Faber & Faber, 1949), p. 35. Much of Nash's correspondence has been preserved at the Tate Gallery Archive, London (hereafter TGA).
31 Nash, *Outline*, p. 90.
32 See Claude Abbott and Anthony Bertram (eds), *Poet and Painter: Being the Correspondence between Gordon Bottomley and Paul Nash 1910–1946* (London: Oxford University Press, 1955).
33 Nash, *Outline*, pp. 123–30.
34 See Haycock, *A Crisis of Brilliance*, pp. 148–9.
35 The details of Nash's holiday are taken from a letter he wrote to Gordon Bottomley in August or early September 1914, TGA TAM 38/12.
36 For Spencer's childhood, see Gilbert Spencer, *Stanley Spencer* (London: Gollancz, 1961). A substantial collection of Spencer's correspondence and unpublished writings has been gathered at the Tate Gallery Archive, London.
37 Marsh to Brooke, [November 1913], cited in Hassall, *Edward Marsh*, p. 252.
38 Spencer to Jacques and Gwen Raverat, 12, 15 and 17 July 1914, Adrian Glew (ed.), *Stanley Spencer: Letters and Writings* (London: Tate Gallery Publishing, 2001) (hereafter *SS*), p. 49.
39 Hassall, *Edward Marsh*, p. 289.
40 Fussell, *The Great War and Modern Memory*, p. 144.
41 Most surviving unpublished material relating to Jones is held in the David Jones Papers at the National Library of Wales, Aberystwyth (hereafter DJP).
42 See Thomas Dilworth, *David Jones in the Great War* (London: Enitharmon, 2012), pp. 19–34, here p. 31.
43 René Hague (ed.), *Dai Greatcoat: A Self-portrait of David Jones in his Letters* (London: Faber & Faber, 1980), pp. 23–4.
44 David Jones, *In Parenthesis* ([1937] London: Faber & Faber, 1969), p. 160. Other scholars have argued that, above all in a 'spiritual sense', Jones was profoundly 'Welsh'. See John Matthias (ed.), *David Jones: Man and Poet* (Maine: National Poetry Foundation, no date), pp. 27–8.
45 William Blissett, *The Long Conversation: A Memoir of David Jones* (Oxford: Oxford University Press, 1981), p. 116.
46 Jones to Grisewood, 24 September 1938, cited in Hague, *Dai Greatcoat*, p. 88.
47 The surviving unpublished material (which is largely in Welsh) relating to Evans is held at the Archive of Bangor University, and at the National Library of Wales, Aberystwyth.
48 See Alan Llwyd, *Gwae Fi Fy Myw: Cofiant Hedd Wyn* (Llanbedr: Argraffiad Cyntaf, 1991), p. 57.

49  J. Dyfnallt Owen, 'Hedd Wyn', *Ceninen* Gŵyl Ddewi, Mawrth 1, 1918 (*Ceninen* St David's Day, 1 March 1918), pp. 15–23.

50  These biographical details are to be found in Diana McVeagh, *Gerald Finzi: His Life and his Music* (Woodbridge: Boydell Press, 2005).

51  See his letter to E. M. Forster, 24 June 1926, Papers of T. E. Lawrence and A. W. Lawrence, Bodleian Library, Oxford (hereafter TEL) MS Eng. c.6737. There is a very substantial collection of unpublished documents, transcripts and photographs in this collection.

52  AC 2 Shaw to John Buchan, 20 June 1927, TEL MS. Eng. c.6737.

53  Lawrence to Andrews, no date [15 March 1934], TEL MS Eng. d.3327.

54  John Mack, *A Prince of our Disorder: The Life of T. E. Lawrence* (Boston: Little, Brown, 1976), p. 38.

55  See Satia, *Spies in Arabia*, pp. 23–39.

56  Lawrence to Flecker [June 1914], TEL MS Eng. d.3327.

# Chapter 2

1  Asquith to Stanley, 24 July 1914, Michael Brock and Eleanor Brock (eds), *H.H. Asquith: Letters to Venetia Stanley* (Oxford and New York: Oxford University Press, 1982), p. 122.

2  See Holger Herwig, *The First World War: Germany and Austria-Hungary 1914–1918* (London: Arnold, 1997), pp. 18–23.

3  Asquith to Stanley, 3 August 1914, Brock and Brock, *H.H. Asquith: Letters*, p. 146. The German ultimatum to Belgium is in George Gooch and Harold Temperley (eds), *British Documents on the Origins of the War, 1898–1914* (London: HMSO, 1926–38) (hereafter *BDOW*), XI, No. 515, p. 286. Asquith by this point had reconciled himself to British intervention; his primary concern was that there should be consensus in the Cabinet, and in Parliament.

4  Grey's speech and the Belgian note are in Viscount Grey of Fallodon, *Twenty-Five Years, 1892–1916* (London: Hodder and Stoughton, 1925), Vol. II, Appendix D, pp. 294–309.

5  'Mr. Redmond and Irish Loyalty', *The Times*, 4 August 1914.

6  'The Empire and War', *The Times*, 3 August 1914.

7  Grey to Goschen, 4 August 1914, *BDOW*, XI, No. 594, p. 314.

8  Goschen to Grey, 6 August 1914, *BDOW*, XI, No. 671, pp. 350–4.

9  Brooke to Loines, 6 July 1914, *LRB*, p. 598.

10  Grey actually wrote in his post-war memoirs that a friend *recalled* his having said this. Grey, *Twenty-Five Years*, Vol. II, p. 20.

11  Asquith to Stanley, 4 August 1914, Brock and Brock, *H.H. Asquith: Letters*, p. 151.

12  'The Declaration of War', *The Times*, 5 August 1914.

13  *New Statesman*, editorials on 1 August 1914 and 8 August 1914.

14 'Notes of the Month', *Welsh Outlook*, September 1914, pp. 375–80.
15 Diary of Eddie Marsh, 30 July 1914, KCA RCB/L/10/5.
16 Brooke to Spencer, 31 July 1914, *LRB*, p. 601.
17 Brooke to Wellesley, 1 August 1914, *LRB*, p. 603.
18 Brooke to Jacques Raverat, 1 August 1914, *LRB*, p. 603.
19 Brooke to Nesbitt, no date [4–5 August 1914] KCA RCB/L/9/1.
20 Brooke to Jacques Raverat, 6 August 1914, KCA RCB/L/3.
21 Brooke to Ward, 8 August 1914, KCA RCB/L/9/13.
22 Brooke to Nesbitt, no date [8 August 1914], *LRB*, p. 606.
23 Rupert Brooke, 'An Unusual Young Man', *New Statesman*, 29 August 1914.
24 Brooke to Wellesley, 15–17 August 1914, *LRB*, p. 608.
25 Brooke to Nesbitt, 24 August 1914, *LRB*, pp. 610–11.
26 Cited in Haycock, *A Crisis of Brilliance*, p. 199.
27 Spencer to Lamb, 12 August 1914, TGA TAM 15A.
28 'Minutes of the Seventy-seventh Meeting of the Executive Committee', 5 August 1914, British Red Cross Society Archive, London (hereafter BRCS), Executive Committee Minutes, 8 December 1912–13 October 1915.
29 Service Card for Kate John Finzi, BRCS; and Medal Card for Finzi, Kate John, TNA WO 372/23/14306.
30 *Reports by the Joint War Committee and the Joint War Finance Committee of the British Red Cross Society and the Order of St. John of Jerusalem in England on Voluntary Aid Rendered to the Sick and Wounded at Home and Abroad and to British Prisoners of War, 1914–1919* (London: HMSO, 1921), p. 189.
31 *Reports by the Joint War Committee*, p. 78; and 'Summary of Six Months' Work from Declaration of War, 2nd August 1914, to 3rd February, 1915', BRCS, *Summaries of Work, 1915*, p. 133.
32 Kate Finzi, *Eighteen Months in the War Zone: The Record of a Woman's Work on the Western Front* (London: Cassell, 1916), 21 October 1914, p. 3.
33 Hamilton Bailey, 'With the British Red Cross in Belgium', *London Hospital Gazette*, December 1914, pp. 41–3.
34 Finzi, *Eighteen Months*, 21 October 1914, p. 4; and 22 October 1914, p. 5.
35 VB GWD, 4 August 1914, pp. 85–7.
36 VB GWD, 6 August 1914, p. 89.
37 VB GWD, 8 August 1914, pp. 90–1.
38 AED, 5 August 1914.
39 Elgar to Alice and Charles Stuart-Wortley, 9 August 1914, cited in Jerrold Northrop Moore, *Edward Elgar: A Creative Life* (Oxford and New York: Oxford University Press, 1987), p. 668.
40 Postcard from Henry Wood to Elgar, 13 August 1914, EBM L1595.
41 'Music and the War', *The Times*, 18 August 1914.

42　AED, 17 August 1914. 'Special Constables' were being recruited to allow serving policemen to enlist in the armed forces.
43　AED, 15 August 1915.
44　Benson to Elgar, 25 August 1914, EBM L3334.
45　Elgar to Frances Colvin, 25 August 1914, EBM L3452.
46　Elgar to Frank Schuster, 25 August 1914, cited in Kennedy, *Portrait of Elgar*, p. 261.
47　CHHPD, 6 September 1914.
48　CHHPD, 7 September 1914.
49　A. W. Lawrence (ed.), *T. E. Lawrence by his Friends* (London: Jonathan Cape, 1937), p. 225.
50　Lawrence to Rieder, 18 September 1914, David Garnett (ed.), *The Letters of T. E. Lawrence* ([1938] London: Spring Books, 1964), p. 185.
51　See John Terraine, *Douglas Haig: The Educated Soldier* (London: Hutchinson, 1963), p. 73; and Peter Simkins, *Kitchener's Army: The Raising of the New Armies, 1914–1916* ([1988] Barnsley: Pen and Sword, 2007), pp. 38–9.
52　*The Times History of the War* (London: Printing House Square, 1915 onwards) (hereafter *THW*), Vol. II, p. 172.
53　'Visé Burned', *The Times*, 18 August 1914.
54　*Punch*, Vol. CXLVII, 26 August 1914, p. 185.
55　John Horne and Alan Kramer, *German Atrocities, 1914: A History of Denial* (New Haven and London: Yale University Press, 2001), p. 177. See also the discussion in Gregory, *The Last Great War*, pp. 47–55.
56　'German Defeat by Belgians', *South Wales Daily News*, 6 August 1914.
57　VB GWD, 6 August 1914.
58　*THW*, Vol. IV, p. 209.
59　Ibid., p. 224.
60　Lawrence James, *Warrior Race: A History of the British at War* (London: Abacus, 2002), p. 404.

# Chapter 3

1　Cited in Terraine, *Douglas Haig*, p. 73.
2　'How Long Will the War Last?', *The Times*, 8 August 1914.
3　'Your King and Country Need You', *The Times*, 5 August 1914.
4　For detailed figures see Pennell, *A Kingdom United*.
5　*The Times*, 27 August 1914.
6　'Cricket Enthusiasts During the War', *Daily Mail*, 11 September 1914.
7　'Another Brave Woman', *Sheffield Daily Telegraph*, 16 November 1914.

8   H. C. Colles (ed.), *College Addresses Delivered to Pupils of the Royal College of Music by Sir C. Hubert H. Parry* (London: Macmillan, 1920), pp. 215–29.
9   CHHPD, 25 September 1914.
10  CHHPD, 24 October 1914.
11  CHHPD, 28 November 1914.
12  Hassall, *Edward Marsh*, pp. 295–6; see TNA ADM 339/3/225 for Brooke's Admiralty Service Card.
13  Brooke to Cox, 3 September 1914, *LRB*, p. 615.
14  Brooke to Nesbitt, 3 September 1914, *LRB*, p. 613.
15  Brooke to Jacques Raverat, 24 September 1914, KCA RCB/L/3.
16  Brooke to Wellesley, Sunday [20 September 1914], *LRB*, pp. 615–16. See Cynthia Asquith, *Diaries 1915–1918* (London: Hutchinson, 1968), 3 July 1915, p. 50, where she writes: 'Eileen Wellesley claims very serious love affair with Rupert Brooke saying that quite unsuspected of everyone else they used to meet in Richmond Park and in Eddie's flat.'
17  Brooke to Nesbitt, no date [23 September 1914], KCA RCB/L/9/1.
18  Diary of Eddie Marsh, 27 September 1914, KCA RCB/L/10/5.
19  Brooke to Nesbitt, no date [17 October 1914], *LRB*, p. 624.
20  Brooke to Bacon, 11 November 1914, *LRB*, pp. 631–3.
21  Brooke to Loines, December 1914, *LRB*, pp. 644–5.
22  Brooke to Nesbitt, 10 November 1914, *LRB*, p. 631.
23  Brooke to Jacques Raverat, 3 December 1914, KCA RCB/L/3.
24  See *New Numbers*, 1: 4 (December 1914), 165–9. The December 1914 issue of the journal was not issued to the public until March 1915.
25  Audoin-Rouzeau and Becker, *14–18, retrouver la Guerre*, p. 24.
26  *THW*, Vol. IV, p. 56.
27  *Reports by the Joint Committee*, p. 285.
28  Finzi, *Eighteen Months*, pp. 26–7.
29  Finzi, *Eighteen Months*, 27 October and 30 October 1914, pp. 15 and 27.
30  Finzi, *Eighteen Months*, 30 October 1914, p. 31. *Punch* carried an article on 9 September 1914, about 'The Two Germanies'. One, it argued, was 'the land of poets, seers, and sages'; the other preached 'rapine in the name of culture'. See *Punch*, Vol. CXLVII, p. 213.
31  Finzi, *Eighteen Months*, 30 October 1914, pp. 30–2.
32  Finzi, *Eighteen Months*, 3 November 1914, pp. 43–4.
33  Finzi, *Eighteen Months*, 31 October 1914, pp. 33–8.
34  Finzi, *Eighteen Months*, 2 December 1914, p. 68.
35  Finzi, *Eighteen Months*, 9 November 1914, pp. 50–1.
36  Finzi, *Eighteen Months*, 1 November 1914, p. 40.
37  *THW*, Vol. IV, pp. 55–63.
38  Nevinson, *Paint and Prejudice*, pp. 70–1.

39  HND, 25 October 1914, MS. Eng. misc. e.618/3.
40  Tatham Meaburn and James Miles, *The Friends' Ambulance Unit 1914–1919: A Record* (London: Swarthmore Press, 1919), p. 7.
41  HND, 10 November 1914, MS. Eng. misc. e.618/3.
42  HND, 12 November 1914, MS. Eng. misc. e.618/3.
43  HND, 13 November 1914, MS. Eng. misc. e.618/3.
44  Walsh, *C. R. W. Nevinson*, pp. 95–6.
45  Medal Card, Nevinson, Richard, TNA WO 372/14/204421.
46  T. A. Malloch, 'The War: Hospital Experiences in France', *The Canadian Medical Association Journal*, 5: 2 (February 1915), 155–65, 157.
47  HND, 14 November 1914, MS. Eng. misc. e.618/3.
48  HND, 15 November 1914, MS. Eng. misc. e.618/3.
49  HND, 24 November 1914, MS. Eng. misc. e.618/3.
50  HND, 14 December 1914, MS. Eng. misc. e.618/4.
51  HND, 19 December 1914, MS. Eng. misc. e.618/4.
52  HND, 22 December 1914, MS. Eng. misc. e.618/4.
53  HND, 12 January 1915, MS. Eng. misc. e.618/4.
54  HND, 23 December 1914, MS. Eng. misc. e.618/4.
55  HND, 30 January 1915, MS. Eng. misc. e.618/4.
56  Nash to Gordon and Emily Bottomley, no date [mid-August–early September 1914], TGA TAM 38/12.
57  Nash to Marsh, no date [August 1914], TGA TAM 38/4.
58  Ibid.
59  Nash to Gordon Bottomley, TGA TAM 38/12.
60  Lance Sieveking, *The Eye of the Beholder* (London: Hulton Press, 1957), p. 48.
61  Nash to Bottomley, October 1914, cited in Anthony Bertram, *Paul Nash: The Portrait of an Artist* (London: Faber & Faber, 1955), p. 86.
62  This is according to an 'undated draft or copy of a letter' by David Jones, cited in Hague, *Dai Greatcoat*, pp. 26–7.
63  J. E. Munby, *A History of the 38th (Welsh) Division* (London: Rees, 1920), p. 2.
64  Rees Jones, London Welsh Battalion, to David Jones, 17 September 1914, DJP P1/2/1. In 1963 David Jones found in his papers a letter from Lloyd George's Private Secretary which suggested that his father had written to Lloyd George to complain about this delay. The existing biographical accounts of David Jones confuse the chronology of these various letters. See Jones to Grisewood, 1 January 1964, in Hague, *Dai Greatcoat*, p. 195.
65  'A Great Speech', *The Times*, 21 September 1914.
66  See the programme for the meeting in DJP CT6/7.
67  *Welsh Army Corps 1914–1919: Report of the Executive Committee* (Cardiff: Western Mail, 1921), p. 3.

68 'Trumpet Call to Welsh Nation', *South Wales Daily News*, 30 September 1914.
69 'Mr Asquith's call to the Men of Wales', *South Wales Daily News*, 3 October 1914.
70 *Welsh Army Corps 1914–1919*, p. 14.
71 'London Welsh Battalions', *South Wales Daily News*, 5 October 1914.
72 'Nonconformists and the Call to Arms', *South Wales Daily News*, 3 October 1914.
73 'Height for Welsh Army', *South Wales Daily News*, 14 October 1914.
74 'The Need for More Recruits', *South Wales Daily News*, 6 November 1914.
75 'A Temperance Company', *South Wales Daily News*, 16 December 1914; 'Bantam Battalion', *South Wales Daily News*, 18 December 1914.
76 Officer Commanding 28th (County of London) Reserve Battalion, the London Regiment, to David Jones, 12 November 1914, DJP P1/2/1.
77 Rees Jones to James Jones, 11 November 1914, DJP P1/2/1.
78 Llwyd, *Gwae fi fy Myw*, p. 180. I am grateful to Sioned Treharne for her translation of this poem.
79 Alan Llwyd, *Stori Hedd Wyn: Bardd y Gadair Ddu. The Story of Hedd Wyn: The Poet of the Black Chair* (Llandybie: Barddas, 2009), p. 51.
80 AED, 28 August 1914.
81 AED, 25 September 1914.
82 AED, 7 December 1914.
83 'New Work by Sir E. Elgar', *The Times*, 8 December 1914.
84 de Launay, 5e Régiment de Cuirassiers, to Elgar, 18 December 1914, EBM L6358.
85 VB GWD, 5 August 1914, p. 88.
86 VB GWD, 7 August 1914, p. 89.
87 VB GWD, 8 August 1914, p. 90.
88 Ibid., p. 91.
89 Brittain to Leighton, 23 August 1914, *LLG*, p. 26.
90 Brittain to Leighton, 27 August 1914, *LLG*, p. 28.
91 Leighton to Brittain, 29 September 1914, *LLG*, p. 30.
92 Leighton to Brittain, 7 October 1914, *LLG*, p. 33.
93 VB GWD, 6 September 1914.
94 VB GWD, 27 December 1914.
95 Spafford was later commissioned in the Staffordshire Regiment. See *London Gazette*, 7 December 1915, p. 12204. See also the discussion in Paul Berry and Mark Bostridge, *Vera Brittain: A Life* (London: Chatto and Windus, 1995).
96 VB GWD, 12 November 1914, p. 124.
97 'Incident at Bach Choir Supper', no date, Margaret Kennedy Collection, Forster, Box 2, Somerville College Archive, Oxford.

98 Leighton to Brittain, 8 December 1914, *LLG*, p. 39.
99 Spencer to Jacques and Gwen Raverat, [first part of the letter undated; then 29 August 1914], TGA 8116.40.
100 Spencer to Gwen Raverat, n. d. [September 1914], *SS*, p. 51.
101 Pennell, *A Kingdom United*, pp. 52–5.
102 Spencer to Lamb, 23 November 1914, *SS*, pp. 51–2.
103 Spencer to Jacques and Gwen Raverat, 23 December 1914, TGA 8116.44.
104 Lawrence to Buchan, 20 June 1927, TEL, MS. Eng. misc. c.6737.
105 Lawrence to Fontana, 19 October 1914, TEL, MS. Eng. misc. d.3333.
106 See Lawrence to Cowley, 29 October 1914, TEL, MS. Eng. misc. d.3327.
107 Michael Yardley, *Backing into the Limelight: A Biography of T. E. Lawrence* (London: Harrap, 1985), p. 57.
108 Medal Card, Lawrence, T. E., TNA WO 372/24/37885.
109 Lawrence to Will Lawrence, 15 November 1914, TEL, MS. Eng. misc. c.6740.
110 Lawrence to Rieder, 24 November 1914, TEL, MS. Eng. misc. d.3338.

# Chapter 4

1 The memorandum is in Lord Hankey, *The Supreme Command 1914–1918* (London: Allen and Unwin, 1961), Vol. 1, pp. 244–50.
2 Churchill to Asquith, 29 December 1914, Martin Gilbert (ed.), *Winston S. Churchill, Vol. III, Companion* (London: Heinemann, 1972) (hereafter CC III), Part 1, pp. 343–5.
3 'Memorandum to the War Council', 1 January 1915, *War Memoirs of David Lloyd George* (London: Odhams Press, 1938), Vol. I, pp. 222–5.
4 Meeting of the War Council, 13 January 1915, *CC III*, Part 1, pp. 407–11.
5 Brooke to Ward, no date [before 15 December 1914], *LRB*, p. 636.
6 Brooke to Cox, 4 January 1915, KCA RCB/L/5.
7 Brooke to Ward, no date [13 or 14 January 1915], *LRB*, pp. 653–4.
8 Brooke to Jacques Raverat, 19 January 1915, *LRB*, p. 656.
9 Brooke to Violet Asquith, 22 February 1915, KCA RCB/L/10/6; see also Violet Bonham Carter, *Winston Churchill As I Knew Him* (London: Eyre & Spottiswoode and Collins, 1965), pp. 360–2. Brooke's references here are to Homer's *Iliad*: Hero's Tower was where Hero, goddess of Aphrodite lived, and would await Leander, who swam across the Hellespont by night to be with her. 'Wine dark' is an epithet for the sea; 'polyphloisbic' means 'loud-roaring'. I am grateful to Claire Wilkinson for her elucidation of these details.
10 Bonham Carter, *Winston Churchill*, p. 363.
11 Brooke to Jacques and Gwen Raverat, 8 March 1915, *LRB*, p. 668.
12 Brooke to Cox, 10 March 1915, *LRB*, pp. 669–70.

13  Brooke to Ward, 17 March 1915, *LRB*, pp. 671–2.
14  Brooke to Cox, 19 March 1915, *LRB*, pp. 674–5.
15  Diary of Sir Ian Hamilton, 3 April 1915, KCA RCB/XC/2.
16  Brooke's Medal Card in the Admiralty records (TNA ADM 337/117/353) states that he died from 'pneumococcus septicaemia'.
17  '"Thoughts by England Given"', *The Times Literary Supplement*, 11 March 1915.
18  'Easter Sermons', *The Times*, 5 April 1915.
19  'Death of Mr. Rupert Brooke', *The Times*, 26 April 1915.
20  Walter de la Mare, 'Rupert Brooke', *Westminster Gazette*, 8 May 1915.
21  See the frontispiece to Rupert Brooke, *1914 & Other Poems* (London: Sidgwick and Jackson, 22nd Impression, 1917).
22  Edward Thomas, 'Rupert Brooke', *English Review*, 20 (April–July 1915), 325–8.
23  Thomas to Frost, 19 October 1916, Edward Thomas Archive, Cardiff University, 424/1/2/1.
24  Edward Dent, 'Rupert Brooke', *The Cambridge Magazine*, 8 May 1915, pp. 390–6. I am grateful to Karen Arrandale for this reference, and for her thoughts on Dent and Brooke.
25  HND, 26 April 1915, MS. Eng. misc. e.618/4.
26  Cutting from *The Nation*, no date, KCA RCB/Xd/21.
27  See Gregory, *The Last Great War*, pp. 62–3.
28  Cited in Johnston, *English Poetry of the First World War*, p. 35.
29  Lawrence to Leeds, 18 April 1915, TEL, MS. Eng. misc. d.3337.
30  Lawrence to Will Lawrence, 21 January 1915, TEL, MS. Eng. misc. c.6740.
31  Lawrence to Hogarth, 18 March 1915, TEL, MS. Eng. misc. d.3335.
32  See Lawrence to Watt, 15 June 1915; and Lawrence to Watt, undated, TEL, MS. Eng. misc. d.3328.
33  Lawrence to Hogarth, 22 March 1915, TEL, MS. Eng. misc. d.3335.
34  The text of the telegram, and many related documents, are reprinted in 'Summary of Historical Documents from the outbreak of War between Great Britain and Turkey 1914 to the outbreak of the Revolt of the Sherif of Mecca in June 1916,' 29 November 1916, TNA FO 882/5.
35  Lawrence to Will Lawrence, no date [June 1915], TEL, MS. Eng. misc. d.6741.
36  Lawrence to Thomas and Sarah Lawrence, 4 June 1915, TEL, MS. Eng. misc. c.6740.
37  Lawrence to Sarah Lawrence, no date [June 1915], TEL, MS. Eng. misc. c.6740.
38  VB GWD, 30 December 1914.
39  VB GWD, 24 January 1915.
40  VB GWD, 19 March 1915.
41  VB GWD, 28 March 1915.

42  VB GWD, 20 March 1915, p. 162.
43  VB GWD, 14 May 1915, p. 197.
44  Brittain to Leighton, 11 May 1915; Brittain to Leighton, 13 May 1915, *LLG*, pp. 98 and 103.
45  See VB GWD, 11 April 1915, pp. 172–3.
46  VB GWD, 28 May 1915, pp. 202–3.
47  VB GWD, 12 May 1915, p. 195.
48  VB GWD, 18 May 1915, p. 199; Brittain to Leighton, 8 May 1915, *LLG*, p. 109.
49  VB GWD, 18 June 1915, and 20 June 1915, pp. 210–11.
50  VB GWD, 27 June 1915, pp. 214–15.
51  Finzi, *Eighteen Months*, 15 January 1915, p. 98.
52  Finzi, *Eighteen Months*, 12 June 1915, p. 151.
53  Finzi, *Eighteen Months*, 23 May 1915, p. 144. Finzi's wording is chronologically misleading. The International Congress of Women at The Hague was held between 28 April and 1 May 1915, and attended by 1,200 delegates from 12 countries. The Congress passed a resolution calling for an on-going process of mediation, and mandated a group led by the American feminist Jane Addams to undertake a 'Peace Mission' to the governments of the warring countries. Addams apparently 'found Sir Edward Grey politely encouraging, expressing his own personal pacific sentiments, but saying nothing about his Government.' Margaret Cole (ed.), *Beatrice Webb's Diaries, 1912–1924* (London: Longmans, Green and Co., 1952), 22 June 1915, p. 40. See also Susan Grayzel, *Women and the First World War* (Longman: London, 2002), pp. 80–4.
54  Finzi, *Eighteen Months*, 14 January 1915, p. 93.
55  Finzi, *Eighteen Months*, 12 June 1915, pp. 150–3.
56  Finzi, *Eighteen Months*, 30 June 1915, p. 159.
57  Spencer to Jacques and Gwen Raverat, 4 April 1915, TGA 8116.48.
58  Spencer to Jacques and Gwen Raverat, 8 May 1915, *SS*, p. 55.
59  Spencer to Lamb, 19 July 1915, TAM 15A.
60  Spencer to Jacques and Gwen Raverat, no date [May 1915], TGA 8116.50.
61  Spencer to Jacques and Gwen Raverat, no date [June 1915], TGA 8116.51.
62  'Futurism at the Friday Club', *The Observer*, 14 February 1915.
63  'The Friday Club', *The Times*, 11 February 1915.
64  Nevinson to *The Times*, 11 February 1915, TGA 7311. The letter was not published.
65  'Painter of Smells at the Front', *Daily Express*, 25 February 1915.
66  'Junkerism in Art', *The Times*, 10 March 1915.
67  Charles Samson was one of the first naval officers to qualify as a pilot, and he commanded a squadron of the Royal Naval Air Service sent to Dunkirk in September 1914. He also equipped a number of cars with protective

armour and led these in expeditions around Dunkirk in October 1914, earning great fame. Kate Finzi was very excited in November 1914 to have seen in Boulogne an armoured train 'daubed with many-hued, very futuristic patches' which, she believed, 'under Commander Samson's guidance played such havoc with the enemy and caused the Kaiser to put a price on that gallant officer's head'. Finzi, *Eighteen Months*, 17 November 1914, pp. 64–5.

68  Walsh, *C. R. W. Nevinson*, p. 139.
69  'Red Cross Orderlies', *Manchester Guardian*, 20 February 1915.
70  See 'Will These Pictures Help the Germans?' *Daily Express*, 25 February 1915. The painting, now entitled *Arrival*, and dated to 1912, is in the Tate Gallery, London.
71  HND, 15 March 1915, MS. Eng. misc. e.618/4.
72  HND, 28 May 1915, MS. Eng. misc. e.619/1.
73  HND, 1 June 1915, MS. Eng. misc. e.619/1.
74  HND, 5 June 1915, MS. Eng. misc. e.619/1.
75  Munby, *A History of the 38th (Welsh) Division*, pp. 11 and 6–7.
76  Programme for an Inspection of the North Wales Brigade at Llandudno, 1 March 1915, DJP CT6/7.
77  Colvin to Elgar, 10 January 1915, EBM L3453.
78  Rachel Cowgill, 'Elgar's War Requiem', in Byron Adams (ed.), *Edward Elgar and his World* (Princeton and Oxford: Princeton University Press, 2007), pp. 317–62.
79  The poem was published, untitled, in *The Times*, 11 August 1914.
80  'To Women', *The Times*, 20 August 1914.
81  'For the Fallen', *The Times*, 21 September 1914.
82  AED, 9 February 1915.
83  Binyon to Elgar, 27 March 1915, EBM L6350.
84  Elgar to Sidney Colvin, no date, EBM L3473.
85  Sidney Colvin to Elgar, 13 April 1915, EBM L3457.
86  AED, 14 April 1915.
87  Sidney Colvin to Elgar, 15 April 1915, EBM L3458.
88  AED, 20 June 1915.
89  Bizarrely, at this point the government was not prepared to release any details about air raids, 'in order to secure the public safety'. See 'Zeppelins near London', *The Times*, 1 June 1915.
90  AED, 3 June 1915.
91  CHHPD, 8 May 1915, and 21 May 1915.
92  See Horne and Kramer, *German Atrocities*, pp. 229–37.
93  See for example 'Barbarism in War', *The Times*, 13 May 1915.
94  CHHPD, 30 April 1915.

95  CHHPD, 3 May 1915.
96  Colles, *College Addresses*, p. 243.
97  CHHPD, 17 May 1915.
98  Parry to Vaughan-Williams, 19 January 1915, Lewis Foreman (ed.), *From Parry to Britten: British Music in Letters, 1900–1945* (London: Batsford, 1987), p. 71.
99  CHHPD, 3 June 1915.
100 'Rioting in London', *The Times*, 13 May 1915.

# Chapter 5

1  *GWI*, Vol. IV, p. 1437.
2  Harris, *Douglas Haig*, p. 155.
3  See 'Meeting of the Dardanelles Committee: Secretary's Notes', 17 June 1915, *CC III*, Part II, pp. 1019–27.
4  Churchill to Asquith, 12 August 1915, *CC III*, Part II, pp. 1130–1; and Churchill to Asquith and Balfour, 21 August 1915, *CC III*, Part II, pp. 1151–5.
5  'Sir J. French's Report', *The Times*, 27 September 1915.
6  'Captured During the British Advance', *Sheffield Daily Telegraph*, 1 October 1915.
7  'British Advance Near Loos', *The Times*, 11 October 1915; and 'Sir J. French: Very Serious Reverse for Enemy', *Sheffield Daily Telegraph*, 12 October 1915.
8  'The British Line Advanced', *The Times*, 15 October 1915.
9  'Repaying the Germans in their own Coin', *The Graphic*, 23 October 1915.
10 'First Calling of Classes', *The Times*, 10 February 1916.
11 See 'Notes of the Month', *Welsh Outlook*, pp. 329–35.
12 See Dilworth, *David Jones*, pp. 57–8.
13 Munby, *A History of the 38th (Welsh) Division*, pp. 13–14.
14 Medal Card, Jones, Walter D, Pte, 22579, TNA WO 372/11/75056.
15 See Dilworth, *David Jones*, pp. 52–9.
16 'The Soldier as Cartoonist', *The Graphic*, 11 December 1915.
17 Lawrence to Thomas and Sarah Lawrence, 27 July 1915, TEL MS. Eng. misc. c.6740.
18 Lawrence to Leeds, 16 November 1915, TEL, MS. Eng. misc. d.3337.
19 See 'Summary of Historical Documents from the outbreak of War between Great Britain and Turkey 1914 to the outbreak of the Revolt of the Sherif of Mecca in June 1916', 29 November 1916, TNA FO 882/5; for a view of the Arab Revolt which also uses Arabic sources, see George Antonius,

*The Arab Awakening: The Story of the Arab National Movement* ([1969] Beirut: Lebanon Bookshop, no date), which also contains the full McMahon-Husein correspondence, the text of the Sykes-Picot Agreement and other important official documents.

20  *Arab Bulletin*, No. 5, 18 June 1916, p. 43, TNA FO 882/25.
21  VB GWD, 27 June 1915.
22  Berry and Bostridge, *Vera Brittain*, p. 81.
23  VB GWD, 22 August 1915, p. 256.
24  VB GWD, 23 August 1915, p. 263.
25  VB GWD, 16 September 1915, p. 273.
26  Leighton to Brittain, 7 September 1915, *LLG*, p. 161.
27  Leighton to Brittain, 11 September 1915, *LLG*, p. 165.
28  Cited in VB GWD, 25 September 1915.
29  Leighton to Brittain, 3 November 1915, *LLG*, pp. 182–3.
30  Brittain to Leighton, 8 November 1915, *LLG*, pp. 185–6.
31  VB GWD, 16 December 1915, p. 294.
32  VB GWD, 27 December 1915, p. 296.
33  See Roper, *The Secret Battle*, pp. 214–18.
34  VB GWD, 4 January 1916, p. 304.
35  Brittain to Edith Brittain, 12 January 1916, VB/PBA Box 3, Folder 3.
36  VB GWD, 13 January 1916.
37  Brittain to Edward Brittain, 24 January 1916, cited in Berry and Bostridge, *Vera Brittain*, p. 102.
38  VB GWD, 23 January 1916, p. 306.
39  'To Monseigneur', Mark Bostridge (ed.), *Because You Died. Poetry and Prose of the First World War and After: Vera Brittain* (London: Virago, 2008), p. 9.
40  'A military hospital', Bostridge, *Because You Died*, p. 15.
41  VB GWD, 29 February 1916, p. 316.
42  VB GWD, 2 March 1916, p. 317.
43  VB GWD, 4 March 1916, p. 320.
44  VB GWD, 6 March 1916, p. 320.
45  See the extract from Spencer's notebook in *SS*, pp. 57–60.
46  Spencer to Florence Spencer, no date [1916], TGA 733.1.722.
47  There is now a website dedicated to the history of this institution, which includes a gallery of photographs taken during the First World War. See http://www.glensidemuseum.org.uk.
48  Spencer to Wood, no date [May 1916], TGA TAM 19/1.
49  Spencer to Marsh, 12 October 1915, cited in Haycock, *A Crisis of Brilliance*, p. 235.
50  Spencer to Lamb, 2 February 1916, *SS*, p. 66.

51 'New English Art Club. Mr. Stanley Spencer's Vivid Work', *The Times*, 30 November 1915.
52 On Spencer's relationship with Chute, see Rothenstein, *Stanley Spencer*, pp. 16–22.
53 Spencer to Jacques and Gwen Raverat, [December] 1915, TGA 8116.56.
54 Spencer to Jacques and Gwen Raverat, [December] 1915, *SS*, p. 66.
55 See Walsh, *C. R. W. Nevinson*, pp. 126–8.
56 'Art and Artists: The London Group', *The Observer*, 28 November 1915.
57 *Modern War Paintings by C. R. W. Nevinson*, with an essay by P. G. Konody (London: Grant Richards, 1917), p. 26.
58 Nevinson, *Paint and Prejudice*, pp. 79–80.
59 See the colourful later account in Nevinson, *Paint and Prejudice*, pp. 82–3.
60 HND, 30 October 1915, MS. Eng. misc. e.619/2.
61 Nevinson, *Life's Fitful Fever*, p. 247.
62 Nevinson, *Paint and Prejudice*, p. 81.
63 Finzi, *Eighteen Months*, 13 August 1915, p. 173.
64 Finzi, *Eighteen Months*, 26 September, and 29 September 1915, p. 184.
65 Finzi, *Eighteen Months*, 3 October 1915, p. 189.
66 Finzi, *Eighteen Months*, 12 September 1915, p. 181.
67 Finzi, *Eighteen Months*, 30 December 1915, p. 217.
68 Sieveking, *The Eye of the Beholder*, p. 55.
69 Nash to Margaret Nash, 28 December 1914, cited in Bertram, *Paul Nash*, p. 88.
70 Sieveking, *The Eye of the Beholder*, p. 57.
71 Nash to Margaret Nash, 30 June 1915, TGA TAM 38/5.
72 Bertram, *Paul Nash*, p. 88.
73 AED, 6 July 1915.
74 AED, 5 October 1915.
75 'Service for All', *The Times*, 16 August 1915. This manifesto repeated calls which writers and others had been making since the Boer War, for example Erskine Childers in the 'Postscript' to his novel *Riddle of the Sands* (London: Nelson, 1903).
76 AED, 4 September 1915.
77 AED, 8 September 1915.
78 AED, 14 October 1915.
79 'The Raid', and 'Reprisals for Air Raids', *The Times*, 15 October 1915.
80 AED, 29 December 1915.
81 Elgar to Alice Stuart-Wortley, 2 January 1916, EBM L4163.
82 CHHPD, 25 July 1915.
83 CHHPD, 23 October 1915.
84 CHHPD, 20, 21 and 22 November 1915.

85 'The London Peace Meeting', *The Times*, 9 December 1915.
86 Arthur Ponsonby's Diary, 5 April 1915, cited in Jones, *Arthur Ponsonby*, p. 96.
87 CHHPD, 13 May 1915.
88 CHHPD, 2 December 1915.
89 J. Vyrnwy Morgan, *The War and Wales* (London: Chapman and Hall, 1916), pp. xvii, 188, and 177.
90 'Notes of the Month', *Welsh Outlook*, December 1915, pp. 371–4.
91 See Lieven Dehandschutter, *Hedd Wynn: Een Welshe tragedie in Vlaanderen; Trasiedi Cymreig yn Fflandrys; A Welsh Tragedy in Flanders* (Brussels: Vormingscentrum, 1992), p. 46. I am grateful to Eluned Lewis for her translation of this poem.
92 'The King's Message to Wales', *The Times*, 7 August 1915.
93 'General Commanding the Mediterranean Expeditionary Force to the Secretary of State for War', 20 May 1915, *The World War I Collection: Gallipoli and the Early Battles 1914–15* (London: The Stationery Office, 2001), p. 378.

# Chapter 6

1 Terraine, *Douglas Haig*, p. 181.
2 *HD*, 29 March 1916, p. 183.
3 *HD*, 8 January 1916, p. 178.
4 'General Townshend Keeps His Sword', *The Times*, 12 May 1916.
5 See the lengthy account of this mission in Lawrence's letter to Sarah Lawrence, 18 May 1916, TEL MS. Eng. d.3342.
6 HND, 3 June 1916, MS. Eng. misc. e.619/4.
7 Elgar to Alice Stuart-Wortley, 3 June 1916, Jerrold Northrop Moore (ed.), *The Windflower Letters: Correspondence with Alice Caroline Stuart-Wortley and her Family* (Oxford: Oxford University Press, 1989), p. 165.
8 HND, 6 June 1916, MS. Eng. misc. e.619/4.
9 CHHPD, 6 June 1916.
10 Robert Blake (ed.), *The Private Papers of Douglas Haig, 1914–1919* (London: Eyre and Spottiswoode, 1952) (hereafter *PPDH*), 7 June 1916, p. 147.
11 *HD*, 30 June 1916, p. 195.
12 *HD*, 9 June 1916, p. 189.
13 *The Battlefields of the Somme* (Péronne: Comité du Tourisme de la Somme, 2004), pp. 14 and 12.
14 'Forward in the West', *The Times*, 3 July 1916.
15 'Sir D. Haig's Report', *Evening Standard and St. James Gazette*, 2 July 1916.
16 'The Way of the War', *The Graphic*, 8 July 1916.

17  *The Battles of the Somme and Ancre* (London: Trustees of the Imperial War Museum, 1999).
18  HND, 21 August 1916, MS. Eng. misc. e.620/1.
19  Antonius, *The Arab Awakening*, p. 248.
20  Sykes to Clayton, 28 December 1915, TNA FO 882/2.
21  Lawrence to Thomas and Sarah Lawrence, 1 July 1916, TEL MS. Eng. c.6740. Lawrence was referring to 'Great Arab Revolt', *The Times*, 22 June 1916, the material for which had been supplied by his office in Cairo.
22  Telegram from R.N.O. Port Sudan to Intrusive, Cairo, 7 June 1916, TNA FO 141/736.
23  Cablegram from Chief, Egyptforce, to Chief, London, 29 June 1916, TNA FO 141/736.
24  See *Arab Bulletin*, No. 100, 20 October 1918, TNA FO 882/27.
25  James Barr, *Setting the Desert on Fire: T. E. Lawrence and Britain's Secret War in Arabia, 1916–18* (London: Bloomsbury, 2007), p. 55.
26  'Extract from Diary (R.S.)', TNA FO 882/5.
27  Barr, *Setting the Desert on Fire*, pp. 64–5.
28  Lawrence, *Seven Pillars*, p. 62.
29  *Arab Bulletin*, No. 32, 26 November 1916, p. 482, TNA FO 882/25.
30  Lawrence to Newcombe, 17 January 1917, TEL MS. Eng. c.6737.
31  HND, 26 March 1916, Misc. e.619/3.
32  'A Monthly Chronicle', *Burlington Magazine*, April 1916.
33  *Catalogue of an Exhibition of Paintings and Drawings of War by C. R. W. Nevinson (Late Private R.A.M.C.)* (London: Leicester Galleries, 1916), cited in Walsh, *C. R. W. Nevinson*, p. 139.
34  'True War Pictures. Mr. Nevinson's Moralities at the Leicester Galleries', *Daily Chronicle*, 30 September 1916.
35  'The War from a New Art Angle', *The Graphic*, 30 September 1916.
36  'Paintings and Drawings of War by Mr. C. R. W. Nevinson', *Athenaum*, October 1916.
37  C. H. Collins Baker, 'War Paintings', *The Saturday Review*, 7 October 1916.
38  'Mr. Nevinson as War Artist', *Observer*, 24 September 1916, cited in Walsh, *C. R. W. Nevinson*, p. 139.
39  'All Done', *Daily Mirror*, 18 October 1916.
40  Nevinson to Rothenstein, 22 October 1916, cited in Walsh, *C. R. W. Nevinson*, p. 151.
41  HND, 8 September 1916, MS. Eng. misc. e.620/1.
42  HND, 15 November 1916, MS. Eng. misc. e.620/1.
43  Carline, *Stanley Spencer at War*, p. 60.
44  Spencer to Wood, no date [May 1916], TGA TAM 19I.
45  Spencer to Florence Spencer, no date [May 1916], TGA 733.3.718.

46  Spencer to Wood, 26 May 1916, TGA TAM 19I.
47  Spencer to Jacques and Gwen Raverat, no date [24 May 1916], TGA 8116.59.
48  Spencer to Lamb, no date, from Tweseldown Camp, TGA TAM 15A.
49  Spencer to Wood, 9 July 1916, TGA TAM 19I.
50  Carline, *Stanley Spencer at War*, pp. 66–7.
51  Spencer to Jacques and Gwen Raverat, no date [September 1916], *SS*, pp. 75–6.
52  VB GWD, 2 March 1916, p. 317.
53  VB GWD, 18 April 1916, p. 325.
54  VB GWD, 4–10 June 1916, p. 325.
55  VB GWD, 1 July 1916, p. 326.
56  VB GWD, 4 and 5 July 1916, pp. 326–7.
57  Brittain to Edith Brittain, 21 July 1916, *LLG*, p. 267.
58  VB GWD, 1 July 1916, p. 326.
59  Brittain to Edith Brittain, 25 August 1916, *LLG*, p. 268.
60  VB GWD, 16–22 September 1916, and 24 September 1916, p. 328.
61  Finzi, *Eighteen Months*, 1 January 1916, p. 227.
62  Finzi, *Eighteen Months*, 10 February 1916, pp. 251 and 258.
63  Finzi, *Eighteen Months*, 'Epilogue', p. 259.
64  'The Zeppelin Campaign', *The Times*, 2 February 1916.
65  'Line of the Raid', *Sheffield Daily Telegraph*, 7 March 1916; 'The Air Raid', *The Times*, 7 March 1916.
66  'Raid by Five Airships', *The Times*, 3 May 1916.
67  See Anthony Hyne, *David Jones: A Fusilier at the Front* (Bridgend: Seren, 1995), pp. 38–95.
68  See René Hague's comments in Hague, *Dai Greatcoat*, p. 58.
69  From Gurney's poem 'First Time In', in John Richards (ed.), *Wales on the Western Front* (Cardiff: University of Wales Press, 1994), pp. 92–3.
70  Munby, *A History of the 38th (Welsh) Division*, p. 16.
71  Ibid., p. 17.
72  *HD*, 9 July 1916, p. 201.
73  See Tim Travers, *The Killing Ground: The British Army, the Western Front & the Emergence of Modern War 1900–1918* (Barnsley: Pen & Sword, 2003), pp. 21 and 169.
74  Munby, *A History of the 38th (Welsh) Division*, p. 19.
75  See Llewelyn Wyn Griffith, *Up to Mametz . . . and Beyond* (Barnsley: Pen and Sword, 2010), p. 144, fn. 4.
76  *HD*, 10 July 1916, p. 202.
77  See 'Introduction', Munby, *A History of the 38th (Welsh) Division*.
78  AED, 29 and 30 January 1916.
79  AED, 4 May 1916.

80  AED, 10 May 1916.
81  Ernest Newman, '"The Spirit of England": Edward Elgar's New Choral Work', *The Musical Times*, 57: 879 (May 1916), 235–9.
82  AED, 9 July 1916.
83  Harris, *Douglas Haig*, p. 231.
84  AED, 15 September 1916.
85  AED, 29 August 1916.
86  Elgar to Alice Stuart-Wortley, 31 August 1916, EBM L4162.
87  CHHPD, 10 March 1916.
88  'Britain's Fight for Right', *The Times*, 2 March 1916.
89  See '"Fight for Right". Sir H. Parry's Music for the Movement', *The Times*, 29 March 1916, for more on the music used by the movement. Elgar had also written a song, called *Fight for Right*, which evidently did not catch on.
90  CHHPD, 11 March 1916.
91  See 'A Fight for Freedom', *The Times*, 14 March 1916.
92  CHHPD, 4 October 1916.
93  Finzi, *Eighteen Months*, p. vii.
94  Gregory, *The Last Great War*, p. 102.
95  Alfred Turner, 'Introduction', Finzi, *Eighteen Months*, pp. xv–xxiii.
96  'Mr. Kipling and Others', *The New Statesman*, 27 January 1917.
97  Wohl, *The Generation of 1914*, p. 92.
98  'All Goes Well', *South Wales Daily News*, 17 July 1916.

# Chapter 7

1  Travers, *The Killing Ground*, p. 185.
2  Terraine, *Douglas Haig*, p. 229.
3  'Fifth Month on the Somme', *The Times*, 1 December 1916.
4  'British Casualties', *Daily Telegraph*, 1 September 1916.
5  See Jenkins, *Asquith*, pp. 412–15.
6  The key documents in this exchange are reproduced in *War Memoirs of David Lloyd George*, Vol. I, pp. 652–66.
7  'Disturbers of the World's Peace', *The Graphic*, 10 March 1917.
8  'Notes of the Month', *Welsh Outlook*, September 1917.
9  The first American troops landed in France in June 1917, prompting a debate which would run into 1918 about how best they should be acclimatised to trench warfare. See Byron Farwell, *Over There: The United States in the Great War, 1917–1918* (New York and London: Norton, 2000).
10  J. P. Harris describes Haig as 'at least temporarily, bowled over' after his first meeting with Nivelle in December 1916. Harris, *Douglas Haig*, p. 280.

11  See *HD*, 12 March 1917 and 14 March 1917, pp. 274–7.
12  See Isabel Hull, *Absolute Destruction: Military Culture and the Practices of War in Imperial Germany* (Ithaca and London: Cornell University Press, 2005), pp. 258–60.
13  Harris, *Douglas Haig*, pp. 281, 306, and 313.
14  'The Battle of Arras', *The Times*, 10 April 1917.
15  See his letter to King George V, 9 April 1917, in *HD*, p. 278.
16  See John Davidson, *Haig: Master of the Field* (London and New York: Nevill, 1953), pp. 14–25, on the French mutinies, and their impact on Haig's decision-making.
17  See *HD*, 19 June and 20 June 1917, pp. 300–1.
18  Cited in Weldon, Jedda, to Arbur, Cairo, 25 January 1917, TNA FO 141/736.
19  Lawrence to K. C., 27 December 1916, TNA FO 882/6.
20  Lawrence to Thomas and Sarah Lawrence, 31 January 1917, TEL MS. Eng. c.6740.
21  'Precis', no date [November 1916], TNA FO 882/5, Sheet 308.
22  *War Memoirs of David Lloyd George*, Vol. II, p. 1076.
23  *Arab Bulletin*, No. 32, 26 November 1916, TNA FO 882/25.
24  'Hejaz Administration', 3 November 1916, TNA FO 882/5; see also 'Route Notes', 8 January 1917, TNA FO 882/6, later reprinted in the *Arab Bulletin*.
25  See Sykes to Clayton, 28 December 1915, TNA FO 882/2.
26  'Feisal's Operations', 30 October 1916, TNA FO 882/5.
27  Lawrence to Wilson, 5 January 1917, TNA FO 882/6.
28  Lawrence to Thomas and Sarah Lawrence, 12 February 1917, TEL MS Eng. c.6740.
29  Cited in Pearson to Wingate, 29 December 1916, TNA FO 736/141.
30  See Barr, *Setting the Desert on Fire*, p. 87.
31  'Victory at Baghdad', *The Times*, 12 March 1917.
32  Lawrence to Wilson, 9 March 1917, TEL MS. Eng. d.3339.
33  See 'Raids on the Railway', T. E. L., *Arab Bulletin*, No. 50, 13 May 1917, FO 882/26.
34  See Lawrence's report of the expedition to General Clayton, 10 July 1917, TEL MS Eng. d.3327.
35  See Arbur, Cairo, to Pearson, Jeddah, 24 January 1917, TNA FO 141/736.
36  See Lawrence's colourful account of 'The Occupation of Akaba', 7 August 1917, TNA FO 882/7.
37  Cited in Barr, *Setting the Desert on Fire*, p. 150.
38  Spencer to Florence Spencer, 25 March 1917, TGA 733.1.722.
39  See Spencer to Florence Spencer, 27 April 1917, TGA 733.1.730.
40  Spencer to Florence Spencer, 21 May 1917, *SS*, p. 85.

41  See Spencer to Chute, March 1917, Rothenstein, *Stanley Spencer*, pp. 17–20.
42  Spencer to Will and Joanna Spencer, 30 July 1917, *SS*, p. 90.
43  Spencer to Jacques and Gwen Raverat, no date [1917/18], TGA 8116.73.
44  Carline, *Stanley Spencer at War*, p. 87.
45  'The Sisters Buried at Lemnos', Bostridge, *Because You Died*, pp. 25–6.
46  Brittain to Edith Brittain, 29 March 1917, VB/PBA Box 3 Folder 3.
47  Brittain to Edith Brittain, 12 December 1916, VB/PBA Box 3 Folder 3.
48  VB GWD, 18 April 1917; and 1 May 1917, pp. 339–40.
49  Berry and Bostridge, *Vera Brittain*, pp. 116–17.
50  Gregory, *The Last Great War*, p. 102.
51  For original Welsh versions of Hedd Wyn's poems, and different English translations, see http://www.lgac.org/poetry/HeddWynPoems.html
52  See Adrian Gregory's discussion of Military Service Tribunals, in *The Last Great War*, pp. 101–8, and for tentative statistics about how many appeals for exemption were granted.
53  Llwyd, *The Story of Hedd Wyn*, p. 71.
54  See Siegfried Sassoon, *Memoirs of an Infantry Officer* ([1930] London: Folio Society, 1974), pp. 110–24.
55  Cited in Bethan Phillips, 'A Fine Day's Work', *Planet*, 72 (December/January 1988–89), 59–64, 60.
56  Evans to a friend, July 1917, cited in Phillips, 'A Fine Day's Work', p. 63.
57  Munby, *A History of the 38th (Welsh) Division*, p. 21.
58  Hyne, *David Jones*, p. 127.
59  'Close Quarters', *The Graphic*, 9 September 1916.
60  'Germany and Peace', *The Graphic*, 20 January 1917.
61  The essay is reprinted in Dilworth, *David Jones*, pp. 127–9.
62  Cited in Dilworth, *David Jones*, pp. 141–4.
63  Munby, *A History of the 38th (Welsh) Division*, p. 22.
64  Cited in Llywd, *Gwae Fi Fy Myw*, p. 223.
65  Private Ivor Watkins, cited in Nigel Steel and Peter Hart, *Passchendaele: The Sacrificial Ground* (London: Cassell, 2001), p. 100.
66  Thomas to Frost, 21 May 1916, Edward Thomas Archive, Cardiff University, 424/1/2/1/14/2/1-34.
67  Nash to Margaret Nash, 12 October 1916, TGA TAM 38/5.
68  Nash to Margaret Nash, 7 March 1917, Nash, *Outline*, pp. 186–9.
69  Nash to Margaret Nash, 6 April 1917, Nash, *Outline*, pp. 194–6.
70  Nash to Margaret Nash, 12 May 1917, Nash, *Outline*, p. 203.
71  Nash to Margaret Nash, 31 May 1917, Nash, *Outline*, pp. 205–6.
72  HND, 20 October 1916, MS. Eng. misc. e.620/1.
73  Walsh, *C. R. W. Nevinson*, pp. 154–5.

## NOTES

74  See 'Political Notes: New Man Power Bill Explained', *The Times*, 5 April 1917.
75  Nevinson to Masterman, 30 June 1917, Walsh, *C. R. W. Nevinson*, p. 159.
76  AED, 5 January 1917.
77  AED, 6 October 1916; the Zeppelin was presumably L31, shot down over Potters Bar on the night of 1/2 October.
78  AED, 12 December 1916.
79  Elgar to Newman, 17 June 1917, Moore, *Edward Elgar: Letters of a Lifetime*, p. 307.
80  AED, 26 August 1917. It is not clear why Kipling objected to the performances; if anything, the loss of his son Jack at Loos in September had intensified his anti-German hostility, and his view that the war had to be continued to the bitter end. See Harry Ricketts, *The Unforgiving Minute: A Life of Rudyard Kipling* (London: Pimlico, 2000), pp. 328–9.
81  Elgar to Newman, 17 June 1917, Moore, *Edward Elgar: Letters of a Lifetime*, p. 307.
82  CHHPD, 20 May 1917.
83  CHHPD, 17 March 1917.
84  Cited in Dibble, *C. Hubert H. Parry*, p. 487.
85  Parry to Howells, 13 April 1917, Christopher Palmer, *Herbert Howells: A Centenary Celebration* (London: Thames Publishing, 1992), p. 19.
86  Parry to Howells, 18 May 1917, Palmer, *Herbert Howells*, p. 19.

# Chapter 8

1  Harris, *Douglas Haig*, p. 374.
2  See Jane Carmichael, *First World War Photographers* (London: Routledge, 1987), pp. 54–5; and 'With Our Troops at the Battle of Flanders', *The Times*, 6 September 1917.
3  'A Flanders Battlefield', *The Graphic*, 20 October 1917; and 'The Battlefield from Above and Below', *The Graphic*, 27 October 1917.
4  'German Blow on Isonzo', *The Times*, 26 October 1917; and 'Tagliamento Fight', *The Times*, 6 November 1917.
5  'Coup d'État in Petrograd', *The Times*, 9 November 1917.
6  'Story of the Great Victory', *The Times*, 23 November 1917.
7  Dehandschutter, *Hedd Wynn*, p. 41.
8  Much of the narrative detail on the battle for Pilckem Ridge is taken from Munby, *A History of the 38th (Welsh) Division*, pp. 22–8.
9  'The Premier', *South Wales Daily News*, 7 September 1917.
10  'Notes of the Month', *Welsh Outlook*, October 1917, pp. 329–35.
11  Dehandschutter, *Hedd Wynn*, p. 41.
12  'Black Chair', *South Wales Daily News*, 7 September 1917.

13 'Notes of the Month', *Welsh Outlook*, October 1917, pp. 329–35.
14 'In Memoriam: Hedd Wyn – Bardd y Gadair Ddu', *Welsh Outlook*, October 1917, p. 336. I am grateful to Siobhan McGurk for her translation of this group of poems.
15 See Llwyd, *The Story of Hedd Wyn*, pp. 175–95.
16 'Introduction', Munby, *A History of the 38th (Welsh) Division*.
17 The picture of the howitzer is now in a private collection. See the reproduction in Dilworth, *David Jones*, p. 162.
18 'The Wrack of War', *The Graphic*, 8 December 1917.
19 See Dilworth, *David Jones*, pp. 176–83.
20 Bullock to Jones, 18 December 1917, DJP CT5/1.
21 Nevinson, *Paint and Prejudice*, pp. 97–105.
22 Walsh, *C. R. W. Nevinson*, pp. 158–64.
23 HND, 16 August 1917, MS. Misc. Eng. e.620/2.
24 Sue Malvern, *Modern Art, Britain, and the Great War: Witnessing, Testimony, and Remembrance* (New Haven and London: Yale University Press, 2004).
25 Both officials are cited in Walsh, *C. R. W. Nevinson*, p. 161.
26 Laurence Binyon, 'Three Artists', *The New Statesman*, June 1917.
27 John Salis, 'The Art of Today', *The New Witness*, July 1917.
28 Haycock, *A Crisis of Brilliance*, p. 275.
29 Nash to Rothenstein, no date [August 1917], TGA TAM 38/7.
30 Nash to Rothenstein, 23 September 1917, TGA TAM 38/7.
31 Nash to Margaret Nash, no date, Nash, *Outline*, p. 207.
32 John Nash to Christine Kühlenthal, no date [November 1917], Alan Freer and Peter Widdowson (eds), *Love Letters From the Front: John Nash to Christine Kühlenthal, France 1916–1917* (Cheltenham: Cyder Press, 2007), p. 102.
33 Nash to Margaret Nash, Nash, *Outline*, pp. 210–11.
34 Malvern, *Modern Art, Britain, and the Great War*, pp. 32–5.
35 Nash to Masterman, 16 November 1917, TGA TAM 38/3.
36 Nash to Masterman, 22 January 1918, TGA TAM 38/3.
37 Lloyd George, *War Memoirs*, Vol. II, p. 1089.
38 Wingate to Robertson, 18 June 1917, TNA FO 882/3.
39 See 'Twenty-Seven Articles', August 1917; Clayton to Lawrence, 14 July 1917; and Wilson to Arbur, Cairo, 13 July 1917, TNA FO 882/7.
40 See Desmond Stewart, *T. E. Lawrence* (London: Hamish Hamilton, 1977), pp. 167–8.
41 Lawrence to Thomas and Sarah Lawrence, 27 August 1917, TEL MS. Eng. c.6740.
42 See Lawrence's report on these two incidents, 'Raid at Haret Ammar', *Arab Bulletin*, No. 65, 8 October 1917, TNA FO 882/26.

43   Lawrence to a friend [Stirling], 24 September 1917, Garnett, *The Letters of T. E. Lawrence*, pp. 237–8.
44   'Raid near Bir-esh-Shediyah', T. E. L., 10 October 1917, FO 882/7.
45   See Joyce to Clayton, 13 September 1917; and Joyce to Clayton, 17 September 1917, TNA FO 882/7.
46   'A Raid', T. E. L., *Arab Bulletin*, No. 73, 16 December 1917, TNA FO 882/26.
47   Lawrence to Leeds, 15 December 1917, TEL MS. Eng. d.3337. Readers of *Seven Pillars of Wisdom* will know that Lawrence claimed that on the guerrilla expedition to the Yarmuk valley he was captured and ill-treated in Deraa. As there is doubt about the accuracy of these claims, I have not repeated them here. The incident at Deraa is discussed in Chapters 11 and 12.
48   'Palestine for the Jews', *The Times*, 9 November 1917.
49   Lawrence expressed this in a letter to Mark Sykes, written on 9 September 1917. The letter was not delivered. See Barr, *Setting the Desert on Fire*, pp. 164–5.
50   'Jerusalem', *The Times*, 11 December 1917.
51   Maud Tree to Elgar, 20 July 1917, EBM L1421.
52   'A. S.', in the *Birmingham Evening Dispatch*, cited in John Norris, 'The Spirit of Elgar: crucible of remembrance', in Foreman, *Oh, My Horses!*, pp. 237–60, p. 251.
53   AED, 1 November 1917.
54   Elgar to Alice Stuart-Wortley, 27 November 1917, cited in Martin Bird, 'An Elgarian Wartime Chronology', in Foreman, *Oh, My Horses!*, pp. 388–456, p. 436.
55   Bird, 'An Elgarian Wartime Chronology', p. 436.
56   Elgar to Alice Stuart-Wortley, 23 December 1917, EBM L4198.
57   AED, 27 December 1917.
58   The journalist Edmund Morel, whom Parry had met at his daughter's house in 1915, was imprisoned under the Defence of the Realm Act in September 1917.
59   CHHPD, 24 November 1917.
60   'The First Seven Divisions', *The Times*, 17 December 1917.
61   CHHPD, 15 December 1917.
62   VB GWD, 27 May 1917.
63   Brittain to Bervon, 9 August 1917, *LLG*, p. 370.
64   Brittain to Edith Brittain, 25 September 1917, VB/PBA Box 3 Folder 3.
65   See Jones, *In Parenthesis*, p. 196, n. 21.
66   Brittain to Bervon, 9 August 1917, *LLG*, p. 370.
67   'The German War', Bostridge, *Because You Died*, pp. 38–9.
68   See Berry and Bostridge, *Vera Brittain*, pp. 126–7.
69   Brittain to Edith Brittain, 12 November 1917, *LLG*, p. 381.

70  Brittain to Edith Brittain, 5 December 1917, *LLG*, p. 383.
71  Norris, 'The Spirit of Elgar', Foreman, *Oh, My Horses!*, pp. 259–60.
72  *War Memoirs of David Lloyd George*, Vol. I, p. 659.
73  Notably, in his later memoir, David Jones used this image when describing the experience of first coming under shellfire, writing: 'Out of the vortex, rifling the air it came – bright, brass-shod, Pandoran; with all-filling screaming the howling crescendo's up-piling snapt.' Jones, *In Parenthesis*, p. 24.
74  See Jean Moorcroft Wilson, *Siegfried Sassoon: The Making of a War Poet. A Biography 1886–1918* (London: Duckworth, 1998), pp. 367–86; Sassoon's statement is reproduced on pp. 373–4.

# Chapter 9

1  'A Case for Enquiry', *The Times*, 12 December 1917.
2  *Lord Riddell's War Diary*, 23 December 1917, p. 300.
3  'Bolshevists Surrender', *The Times*, 12 February 1918.
4  See Harris, *Douglas Haig*, p. 433. Haig told the King that he had 100,000 men fewer than in 1917. See *HD*, 29 March 1918, p. 395.
5  Davidson, *Haig*, p. 85.
6  *HD*, 23 March 1918, p. 391.
7  *HD*, 25 March 1918, p. 393.
8  Haig's Diary, 3 April 1918, *PPDH*, pp. 300–1.
9  *HD*, 9 April 1918, p. 400.
10  Cited in Davidson, *Haig*, footnote on p. 91.
11  See *HD*, 12 April 1918, p. 403.
12  Haig's Diary, 26 April 1918, *PPDH*, p. 305.
13  See Hull, *Absolute Destruction*, p. 302.
14  For Pershing's orders, which ironically were very similar to those given to Haig when he was given the command of the BEF, see Farwell, *Over There*, p. 87.
15  Haig's Diary, 1 May 1918, *PPDH*, p. 307.
16  Hankey, *The Supreme Command*, Vol. 2, p. 813.
17  *HD*, 1 June 1918, p. 417.
18  See Farwell, *Over There*, pp. 168–75.
19  See William Manchester, *The Arms of Krupp, 1587–1968* (London: Michael Joseph, 1969), pp. 343–5.
20  There were 951,000 German casualties from March to July 1918, and 1,960,000 cases of sickness, many of these caused by influenza. See Martin Kitchen, *The German Offensives of 1918* (Stroud: Tempus, 2001), p. 208.
21  Ernst Jünger, *Werke, Band 1, Tagebücher I, Der Erste Weltkrieg* ([1920] Stuttgart: Klett, n.d.), p. 283.
22  Haig's Diary, 21 July 1918, *PPDH*, p. 320.

23  *HD*, 23 July 1918, p. 433.
24  See S. C. Rolls, *Steel Chariots in the Desert* ([1937] London: Leonaur, 2005).
25  Liman von Sanders, *Five Years in Turkey*, trans. Reichmann (Maryland: U. S. Naval Institute, 1927), pp. 196–7. See p. 174 for a full breakdown of the Asia Corps.
26  *Arab Bulletin*, No. 90, 24 May 1918, TNA FO 882/27.
27  *Arab Bulletin*, No. 78, 11 February 1918, TNA FO 882/27.
28  See his account in *Arab Bulletin*, No. 79, 18 February 1918, TNA FO 882/27.
29  *Arab Bulletin*, No. 106, 22 October 1918, TNA FO 882/27.
30  This episode is recounted in *Seven Pillars of Wisdom*, pp. 410–11.
31  See Franz von Papen, *Memoirs*, trans. Connell (London: Deutsch, 1952), p. 80; and Sanders, *Five Years*, p. 262.
32  Clayton to Wilson, 6 May 1918, TNA FO 882/3.
33  Lawrence to Richards, 15 July 1918, TEL MS Eng. d.3338.
34  Lawrence to Thomas and Sarah Lawrence, 15 July 1918, TEL MS Eng. c.6740.
35  Spencer to Florence Spencer, 24 February 1918, *SS*, p. 91.
36  Spencer to Wood, 3 March 1918, *SS*, pp. 91–2.
37  Spencer to Florence Spencer, 12–21 April 1918, TGA 733.1.750.
38  Spencer to Wood, 3 May 1918, TGA TAM 19I.
39  Yockney, Ministry of Information, to Spencer, received 10 May 1918, TGA 733.1.749.
40  Spencer to Lamb, 3 June 1918, *SS*, p. 92.
41  Spencer to Florence Spencer, 27 June 1918, *SS*, pp. 92–3.
42  AED, 7 January 1918.
43  AED, 15 January 1918.
44  EED, 6 March 1918.
45  AED, 15 March 1918; and EED, 15 March 1918.
46  EED, 29 January 1918; also 'Empire War Exhibits', *The Times*, 7 January 1918.
47  EED, 6 March 1918; 'The War in Colour', *The Times*, 4 March 1918.
48  AED, 24 March 1918.
49  Cited in Bird, 'An Elgarian Wartime Chronology', p. 439.
50  EED, 3 April 1918.
51  See 'Loss of the Ridge'; and 'German Gains on the Belgian Frontier', *The Times*, 17 April 1918.
52  Mott to Elgar, 11 May 1918, EBM L6371.
53  EED, 25 May 1918.
54  EED, 30 May 1918.
55  CHHPD, 21 June 1918.
56  CHHPD, 14 June 1918.

57 'The Power of the Vote', *The Times*, 13 March 1918.
58 CHHPD, 13 March 1918.
59 Parry to Millicent Fawcett, 18 March 1918, cited in Charles Graves, *Hubert Parry: His Life and Works* (London: Macmillan, 1926), Vol. II, p. 93.
60 CHHPD, 4 July 1918.
61 Brittain to Edith Brittain, 31 March 1918, *LLG*, pp. 392–3.
62 See war diary of the Matron-in-Chief, BEF, 20 May 1918, TNA WO95/3990. The whole diary has been transcribed at http://www.scarletfinders.co.uk, accessed on 13 February 2013.
63 The separate raid on Etaples which Brittain describes hearing about *after* her return to London, would appear to be that of the night of 30/31 May 1918. See war diary of the Matron-in-Chief, BEF, 1 June 1918, TNA WO95/3990; and Brittain, *Testament of Youth*, p. 432.
64 'Vengeance is Mine', Bostridge, *Because You Died*, p. 49. It is not clear whether this poem was written in Etaples, after the raid Brittain experienced, or later in London, after hearing about the second raid on 30/31 May.
65 Brittain to Edward Brittain, 5 June 1918, *LLG*, p. 398.
66 'To My Brother', Bostridge, *Because You Died*, p. 52.
67 See Berry and Bostridge, *Vera Brittain*, p. 127.
68 'Welshmen's Record in the War', *The Times*, 2 March 1918.
69 'Captive Civilisation and the Black Knight of Prussia', *The Graphic*, 13 July 1918.
70 Munby, *A History of the 38th (Welsh) Division*, pp. 41–2.
71 See the brochure 'Brittains Limited' (1932), in the VB/PBA, Box 3 Folder 2.
72 Berry and Bostridge, *Vera Brittain*, pp. 91–2.
73 HND, 22 November 1917, Misc. Eng. e.620/3.
74 Cited in Walsh, *C. R. W. Nevinson*, p. 175.
75 Ibid.
76 HND, 4 December 1917, Misc. Eng. e.620/3.
77 See Walsh, *C. R. W. Nevinson*, pp. 174–8.
78 HND, 22 December 1917, Misc. Eng. e.620/3.
79 HND, 21 January 1918, Misc. Eng. e.620/3.
80 'Battle Pictures', *The Times*, 2 March 1918.
81 HND, 18 February 1918, Misc. Eng. e.620/3.
82 The whole preface, dated March 1918, is reprinted in Nevinson, *Paint and Prejudice*, pp. 107–10.
83 'An Aesthetic Contrast', *The Times*, 4 March 1918.
84 '"Duds" for the Imperial War Museum', *Saturday Review*, 16 March 1918.
85 See Malvern, *Modern Art, Britain, and the Great War*, p. 54.
86 'Mr. Nevinson's War Pictures', *Saturday Review*, 25 May 1918.
87 HND, 4 March and 5 March 1918, Misc. Eng. e.620/3.

88  HND, 8 April 1918, Misc. Eng. e.620/3.
89  HND, 5 June 1918, Misc. Eng. e.620/3.
90  Malvern, *Modern Art, Britain, and the Great War*, p. 182.
91  Hynes, *A War Imagined*, p. 223.
92  Nash to Bottomley, 16 July 1918, Abbott and Bertram, *Poet and Painter*, p. 99.
93  Cited in Ronald Blythe, *First Friends: Paul and Bunty, John and Christine – and Carrington* (Denby: Fleece Press, 1998), pp. 150–1.
94  Cited in Malvern, *Modern Art, Britain, and the Great War*, p. 64.
95  'Gaudier-Brzeska and War Pictures', *The Saturday Review*, 1 June 1918.
96  Cutting from the *Liverpool Post*, 18 May 1918, TGA TAM 38/21.
97  See Jones, *Arthur Ponsonby*, pp. 116–18.
98  See Lloyd George, *War Memoirs*, Vol. II, Appendix D, pp. 1510–17.

# Chapter 10

1  Haig to Wilson, 24 July 1918, *HD*, p. 434.
2  *HD*, 29 July 1918, p. 436. Emphasis in the original.
3  Christy Campbell, *Band of Brigands: The Extraordinary Story of the First Men in Tanks* (London: Harper Press, 2007), p. 386.
4  Kitchen, *The German Offensives of 1918*, p. 230.
5  Harris, *Douglas Haig*, p. 495.
6  Erich Ludendorff, *Meine Kriegserinnerungen 1914–1918* (Berlin: Mittler und Sohn, 1919), p. 547.
7  *HD*, 21 August 1918, p. 448.
8  *HD*, 22 August 1918, p. 448.
9  Maurice Hankey noted as late as 23 July 1918 that Lloyd George was still considering candidates to replace Haig. See *The Supreme Command*, Vol. 2, p. 828.
10  Haig's Diary, 29 August 1918, *PPDH*, pp. 325–6. Wilson's telegram is cited in the same diary entry.
11  *HD*, 10 September 1918, p. 458.
12  Cited in David Woodward, *Lloyd George and the Generals* ([1983] London: Frank Cass, 2004), p. 333.
13  Hull, *Absolute Destruction*, pp. 260–2.
14  Haig's Diary, 6 October 1918, *PPDH*, p. 330.
15  The speech in which Wilson initially outlined his 'Fourteen Points' on 8 January 1918 is reproduced in Arthur Keith (ed.), *Speeches and Documents on International Affairs, 1918–1937* (London: Oxford University Press, 1938), Vol. I, pp. 1–8.
16  See Lloyd George's comments in *Lord Riddell's War Diary*, 19 October 1918, and 10 November 1918, pp. 374 and 380.

17  See the summary of the views Haig presented to the government in *HD*, 19 October 1918, and 21 October 1918, pp. 475–7.
18  *Lord Riddell's War Diary*, 27 October 1918, p. 376.
19  On the Turkish collapse, see David Stephenson, *1914–1918: The History of the First World War* (London: Penguin, 2005), pp. 483–5.
20  On the Austrian collapse, see Herwig, *The First World War*, pp. 433–40.
21  On the philosophy of a 'final struggle' (*Endkampf*) in 1918, see Hull, *Absolute Destruction*, pp. 309–19.
22  See Herwig, *The First World War*, pp. 440–6.
23  Cited in *PPDH*, 12 November 1918, p. 343.
24  *Arab Bulletin*, No. 106, 22 October 1918, TNA FO 882/27; the narrative details which follow are taken from this report.
25  The full text of both Hague Conventions can be seen at the website of the Avalon Project, run by the Law School at Yale University, http://avalon.law.yale.edu.
26  Audoin-Rouzeau and Becker, *14–18, retrouver la Guerre*, pp. 54–5.
27  Telegram from Pearson, Jeddah, to Arbur, Cairo, 20 January 1917, TNA FO 141/736.
28  *Arab Bulletin*, No. 106, 22 October 1918, TNA FO 882/27.
29  See James, *The Golden Warrior*, pp. 298–303.
30  Rolls, *Steel Chariots*, p. 247.
31  See Earl Winterton, *Fifty Tumultuous Years* (London: Hutchinson, 1955), pp. 70–3. Winterton did not allude to the earlier killing of prisoners.
32  Lawrence to Yale, 22 October 1929, TEL MS. Eng. c.6737.
33  See the account in James, *The Golden Warrior*, p. 308.
34  For Lawrence's political dealings in Damascus see Knightley and Simpson, *The Secret Lives*, pp. 86–97.
35  Lawrence to Scott, 14 October 1918, TEL MS. Eng. d.3328.
36  CHHPD, 23 July 1918.
37  CHHPD, 3 August 1918.
38  'Sir Hubert Parry', *The Times*, 17 October 1918.
39  'The Late Sir Hubert Parry', *The Times*, 10 October 1918.
40  'That Which Remaineth (In Memory of Captain E. H. Brittain, M.C.)', Bostridge, *Because You Died*, p. 55.
41  Berry and Bostridge, *Vera Brittain*, pp. 128–9.
42  'Court Circular' *The Times*, 19 September 1918.
43  'To a V.C.', Bostridge, *Because You Died*, p. 65. After the publication of *Testament of Youth* in 1933, Brittain discovered from Hudson that shortly before Edward's death evidence had come to light of homosexual relations between him and other men in his unit, raising the suspicion that he might have deliberately courted danger in the subsequent Austrian offensive, preferring death to disgrace. Given Vera Brittain's sheltered and conventional

upbringing, it is unsurprising that she had no understanding of her brother's sexuality while he was alive. See Berry and Bostridge, *Vera Brittain*, pp. 128–35.

44  'To My Brother', Bostridge, *Because You Died*, p. 52.
45  Brittain, *Testament of Youth*, p. 448.
46  Ibid., p. 462.
47  Nevinson, *Paint and Prejudice*, pp. 114–15.
48  Spencer to Florence Spencer, 16 September 1918, TGA 733.1.754.
49  See the account in *A Short History of the South Wales Borderers 24th Foot and the Monmouthshire Regiment* (Cardiff: Western Mail and Echo, no date), pp. 75–6.
50  Carline, *Stanley Spencer at War*, pp. 97–105.
51  See 'Ten Days in 1918', written in 1936, excerpted in *SS*, pp. 94–6.
52  Spencer to Lamb, 6 October 1918, TGA TAM 15A.
53  Spencer to Jacques and Gwen Raverat, 6 October 1918, TGA 8116.78.
54  Spencer to Florence Spencer, no date, from hospital, TGA 733.1.761.
55  Spencer to William and Anna Spencer, 23 October 1918, TGA 733.1.760.
56  Spencer to Florence Spencer, [November] 1918, *SS*, p. 98.
57  EED, 5 June 1918.
58  See Trowell, 'The Road to Brinkwells'.
59  Trowell, 'The Road to Brinkwells'.
60  EED, 5 August 1918.
61  EED, 7 October 1918.
62  AED, 8 October 1918.
63  Elgar to Binyon, 5 November 1918, cited in Kennedy, *Portrait of Elgar*, p. 277.
64  I take this phrase from Milton's *L'Allegro* (1631).
65  Sidney Colvin to Elgar, 12 November 1918, EBM L3477.
66  Legge to Elgar, 17 November 1918, EBM L2510.
67  Elgar to Sidney Colvin, 14 November 1918, EBM L3479.
68  EED, 11 November 1918, and 12 November 1918.
69  'South Wales Scenes', *South Wales Daily News*, 12 November 1918.

# Chapter 11

1  Ross Anderson, *The Forgotten Front: The East African Campaign, 1914–1918* (Stroud: Tempus, 2004), p. 294.
2  Martin Niemöller, *Vom U-Boot zur Kanzel* (Berlin: Martin Warneck, 1934), p. 140.
3  For the full armistice terms see James Edmonds, *The Occupation of the Rhineland 1918–1929* (London: HMSO, 1987), Appendix 1.

4   See 'Great Naval Surrender', and 'Der Tag', *The Times*, 22 November 1918; and 'After the Great Surrender', *The Times*, 23 November 1918.
5   See 'Calendar of Principal Events', Edmonds, *The Occupation of the Rhineland*, pp. xix–xxv.
6   'End of Conscription', *South Wales Daily News*, 12 November 1918.
7   For the full terms of the treaty see Keith, *Speeches and Documents on International Affairs, 1918–1937*, Vol. I, pp. 9–61.
8   See Satia, *Spies in Arabia*, pp. 165ff.
9   See Fiona Reid, *Broken Men: Shell Shock, Treatment and Recovery in Britain 1914–1930* (London and New York: Continuum, 2010).
10  Former T. E. Lawrence to William Yale, 22 October 1929, TEL, MS. Eng. c.6737.
11  'The Arab March on Damascus', *The Times*, 17 October 1918.
12  The memorandum is reproduced in Garnett, *The Letters of T. E. Lawrence*, pp. 265–9.
13  James, *The Golden Warrior*, p. 325.
14  'The Arab Campaign', *The Times*, 26 November 1918.
15  'The Arab Epic', *The Times*, 27 November 1918.
16  'The Arab Epic', *The Times*, 28 November 1918.
17  Lawrence to Doughty, 25 December 1918, TEL, MS. Eng. d.3332.
18  See the excerpt from Lawrence's diary of the Conference in Garnett, *The Letters of T. E. Lawrence*, pp. 273–4.
19  See James, *The Golden Warrior*, pp. 359–65.
20  Arnold Lawrence to T. E. Lawrence, 7 April 1919, TEL, MS. Eng. c.6741.
21  See the account by the pilot of an accompanying machine in Garnett, *The Letters of T. E. Lawrence*, pp. 276–9.
22  'The Syrian Question', *The Times*, 11 September 1919.
23  The memorandum is reproduced in Garnett, *The Letters of T. E. Lawrence*, pp. 288–91.
24  James, *The Golden Warrior*, p. 374.
25  Lawrence to Curzon, 27 September 1919, TEL MS. Eng. d.3327.
26  See Garnett, *The Letters of T. E. Lawrence*, pp. 282–7.
27  Lawrence to Lloyd George, September 1919, TEL MS. Eng. d.3327.
28  See 'Honour for Colonel Lawrence', *The Times*, 7 November, 1919.
29  Satia, *Spies in Arabia*, p. 165; see also pp. 181–2.
30  Cited in James, *The Golden Warrior*, p. 327.
31  Brittain, *Testament of Youth*, pp. 467–74.
32  Ibid., pp. 468–9.
33  'After Three Years', Bostridge, *Because You Died*, p. 69; and 'Epitaph on my Days in Hospital', Ibid., p. 75.
34  Gorham, *Vera Brittain*, pp. 138–48.

35  Brittain, *Testament of Youth*, p. 481.
36  Vera Brittain, 'The Point of View of a Woman Student', *The Oxford Outlook*, 1: 1 (May 1919), 121–5.
37  Vera Brittain, 'The Degree and "The Times"', *The Oxford Outlook*, 1: 4 (November 1919), 279–84.
38  The literature on Vera Brittain attributes Ruffer's death to pneumonia, which was frequently a fatal development of the 'Spanish flu'.
39  Brittain, *Testament of Youth*, p. 484.
40  See Berry and Bostridge, *Vera Brittain*, pp. 145–8; and Brittain, *Testament of Youth*, pp. 488–93.
41  'The Lament of the Demobilised', Bostridge, *Because You Died*, p. 87.
42  Kennedy, *Portrait of Elgar*, p. 280.
43  'London Symphony Orchestra', *The Times*, 28 October 1919.
44  Elgar to Jaeger, 4 October 1900, Kennedy, *Portrait of Elgar*, p. 119.
45  Trowell, 'The Road to Brinkwells', p. 376.
46  Kennedy, *Portrait of Elgar*, p. 283.
47  Cited in Kennedy, *Portrait of Elgar*, p. 288.
48  'Passing of the Unknown', *The Times*, 12 November 1920; see also Norris, 'The Spirit of Elgar', p. 253.
49  Elgar to Griffith, 8 December 1919, Moore, *Letters of a Lifetime*, p. 330.
50  Nash, *Outline*, p. 218.
51  On this exhibition see Malvern, *Modern Art*, pp. 69–75.
52  Bottomley to Nash, 23 November 1918, cited in Abbott and Bertram, *Poet and Painter*, p. 102.
53  Nevinson, *Paint and Prejudice*, p. 122.
54  Ibid., p. 117.
55  HND, 2 April 1919, Misc. Eng. e.621/1.
56  See Walsh, *C. R. W. Nevinson*, pp. 189–90.
57  Ibid., p. 196.
58  'Deaths', *The Times*, 9 June 1919.
59  Nevinson, *Paint and Prejudice*, p. 140.
60  HND, 2 May 1919, Misc. Eng. e.621/1.
61  Nevinson, *Paint and Prejudice*, p. 125.
62  HND, 10 November 1918, Misc. Eng. e.621/2.
63  Walsh, *C. R. W. Nevinson*, p. 203.
64  See HND, 10 December 1918, Misc. Eng. e.621/2.
65  See HND, 14 December and 7 December 1918, Misc. Eng. e.621/2.
66  Richard Aldington, *Images of War* (London: Beaumont Press, 1919); Nash's original black and white pen drawings for Aldington's book are reproduced in another limited edition, Blythe, *First Friends*.

67  See the sympathetic account of this episode in Bertram, *Paul Nash*, pp. 106–7; and Nash's own version in his letter to Gordon Bottomley, July 1920, cited in Abbott and Bertram, *Poet and Painter*, pp. 119–22.
68  See Abbott and Bertram, *Poet and Painter*, p. 126, fn. 3.
69  See the two letters from Spencer to Chute, dated January and March 1917, cited in Rothenstein, *Stanley Spencer*, pp. 17–20.
70  See Spencer to Lamb, no date [April, 1920], *SS*, p. 109.
71  Spencer to Florence Spencer, 16 December 1918, *SS*, p. 102.
72  See the later account in *SS*, p. 103.
73  See Carline, *Stanley Spencer at War*, p. 112.
74  Spencer to Hilda Carline, 1923, cited in Carline, *Stanley Spencer at War*, p. 112.
75  Spencer to Lamb, 20 July 1919, cited in Carline, *Stanley Spencer at War*, p. 112.
76  See Carline, *Stanley Spencer at War*, p. 117, fn. 6.
77  See Rothenstein, *Stanley Spencer*, pp. 20–1.
78  Spencer, *Stanley Spencer*, p. 154.
79  Cited in *SS*, p. 102.
80  Both cards are reproduced in Dilworth, *David Jones*, pp. 201–3.
81  See his letter to René Hague, 9–15 July 1973, cited in Hague, *Dai Greatcoat*, pp. 245–50.

## Chapter 12

1  Rupert Brooke, *The Collected Poems, with a Memoir by Edward Marsh* (London: Sidgwick and Jackson, 1918).
2  Audoin-Rouzeau and Becker, *14–18, retrouver la Guerre*, p. 183. See also Jay Winter, *Sites of Memory, Sites of Mourning: The Great War in European Cultural History* (Cambridge: Cambridge University Press, 1995); and Jay Winter and Emmanuel Sivan (eds), *War and Remembrance in the Twentieth Century* (Cambridge: Cambridge University Press, 1999).
3  J. Dyfnallt Owen, 'Hedd Wyn', *Ceninen Gŵyl Ddewi*, Mawrth 1, 1918 (*Ceninen* St David's Day, 1 March 1918), pp. 15–23.
4  J. J. Williams (ed.), *Cerddi'r bugail: cyfrol goffa Hedd Wyn* (Cardiff: William Lewis, 1918).
5  Llwyd, *The Story of Hedd Wyn*, p. 195.
6  John Masefield, *The Old Front Line* ([1917] Barnsley: Pen and Sword, 2003).
7  Llwyd, *The Story of Hedd Wyn*, p. 205.
8  Ibid., p. 201.
9  See for a survey of these developments, Todman, *The Great War*.
10  Finzi, *Eighteen Months*, 12 November 1914, p. 58.
11  Brittain to Edith Brittain, 16 December 1916, VB/PBA Box 3 Folder 3.

12  Richard Aldington, *Lawrence of Arabia: A Biographical Enquiry* (London: Collins, 1955), p. 13.
13  Lawrence, *Seven Pillars*, 'Author's Preface'.
14  Cited in James, *The Golden Warrior*, p. 338.
15  Lawrence, *Seven Pillars*, p. 9.
16  This phrase was in the introduction to the '1922 Edition' of *Seven Pillars of Wisdom*, part of which was cut from the 1926 edition. See Garnett, *The Letters of T. E. Lawrence*, p. 262.
17  Lawrence, *Seven Pillars*, p. 10.
18  Ibid., pp. 348–53, p. 353.
19  See James, *The Golden Warrior*, pp. 245–63; and Aldington, *Lawrence of Arabia*, pp. 204–7.
20  Lawrence, *Seven Pillars*, p. 507.
21  Satia, *Spies in Arabia*, p. 188.
22  Lawrence to Davies, 28 February 1935, TEL MS. Eng. d.3342.
23  'Too Big for Wealth and Glory', *Daily Sketch*, 20 May 1935.
24  Berry and Bostridge, *Vera Brittain*, p. 264.
25  Brittain, *Testament of Youth*, p. 370.
26  Ibid., p. 467.
27  Ibid., pp. 286 and 468.
28  Ibid., p. 634.
29  Ibid., p. 476.
30  Ibid., p. 635.
31  Ibid., pp. 471–2.
32  Ibid., p. 661.
33  Ibid., p. 656.
34  Spencer to Sadler, 21 February 1922, *SS*, pp. 114–15.
35  See Spencer to Florence Spencer [September/October 1923], *SS*, pp. 124–5.
36  Cited in Carline, *Stanley Spencer at War*, pp. 195 and 175. See pp. 145–60 and 176–99 for more of Spencer's commentary on the Burghclere paintings.
37  Spencer to Hilda Carline, September 1923, cited in Carline, *Stanley Spencer at War*, p. 153.
38  On Spencer's relationship with Hilda Carline, see Rothenstein, *Stanley Spencer*, pp. 23–47.
39  Dilworth, *David Jones*, p. 216.
40  Jones, *In Parenthesis*, p. xv.
41  Hague, *Dai Greatcoat*, p. 28.
42  Stanley Honeyman, cited in Hague, *Dai Greatcoat*, p. 147.
43  See Fussell, *The Great War*, pp. 144–54; and Dilworth, *David Jones*, pp. 216–17.

44  Jones, *In Parenthesis*, Dedication.
45  Jones, *In Parenthesis*, pp. xii–xiii.
46  William Blissett, *The Long Conversation: A Memoir of David Jones* (Oxford: Oxford University Press, 1981), p. 12.
47  Jones, *In Parenthesis*, p. xiii.
48  Ibid., p. 138.
49  Ibid., pp. 122–3.
50  Ibid., p. 95.
51  Ibid., pp. 180–1.
52  It is not clear from *In Parenthesis* whether the dissenting General is Phillips, the Commander of the 38th (Welsh) Division, or Brigadier-General Price-Davies. Both were dismissed from their posts after Mametz Wood.
53  Jones, *In Parenthesis*, p. 173.
54  Johnson, *English Poetry*, pp. 284–340, p. 285.
55  Jones, *In Parenthesis*, p. ix.
56  Hague, *Dai Greatcoat*, p. 58.
57  Guy Davenport lists *In Parenthesis*, alongside *Seven Pillars of Wisdom* and Spencer's paintings in the Sandham Memorial Chapel, as the 'transcendentally great works of art' which have depicted the First World War. See his 'In Love With All Things Made', Matthias, *David Jones*, pp. 73–6, p. 73.
58  See Bernard Porter, 'Elgar and Empire: Music, Nationalism, and the War', Foreman, *Oh, My Horses!*, pp. 133–74.
59  Foreman, *Oh, My Horses!*
60  A recent example is Lawrence Sondhaus, *World War One: The Global Revolution* (Cambridge: Cambridge University Press, 2011), the front cover of which carries a reproduction of Nevinson's *Explosion* (1916).
61  Claire Tylee, *The Great War and Women's Consciousness: Images of Militarism and Womanhood in Women's Writings, 1914–64* (London: Macmillan, 1990), pp. 99–100.
62  Jane Potter, *Boys in Khaki, Girls in Print: Women's Literary Responses to the Great War 1914–1918* (Oxford: Oxford University Press, 2005), p. 224.
63  *Hedd Wyn*, directed by Paul Turner (1992).
64  See 'Hedd Wyn: The Belgian Legacy', *Daily Post*, 31 July 2012.
65  'Notes of the Month', *Welsh Outlook*, October 1914, pp. 415–19.
66  See for example Gullace, 'The Blood of our Sons.'

# Conclusion

1  Watson, *Fighting Different Wars*, p. 4.
2  See Audoin-Rouzeau and Becker, *14–18, retrouver la Guerre*, pp. 109–95 for an extended discussion.

3  Gregory, *The Last Great War*, p. 39.
4  See Peter Mandler, 'The Problem with Cultural History', *Cultural and Social History*, 1: 1 (1994), 94–117.
5  Asquith to Stanley, 3 August 1914, Brock and Brock, *H. H. Asquith Letters to Venetia Stanley*, p. 148.
6  See Gregory, *The Last Great War*, pp. 9–11.
7  See Watson, *Fighting Different Wars*, pp. 300–1.
8  Lawrence to Lewis, 16 November 1934, TEL MS. Eng. d.3327.
9  Todman, *The Great War*, p. 221.
10  Alice Elgar referred to the Germans as 'demons' in her diary *before* her husband decided to use his music from the 'Demons' Chorus' in *Gerontius* to portray them (see AED, 27 January 1915). She frequently described them also as 'brutes', and 'barbarians'. Clearly the idea of the Germans as demonic was abroad in the Elgar household from very early in the war.
11  Brooke to Maurice Brown and Ellen van Volkenburg, early October 1914, cited in Mike Read, *Forever England: The Life of Rupert Brooke* (Edinburgh: Mainstream Publishing, 1997), p. 225.
12  Cited in Carline, *Stanley Spencer at War*, p. 93.
13  Speaking on St David's Day 1918, of the achievements of 'the boys of Wales', Lloyd George said 'they were the first to eject the Turks out of Bethlehem where the Saviour was born. . . . They were the first on the Mount of Olives'. 'Welshmen's Record in the War', *The Times*, 2 March 1918.
14  John Keegan, *The First World War* (London: Hutchinson, 1998), p. 321.
15  A. J. P. Taylor, *The First World War: An Illustrated History* (London: Penguin, 1966), p. 140.
16  John Terraine, *The Smoke and the Fire: Myths and Anti-Myths of War 1861–1945* (London: Sidgwick & Jackson, 1980), p. 108.
17  http://www.royalexchange.co.uk/event.aspx?id=583, accessed 27 September 2013.
18  Wohl, *The Generation of 1914*, p. 95.
19  See Harris, *Douglas Haig*, p. 327; and Moorcroft, *Siegfried Sassoon*, pp. 353–4.
20  See Daniel Grimley, '"Music in the midst of desolation": structures of mourning in Elgar's *The Spirit of England*', in J. P. E. Harper-Scott and Julian Rushton (eds), *Elgar Studies* (Cambridge: Cambridge University Press, 2007), pp. 220–37.
21  Satia, *Spies in Arabia*, p. 181.
22  Lawrence to Elgar, 12 October 1932, TEL MS. Eng. d.3327.
23  Cited in Satia, *Spies in Arabia*, p. 177.
24  Esmee Sartorius, 'August 1914', in *Fifty Amazing Stories of the Great War* (London: Odhams Press, 1936), p. 75.

# FURTHER READING

There is a rich and varied literature on the First World War, and it grows constantly. There are many collections of published primary documents, as well as memoirs written by great numbers of those involved, from statesmen and generals through to ordinary soldiers and volunteer nurses. Many of the memoir writers were gifted literary figures, as were some of the key actors in different fields. Historians of great quality have been attracted to the subject since the 1920s, and a flourishing school has emerged since the 1990s, concerned to repudiate some of the long-established paradigms in the subject and to take advantage of insights offered by the 'new cultural history'. The suggestions made below can be no more than starting points.

## Published primary documents

There are a number of valuable collections of documents relating to the British conduct of the war. On the origins of the war see

George Gooch and Harold Temperley (eds), *British Documents on the Origins of the War, 1898–1914* (London: His Majesty's Stationery Office, 1926–38), 11 volumes.

On the conduct of military operations, and particularly on Churchill's role in these, see

Martin Gilbert (ed.), *Winston S. Churchill, Vol. III, Companion, Part I: Documents July 1914-April 1915* (London: Heinemann, 1972).
—*Winston S. Churchill, Vol. III, Companion, Part 2: Documents May 1915-December 1916* (London: Heinemann, 1972).
—*Winston S. Churchill, Vol. IV, Companion: Documents 1917–1922* (London: Heinemann, 1977).
*The World War I Collection: Gallipoli and the Early Battles 1914–15* (London: The Stationery Office, 2001).
*Lord Kitchener and Winston Churchill: The Dardanelles Commission Part I, 1914–1915* (London: The Stationery Office, 2000).
*British Battles of World War I, 1914–15* (London: The Stationery Office, 2000).

See also the multi-volume, multi-authored history of the war 'based on official documents', produced in the 1920s and 1930s. During the war several 'histories' were published, typically with many photographs. These include:

*The Times History of the War* (London: Printing House Square, 1915 onwards), 22 volumes.

J. A. Hammerton (ed.), *The War Illustrated Album de Luxe: The Story of the Great European War told by Camera, Pen and Pencil* (London: Amalgamated Press, 1915–17), 8 volumes.

There are now numerous websites which provide transcriptions of important British foreign policy documents, and treaties from the period 1914–19. For printed transcriptions of important documents from the final period of the war, see

Arthur Keith (ed.), *Speeches and Documents on International Affairs, 1918–1937* (London: Oxford University Press, 1938), Vol. I.

For a critique of the British government's decision to go war by a leading light of the Union of Democratic Control, see

E. D. Morel, *Truth and the War* (London: National Labour Press, 1916).

A contemporary document which was widely read and hugely influential is

*Report of the Committee on Alleged German Outrages Appointed by his Britannic Majesty's Government and Presided Over by the Right Hon. Viscount Bryce, O.M.* (London: HMSO, 1915).

For First World War photographs, posters and ephemera, see

Jane Carmichael, *First World War Photographers* (London: Routledge, 1987).
Maurice Richards (ed.), *Posters of the First World War* (London: Evelyn, Adams, and Mackay, 1968).
Maurice Rickards and Michael Moody (eds), *The First World War: Ephemera, Mementoes, Documents* (London: Jupiter, 1975).

## Wartime correspondence and diaries

There are many available primary sources from the war in this form. An invaluable source for understanding the British decision to go to war is

Michael Brock and Eleanor Brock (eds), *H.H. Asquith: Letters to Venetia Stanley* (Oxford and New York: Oxford University Press, 1982).

An earlier biography which contains much primary material, and which is still worth reading, is

Roy Jenkins, *Asquith: Portrait of a Man and an Era* (New York: Dutton, 1966).

See also, for fascinating insights

*Lord Riddell's War Diary 1914–1918* (London: Nicholson and Watson, 1933).
A. J. P. Taylor (ed.), *Lloyd George: A Diary by Frances Stevenson* (London: Hutchinson, 1971).
Margaret Cole (ed.), *Beatrice Webb's Diaries, 1912–1924* (London: Longmans, Green and Co., 1952).
Cynthia Asquith, *Diaries 1915–1918* (London: Hutchinson, 1968).
Violet Bonham Carter, *Winston Churchill As I Knew Him* (London: Eyre & Spottiswoode and Collins, 1965).

## Post-war memoirs by politicians

Although all of these memoirs are marked by efforts at self-justification, many of them also reprint verbatim valuable primary documents.

Viscount Grey of Fallodon, *Twenty-Five Years, 1892–1916* (London: Hodder and Stoughton, 1925), 2 volumes.
Winston Churchill, *The World Crisis* (London: Thornton Butterworth, 1923–31), 6 volumes.
*War Memoirs of David Lloyd George* (Boston, MA: Little, Brown, and Company, 1933), 6 volumes; note that there are abridged later editions available!
H. H. Asquith, *Memories and Reflections 1895–1927* (London: Cassell, 1928), 2 volumes.

For an understanding of British strategy, written by the Secretary to various Cabinet Committees which directed the war, and which also contains many primary documents, see

Lord Hankey, *The Supreme Command 1914–1918* (London: Allen and Unwin, 1961), 2 volumes.

## General histories of the war

In recent years, several eminent historians have written excellent general histories of the First World War. See, among others:

Lawrence Sondhaus, *World War One: The Global Revolution* (Cambridge: Cambridge University Press, 2011).
David Stephenson, *1914–1918: The History of the First World War* (London: Penguin, 2005).
Hew Strachan, *The Oxford Illustrated History of the First World War* (Oxford and New York: Oxford University Press, 1998).
John Keegan, *The First World War* (London: Hutchinson, 1998).
Niall Ferguson, *The Pity of War* (London: Allen Lane, 1998).
Martin Gilbert, *First World War* (London: Weidenfeld and Nicolson, 1994).

Older histories of the war often tell you as much about the time they were written as about the war. See for interesting examples:

A. J. P. Taylor, *The First World War: An Illustrated History* (London: Hamish Hamilton, 1963).
James Edmonds, *A Short History of World War I* (London: Oxford University Press, 1951).
Basil Liddell-Hart, *History of the First World War* ([1933] London: Pan Books, 1972).

One of the earliest histories, by Vera Brittain's one-time tutor, is still worth reading:

C. R. M. F. Cruttwell, *A History of the Great War 1914–1918* (Oxford: Clarendon Press, 1934).

## Broader cultural histories

There is a distinguished tradition of writing about British society and the cultural imagination of the First World War. See in reverse chronological order:

Adrian Gregory, *The Last Great War: British Society and the First World War* (Cambridge: Cambridge University Press, 2008).
Janet Watson, *Fighting Different Wars: Experience, Memory, and the First World War in Britain* (Cambridge: Cambridge University Press, 2006).
Dan Todman, *The Great War: Myth and Memory* (London: Hambledon and London, 2005).
Jay Winter and Antoine Prost (eds), *The Great War in History: Debates and Controversies, 1914 to the Present* (Cambridge: Cambridge University Press, 2005).
Gail Braybon (ed.), *Evidence, History and the Great War: Historians and the Impact of 1914–18* (New York: Berghahn, 2004).
Trudi Tate, *Modernism, History and the First World War* (Manchester: Manchester University Press, 1998).
Stephen Constantine, Maurice Kirby, and Mary Rose, *The First World War in British History* (London and New York: Edward Arnold, 1995).
Adrian Caesar, *Taking it Like a Man: Suffering, Sexuality, and the War Poets; Brooke, Sassoon, Owen, Graves* (Manchester: Manchester University Press, 1993).
Samuel Hynes, *A War Imagined: The First World War and English Culture* (London: Bodley Head, 1990).
Modris Eksteins, *Rites of Spring: The Great War and the Birth of the Modern Age* (London: Bantam, 1989).
Cecil Eby, *The Road to Armageddon: The Martial Spirit in English Popular Literature 1870–1914* (London and Durham: Duke University Press, 1987).
Ted Bogacz, '"A Tyranny of Words": Language, Poetry, and Antimodernism in England in the First World War'. *Journal of Military History*, 58: 3 (September 1986), 643–68.

Robert Wohl, *The Generation of 1914* (London: Weidenfeld and Nicolson, 1980).
Bernard Bergonzi, *Heroes' Twilight: A Study of the Literature of the Great War* (London: Macmillan, 1980).
Paul Fussell, *The Great War and Modern Memory* (London and New York: Oxford University Press, 1975).
John Johnston, *English Poetry of the First World War: A Study in the Evolution of Lyric and Narrative Form* (Princeton: Princeton University Press, 1964).

## Social history of the war

To a significant extent, the most recent cultural histories have supplanted the older 'social histories', but there are still recent works which illuminate significant aspects of the British experience at home during the war. See

Catriona Pennell, *A Kingdom United: Popular Responses to the Outbreak of the First World War in Great Britain and Ireland* (Oxford: Oxford University Press, 2012).
John Horne and Alan Kramer, *German Atrocities, 1914: A History of Denial* (New Haven and London: Yale University Press, 2001).
Lawrence James, *Warrior Race: A History of the British at War* (London: Little, Brown, 2001).

Still valuable are texts such as:

Gary Messinger, *British Propaganda and the State in the First World War* (Manchester: Manchester University Press, 1992).
Arthur Marwick, *The Deluge: British Society and the First World War* (Basingstoke: Macmillan, 1991).
Jim Bourne, *Britain and the Great War 1914–1918* (London: Edward Arnold, 1989).
Zara Steiner, *Britain and the Origins of the First World War* (Basingstoke: Macmillan, 1971).

For an introduction to the Union of Democratic Control, see

Raymond Jones, *Arthur Ponsonby: The Politics of Life* (London: Christopher Helm, 1989).

## The British Army, the Western Front and the generals

Two recent works will help to unlock the complexity of the structure and operation of the British Army during the First World War:

Peter Simkins, *Kitchener's Army: The Raising of the New Armies, 1914–1916* ([1988] Barnsley: Pen and Sword, 2007).
Charles Messenger, *Call to Arms: The British Army 1914–18* (London: Phoenix, 2006).

There are literally hundreds of books on the Western Front. An interesting recent development is the appearance of books largely structured around witness testimony and oral histories. See for example:

Paul Hart, *1918: A Very British Victory* (London: Weidenfeld and Nicolson, 2008).
Malcolm Brown (ed.), *The Imperial War Museum Book of the First World War* (London: Pan, 2001).
—*The Imperial War Museum Book of the Western Front* (London: Pan, 2001).
Martin Middlebrook, *The First Day on the Somme* (London: Military Book Society, 1971).
Max Arthur (ed.), *Last Post: The Final Word from our First World War Soldiers* (London: Weidenfeld and Nicolson, 2005).

In recent years several authors have argued that the British Army developed into a sophisticated and technologically advanced force by the end of the war. See above all

Tim Travers, *How the War Was Won: Command and Technology in the British Army on the Western Front, 1917–1918* (Barnsley: Pen and Sword, 2005).
—*The Killing Ground: The British Army, the Western Front & the Emergence of Modern War 1900–1918* (Barnsley: Pen & Sword, 2003).
Gary Sheffield, *Forgotten Victory. The First World War: Myths and Realities* (London: Review Books, 2002).
John Terraine, *1914–1918: Essays on Leadership & War* (Reading: Western Front Association, 1998).

On the opening stages of the war, one of the classic literary accounts is still worth reading:

Barbara Tuchman, *August 1914* (London: Macmillan, 1980).

And there are some useful histories of the Christmas truce of 1914. One which considers other similar informal arrangements by front-line soldiers in different theatres is

Marc Ferro, Malcolm Brown, Rémy Cazals, Olaf Mueller, *Meetings in No Man's Land: Christmas 1914 and Fraternization in the Great War* (London: Constable & Robinson, 2007).

See also

Stanley Weintraub, *Silent Night: The Remarkable Christmas Truce of 1914* (New York: Pocket Books, 2002).

An influential earlier text on Passchendaele is

Leon Wolff, *In Flanders Fields: Passchendaele 1917* ([1959] London: Penguin, 2001).

The German offensives of 1918 have been addressed in a range of books, including

Lyn MacDonald, *To the Last Man: Spring 1918* (London: Viking, 1998).

Martin Kitchen, *The German Offensives of 1918* (Stroud: Tempus, 2001).
Martin Middlebrook, *The Kaiser's Battle* ([1978] London: Penguin, 2000).

On the use of chemical weapons, see

Rob Evans, *Gassed* (London: Stratus, 2000).
William van der Kloot, 'April 1915: Five Future Nobel Prize-Winners Inaugurate Weapons of Mass Destruction and the Academic-Industrial-Military Complex'. *Notes and Records of the Royal Society of London*, 58: 2 (May 2004), 149–60.

An excellent recent book on the development and use of tanks is

Christy Campbell, *Band of Brigands: The Extraordinary Story of the First Men in Tanks* (London: Harper Press: 2007).

On the American contribution, see

Byron Farwell, *Over There: The United States in the Great War, 1917–1918* (New York and London: Norton, 2000).

There is a growing interest in the fate of those who fell foul of military discipline during the war. See

Cathryn Corns and John Hughes-Wilson, *Blindfold and Alone: British Military Executions in the Great War* (London: Cassell, 2001).

For the immediate aftermath of the war in the West, see

James Edmonds, *The Occupation of the Rhineland 1918–1929* (London: HMSO, 1987).

## Haig and the generals

There are two vital publications with extensive selections from Haig's own writing:

Gary Sheffield and John Bourne (eds), *Douglas Haig: War Diaries and Letters 1914–1918* (London: Weidenfeld and Nicolson, 2005).
Robert Blake (ed.), *The Private Papers of Douglas Haig, 1914–1919* (London: Eyre and Spottiswoode, 1952).

After nearly a century some balanced appraisals of Haig are now being produced. See in particular:

Gary Sheffield, *The Chief: Douglas Haig and the British Army* (London: Aurum Press, 2011).
J. P. Harris, *Douglas Haig and the First World War* (Cambridge: Cambridge University Press, 2008).
Elizabeth Greenhalgh, 'Myth and Memory: Sir Douglas Haig and the Imposition of Allied Unified Command in March 1918'. *Journal of Military History*, 68: 3 (July 2004), 771–820.

Dominick Graham and Shelford Bidwell, *Coalitions, Politicians and Generals: Aspects of Command in Two World Wars* (London: Brassey's, 1993).

See, for earlier efforts to defend Haig, in chronological order:

Duff Cooper, *Haig* (London: Faber & Faber, 1935).
John Davidson, *Haig: Master of the Field* (London and New York: Nevill, 1953).
John Terraine, *Douglas Haig: The Educated Soldier* (London: Hutchinson, 1963).

And, for representative denunciations, see

Denis Winter, *Haig's Command: A Reassessment* (London: Viking, 1991).
John Laffin, *British Butchers and Bunglers of World War One* (Stroud: Sutton, 1988).

Churchill's analysis of Haig, originally published in 1935, is lively and balanced:

Winston Churchill, *Great Contemporaries* (London: Reprint Society, 1941), pp. 183–95.

For fuller accounts of the tension between Lloyd George, Haig and other senior officers, see

David Woodward, *Lloyd George and the Generals* ([1983] London: Frank Cass, 2004).
John Grigg, *Lloyd George: War Leader 1916–1918* (London: Allen Lane, 2002).

## The war at sea

Anyone seriously interested in this topic should read the foremost historian of the Royal Navy, Arthur Marder. There are also numerous surveys, more detailed essays, and memoirs. See among others

John Jellicoe, *The Grand Fleet 1914–16: Its Creation, Development and Work* (London and New York: Cassell, 1919).
Arthur Marder, *From the Dreadnought to Scapa Flow: A History of the Royal Navy in the Fisher Era* (London: Oxford University Press, 1961–70), 5 volumes.
Nigel Steel and Peter Hart, *Jutland 1916: Death in the Grey Wastes* (London: Cassell, 2003).
V. E. Tarrant, *Jutland: the German Perspective* (London: Cassell, 2001).
Richard Hough, *The Great War at Sea, 1914–1918* (Oxford and New York: Oxford University Press, 1983).
Robert Massie, *Dreadnought: Britain, Germany, and the Coming of the Great War* (New York: Random House, 1991).
Nicholas Lambert, '"Our Bloody Ships" or "Our Bloody System"? Jutland and the Loss of the Battle Cruisers, 1916'. *The Journal of Military History*, 62: 1 (January 1998), 29–55.

## The Dardanelles, Gallipoli, Mesopotamia and other 'side shows'

The aura of romance and tragedy around the Gallipoli campaign has attracted many notable writers. A recent account with much fascinating oral testimony is

Nigel Steel and Peter Hart, *Defeat at Gallipoli* (London: Macmillan, 1994).

See also

Field Marshal Lord Carver, *The Turkish Front, 1914–1918: The Campaigns at Gallipoli, in Mesopotamia, and in Palestine* (Basingstoke: Sidgwick and Jackson, 2003).
Robert Rhodes James, *Gallipoli* (London: Batsford, 1965).
Peter Doyle and Matthew Bennett, 'Military Geography: The Influence of Terrain on the Outcome of the Gallipoli Campaign, 1915'. *The Geographical Journal*, 65: 1 (March 1999), 12–36.
Arthur Marder, *From the Dardanelles to Oran: Studies of the Royal Navy in War and Peace 1915–1940* (London: Oxford University Press, 1974).
Ross Anderson, *The Forgotten Front: The East African Campaign, 1914–1918* (Stroud: Tempus, 2004).

For one of the outstanding literary accounts of any campaign in the war, see

Alan Moorehead, *Gallipoli* (London: Hamish Hamilton, 1956).

As most of the English-language accounts have little to say about the Turkish perspective or experience, an invaluable alternative view is provided by the account of the German general who commanded the Turks in the field for most of the war. This memoir was written very shortly after the end of the conflict.

Liman von Sanders, *Five Years in Turkey,* trans. Reichmann (Maryland: U. S. Naval Institute, 1927).

A still valuable book using Arabic sources, and which also reprints important primary documents, is

George Antonius, *The Arab Awakening: The Story of the Arab National Movement* ([1969] Beirut: Lebanon Bookshop, no date).

## On aviation

As well as general surveys, there are detailed essays on individual campaigns. See for example:

Neil Hanson, *First Blitz: The Secret German Plan to Raze London to the Ground in 1918* (London: Corgi, 2009).

Peter Hart, *Aces Falling: The War Above the Trenches 1918* (London: Weidenfeld and Nicolson, 2007).
John Mordike, 'General Sir Edmund Allenby's joint operations in Palestine, 1917–1918'. *RAF Air Power Review*, 5: 4 (Winter 2002), 16–40.

Two of the outstanding memoirs of the war were written by pilots who survived. See

V. M. Yeates, *Winged Victory* (London: Jonathan Cape, 1934).
Cecil Day Lewis, *Sagittarius Rising* (London: Peter Davies, 1936).

## Wales and the war, and Hedd Wyn

There is no single recent book which addresses specifically the Welsh experience of the war in all its complexity. For a contemporary view, and details on the 'Welsh Army Corps' and other Welsh units, see

J. Vyrnwy Morgan, *The War and Wales* (London: Chapman and Hall, 1916).
J. E. Munby, *A History of the 38th (Welsh) Division* (London: Rees, 1920).
*Welsh Army Corps 1914–1919: Report of the Executive Committee* (Cardiff: Western Mail, 1921).
*A Short History of the South Wales Borderers 24th Foot and the Monmouthshire Regiment* (Cardiff: Western Mail and Echo, no date).

A useful small book, actually intended for schools but including many fascinating primary sources, is

Keith Strange, *Wales and the First World War* (Bridgend: Mid-Glamorgan County Supplies Department, no date).

For more recent scholarly articles, see

Tecwyn Lloyd, 'Welsh Public Opinion and the First World War'. *Planet*, 10 (1972), 25–37.
Gervase Phillips, 'Dai Bach y Soldier: Welsh Soldiers in the British Army'. *Llafur*, 6: 2 (1993), 94–105.

The most detailed and balanced account of the battle for Mametz Wood also contains much valuable material on the formation and training of the 38th (Welsh) Division:

Colin Hughes, *Mametz: Lloyd George's 'Welsh Army' at the Battle of the Somme* (London: Gliddon Books, 1990).

There are some notable memoirs which illuminate aspects of the specifically Welsh experience of the war, above all:

Llewelyn Wyn Griffith, *Up to Mametz . . . and Beyond* (Barnsley: Pen and Sword, 2010).
Frank Richards, *Old Soldiers Never Die* (London: Faber & Faber, 1964).

Two useful anthologies of 'Welsh' writing on the war have been published, although both take a fairly broad view of who might be considered 'Welsh'!

Alan Llwyd, *Out of the Fires of Hell: Welsh Experience of the Great War 1914–1918 in Prose and Verse* (Llandysul: Gomer, 2008).
John Richards (ed.), *Wales on the Western Front* (Cardiff: University of Wales Press, 1994).

The original publication of Hedd Wyn's collected poems is:

J. J. Williams (ed.), *Cerddi'r bugail: cyfrol goffa Hedd Wyn* (Cardiff: William Lewis, 1918).

Much of the writing on Hedd Wyn is in Welsh, but there are English and Flemish translations alongside some of these:

Alan Llywd, *Gwae Fi Fy Myw: Cofiant Hedd Wyn* (Llanbedr: Argraffiad Cyntaf, 1991).
—'Hedd Wyn – Soldier Poet?' *Poetry Wales*, 28: 2 (October 1992), 49–51.
Alan Llwyd, *Stori Hedd Wyn: Bardd y Gadair Ddu. The Story of Hedd Wyn: The Poet of the Black Chair* (Llandybie: Barddas, 2009).
Lieven Dehandschutter, *Hedd Wynn: Een Welshe tragedie in Vlaanderen; Trasiedi Cymreig yn Fflandrys; A Welsh tragedy in Flanders* (Brussels: Vormingscentrum, 1992).
Bethan Phillips, 'A Fine Day's Work'. *Planet*, 72 (December/January 1988–89), 59–64.

To position Hedd Wyn in a wider context, see

Dafydd Johnston, *A Guide to Welsh Literature c. 1900–1996* (Cardiff: University of Wales Press, 1998).

And for war memorials in Wales, see

Angela Gaffney, *Aftermath: Remembering the Great War in Wales* (Cardiff: University of Wales Press, 1998).

## Nursing

A vital contemporary source is

*Reports by the Joint War Committee and the Joint War Finance Committee of the British Red Cross Society and the Order of St. John of Jerusalem in England on Voluntary Aid Rendered to the Sick and Wounded at Home and Abroad and to British Prisoners of War, 1914–1919* (London: HMSO, 1921).

Kate Finzi's contemporary account is one of several published during the war. It has recently been re-issued.

Kate Finzi, *Eighteen Months in the War Zone: The Record of a Woman's Work on the Western Front* (London: Cassell, 1916).

See, for interesting comparisons

Violetta Thurstan, *Field Hospital and Flying Column* (London: Putnam, 1915).
Sister Martin-Nicholson, *My Experience on Three Fronts* (London: Allen & Unwin, 1916).
Olive Dent, *A V.A.D. in France* (London: Grant Richards, 1917).
Enid Bagnold, *A Diary Without Dates* (London: Heinemann, 1918).
T. A. Malloch, 'The War: Hospital Experiences in France'. *The Canadian Medical Association Journal*, 5: 2 (February 1915), 155–65.

Much of the literature on women and on women's writing and the war refers to nursing. See also

Christine Hallett, *Containing Trauma: Nursing Work in the First World War* (Manchester: Manchester University Press, 2009).
Janet Watson, 'War in the Wards: The Social Construction of Medical Work in First World War Britain'. *Journal of British Studies*, 41: 4 (2002), 484–510.
Henriette Donner, 'Under the cross – why VADs performed the filthiest task in the dirtiest war: Red Cross women volunteers, 1914–1918'. *Journal of Social History*, 30 (1997), 687–704.
Tatham Meaburn and James Miles, *The Friends' Ambulance Unit 1914–1919: A Record* (London: Swarthmore Press, 1919).

An earlier popular history which contains many first-hand accounts is

Lyn MacDonald, *The Roses of No Man's Land* (London: Michael Joseph, 1980).

## On 'Shell-shock' and war-related trauma

There is an extensive literature on these topics. See for starting points:

Michael Roper, *The Secret Battle: Emotional Survival in the Great War* (Manchester: Manchester University Press, 2009).
Ben Shephard, *A War of Nerves: Soldiers and Psychiatrists, 1914–1994* (London: Jonathan Cape, 2000).
Tracey Loughran, 'Evolution, repression and shell shock: emotion and instinct in theories of war neuroses c.1914–1919'. *Manchester Papers in Economic and Social History*, 58 (September 2007), 1–24.
Jay Winter, 'Shell shock and the cultural history of the Great War'. *Journal of Contemporary History*, 35: 1 (2000), 7–11.
John Talbott, 'Soldiers, Psychiatrists, and Combat Trauma'. *Journal of Interdisciplinary History*, 27: 3 (Winter 1997), 437–54.
Eric Leed, *No Man's Land: Combat and Identity in World War I* (Cambridge: Cambridge University Press, 1981).
Ted Bogacz, 'War Neurosis and Cultural Change in England, 1914–1922: The Work of the War Office Committee of Enquiry into "Shell Shock"'. *Journal of Contemporary History*, 24 (April 1989), 227–56.

## On music in Britain before and during the First World War

There are many relevant letters in

Lewis Foreman (ed.), *From Parry to Britten: British Music in Letters, 1900–1945* (London: Batsford, 1987).

For a discussion which is relevant to Elgar and Parry, see

Jeffrey Richards, *Imperialism and Music: Britain 1876–1953* (Manchester: Manchester University Press, 2001).

See also this interesting contemporary piece by Britain's most important music critic

Ernest Newman, 'The War and the Future of Music'. *The Musical Times*, 55: 859 (September 1914), 571–2.

## On Edward Elgar

There is a huge literature on Elgar, with many biographies, and specialist appreciations of his music. The recent discovery of the importance of his relationship with Vera Hockmann at the very end of his life is prompting a reappraisal which has not yet been reflected in older biographies. Still the best general biographies are

Michael Kennedy, *Portrait of Elgar* (Oxford and New York: Oxford University Press, 1987).
Jerrold Northrop Moore, *Edward Elgar: A Creative Life* (Oxford and New York: Oxford University Press, 1987).

For a short introduction to the composer, see

Jerrold Northrop Moore, *Spirit of England: Edward Elgar in his World* (London: Heinemann, 1984).

Several editions of Elgar's correspondence have been published, and two provide vital insights. See

Jerrold Northrop Moore (ed.), *The Windflower Letters: Correspondence with Alice Caroline Stuart-Wortley and her Family* (Oxford: Oxford University Press, 1989).
—*Edward Elgar: Letters of a Lifetime* (Oxford: Clarendon Press, 1990).

A recent publication with several valuable essays in it about Elgar's experience of the First World War is

Lewis Foreman (ed.), *Oh, My Horses! Elgar and the Great War* (Rickmansworth: Elgar Editions, 2001).

On *The Spirit of England*, see also

Rachel Cowgill, 'Elgar's War Requiem', in Byron Adams (ed.), *Edward Elgar and his World* (Princeton and Oxford: Princeton University Press, 2007), pp. 317–62.
Daniel Grimley, '"Music in the midst of desolation": structures of mourning in Elgar's *The Spirit of England*', in J. P. E. Harper-Scott and Julian Rushton (eds), *Elgar Studies* (Cambridge: Cambridge University Press, 2007), pp. 220–37.

For important wartime commentaries on *The Spirit of England*, see

Ernest Newman, '"The Spirit of England": Edward Elgar's New Choral Work'. *The Musical Times*, 57: 879 (May 1916), 235–9.
—'Elgar's "Fourth of August"'. *The Musical Times*, 58: 893 (July 1917), 295–7.

Elgar's anthem *Give unto the Lord* is almost unmentioned in the broader literature. See, for interesting details of this work and its performance

John Allison, *Edward Elgar: The Sacred Music* (Bridgend: Poetry Wales, 1994).
E. Wulstan Atkins, *The Elgar-Atkins Friendship* (Newton Abbott: David & Charles, 1984).

## On Hubert Parry

The best biography is that by Jeremy Dibble, although Graves' older account is still useful. Benoliel focuses more on his actual music. See

Jeremy Dibble, *C. Hubert H. Parry: His Life and Music* (Oxford: Oxford University Press, 1992).
Charles Graves, *Hubert Parry: His Life and Works* (London: Macmillan, 1926), 2 volumes.
Bernard Benoliel, *Parry before Jerusalem: Studies of his Life and Music with Excerpts from his Published Writings* (Aldershot: Ashgate, 1997).
Anthony Boden, *The Parrys of the Golden Vale: Background to Genius* (London: Thames Publishing, 1998).

A valuable primary source is

H. C. Colles (ed.), *College Addresses Delivered to Pupils of the Royal College of Music by Sir C. Hubert H. Parry* (London: Macmillan, 1920).

## On Rupert Brooke

Older biographies of Brooke, and the edited selection of his letters published in 1968 present a one sided-view of the man, concealing his sexuality, and some of the less attractive sides of his character. For a fuller understanding see

Nigel Jones, *Rupert Brooke: Life, Death, and Myth* (London: Richard Cohen, 1999).
Keith Hale (ed.), *Friends and Apostles: The Correspondence of Rupert Brooke and James Strachey 1905–1914* (New Haven and London: Yale University Press, 1998).

Pippa Harris (ed.), *Song of Love: The Letters of Rupert Brooke and Noel Oliver 1909–1915* (London: Bloomsbury, 1991).

There are many editions of Brooke's poems, and Eddie Marsh's memoir of 1918 is a valuable contemporary document.

Rupert Brooke, *1914 & Other Poems* (London: Sidgwick and Jackson, 1915).
*Rupert Brooke: The Collected Poems, with a Memoir by Edward Marsh* (London: Sidgwick and Jackson, 1918).

The older literature can still be helpful, providing that its one-sidedness is recognized:

Geoffrey Keynes (ed.), *The Letters of Rupert Brooke* (London: Faber & Faber, 1968).
Christopher Hassall, *Edward Marsh: Patron of the Arts* (London: Longman, 1959).
—*Rupert Brooke: a Biography* (London: Faber & Faber, 1964).
Mike Read, *Forever England: The Life of Rupert Brooke* (Edinburgh: Mainstream Publishing, 1997).

# On David Jones

There is not at present an authoritative biography of Jones, but one by Thomas Dilworth is in preparation. In the meantime see two books which reproduce primary source material from 1914 to 1918:

Thomas Dilworth, *David Jones in the Great War* (London: Enitharmon, 2012).
Anthony Hyne, *David Jones: A Fusilier at the Front* (Bridgend: Seren, 1995).

See also

David Blamires, *David Jones: Artist and Writer* (Manchester: Manchester University Press, 1978).
Keith Alldritt, *David Jones: Writer and Artist* (London: Constable, 2003).

Two books which contain many of Jones' later thoughts about the war are

René Hague (ed.), *Dai Greatcoat: A Self-Portrait of David Jones in his Letters* (London: Faber and Faber, 1980).
William Blissett, *The Long Conversation: A Memoir of David Jones* (Oxford: Oxford University Press, 1981).

For essays on different aspects of Jones' life and work, see

John Matthias (ed.), *David Jones: Man and Poet* (Maine: National Poetry Foundation, no date).
Roland Mathias (ed.), *David Jones: Eight Essays on his Work as Writer and Artist* (Llandysul: Gomer, 1976).

An essay which, alone in the vast ocean of critical literature on First World War writing, considers seriously the challenge writers faced in publishing anything which came close to replicating the obscene language of the British soldier is

William Blissett, 'The Efficacious Word', in Roland Mathias (ed.), *David Jones: Eight Essays on his Work as Writer and Artist* (Llandysul: Gomer, 1976), pp. 22–49.

Jones' great poetic memoir has been published in several later editions, and some of his later writings refer to his First World War experience:

David Jones, *The Sleeping Lord and other Fragments* (London: Faber & Faber, 1974).
—*The Dying Gaul and other Writings* (London: Faber & Faber, 1978).

Anyone struggling to understand *In Parenthesis* should use

Thomas Dilworth, *Reading David Jones* (Cardiff: University of Wales Press, 2008).

## On T. E. Lawrence, or 'Lawrence of Arabia'

For primary sources on Lawrence see

David Garnett (ed.), *The Letters of T. E. Lawrence* ([1938] London: Spring Books, 1964).
Malcolm Brown (ed.), *The Letters of T. E. Lawrence* (Oxford: Oxford University Press, 1991).
*The Home Letters of T. E. Lawrence and his Brothers* (Oxford: Blackwell, 1954).
*Secret Despatches from Arabia by T. E. Lawrence* (London: Golden Cockerel, 1937).

And for later first-hand writings, see

A. W. Lawrence (ed.), *T. E. Lawrence by his Friends* (London: Jonathan Cape, 1937).
Robert Graves and Liddell Hart (eds), *T. E. Lawrence to his Biographers* ([1938] New York: Doubleday, 1968).

There are numerous biographies of Lawrence. Aldington's first deconstruction of 'Lawrence of Arabia' is still worth reading; Mack's psychoanalytical reading is full of insights; and Lawrence James' recent study is balanced and detailed.

Richard Aldington, *Lawrence of Arabia: A Biographical Enquiry* (London: Collins, 1955).
Phillip Knightley and Colin Simpson, *The Secret Lives of Lawrence of Arabia* (London: Literary Guild, 1969).
John Mack, *A Prince of our Disorder: The Life of T. E. Lawrence* (Boston: Little, Brown, 1976).
Desmond Stewart, *T. E. Lawrence* (London: Hamish Hamilton, 1977).
Michael Yardley, *Backing into the Limelight: A Biography of T. E. Lawrence* (London: Harrap, 1985).
Lawrence James, *The Golden Warrior: The Life and Legend of Lawrence of Arabia* (London: Abacus, 1995).

A recent and thought-provoking study which has much useful interpretative material on Lawrence is

Priya Satia, *Spies in Arabia: The Great War and the Cultural Foundations of Britain's Covert Empire in the Middle East* (Oxford: Oxford University Press, 2008).

There are numerous essays on aspects of Lawrence's involvement in the desert war. Consider among others:

James Barr, *Setting the Desert on Fire: T. E. Lawrence and Britain's Secret War in Arabia, 1916–18* (London: Bloomsbury, 2007).
Maxwell Orme Johnson, 'The Arab Bureau and the Arab Revolt: Yanbu' to Aqaba'. *Military Affairs*, 46: 4 (December 1982), 194–201.
J. A. English, 'Kindergarten Soldier: The Military Thought of Lawrence of Arabia'. *Military Affairs*, 51: 1 (January 1987), 7–11.
Linda J. Tarver, 'In Wisdom's House: T. E. Lawrence in the Near East'. *Journal of Contemporary History*, 13: 3 (July 1978), 585–608.

Lawrence's later book, published posthumously, tells us much about him, and is much less well known than it should be!

T. E. Lawrence, *The Mint: A Day-book of the R.A.F. Depot between August and December 1922 with later Notes by 352087 A/c Ross* (London: Jonathan Cape, 1955).

Several who served alongside Lawrence in the desert have left us memoirs. See for example:

S. C. Rolls, *Steel Chariots in the Desert* ([1937] London: Leonaur, 2005).
Earl Winterton, *Fifty Tumultuous Years* (London: Hutchinson, 1955).

## On Vera Brittain

For valuable primary source material, see

Vera Brittain, *Verses of a V.A.D.* (London: Erskine MacDonald, 1918).
—*Poems of the War and After* (London: Gollancz, 1934).
Alan Bishop and Mark Bostridge (eds), *Letters from a Lost Generation: First World War Letters of Vera Brittain and Four Friends* (London: Little, Brown, 1998).
Mark Bostridge (ed.), *Because You Died. Poetry and Prose of the First World War and After: Vera Brittain* (London: Virago, 2008).

Bear in mind that Vera Brittain's published 'Great War Diary' has been edited:

Alan Bishop (ed.), *Vera Brittain: Chronicle of Youth. Great War Diary 1913–1917* (London: Phoenix Press, 2000).

The best biographies are

Paul Berry and Mark Bostridge, *Vera Brittain: A Life* (London: Chatto and Windus, 1995).
Deborah Gorham, *Vera Brittain: A Feminist Life* (Oxford: Blackwell, 1996).

See also

Andrea Peterson, 'Shell-shocked in Somerville: Vera Brittain's post-traumatic stress disorder', in Angela Smith (ed.), *Gender and warfare in the Twentieth Century: Textual Representations* (Manchester: Manchester University Press, 2004), pp. 33–52.

## On women and the war

The contribution of women to the war effort was the subject of much contemporary comment. See for example

Edith Abbott, 'The War and Women's Work in England'. *Journal of Political Economy*, 25: 7 (July 1917), 641–78.

There is now a well-established tradition of writing about women's experience of the war, which is recently broadening to consider gender more widely. See

Nicoletta Gullace, *'The Blood of our Sons': Men, Women, and the Renegotiation of British Citizenship during the Great War* (London: Palgrave Macmillan, 2004).
Susan Grayzel, *Women and the First World War* (Longman: London, 2002).
Susan Kingsley Kent, 'The Politics of Sexual Difference: World War I and the Demise of British Feminism'. *Journal of British Studies*, 27: 3 (July 1988), 232–53.
Philippa Levine, '"Walking the Streets in a Way No Decent Woman Should": Women Police in World War I'. *Journal of Modern History*, 66: 1 (March 1994), 34–78.
Angela Woolacott, '"Khaki fever" and its Control: Gender, Class, Age, and Sexual Morality on the British Homefront in the First World War'. *Journal of Modern History*, 58: 3 (September 1986), 643–68.

See the relevant essays in

Margaret Randolph Higonnet, Jane Jenson, Sonya Michel and Margaret Collins Weitz (eds), *Behind the Lines: Gender and the Two World Wars* (London and New Haven: Yale University Press, 1987).

## On women's writing from the First World War

Since the 1970s a considerable body of women's writing from the war has been published and analysed. Most of these books discuss Vera Brittain, and a few make brief reference to Kate Finzi. See

Jane Potter, *Boys in Khaki, Girls in Print: Women's Literary Responses to the Great War 1914–1918* (Oxford: Oxford University Press, 2005).
Angela Smith, *Women's Writing of the First World War: An Anthology* (Manchester: Manchester University Press, 2000).

Linda Anderson, *Women and Autobiography in the Twentieth Century* (London: Prentice Hall/Harvester Wheatsheaf, 1997).

Sharon Ouditt, *Fighting Forces, Writing Women: Identity and Ideology on the First World War* (London: Routledge, 1994).

Claire Tylee, *The Great War and Women's Consciousness: Images of Militarism and Womanhood in Women's Writings, 1914–64* (London: Macmillan, 1990).

## On Richard Nevinson

The best study of Nevinson in the First World War is

Michael Walsh, *C. R. W. Nevinson: This Cult of Violence* (New Haven and London: Yale University Press, 2002).

See also

Jonathan Black, 'A Curious, Cold Intensity: C.R.W. Nevinson as a War Artist, 1914–1918', in Richard Ingleby, Jonathan Black, David Cohen and Gordon Cooke (eds), *C.R.W. Nevinson: The Twentieth Century* (London: Merrell Holberton, 1999).

Nevinson's own autobiography needs to be treated with caution, and his mother's earlier memoir makes only brief reference to him!

C. R. W. Nevinson, *Paint and Prejudice* (London: Methuen, 1937).

Margaret Nevinson, *Life's Fitful Fever* (London: Black, 1926).

Many of Nevinson's pictures were reproduced during the war for publication. See

*Modern War Paintings by C. R. W. Nevinson*, with an essay by P. G. Konody (London: Grant Richards, 1917).

## On Paul Nash

There is a larger biographical corpus on Nash, but most of it is disappointingly vague about his First World War experience. See

Anthony Bertram, *Paul Nash: The Portrait of an Artist* (London: Faber & Faber, 1955).

Margot Eates, *Paul Nash: The Master of the Image, 1889–1946* (London: Murray, 1973).

John Rothenstein, *Paul Nash* (London: Beaverbrook Newspapers, 1961).

James King, *Interior Landscapes: A Life of Paul Nash* (London: Weidenfeld and Nicolson, 1987).

For books which include letters to and from Paul Nash from the war years, see:

Paul Nash, *Outline: An Autobiography and Other Writings* (London: Faber & Faber, 1949). Note that the recent paperback edition of this book *does not* contain the letters!

Claude Abbott and Anthony Bertram (eds), *Poet and Painter: Being the Correspondence between Gordon Bottomley and Paul Nash 1910–1946* (London: Oxford University Press, 1955).

Ronald Blythe, *First Friends: Paul and Bunty, John and Christine – and Carrington* (Denby: Fleece Press, 1998).

Nash's drawings to illustrate one of the first books of post-war poetry by an important author are reproduced in black and white in the volume above. See, for the original colour drawings, and the poems they accompanied:

Richard Aldington, *Images of War* (London: Beaumont Press, 1919).

## Stanley Spencer

By far the best introduction to Spencer is the edited volume of his writings by Adrian Glew. There are several other studies which include much primary source material from the war and comment on his post-war representations.

Adrian Glew (ed.), *Stanley Spencer: Letters and Writings* (London: Tate Gallery Publishing, 2001).

John Rothenstein, *Stanley Spencer. The Man: Correspondence and Reminiscences* (Athens, Ohio: Ohio University Press, 1979).

Richard Carline, *Stanley Spencer at War* (London: Faber & Faber, 1978).

Timothy Hyman and Patrick Wright (eds), *Stanley Spencer* (London: Tate Gallery Publishing, 2001).

Duncan Robinson, *Stanley Spencer: Visions from a Berkshire Village* (Oxford: Phaidon, 1979).

For an illuminating personal account of Spencer's childhood, see his brother's memoir:

Gilbert Spencer, *Stanley Spencer* (London: Gollancz, 1961).

## On painting and the war

There is a flourishing branch of art history dedicated to British artists and the war. See for starting points:

Paul Gough, *A Terrible Beauty: British Artists in the First World War I* (Bristol: Sansom, 2010).

David Boyd Haycock, *A Crisis of Brilliance: Five Young British Artists and the Great War* (London: Old Street Publishing, 2009).

Sue Malvern, *Modern Art, Britain, and the Great War: Witnessing, Testimony, and Remembrance* (New Haven and London: Yale University Press, 2004).
Barbara Jones and Bill Howell, *Popular Arts of the First World War* (London: Studio Vista, 1972).
Christopher Hassall, *Edward Marsh: Patron of the Arts* (London: Longman, 1959).

On the larger international context, see

Richard Cork, *Vorticism and Abstract Art in the First Machine Age* (London: Gordon Fraser, 1976).
—*A Bitter Truth: Avant-garde Art and the Great War* (New Haven and London: Yale University Press, 1994).
M. R. D. Foot, *Art and War: Twentieth Century Warfare as Depicted by War Artists* (London: Headline, 1990).

## The construction of memory

One of the foundations stones of this literature has recently been re-issued:

John Masefield, *The Old Front Line* ([1917] Barnsley: Pen and Sword, 2003).

In recent years there has been a huge interest in this topic, extending previous work on war memorials. See for an introduction:

Jay Winter, *Sites of Memory, Sites of Mourning: The Great War in European Cultural History* (Cambridge: Cambridge University Press, 1995).
Jay Winter and Emmanuel Sivan (eds), *War and Remembrance in the Twentieth Century* (Cambridge: Cambridge University Press, 1999).
Martin Evans and Ken Lunn (eds), *War and Memory in the Twentieth Century* (Oxford: Berg, 1997).
Nicholas J. Saunders, 'Crucifix, Calvary, and Cross: Materiality and Spirituality in Great War Landscapes'. *World Archaeology*, 35: 1 (June 2003), 7–21.

## Other memoirs

There is an extraordinarily rich seam of English-language memoirs of the First World War, many produced by writers of great distinction. Others are still emerging. See, for some of the most influential examples (many of which are available in reprints), in order of publication:

Ford Madox Ford, *No More Parades* (London: Duckworth, 1925).
Edmund Blunden, *Undertones of War* (London: Cobden-Sanderson, 1928).
Siegfried Sassoon, *Memoirs of an Infantry Officer* (London: Faber and Gwyer, 1928).
Robert Graves, *Goodbye to All That* (London: Jonathan Cape, 1929).
Richard Aldington, *Death of a Hero* (Paris: Babou and Kahane, 1930).
Siegfried Sassoon, *Memoirs of an Infantry Officer* (London: Faber & Faber, 1930).

Henry Williamson, *The Patriot's Progress* (London: Geoffrey Bles, 1930).
Frederick Manning, *Her Privates We* (London: Peter Davies, 1930).
Llewelyn Wyn Griffith, *Up to Mametz* (London: Faber & Faber, 1931).
Vera Brittain, *Testament of Youth* (London: Victor Gollancz, 1933).
T. E. Lawrence, *Seven Pillars of Wisdom* (London: Jonathan Cape, 1935).
Siegfried Sassoon, *Sherston's Progress* (London: Faber & Faber, 1936).
David Jones, *In Parenthesis* (London: Faber & Faber, 1937).
Captain J. C. Dunn (ed.), *The War the Infantry Knew* (London: King & Son, 1938).

To balance these memoirs, which are for the most part tales of disillusion, have a look at this anthology from the same period, which contains a much more interesting selection than its title suggests:

*Fifty Amazing Stories of the Great War* (London: Odhams Press, 1936).

A memoir which captures perhaps better than any other the awfulness of the war in the trenches only appeared fairly recently:

Edmund Campion Vaughan, *Some Desperate Glory: The Diary of a Young Officer, 1917* (London: Macmillan, 1985).

## War poetry

There are numerous anthologies of English-language war poetry available, and many books about individual poets. For some of the most influential, see

Wilfred Owen, *Collected Letters* (London: Oxford University Press, 1967).
—*The War Poems of Wilfred Owen* (London: Chatto and Windus, 1994).
Dominic Hibberd, *Wilfred Owen: A New Biography* (London: Weidenfeld and Nicolson, 2002).
Siegfried Sasson, *Collected Poems* (London: Faber & Faber, 2002).
Rupert Hart-Davis (ed.), *Siegfried Sassoon: Diaries 1915–1918* (London: Book Club Associates, 1983).
Jean Moorcroft Wilson, *Siegfried Sassoon: The Making of a War Poet. A Biography 1886–1918* (London: Duckworth, 1998).
Jan Marsh, *Edward Thomas: A Poet for his Country* (London: Elek, 1978).
Matthew Hollis, *Now All Roads Lead to France: The Last Years of Edward Thomas* (London: Faber & Faber, 2012).
Ivor Gurney, *Severn & Somme* (London: Sidgwick & Jackson, 1917).
Edmund Blunden, *Poems of Ivor Gurney 1890–1937* (London: Chatto & Windus, 1973).
Michael Hurd, *The Ordeal of Ivor Gurney* (Oxford: Oxford University Press, 1978).
Jon Stallworthy, *Anthem for Doomed Youth: Twelve Soldier Poets of the First World War* (London: Constable, 2002).
David Bond, *Minds at War: The Poetry and Experience of the First World War* (Burgess Hill: Saxon Books, 1996).

David Roberts, *Out in the Dark: Poetry and the First World War in Context* (Burgess Hill: Saxon Books, 1998).
Jon Silkin, *The Penguin Book of First World War Poetry* (Harmondsworth: Penguin, 1996).
I. M. Parsons (ed.), *Men Who March Away: Poems of the First World War* (London: Heinemann, 1965).

## International perspectives

Virtually all the titles above are concerned with the British experience. For recent texts which place this in comparative perspective see

Annika Mombauer, 'The First World War: Inevitable, Avoidable, Improbable or Desirable? Recent Interpretations of War Guilt and the War's Origins'. *German History*, 25: 1 (2007), 78–95.
Jay Winter and Antoine Prost (eds), *The Great War in History: Debates and Controversies, 1914 to the Present* (Cambridge: Cambridge University Press, 2005).
Stéphane Audoin-Rouzeau and Annette Becker, *1914–1918: Understanding the Great War*, trans. Temerson (London: Profile, 2002).
Jay Winter, *The Experience of World War I* (London: Guild Publishing, 1989).
Marc Ferro, *The Great War, 1914–1918*, trans. Stone (London: Routledge & Kegan Paul, 1973).

For useful selections of first-hand international accounts, including poetry, prose and drawings, see

Tim Cross (ed.), *The Lost Voices of World War I: An International Anthology of Writers, Poets, & Playwrights* (London: Bloomsbury, 1988).
Peter Vansittart (ed.), *Voices from the Great War* (London: Jonathan Cape, 1981).

## German memoirs and perspectives

Some of the most important German memoirs of the war have been published in English translation. See among others

Ernst Jünger, *Storm of Steel*, trans. Hofmann (London: Penguin, 2004).
Ex-Kaiser Wilhelm II, *My Memoirs: 1878–1918* (London and New York: Cassell, 1922).
Erich Maria Remarque, *All Quiet on the Western Front*, trans. Wheen (London: Putnam, 1929).

In German see

Ernst Jünger, *Werke, Band 1. Tagebücher I, Der Erste Weltkrieg* ([1920] Stuttgart: Klett, n.d.).
Erich Maria Remarque, *Im Westen Nichts Neues* (Berlin: Propylaen, 1929).

For an account of submarine warfare from a U-boat commander who went on to be a dissident under the Nazis, see

Martin Niemöller, *Vom U-Boot zur Kanzel* (Berlin: Martin Warneck, 1934).

For a recent account which provides a useful alternative to the usual perspective, see

Christopher Duffy, *Through German Eyes: The British and the Somme in 1916* (London: Phoenix, 2007).

In German, see for a fascinating look at the Gallipoli campaign:

E. R. Prigge, *Der Kampf um die Dardanellen* (Weimar: Kiepenheuer, 1916).

Many British histories quote one line from Ludendorff's memoirs (on the 'black day' of the German Army) without context. The original text, written shortly after the Armistice in 1918, is very revealing, as is Hindenburg's account. Both books contain excellent maps.

Erich Ludendorff, *Meine Kriegserinnerungen 1914–1918* (Berlin: Mittler und Sohn, 1919).

Paul von Hindenburg, *Aus meinem Leben* (Leipzig: Hirzel, 1934).

For an overview of the war from the German and Austrian perspective, see

Holger Herwig, *The First World War: Germany and Austria-Hungary 1914–1918* (London: Arnold, 1997).

An important book which has recently tried to contextualize aspects of the First World War in terms of German 'military culture' is

Isabel Hull, *Absolute Destruction: Military Culture and the Practices of War in Imperial Germany* (Ithaca and London: Cornell University Press, 2005).

And for a painter who makes a fascinating comparison with Nevinson or Nash, see

Thomas Compère-Morel (ed.), *Otto Dix: Der Krieg* (Milan: 5 Continents, 2003).

## An important French text

One French novel above all others exercised a great influence on many British writers in the post-war period:

Henri Barbusse, *Le Feu (Journal d'une Escouade). Basé sur des expériences s'est produite lors de la Première Guerre Mondiale* (Paris: Flammarion, 1916).

This was published in English in 1926 and is now available in many editions, including

Henri Barbusse, *Under Fire* (London: Penguin, 2003).

# INDEX

Abbott, Maurice 187, 201
Abercrombie, Lascelles 18
Achnasheen 14
Agadir crisis 33
Ahmed, Salim (Dahoum) 29
Akaba 155–6, 182–5, 198, 235
Aldington, Richard 244, 255, 258, 263, 271, 278
Allenby, Edmund 182, 184–6, 197, 199, 218–19, 222, 235, 237, 256
America 17, 86, 150, 168, 201, 258, 267
American Army 150, 193, 196–7, 203, 213–16, 228
Amiens 194, 214
Anglesey 25, 95
Anglo-Persian Oil Company 29
*Anglo-Saxon Chronicle, The* 25
Antwerp 34, 39–40, 46, 48–9, 51, 58–9, 67, 74, 82, 99, 275, 277–8
Arabia 6, 75, 87–8, 129–30, 132, 154–5, 234–7, 281
Arab Revolt 7, 130–2, 152–6, 186, 220, 234–8, 255–7
Arras 143–4, 150–1, 159, 214, 277
Ashmolean Museum 28, 186
Asquith, Henry 18, 33–6, 44, 50, 51, 53, 68, 69, 82, 101, 103, 104, 148, 159, 166, 168, 191, 274
Asquith, Violet 17, 83
Austria 20, 33–5, 55, 79, 149, 215, 216, 217, 232, 279
Aveling, George 99

Bach, Johann Sebastian 24, 73, 119, 158, 203, 223
Baghdad 154, 198
Bala 26
Balfour, Arthur 154
Balfour Declaration 186, 256
Balkans 33

Balkan Wars 11
Bank of England 12
Beatty, David 216
Beaufort Hospital 110–12, 134–5, 168, 200, 246, 260–1
Bede, the Venerable 25
Beethoven, Ludwig van 24
Belgium 3, 8, 34–6, 39, 43, 44–8, 50–1, 55, 59, 68, 71, 77, 93, 128, 134, 149, 162, 163, 168, 207, 212, 220, 228, 232, 241, 247, 269, 275
    'Belgian atrocities' 47–8, 51, 57, 63, 71, 77, 98, 108, 234, 279
Benson, Arthur 12, 42
Berkshire 24
Berlin 33, 35, 83, 217
Berlin–Baghdad railway 29
Bethmann-Hollweg, Chancellor Theobald von 35, 149
Billing Case 3
Binyon, Laurence 95–7, 117, 121, 140–1, 160, 167, 179, 187, 227–8, 240, 249, 254, 267, 274, 280
Birmingham 26, 161, 179, 187
*Blackadder Goes Forth* 270–1
Black Sea 29, 79
Blake, William 23, 142–3, 158, 263
Bloomsbury Group 17
Blunden, Edmund 1, 258, 278, 279
Boer War 11
Bone, Muirhead 24, 165, 200, 243
Bottomley, Emily 23, 67
Bottomley, Gordon 23, 67, 242
Boulogne 6, 62, 64, 65, 66, 90, 114, 115, 136, 188, 221, 278
Brett, Dorothy 21
British Army, units
    Artists' Rifles 67–9, 70, 116, 180

15th Battalion (London Welsh) Royal Welch Fusiliers  26, 68–70, 94–5, 137, 160, 161, 163, 173, 174, 205, 262, 278
143rd Field Ambulance  157
17th Battalion Royal Welch Fusiliers  104
7th Battalion Royal Berkshire Regiment  158, 200, 225
7th Battalion South Wales Borderers  225
68th Field Ambulance  157
66th Field Ambulance  135, 156
10th Battalion South Wales Borderers  139, 174
38th (Welsh) Division  94–5, 104, 137, 173–4, 265
Hampshire Regiment  164, 182
Irish Regiment  40
Machine Gun Corps  164
Oxford and Bucks Light Infantry  225
British Red Cross Society  38–40, 62–3, 65, 90, 141
Brittain, Arthur  19, 207
Brittain, Edward  19–20, 41, 72, 73, 90, 108, 109, 136, 159, 188, 203, 204, 207, 212, 223–4, 258
Brittain, Vera  1, 4, 86, 144, 278
  background and personality  5–8, 19–20, 27, 30–1, 106, 159
  and enlistment  41, 72–4, 99
  and nursing  43, 89–90, 105–10, 112, 114, 135–6, 158–9, 188–9, 203–4, 258, 274
  reaction to the end of the war  224, 238–40
  reaction to the war  40–1, 48, 51, 78, 89–90, 166, 205, 211–12, 223–4, 253–4, 273–6
  works
    'Great War Diary'  20, 159, 168, 188, 257, 287nn. 17, 19
    *Testament of Youth*  257–9, 264, 276
    *Verses of a V.A.D.*  158, 189, 204, 223, 240
  and writing  121, 159, 168, 188, 190, 204, 223–4, 238–40

*see also* Brittain, Edward; Leighton, Roland; Somerville College
Broadheath  12
Brooke, Rupert  6, 7, 23, 25, 36, 62, 63, 70, 73, 74, 88, 91, 120, 158, 258, 268
  background and personality  4–5, 16–18, 31
  and the Dardanelles  82–5
  death and memorialization  85–6, 175
  and Germany  30, 275
  reaction to the war  8–9, 36–8, 51, 53, 56–60, 78, 121, 190, 211, 253–4, 273, 277–8, 281
  works
    war sonnets  60–1, 90, 106–7, 109, 114, 122, 136, 141, 247, 249, 251, 274–5, 282
Browne, Denis  18, 56, 58
Brussels  39
Bryce Report  98–9
Burns, John  35
Buxton  5, 19, 21, 40, 72, 89, 90, 105, 106, 158

Cairo  77, 84, 87, 106, 121, 124, 129, 130, 153, 156, 184, 220–2, 234, 236
Calais  34, 56, 150, 196
Camberwell School of Arts and Crafts  25, 248
Cambrai, Battle of  173, 193
Cambridge University  16–17, 38, 57, 61, 86
Carcemish  29, 186
Cardiff  26, 53, 68, 95, 228
Carrington, Dora  21
Catlin, George  258
Chapman, Thomas  27, 88, 236
Cheltenham Ladies' College  23
Chotek, Sophie  33
*Christian Herald*  25, 163
Churchill, Winston  17, 18, 36, 48, 56–7, 67, 79, 82, 83, 87, 89, 101–2, 191, 214, 278
Chute, Desmond  111, 158, 245, 248
citizenship  2, 271
City of Oxford High School  28

Clayton, Gilbert  77, 129–30, 153, 156, 199
Clemenceau, Georges  195, 236–7
Colvin, Frances  42
Colvin, Sidney  95, 97, 228
conscription  55, 69, 104, 114, 117–20, 144, 159, 165–6, 174, 191, 193, 194, 202, 209, 213, 232
Constantinople  75, 79–80, 88, 101, 129
Cookham  24–5, 74–5, 91–2, 110, 157, 158, 200, 201, 245, 246, 247, 260
Cowgill, Rachel  95–6
Cox, Katharine  17–18, 57, 82, 84

*Daily Express*  93
*Daily Mail*  21, 55
Damascus  75, 87–8, 153, 155, 184, 186, 215–18, 221–2, 234, 235, 256
Dannreuther, Edward  14
Dardanelles  3, 79–82, 83, 84, 86, 87, 99, 101, 111, 115, 116, 216, 276, 278
Dent, Edward  57, 86
Deraa  184, 218, 234, 256
Dilworth, Thomas  25, 162
Dingwall  14
Duncan, George  197
Dunkirk  34, 48, 57–9, 65–6, 92, 94, 121, 134, 222, 279

Edward VII, King  15
Egypt  15, 29, 76–7, 84, 87–8, 105, 129–30, 133, 154, 179, 182, 199, 212, 220, 222, 236
Elgar, Alice  7, 12–14, 16, 41–3, 71, 96, 97, 98, 117, 140, 141, 142, 166, 187, 201, 223, 227, 240, 241, 268
Elgar, Carice  14, 41, 98
Elgar, Edward  15, 22, 119, 211–12, 223, 248
  background  4–7, 9, 12–14
  and the Battle of Jutland  124
  and conscription  117, 166, 202
  and the end of the war  226, 240–1, 254, 280
  health and hypochondria  13, 141–2, 166–7, 186–7, 201–2
  and Kipling  166, 186–7
  love for Germany  30, 51, 166–7, 227
  personality  12–14, 30–1, 42–3
  public perception of  12–14, 266–8
  reaction to the war  41, 78, 168, 274–5, 280–1
  sympathy for Belgium  71–2
  works
    *Carillon*  71, 116–17, 228, 267
    Concerto for Cello  201, 226–7, 240–1, 267
    *Dream of Gerontius, The*  12, 141, 167, 240
    *Enigma Variations*  12, 167, 267–8
    *Fringes of the Fleet*  166, 186–7
    *Give unto the Lord*  11–14
    'Land of Hope and Glory'  42, 228, 267
    *Le Drapeau Belge*  267
    *The Music Makers*  13
    *Polonia*  116–17
    Quintet for Piano and Strings  226–7, 240
    *The Sanguine Fan*  166
    *Sospiri*  42
    *The Spirit of England/For the Fallen*  95–7, 99, 121, 140–1, 145, 159, 166–7, 187–90, 241, 254, 267, 273, 282
    *Starlight Express*  117, 140
    String Quartet  226–7, 240
    2nd Symphony  97, 141
    *Une Voix dans le Désert*  116, 140, 267
    Violin Sonata  226–7, 240
Entente Cordiale  33–5
Etaples  6, 64, 161, 188, 203–4
Eton College  15
Evans, Ellis (Hedd Wyn)  4, 9, 163, 181
  background and personality  5–7, 26–7, 30–1
  death and memorialization  174–5, 250–3, 269–70
  and enlistment  119–20, 144, 156, 193
  at Passchendaele  173–4
  reaction to the war  51, 54, 70–1, 78, 121–2, 168, 275, 281

works
   'Gwladgarwch' ('Patriotism') 70–1, 78
   'In Memoriam' 159–60, 253
   'Plant Trawsfynydd' ('The Children of Trawsfynydd') 120
   'Rhyfel' ('War') 160, 190
   'Yr Arwr' ('The Hero') 160

Fabian Society 17
Fawcett, Millicent 203
Feisal, Emir 88, 129, 132, 152–5, 168, 183–4, 199, 219, 221–2, 234–7
Ferdinand, Archduke Franz 33
film 128, 145, 168, 237–8, 253, 255
   *Battle of the Ancre and the Advance of the Tanks* 147–8
   *Battle of the Somme* 128, 142
Finzi, Douglas 27
Finzi, Felix 27
Finzi, Gerald 14, 27
Finzi, Kate 4, 8, 65, 73, 77, 113, 144, 163, 266
   background and personality 5, 27, 31
   and nursing 38–40, 43, 62–4, 90–1, 114–16, 188, 221, 253
   reaction to the war 51, 78, 136–7, 169, 189, 248, 273–5, 278
   works
      *Eighteen Months* 7, 121, 145, 167–8, 190, 211, 250, 268
Flanders 3, 5, 6, 48, 50, 60, 61, 62, 66, 79, 80, 83, 86, 93, 94, 110, 116, 121, 122, 134, 138, 150, 152, 165, 179, 180, 183, 193, 196, 199, 240, 253
Foch, Ferdinand 194, 214, 216–17
Ford, Madox Ford 244, 263
France 21–2, 33–5, 37, 44–6, 48, 50–2, 55, 58, 62, 64, 68, 74, 75, 88, 89–90, 93, 96, 99, 102, 104, 110, 123, 125, 127, 128, 134, 137, 142, 144, 149, 150, 159, 161, 163, 164, 166, 177, 180, 181, 188, 189, 193, 194, 197, 200–2, 204–5, 207, 212, 213, 215, 220, 228, 232, 242, 245, 259, 282

French, John 46–7, 80, 102–4
Friends Ambulance Unit 5, 65–6
Frost, Robert 18, 86, 164
Fry, Roger 23
Fussell, Paul 25, 263
Futurism 21–2, 30, 65–6, 83, 86, 93, 113, 133, 165, 241, 242, 282

Gallipoli campaign 6, 80–1, 84, 87, 101–2, 105, 113, 120, 124, 128, 129, 133, 198, 276
Gaudier-Breszka, Henri 18
George V, King 33, 83, 103, 125, 235, 236, 1414
*Georgian Poetry* 17
Germany 10, 11, 22, 29, 30, 33, 34–7, 41–2, 44, 50–2, 55–9, 79, 97, 105, 117, 119, 123, 128, 149–50, 160, 162, 166–7, 168, 207, 212, 216–17, 226, 232, 236, 242, 247, 257, 259, 267, 273, 275, 279
   German offensives 1918 194–7
   German 'Peace Offensive' 149–50
Gertler, Mark 21
Gibson, Wilfred 18
Gildas, Saint 25
Gill, Eric 246, 248, 262
Gill, Petra 262
Gloucester 14, 44, 99
Gloucestershire 18
*Graphic, The* 102, 104, 105, 121, 127, 133, 149, 162, 168, 173, 176, 205, 207, 247, 263
Graves, Robert 1, 7, 160, 255, 263, 278, 279
Gregory, Adrian 9, 86, 144, 273
Grey, Edward 16, 33–6, 51, 105, 191
Gurney, Ivor 14, 99, 138, 167–8, 187, 190, 202

Hague, René 26, 262, 266
Haig, Douglas 44, 53, 80, 102, 104, 110, 123–7, 137, 139–40, 142, 144, 145, 147–52, 183, 191, 193–7, 200, 201, 214–16, 252, 271
Hamilton, Ian 80, 84, 101–2, 120, 133
Hampstead 12, 20, 42, 114, 209
Handel, George Frideric 24

Hartrick, Archibald  25, 104, 162
Hawaii  17
Hejaz  6, 87–8, 129–30, 153–4, 199, 236
  Hejaz railway  75, 88, 129, 154–5, 183–4, 198, 218, 235
Herbert, George  111
Highnam Court  14, 16, 43–4, 118, 187, 222
Hiles, Barbara  21
Hindenburg, Paul von  212
Hindenburg Line  150, 214–15
Hogarth, David  28–9, 87, 88
Hokusai, Katsushika  24
Horne, John  48, 98
Howells, Herbert  14, 167
Husein Ibn Ali, Sherif  87–8, 105, 129–32, 154, 186, 199, 231, 236

Imperial War Museum  128, 178, 209, 250–1, 257, 268
Iona, Isle of  14
Iraq  29, 75
Ireland  9, 12, 16, 36, 127, 200, 233, 247, 249
Italy  21, 22, 34, 66, 123, 183, 189, 193, 203, 223

Jellicoe, John  152
Jesus College, Oxford  28
Joffre, Joseph  123, 125, 150
Jones, David  4, 6, 160, 254, 257
  background and personality  5–6, 25–6, 30
  in the infantry  94–5, 104–5, 121–2, 137–40, 161–3, 173, 205–6, 212, 247
  post-war writing  262–6, 276, 278, 282
  reaction to the war  9, 53–4, 68–70, 78, 273
  wartime drawings and writings  105, 138, 161–3, 168, 175–7, 190, 205, 207, 211, 247–9, 253, 274–5, 282
Jones, James  25–6, 68, 70, 162, 163, 176, 247, 248
Jünger, Ernst  197
Junner, Sarah  27, 88
Jutland, Battle of  124–5

Kandinsky, Wassily  21
Keynes, John Maynard  57, 277
King's College, Cambridge  16–17
Kitchener, Lord Herbert  29, 44–5, 53, 68, 75, 79, 87, 94, 101–3, 120, 125, 191, 213, 250
Konody, Paul  113, 133
Kramer, Alan  48, 98

Lairg  14
Lake District  23–4
Lamb, Henry  25, 38, 74, 91, 135, 226
Lawrence, D. H.  17, 244
Lawrence, Thomas Edward  108, 168, 244
  and the Arab Revolt  129–32, 152–6, 182–6, 198–9, 218–22
  background and personality  4–7, 27–31
  as an intelligence officer in Cairo  86–8, 105, 124
  and post-war peacemaking  234–8
  reaction to the war  43–4, 51, 77–8, 121, 190, 212, 248, 254, 273–4, 276, 280–1
  *Seven Pillars of Wisdom*  30, 132, 234, 255, 281
Lebanon  28, 29, 75, 129, 155, 218, 237
Leete, Reginald  53
Le Havre  40, 51, 57, 104
Leighton, Roland  19–20, 41, 54, 72–4, 86, 89–90, 106–10, 135, 158–9, 189, 238, 258
Lenin, Vladimir Ilyich  21, 173
Levant  6
Lewis, Cecil Day  274
Lewis, Percy Wyndham  21
Liège  38
'literature of disillusion'  1, 2, 253, 256, 263, 270
Littlehampton  15, 16, 43
Lloyd George, David  34, 68–9, 79, 82, 89, 95, 148–50, 152, 153, 154, 163, 166, 168, 171, 174, 182, 190, 191, 193–5, 200, 205, 210, 212, 214–17, 229, 236–7, 276
London  2, 5, 9, 11, 12, 13, 14, 17, 18, 20, 21, 22, 23, 24, 25, 27, 35, 36, 37, 40, 41, 53, 56, 59, 62,

63, 65, 67, 68, 69, 71, 77, 87, 89, 92, 93, 97–9, 101, 104, 106, 107, 108, 111, 116, 117, 118, 121, 128, 129, 130, 133, 134, 135, 141, 142, 143, 152, 156, 158, 159, 177, 179, 182, 186, 187, 188, 189, 190, 194, 200, 201, 203, 204, 205, 206, 209, 214, 224, 227, 228, 234, 236, 238, 240, 241, 243, 245, 248, 268, 274, 279, 280, 282
Loos  3, 101–4, 106, 115, 251
'lost generation'  1, 258
Louvain  47, 71
Ludendorff, Erich  195, 212, 214, 217
*Lusitania*  3, 80, 86, 89, 91, 98, 99

*Mabinogion*  26, 263
Macedonia  6, 156–7, 246, 260–2, 269, 276, 279
Mack, John  28
McMahon, Henry  76, 105, 154
McMahon–Husein letters  105, 256
Magdalen College, Oxford  28
Maidenhead  24, 74
   Maidenhead Technical Institute  24
Malta  6, 83, 136, 158–9
Mametz Wood  125, 127, 139–40, 161–2, 175, 264–6, 278
*Manchester Guardian*  94
Manning, Frederick  257
Marinetti, Filippo  21–2, 66, 93
Marne
   Battle of the  47
   Second Battle of the  197
Marsh, Eddie  17–18, 23–5, 36, 37, 56, 58, 67, 83, 84, 85, 111, 249, 282
Martin, George  11, 14
Masterman, Charles  165–6, 177, 178, 182, 207, 209, 243
Maubeuge  46
Maurice Debate  3, 210
Medina  75, 129–30, 154, 183, 231, 235
Mediterranean Sea  29, 34, 75, 79, 83, 87, 135, 154, 158, 159, 231, 245, 251, 262
Mesopotamia  29, 75–6, 105, 124, 129, 135, 154, 217, 232, 235, 237, 256

Middleton, Kate  15
Milton, John  14, 25, 158, 200
Modigliani, Amedeo  21
Monro, Charles  102
Mons  3, 46–7, 62, 99
Morgan, John, *The War and Wales*  119–20
Morley, John  35
Mott, Charles  166, 202, 206, 212
Mull, Isle of  14
*Musical Times, The*  141

Namier, Lewis  43, 77
Nash, John  23, 67, 180, 182, 209
Nash, Margaret (née Odeh)  23, 116, 180, 181, 182, 245
Nash, Paul  4, 6, 18, 20–2, 168, 255, 281
   background and personality  5, 23–5, 30–1
   contribution to post-war memory  250–1, 254, 268, 273, 274, 277, 280, 282
   as a junior officer  165
   as an Official War Artist  179–82, 209–10, 241–2, 244
   post-war breakdown  244–5
   reaction to the war  67, 78, 191, 248, 274
   works
      illustrations for *Images of War*  244–5
      *The Menin Road*  244
      *Void*  210–11
      *We Are Making a New World*  210–11, 250, 276
Nesbitt, Cathleen  18, 37, 38, 57, 59, 84
Nevinson, Henry  7, 20, 65–6, 86, 94, 124, 125, 128, 134, 165, 207, 208, 209, 243
Nevinson, Kathleen (née Knowlman)  21, 66, 114, 209, 243
Nevinson, Margaret  20, 22, 113, 114
Nevinson, Richard  86, 120, 138, 222, 250–1, 268
   background and personality  5–7, 20–2, 25, 30–1
   and the end of the war  224, 241–5, 248
   and enlistment  134, 144, 165

and nursing 4, 65–6, 92–4, 112–14, 132–3
as Official War Artist 165–6, 177–81, 206–9, 241
reaction to the war 64, 73, 99, 121–2, 145, 168, 191, 211, 254, 274, 279
works
   *After a Push* 177–8
   *Arrival* 22, 94
   *Bursting Shell* 112–13
   *Declaration of War* 93
   *Deserted Trench* 113
   *First Searchlights at Charing Cross* 93
   *A Group of Soldiers* 207–9
   *Harvest of Battle* 242–4
   *He Gained a Fortune but he Gave a Son* 207
   *La Guerre de Trous* 112
   *La Mitrailleuse* 133, 175–6
   *La Patrie* 134
   *Motor Ambulance Driver* 134
   *In the Observation Ward* 113, 115
   *Paths of Glory* 208–9, 243, 276, 282
   *Pursuing a Taube* 134
   *A Taube Pursued by Commander Samson* 93
   *War Profiteers* 206–7
*see also* Futurism; Vorticism
Newcastle-under-Lyme 19
Newman, Henry 12, 167
*New Numbers* 61, 85
*New Statesman* 36, 37, 145
Nicholson, Ben 21
Nivelle, Robert 150–2
Norfolk 18, 37
North Sea 34, 45, 79, 124, 231

*Observer*, newspaper 21, 93, 113, 133, 227, 228
Olivier, Noel 17, 18
Olympic Games 12, 268
O'Shaughnessy, Arthur 12
Ostend 34, 39–40, 43, 48, 152
Ottoman Empire 28, 29, 51, 75–7, 79, 87–8, 105, 128, 130, 216, 217, 220, 232, 253, 256, 276

Owen, J. Dynallt 27, 282
Oxford 43, 141, 186, 199
Oxford University 15, 19–20, 23, 28–9, 41, 43, 72–4, 89–90, 105, 110, 120, 159, 237, 238–9, 257

Palestine 29, 75, 87, 129, 152–3, 155, 182–4, 186, 194, 197–9, 215, 217–18, 220, 235, 237, 269
Palestine Exploration Fund 29
'Pals' battalions 69–70, 95, 213, 277
Papen, Franz von 199
Paris 21, 22, 46–7, 123, 194, 196–7, 216, 217, 232, 236, 237, 242
Parry, Charles Hubert Hastings 7, 9, 13, 51, 73, 125
   background and personality 5, 14–16, 31, 44
   and conscription 117–19
   death and funeral 222–3
   and Germany 30, 51, 98, 275
   reaction to the war 4, 6, 43, 55–6, 63, 77, 78, 99, 120–1, 142–4, 168, 228, 274–5, 279–80
   and Turkey 276
   works
      *Blest Pair of Sirens* 14
      Chorale Preludes 119
      'Hymn to Aviators' 119, 267
      *I Was Glad* 15
      'Jerusalem' 142–3, 167, 203, 267–8, 279
      *Judith* 15
      'Naval Ode', *The Chivalry of the Sea* 187–8, 189, 267
      *Songs of Farewell* 119, 143, 188, 211, 223
Parry, Dorothea 15
Parry, Maude 14, 15, 118, 202
Partridge, Bernard 47
Passchendaele 196, 216
   Battle of 6, 171–82, 193, 203, 206, 214, 242, 277, 282
Pershing, George 196
Pétain, Phillippe 151–2
Ponsonby, Arthur 15–16, 56, 117–19
Portuguese Expeditionary Force 195–6
Pownall, Frank 99

propaganda 2, 98, 128, 165, 208, 259, 264, 268, 276
Prussia 34, 37, 55–6, 59, 63, 93, 149, 178, 205, 275
*Punch* 47, 292n. 30

Raverat, Gwen 25, 74, 91, 92, 112, 135, 158, 225, 226
Raverat, Jacques 18, 25, 37, 57, 74, 83, 84, 91, 92, 112, 135, 138, 226
Redmond, John 35
Red Sea 29, 129–30, 154–5
Remarque, Erich Maria 262
Richardson, Victor 108, 159, 188, 258
Richmond, William 23
Richter, Hans 30, 167
Riddell, George 148, 193, 194, 216
Roberts, Lizzie 27
Robertson, William 104, 129, 182–3, 193–4
Rolls, S. C. 198
Rootham, Cyril 96
Roper, Michael 3, 108
Rossetti, Gabriel Dante 23
Royal College of Music 4, 14, 43, 55, 118, 125, 143, 167
Royal Naval Division 8, 48, 56–9, 82–4, 147, 277
Royal Navy 11, 16, 29, 45, 76, 130
Royal Welch Fusiliers 9, 70, 104, 160, 174, 205
Rugby 18, 36
Rugby School 16, 57
Russia 17, 29, 34, 37, 68, 75, 79, 101, 123, 125, 148–50, 168, 173, 186, 193, 212, 233
Rutherston, John 24

Sadler, Michael 24
St Hilda's College, Oxford 23
St Monica's School 19
Salonica 102, 112, 129, 135, 156–8, 200, 215, 225, 245
Samson, Charles 93, 297n. 67
Sanders, Liman von 198
Sarajevo 33, 36
Sassoon, Siegfried 1, 17, 23, 160, 191, 240, 258, 263, 277, 278, 279, 281
Satia, Priya 1, 29, 232–3, 237, 257, 281

Schreiner, Olive 19, 20
Schubert, Franz 24
Schuster, Frank 43, 142
Scotland 9, 14, 41
secret diplomacy 9, 51, 56, 256
Servia/Serbia 20, 33–4, 68, 148, 168
Severini, Gino 21–2, 242
Shakespeare, William 25, 157, 158, 176, 263
Shaw, George Bernard 15
Shelley, William 26
shell shock 63, 113, 115, 238, 262
Sinai desert 29–30, 75, 153, 156, 182–3
Slade School of Drawing, Painting, and of Sculpture 20–1, 23–5, 243, 247
Somerville College, Oxford 19, 73, 89, 110, 238–9, 257
Somme, Battle of the 6, 12, 123, 125–8, 134, 136, 139–40, 142, 145, 147–8, 149, 150, 151, 161, 164, 194, 204, 206, 213–14, 250, 264, 266, 276–8, 283
*Song of Roland* 25
South Africa 11, 123, 127
Southampton 40, 102, 104, 158, 245
Spafford, Bertram 72–3
Spanish flu 197, 215, 217, 223, 224, 231, 236, 238
Spencer, Gilbert 24, 38, 74, 91–2, 111, 112, 246
Spencer, Stanley 4, 18, 21, 37, 116, 144, 228, 248, 254
  background and personality 5, 24–5, 31
  and Germany 30
  in the infantry 200–1, 225–6
  and nursing 4, 6, 91–2, 110–12, 114, 121, 134–5, 156–8, 168
  as Official War Artist 225, 241, 245–7
  reaction to the war 7, 38, 51, 54, 74–5, 77–8, 99, 274, 276, 278, 279
  works
    *The Centurion's Servant* 111
    paintings for the Sandham Memorial Chapel 259–63
    *Swan Upping, Cookham* 245

*Travoys Arriving with Wounded at a Dressing Station at Smol, Macedonia* 245–6
Spencer, William 24, 74, 158
Staffa, Isle of 14
Stanford, Charles 13, 56, 223
Staniforth, J. M. 49, 69
Stanley, Venetia 33, 34, 36, 274
Strachey, James 16, 57
Strachey, Lytton 27, 57
Stuart-Wortley, Alice 14, 41, 117, 142, 187
Suez Canal 29, 75
suffrage for women 5, 12, 15, 19, 20, 23, 31, 73, 202–3, 267, 280
Surrey 19
Switzerland 27, 217
Sydney, Philip 84–5, 120
Sykes, Mark 128
Sykes-Picot Agreement 128–9, 153, 186, 234, 237, 256
Syria 28, 29, 75, 87, 105, 129, 130, 153–4, 155, 182–4, 186, 198, 218, 234–7

Taatamata 17, 83
Tafas massacre 219–21, 234
Tahiti 17
tanks 133–4, 147–8, 164, 172–3, 196, 197, 201, 209, 213–14, 236, 255
Tax Resistance League 23
Territorial Army 37, 38, 67, 69, 74, 80
Thatcher, Margaret 12
Thiepval 12, 125, 142
Thomas, Edward 18, 85–6, 164
Thomas, Lowell 7, 237, 255, 257
Thurlow, Geoffrey 110, 159, 258
*Times, The* 10, 21, 22, 33, 35, 36, 40, 42, 47, 48, 50, 53, 54, 55, 68, 71, 72, 85, 89, 93, 95, 96, 99, 102, 111, 117, 127, 129, 137, 148, 151, 173, 186, 188, 193, 201, 209, 224, 234, 235, 237, 240, 243, 257
*Times Literary Supplement, The* 85, 95

Tonks, Henry 20, 243
Trawsfynydd 26–7, 120, 160, 252–3

Union of Democratic Control 51, 56, 118–19, 144, 212, 267, 279
Uppingham School 19–20, 110, 207

Vaughan, Henry 143
Vaughan-Williams, Ralph 14, 99, 167, 274
Versailles 194
    Treaty of 232, 238, 254, 258–9, 263, 277
Voluntary Aid Detachment (VAD) 38–9, 107, 158, 161, 203–4, 224
Vorticism 22, 133, 168, 179, 208, 210, 242, 245, 268

Wagner, Richard 14
Wales 9, 26, 36, 68–70, 78, 94, 95, 119–20, 144, 160, 174–5, 251, 254, 269, 278
Watson, Janet 9, 273, 278, 282
Wellesley, Eileen 18, 37, 57, 84
*Welsh Outlook* 36, 120, 150, 174, 269
Whelan, Peter, *The Accrington Pals* 277
Whistler, James 24
William, Prince 15
Wingate, Reginald 76, 129, 154, 156, 182, 183
Wood, James 134–5, 200
Woolley, Leonard 29–30
Worcester 12, 14
    Worcester Cathedral 12
Worcestershire 5, 141

Ypres (Leper) 48–50, 62, 65, 80, 89, 113, 121, 152, 161, 163–5, 171, 173, 175, 177–80, 188–9, 195–6, 210–11, 216, 241–2, 244, 269, 273

Zeebrugge 34, 48, 152
Zeppelin raids 3, 79, 97–9, 107, 116, 117, 137, 166, 206